KU-195-837

BLADE OF HEAVEN

THE ULTIMATE CLASH IS ABOUT TO BEGIN!

When Soma, a human, is accused of stealing the Heaven King's Sword, the otherwordly order is knocked out of balance. Heavenly beings and demons clash for ultimate supremacy. The hope for salvation rests with Soma, the heavenly princess, and the Blade of Heaven—each holds the key to preventing all Hell from breaking loose!

TEEN
AGE 13+

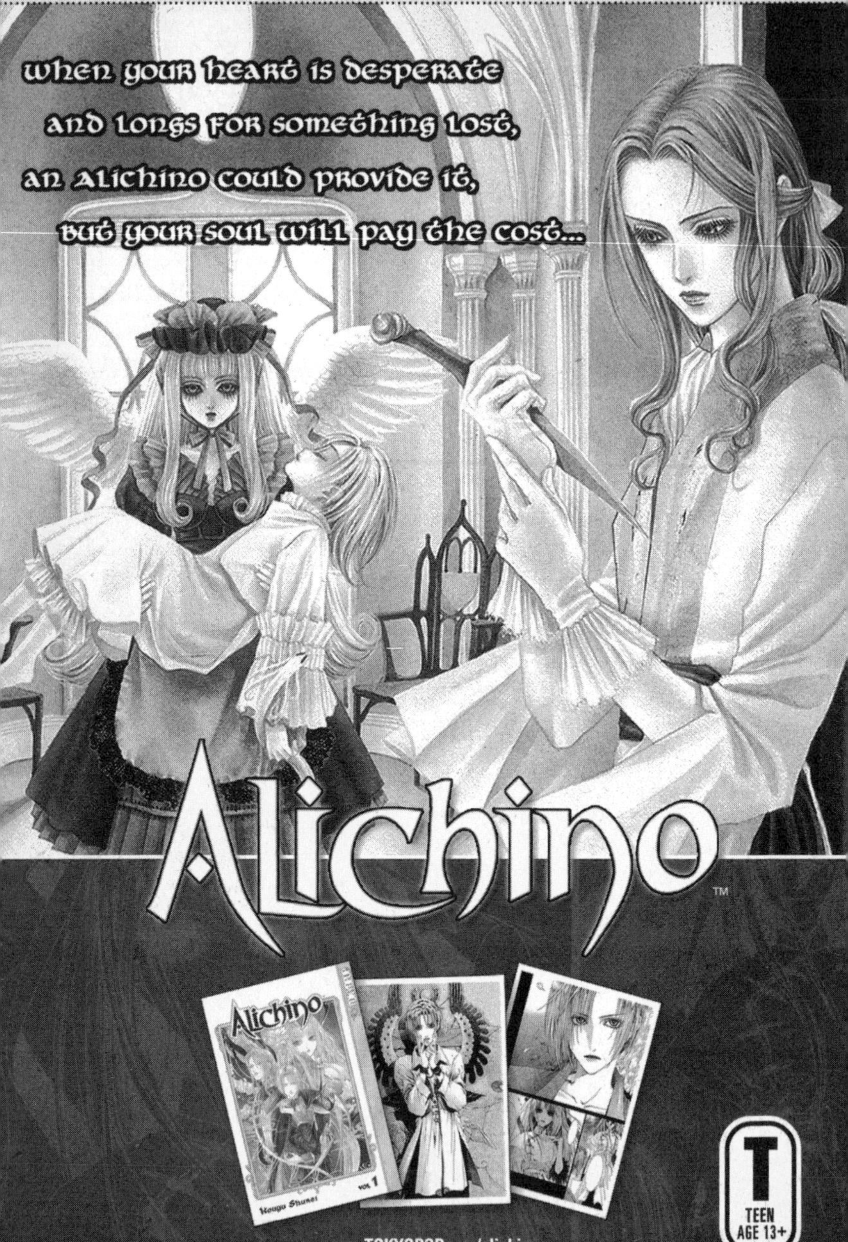
when your heart is desperate
and longs for something lost,
an alichino could provide it,
but your soul will pay the cost...
Alichino™
Alichino
Kouyu Shurei
VOL 1
T
TEEN
AGE 13+

STOP!

This is the back of the book.
You wouldn't want to spoil a great ending!

This book is printed "manga-style," in the authentic Japanese right-to-left format. Since none of the artwork has been flipped or altered, readers get to experience the story just as the creator intended. You've been asking for it, so TOKYOPOP® delivered: authentic, hot-off-the-press, and far more fun!

DIRECTIONS

If this is your first time reading manga-style, here's a quick guide to help you understand how it works.

It's easy... just start in the top right panel and follow the numbers. Have fun, and look for more 100% authentic manga from TOKYOPOP®!

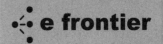

© Minari Endoh/ICHIJINSHA

DAZZLE
BY MINARI ENDOH

When a young girl named Rahzel is sent off to see the world, she meets Alzeido, a mysterious loner on a mission to find his father's killer. The two don't exactly see eye-to-eye, until Alzeido opens his heart to Rahzel. On the long and winding road, the duo crosses paths with various characters...including one who wants to get a little too close to Rahzel!

An epic coming-of-age story from an accomplished manga artist!

T TEEN AGE 13+

© CHIHO SAITOU and IKUNI & Be-PaPas

THE WORLD EXISTS FOR ME
BY BE-PAPAS AND CHIHO SAITOU

Once upon a time, the source of the devil R's invincible powers was *The Book of S & M*. But one day, a young man stole the book without knowing what it was, cut it into strips and used it to create a girl doll named "S" and a boy doll named "M." With that act, the unimaginable power that the devil held from the book was unleashed upon the world!

From the creators of the manga classic *Revolutionary Girl Utena!*

T TEEN AGE 13+

© Keitaro Arima

TSUKUYOMI: MOON PHASE
BY KEITARO ARIMA

Cameraman Kouhei Midou is researching Schwarz Quelle Castle. When he steps inside the castle's great walls, he discovers a mysterious little girl, Hazuki, who's been trapped there for years. Utilizing her controlling charm, Hazuki tries to get Kouhei to set her free. But this sweet little girl isn't everything she appears to be...

The manga that launched the popular anime!

T TEEN AGE 13+

EDITORS' PICKS TOKYOPOP MANGA SUPPLEMENT

BY HO-KYUNG YEO

HONEY MUSTARD

I'm often asked about the title of *Honey Mustard*. What does a condiment have to do with romance and teen angst? One might ask the same thing about a basket of fruits, but I digress. Honey mustard is sweet with a good dose of bite, and I'd say that sums up this series pretty darn well, too. Ho-Kyung Yeo does a marvelous job of balancing the painful situations of adolescence with plenty of whacked-out humor to keep the mood from getting *too* heavy. It's a good, solid romantic comedy...and come to think of it, it'd go great with that sandwich.

~Carol Fox, Editor

BY YURIKO NISHIYAMA

REBOUND

At first glance, *Rebound* may seem like a simple sports manga. But on closer inspection, you'll find that the real drama takes place off the court. While the kids of the Johnan basketball team play and grow as a team, they learn valuable life lessons as well. By fusing the raw energy of basketball with the apple pie earnestness of an afterschool special, Yuriko Nishiyama has created a unique and heartfelt manga that appeals to all readers, male and female.

~Troy Lewter, Editor

Honey Mustard © Ho-Kyung Yeo, HAKSAN PUBLISHING CO., LTD. Rebound © Yuriko Nishiyama.

SPOTLIGHT
TOKYOPOP MANGA SUPPLEMENT

LOVELESS
BY YUN KOUGA

The mystery behind the death of his older brother was only the beginning...

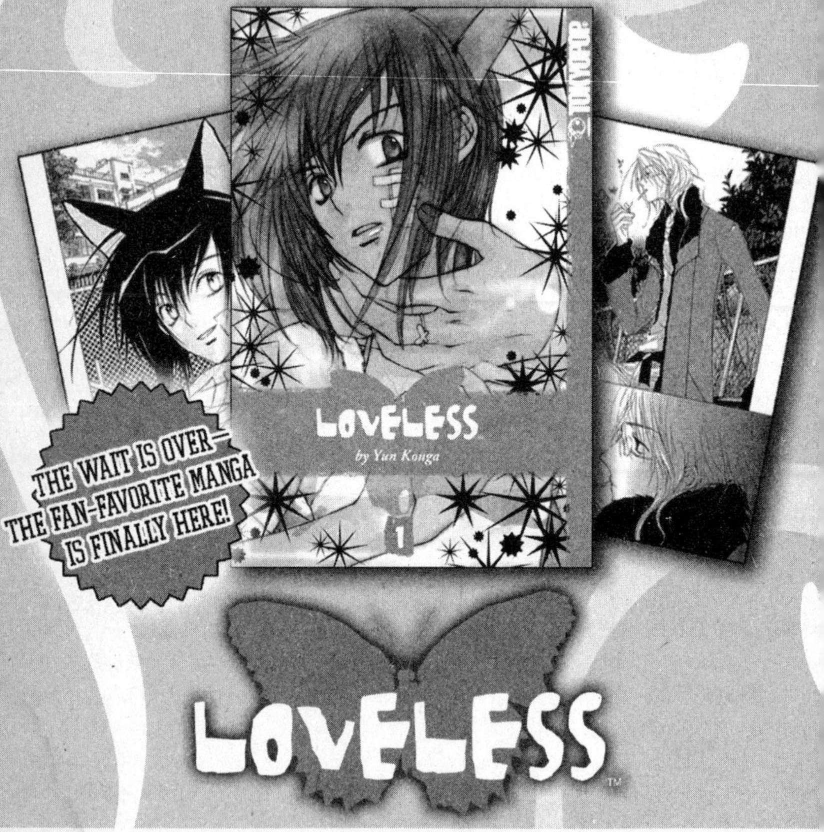
TOKYOPOP
LOVELESS
by Yun Kouga
1
THE WAIT IS OVER—
THE FAN-FAVORITE MANGA
IS FINALLY HERE!
LOVELESS™

After discovering a posthumous message from his brother indicating he was murdered, twelve-year-old Ritsuka becomes involved in a shadowy world of spell battles and secret names. Together with the mysterious Soubi, Ritsuka begins the search to uncover the truth behind the murder! But in a world where mere words have unbelievable power, how can you find true friendship when your very name is Loveless?

OT
OLDER TEEN
AGE 16+

FOR MORE INFORMATION VISIT: WWW.TOKYOPOP.COM/LOVELESS

Serial Publication

Publication

第4巻

RG VEDA

聖伝

氷城炎獄篇

新書館

STORY BY

大川七瀬

AGEHA OHKAWA

COMIC BY

もこなあぱぱ

MOKONA

WINGS

WINGS COMICS

PLANNING

CLAMP

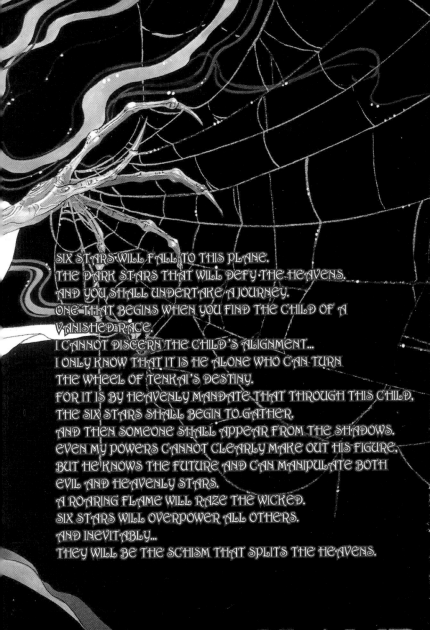

SIX STARS WILL FALL TO THIS PLANE.
THE DARK STARS THAT WILL DEFY THE HEAVENS.
AND YOU SHALL UNDERTAKE A JOURNEY.
ONE THAT BEGINS WHEN YOU FIND THE CHILD OF A
VANISHED RACE.
I CANNOT DISCERN THE CHILD'S ALIGNMENT...
I ONLY KNOW THAT IT IS HE ALONE WHO CAN TURN
THE WHEEL OF TENKAI'S DESTINY.
FOR IT IS BY HEAVENLY MANDATE THAT THROUGH THIS CHILD,
THE SIX STARS SHALL BEGIN TO GATHER.
AND THEN SOMEONE SHALL APPEAR FROM THE SHADOWS.
EVEN MY POWERS CANNOT CLEARLY MAKE OUT HIS FIGURE,
BUT HE KNOWS THE FUTURE AND CAN MANIPULATE BOTH
EVIL AND HEAVENLY STARS.
A ROARING FLAME WILL RAZE THE WICKED.
SIX STARS WILL OVERPOWER ALL OTHERS.
AND INEVITABLY...
THEY WILL BE THE SCHISM THAT SPLITS THE HEAVENS.

PLANNING **CLAMP**

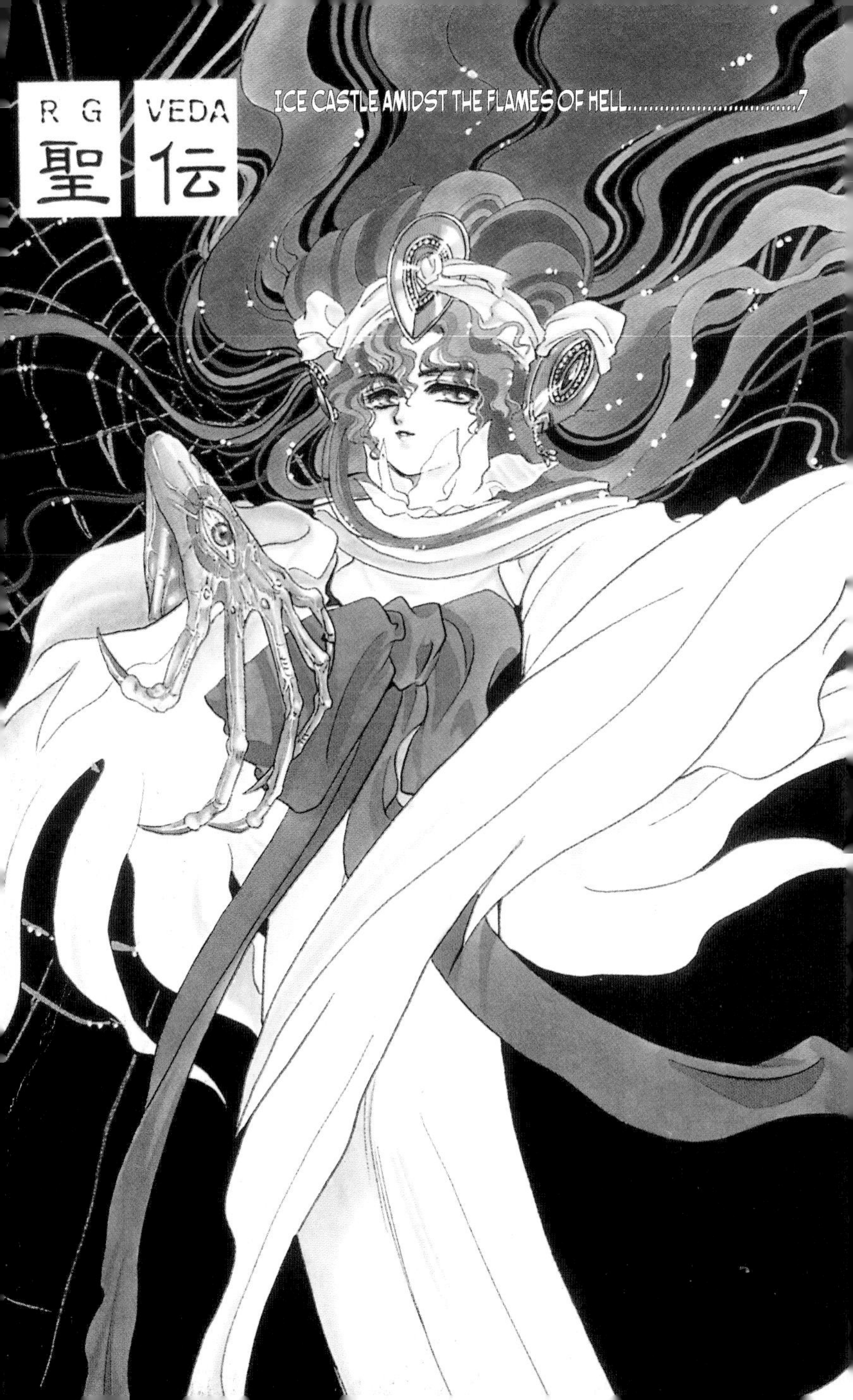
RG VEDA
聖伝

H O S H I G A N A G A R E R U

YOU WILL BE THE SCHISM THAT SPLITS HEAVEN.

CLAMP MEMBERS

Main

STORY
大川七瀬 AGEHA OHKAWA

COMIC
もこなあぱぱ MOKONA

Book Designer
大川七瀬
AGEHA OHKAWA

Director
もこなあぱぱ
MOKONA

Short Comic
猫井みっく
TSUBAKI NEKOI

Art Assistants
猫井みっく TSUBAKI NEKOI
五十嵐さつき SATSUKI IGARASHI

PLANNING & PRESENTED by

CLAMP

RG 聖 VEDA 伝

VOLUME 4

BY
CLAMP

HAMBURG // LONDON // LOS ANGELES // TOKYO

RG Veda Vol. 4
created by CLAMP

Translation - Haruko Furukawa
English Adaptation - Christine Schilling
Copy Editor - Peter Ahlstrom
Retouch and Lettering - Fawn Lau
Production Artists - Fawn Lau and Jason Milligan
Cover Design - Jorge Negrete

Editor - Carol Fox
Digital Imaging Manager - Chris Buford
Production Managers - Jennifer Miller and Mutsumi Miyazaki
Managing Editor - Lindsey Johnston
VP of Production - Ron Klamert
Publisher and E.I.C. - Mike Kiley
President and C.O.O. - John Parker
C.E.O. - Stuart Levy

A  Manga

TOKYOPOP Inc.
5900 Wilshire Blvd. Suite 2000
Los Angeles, CA 90036

E-mail: info@TOKYOPOP.com
Come visit us online at www.TOKYOPOP.com

ISBN: 1-59532-487-9

First TOKYOPOP printing: January 2006
10 9 8 7 6 5 4 3 2 1
Printed in the USA

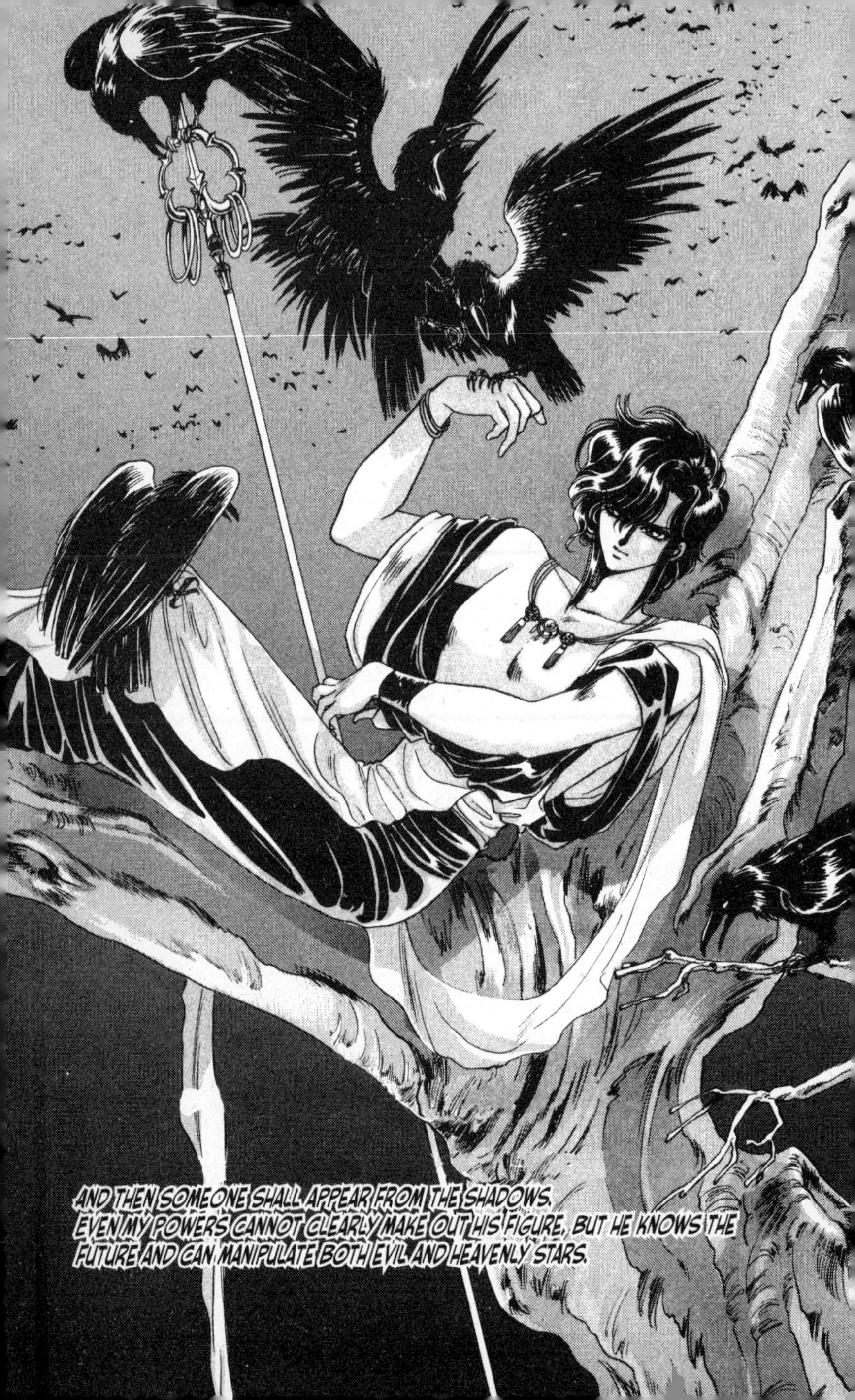
AND THEN SOMEONE SHALL APPEAR FROM THE SHADOWS.
EVEN MY POWERS CANNOT CLEARLY MAKE OUT HIS FIGURE, BUT HE KNOWS THE FUTURE AND CAN MANIPULATE BOTH EVIL AND HEAVENLY STARS.

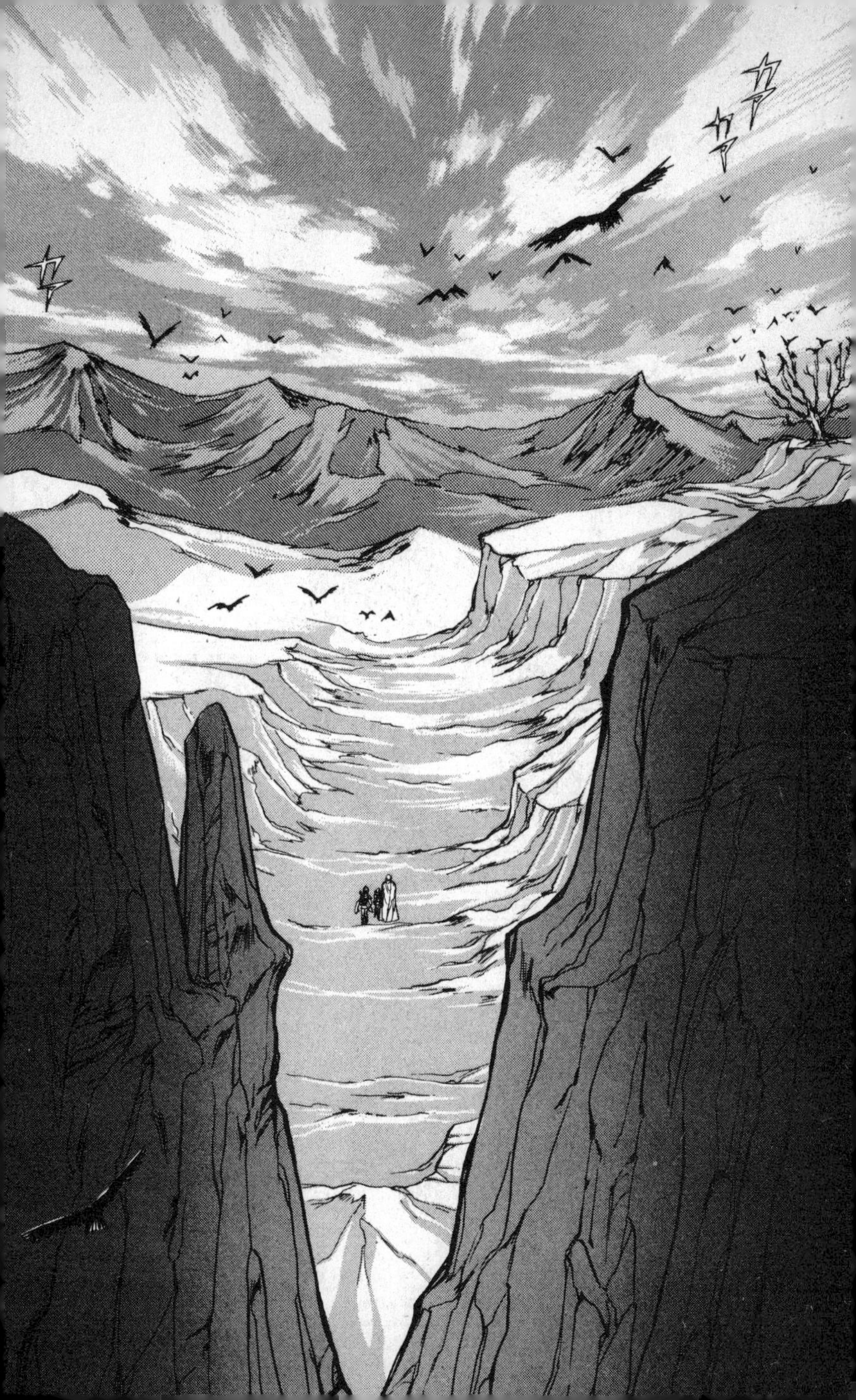
カァ
カァ
カァ

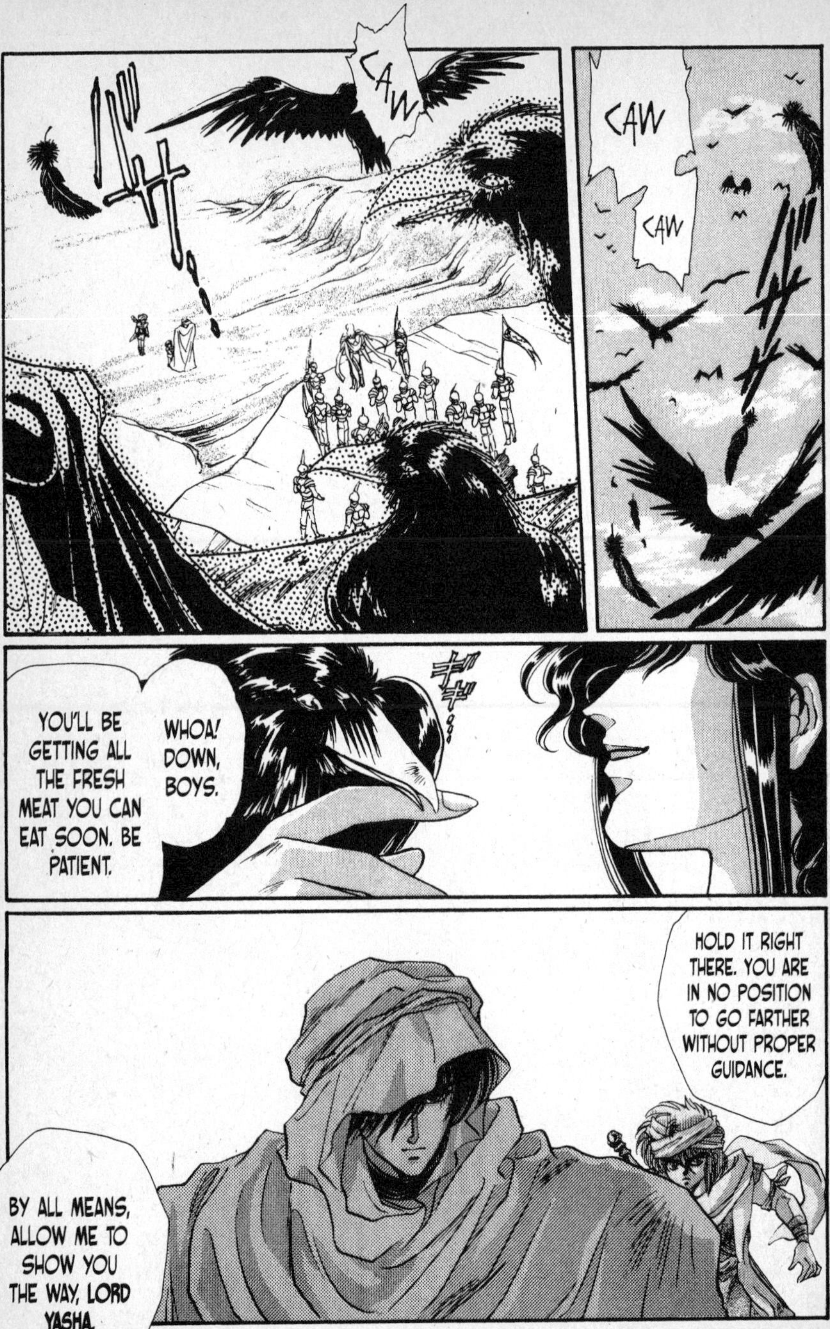
CAW
CAW
CAW
WHOA! DOWN, BOYS.
YOU'LL BE GETTING ALL THE FRESH MEAT YOU CAN EAT SOON. BE PATIENT.
HOLD IT RIGHT THERE. YOU ARE IN NO POSITION TO GO FARTHER WITHOUT PROPER GUIDANCE.
BY ALL MEANS, ALLOW ME TO SHOW YOU THE WAY, LORD YASHA.

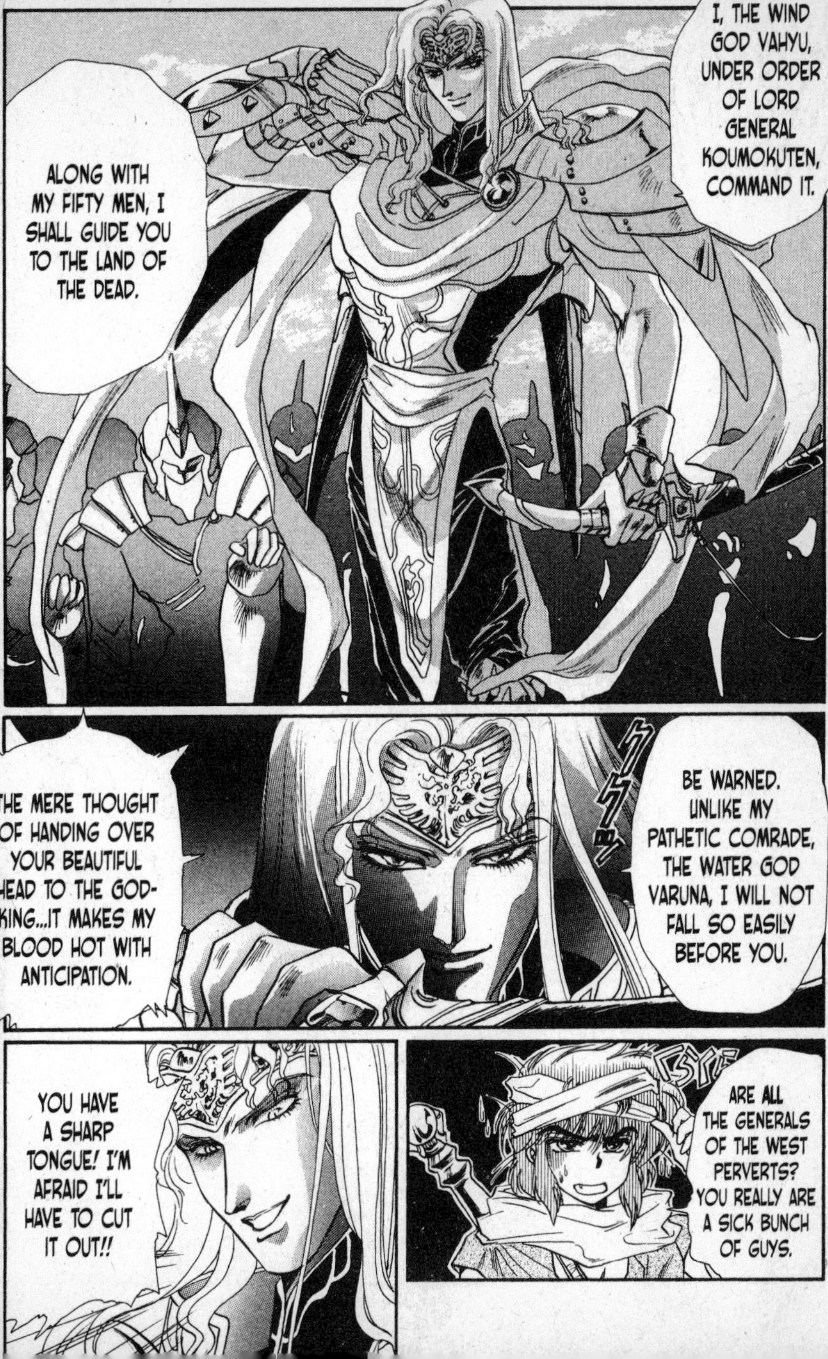
I, THE WIND GOD VAHYU, UNDER ORDER OF LORD GENERAL KOUMOKUTEN, COMMAND IT.
ALONG WITH MY FIFTY MEN, I SHALL GUIDE YOU TO THE LAND OF THE DEAD.
BE WARNED. UNLIKE MY PATHETIC COMRADE, THE WATER GOD VARUNA, I WILL NOT FALL SO EASILY BEFORE YOU.
THE MERE THOUGHT OF HANDING OVER YOUR BEAUTIFUL HEAD TO THE GOD-KING...IT MAKES MY BLOOD HOT WITH ANTICIPATION.
ARE ALL THE GENERALS OF THE WEST PERVERTS? YOU REALLY ARE A SICK BUNCH OF GUYS.
YOU HAVE A SHARP TONGUE! I'M AFRAID I'LL HAVE TO CUT IT OUT!!

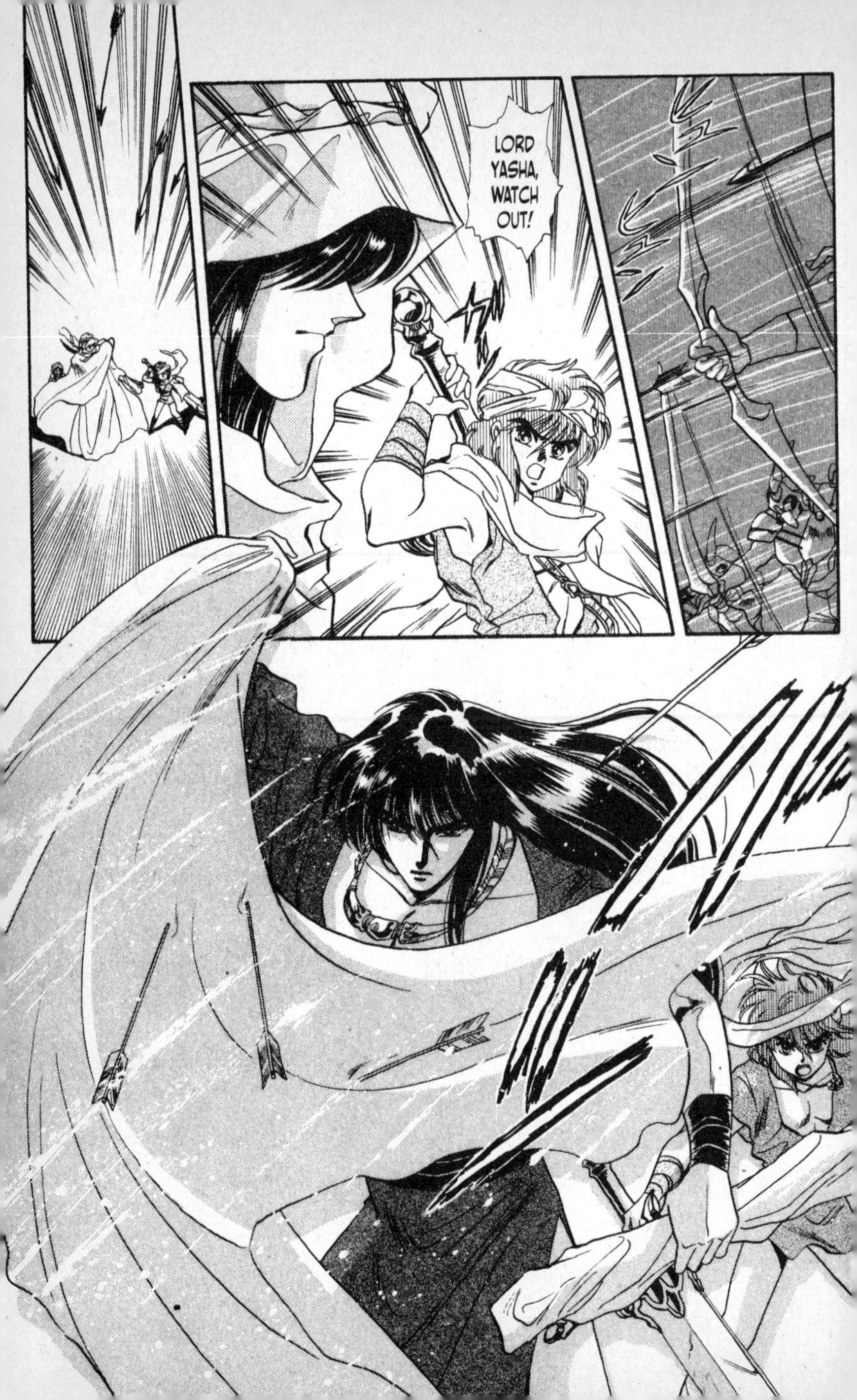
LORD YASHA, WATCH OUT!

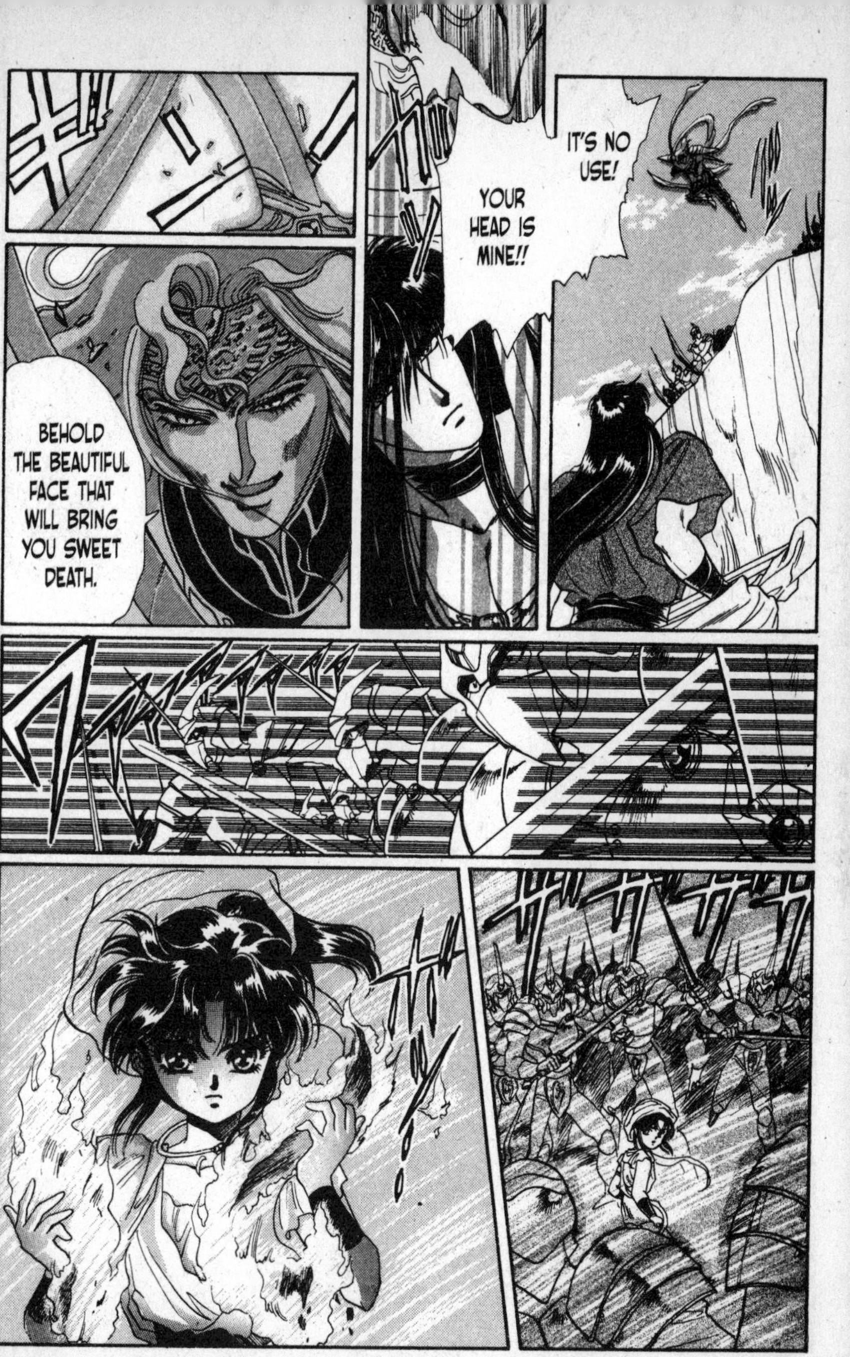
IT'S NO USE!
YOUR HEAD IS MINE!!
BEHOLD THE BEAUTIFUL FACE THAT WILL BRING YOU SWEET DEATH.

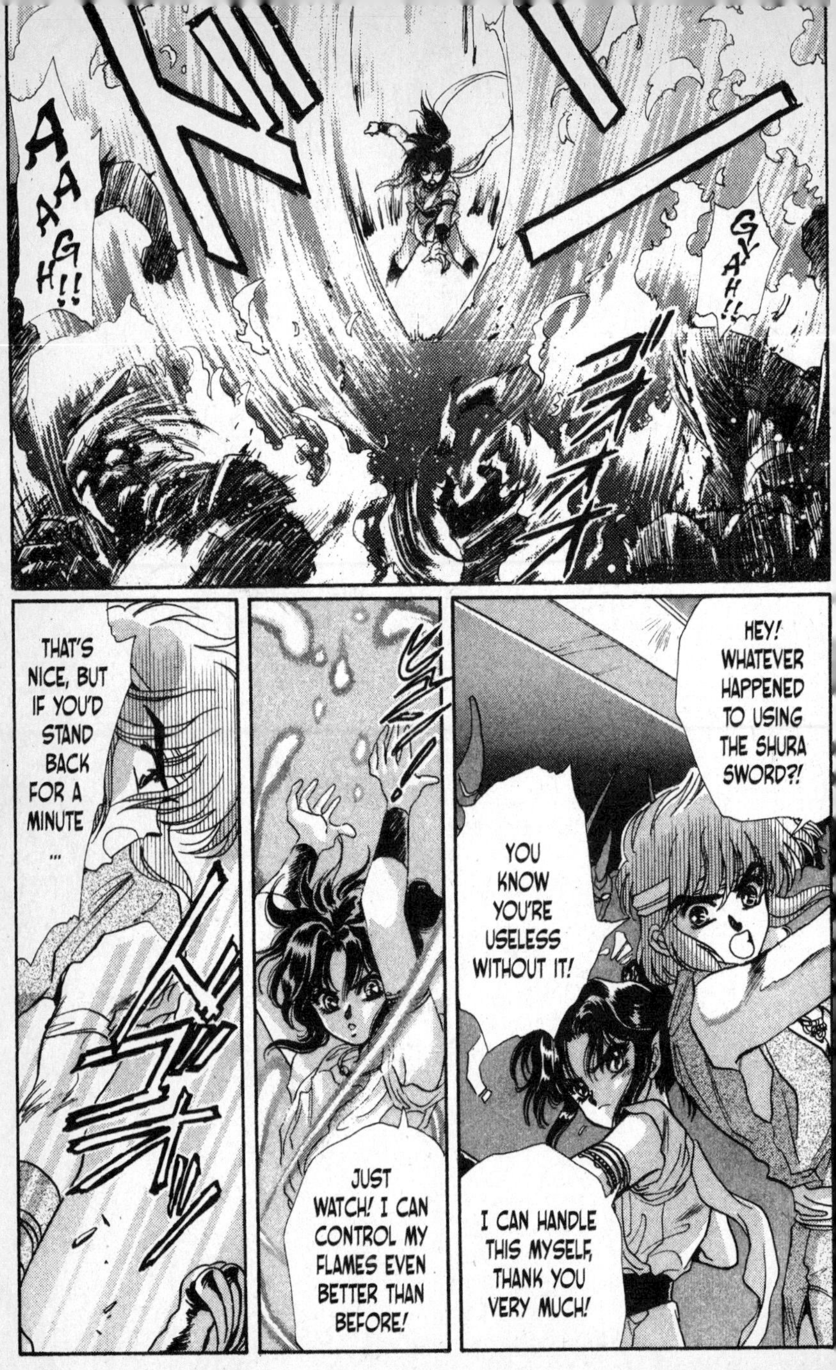
GYAH!!
AAAGH!!
HEY! WHATEVER HAPPENED TO USING THE SHURA SWORD?!
YOU KNOW YOU'RE USELESS WITHOUT IT!
I CAN HANDLE THIS MYSELF, THANK YOU VERY MUCH!
JUST WATCH! I CAN CONTROL MY FLAMES EVEN BETTER THAN BEFORE!
THAT'S NICE, BUT IF YOU'D STAND BACK FOR A MINUTE ...

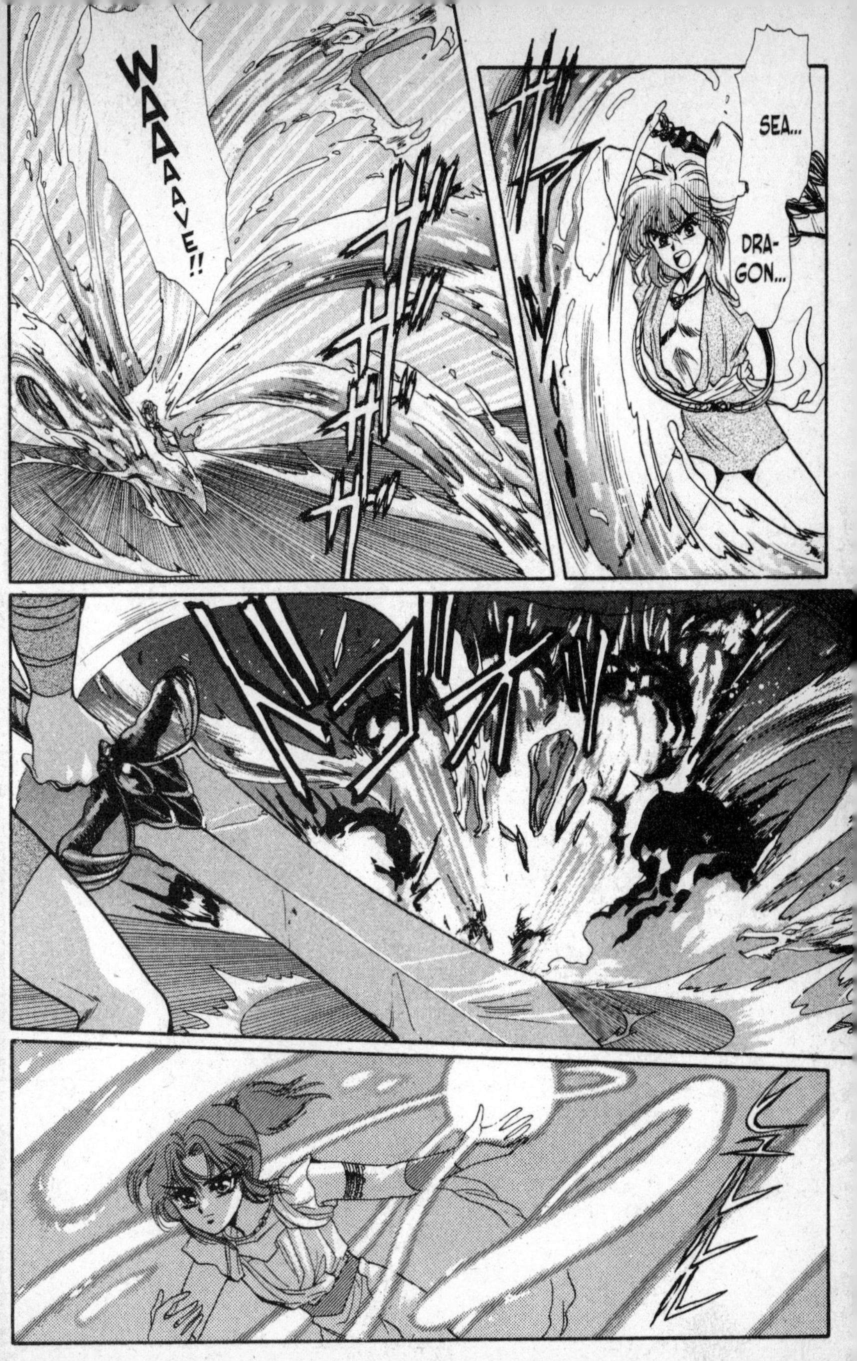
SEA...
DRA-
GON...
WAAAAAVE!!

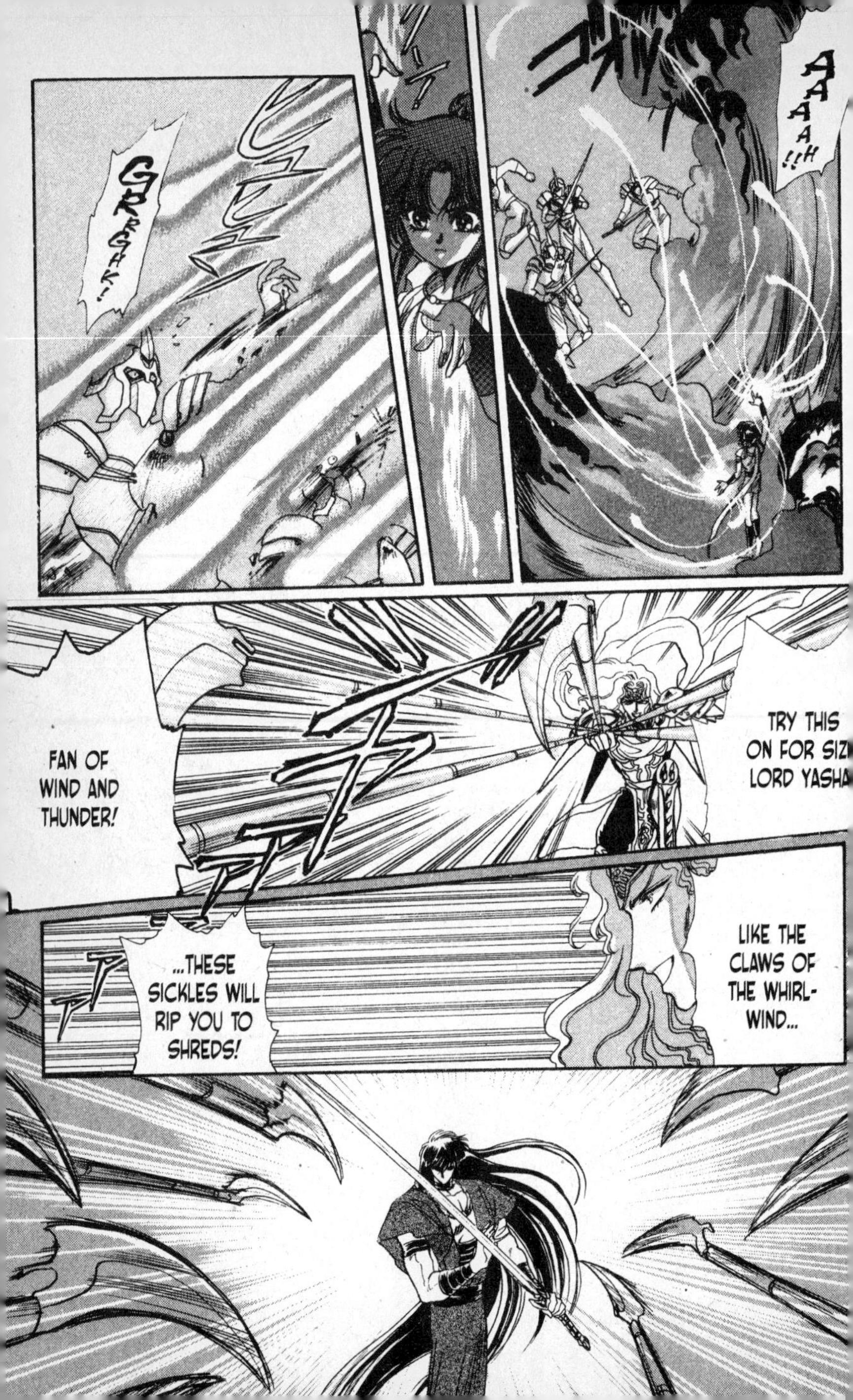
AAAAAH!!
GRRRGHK!
TRY THIS ON FOR SIZ LORD YASHA
FAN OF WIND AND THUNDER!
LIKE THE CLAWS OF THE WHIRL-WIND...
...THESE SICKLES WILL RIP YOU TO SHREDS!

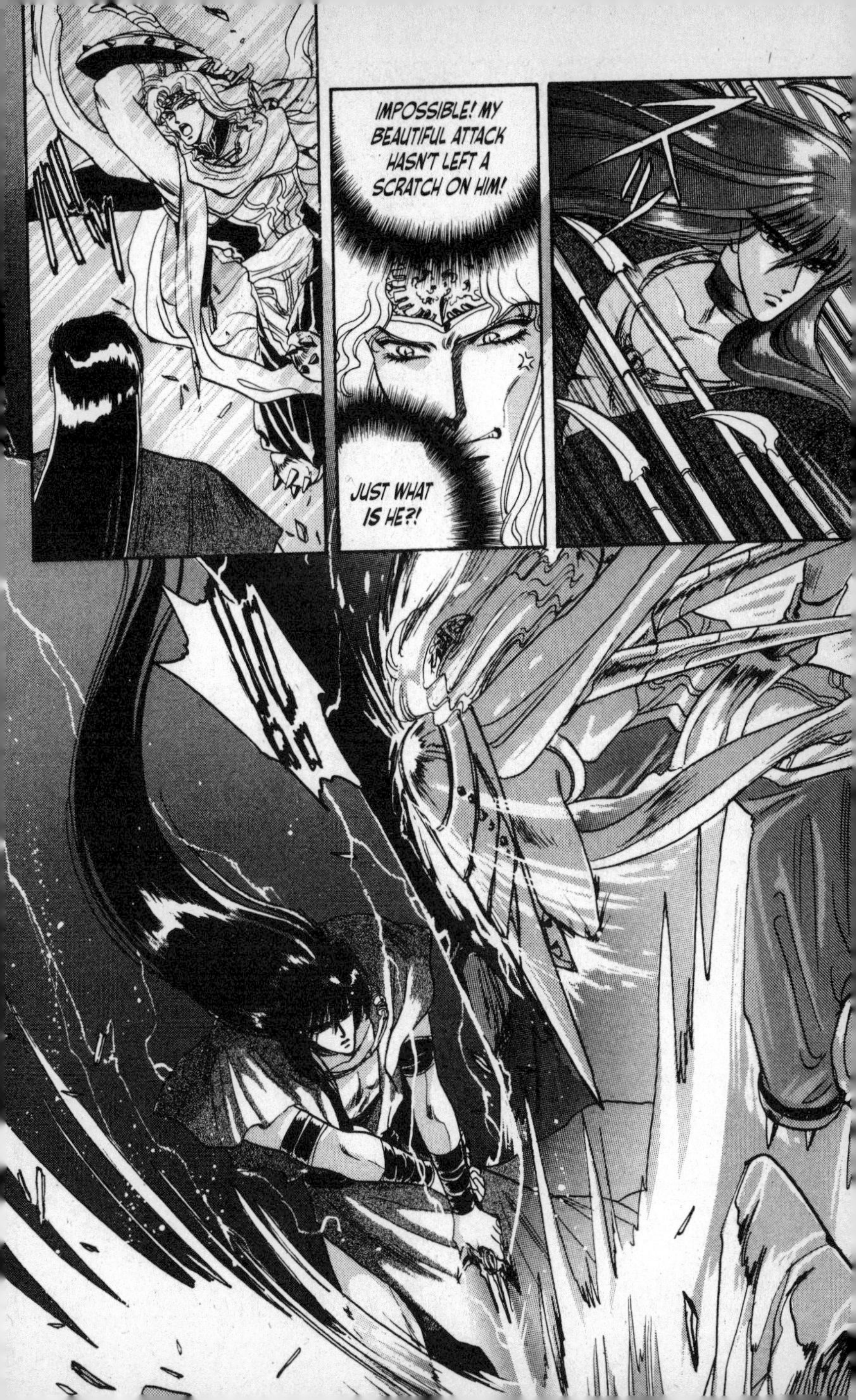
IMPOSSIBLE! MY BEAUTIFUL ATTACK HASN'T LEFT A SCRATCH ON HIM!
JUST WHAT IS HE?!

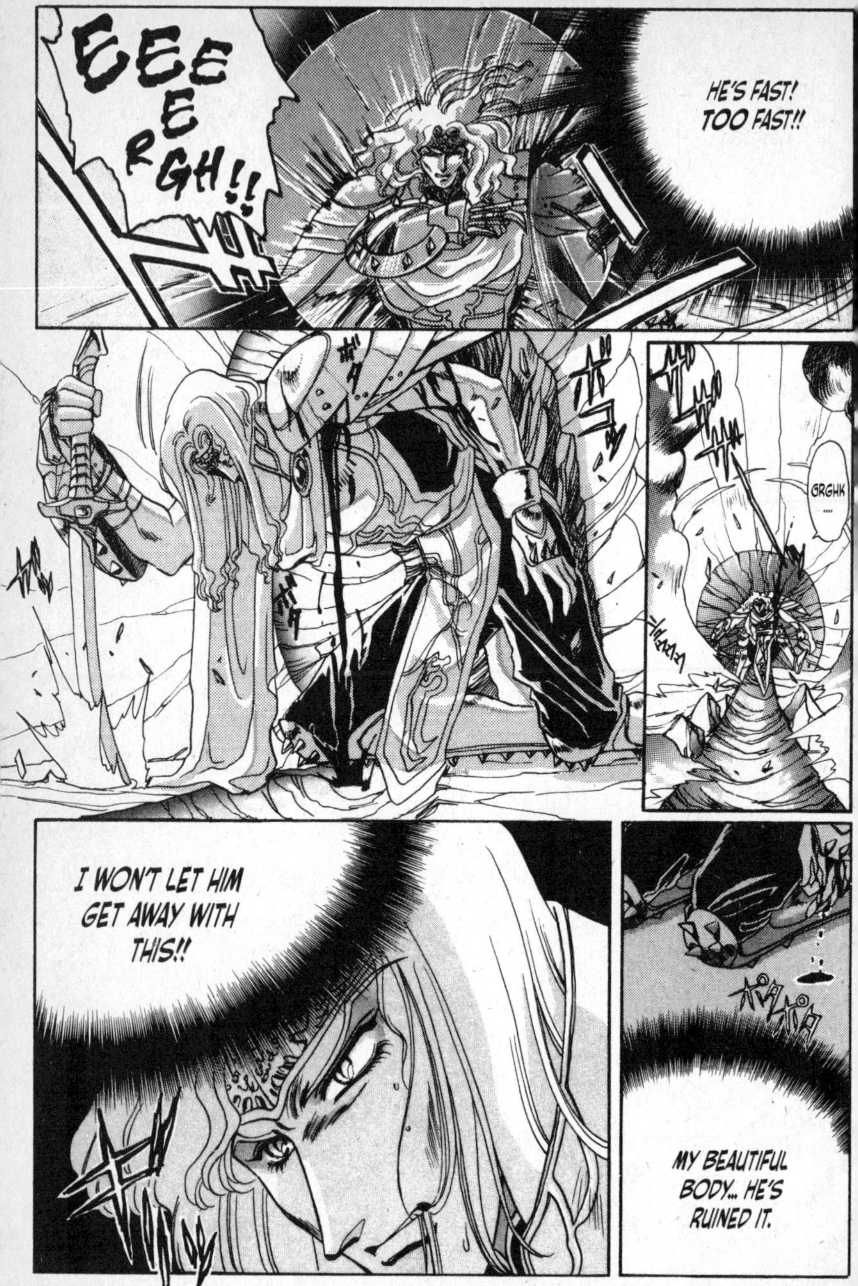
HE'S FAST! TOO FAST!!
EEEEERGH!!
GRGHK...
MY BEAUTIFUL BODY... HE'S RUINED IT.
I WON'T LET HIM GET AWAY WITH THIS!!

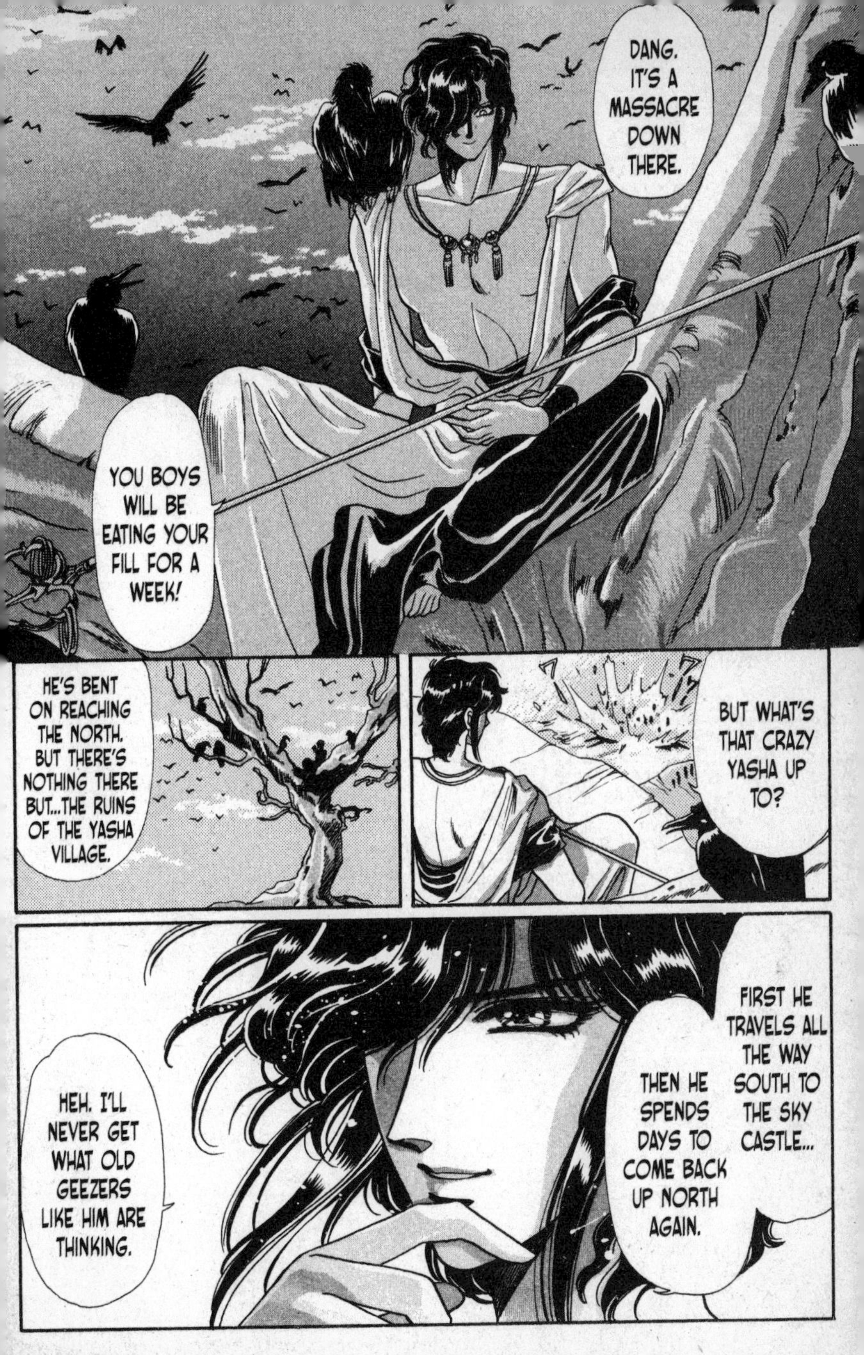
DANG. IT'S A MASSACRE DOWN THERE.
YOU BOYS WILL BE EATING YOUR FILL FOR A WEEK!
BUT WHAT'S THAT CRAZY YASHA UP TO?
HE'S BENT ON REACHING THE NORTH. BUT THERE'S NOTHING THERE BUT...THE RUINS OF THE YASHA VILLAGE.
FIRST HE TRAVELS ALL THE WAY SOUTH TO THE SKY CASTLE...
THEN HE SPENDS DAYS TO COME BACK UP NORTH AGAIN.
HEH. I'LL NEVER GET WHAT OLD GEEZERS LIKE HIM ARE THINKING.

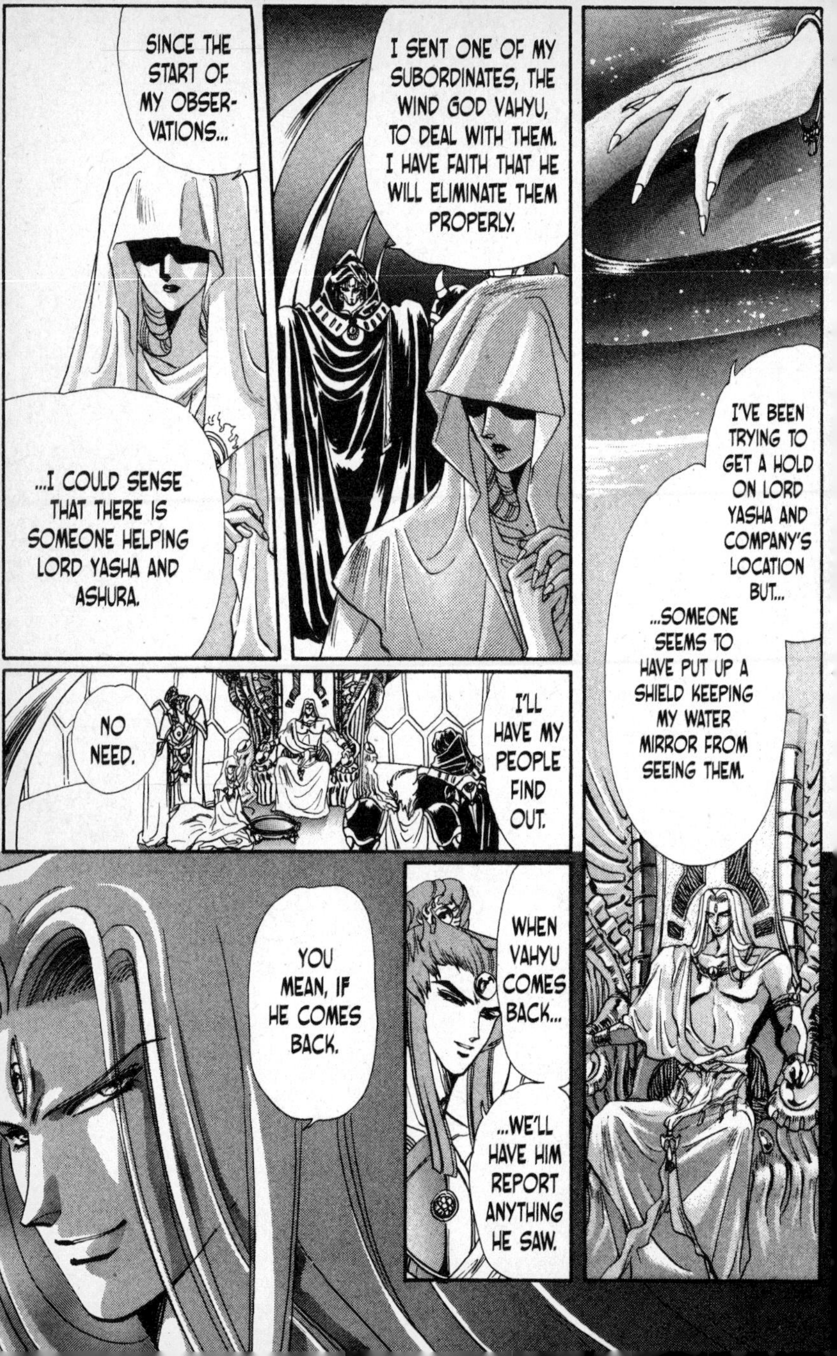
I'VE BEEN TRYING TO GET A HOLD ON LORD YASHA AND COMPANY'S LOCATION BUT...
...SOMEONE SEEMS TO HAVE PUT UP A SHIELD KEEPING MY WATER MIRROR FROM SEEING THEM.
I SENT ONE OF MY SUBORDINATES, THE WIND GOD VAHYU, TO DEAL WITH THEM. I HAVE FAITH THAT HE WILL ELIMINATE THEM PROPERLY.
SINCE THE START OF MY OBSER-VATIONS...
...I COULD SENSE THAT THERE IS SOMEONE HELPING LORD YASHA AND ASHURA.
I'LL HAVE MY PEOPLE FIND OUT.
NO NEED.
WHEN VAHYU COMES BACK...
...WE'LL HAVE HIM REPORT ANYTHING HE SAW.
YOU MEAN, IF HE COMES BACK.

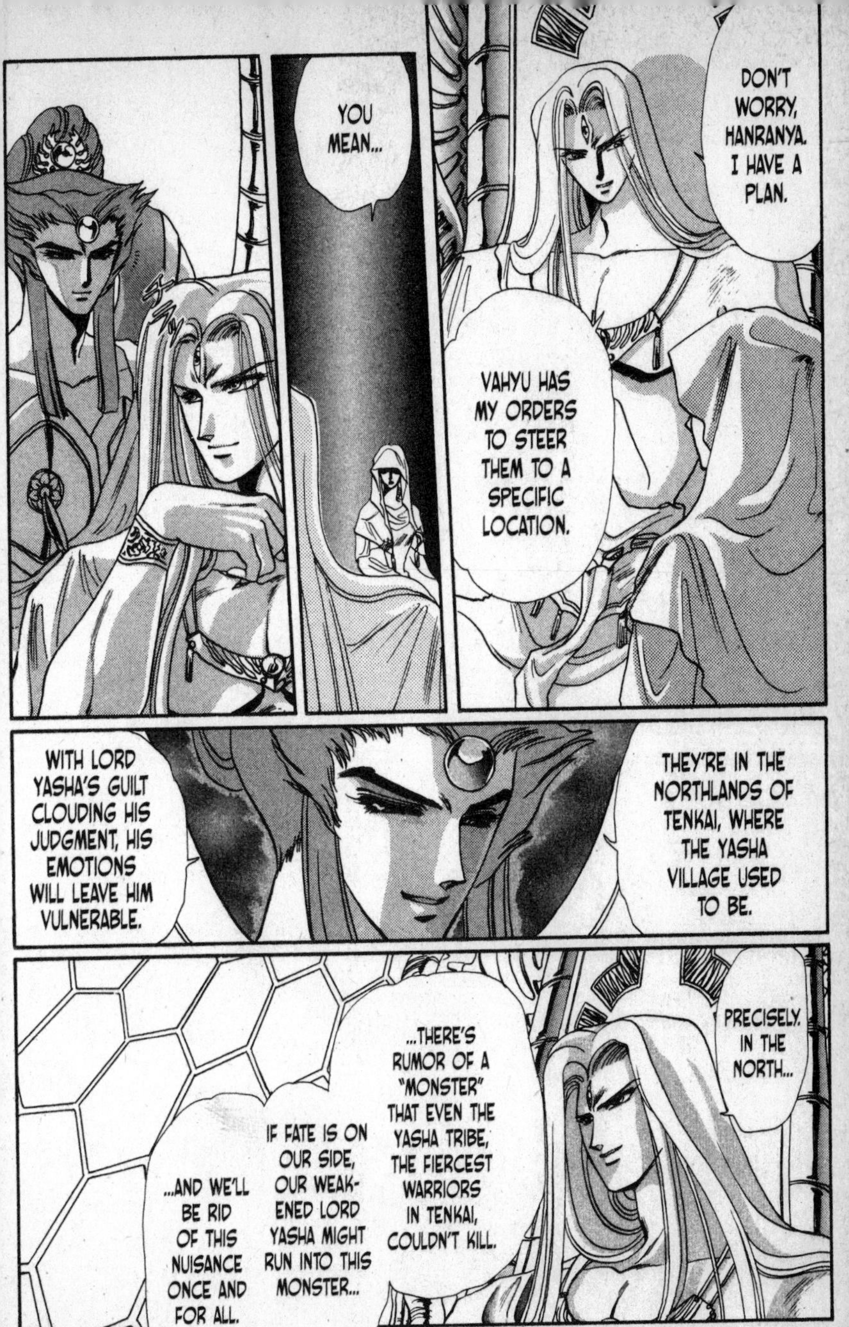
DON'T WORRY, HANRANYA. I HAVE A PLAN.
VAHYU HAS MY ORDERS TO STEER THEM TO A SPECIFIC LOCATION.
YOU MEAN...
THEY'RE IN THE NORTHLANDS OF TENKAI, WHERE THE YASHA VILLAGE USED TO BE.
WITH LORD YASHA'S GUILT CLOUDING HIS JUDGMENT, HIS EMOTIONS WILL LEAVE HIM VULNERABLE.
PRECISELY. IN THE NORTH...
...THERE'S RUMOR OF A "MONSTER" THAT EVEN THE YASHA TRIBE, THE FIERCEST WARRIORS IN TENKAI, COULDN'T KILL.
IF FATE IS ON OUR SIDE, OUR WEAK-ENED LORD YASHA MIGHT RUN INTO THIS MONSTER...
...AND WE'LL BE RID OF THIS NUISANCE ONCE AND FOR ALL.

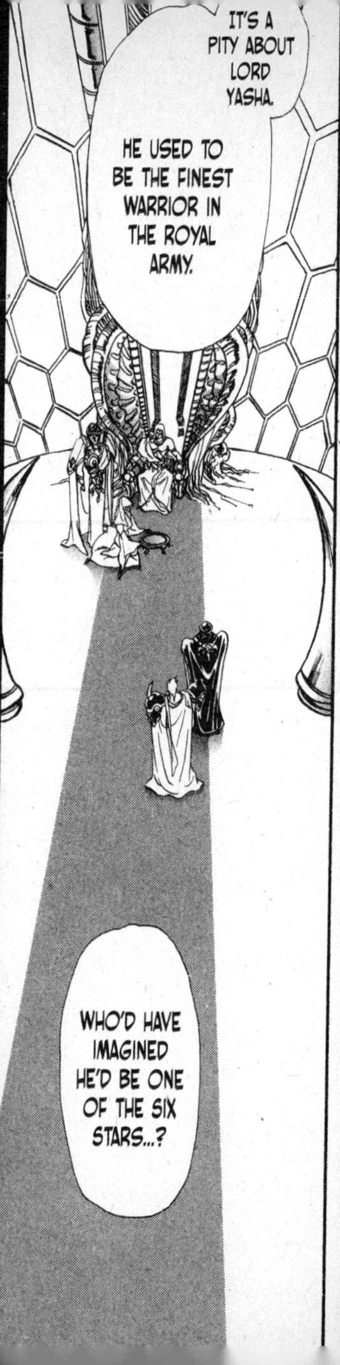
IT'S A PITY ABOUT LORD YASHA.
HE USED TO BE THE FINEST WARRIOR IN THE ROYAL ARMY.
WHO'D HAVE IMAGINED HE'D BE ONE OF THE SIX STARS...?

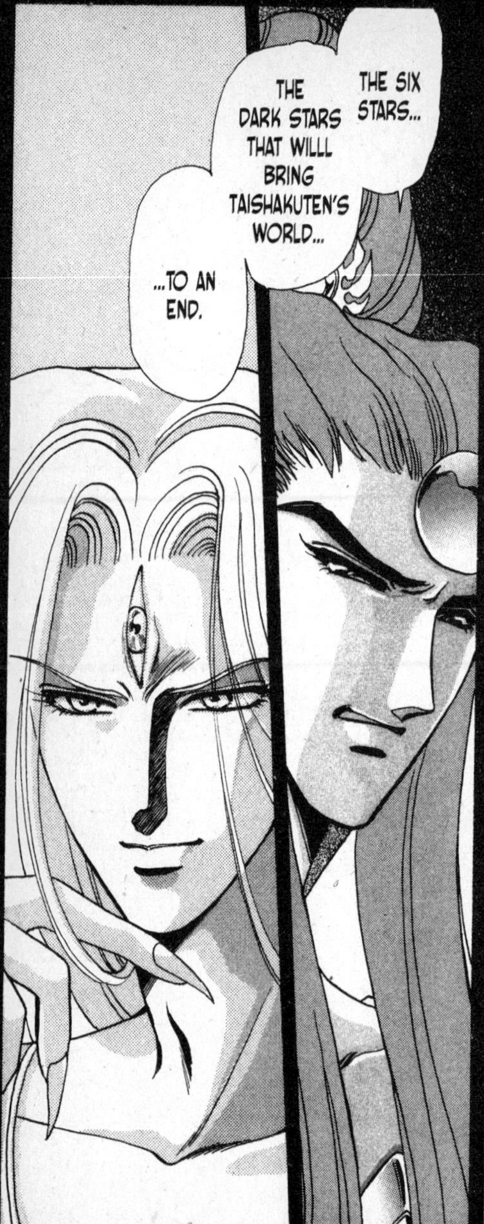
THE SIX STARS...
THE DARK STARS THAT WILLL BRING TAISHAKUTEN'S WORLD...
...TO AN END.

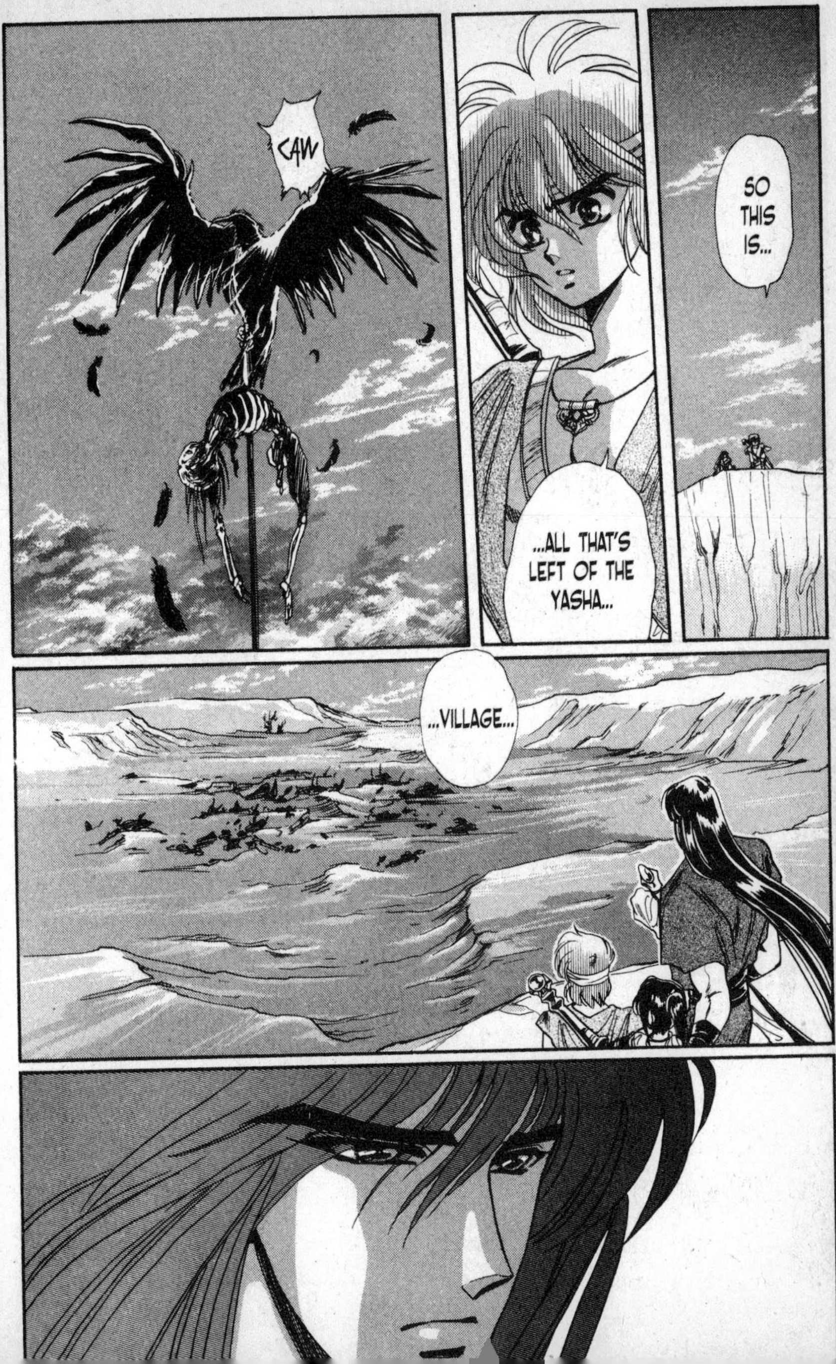
SO THIS IS...
...ALL THAT'S LEFT OF THE YASHA...
CAW
...VILLAGE...

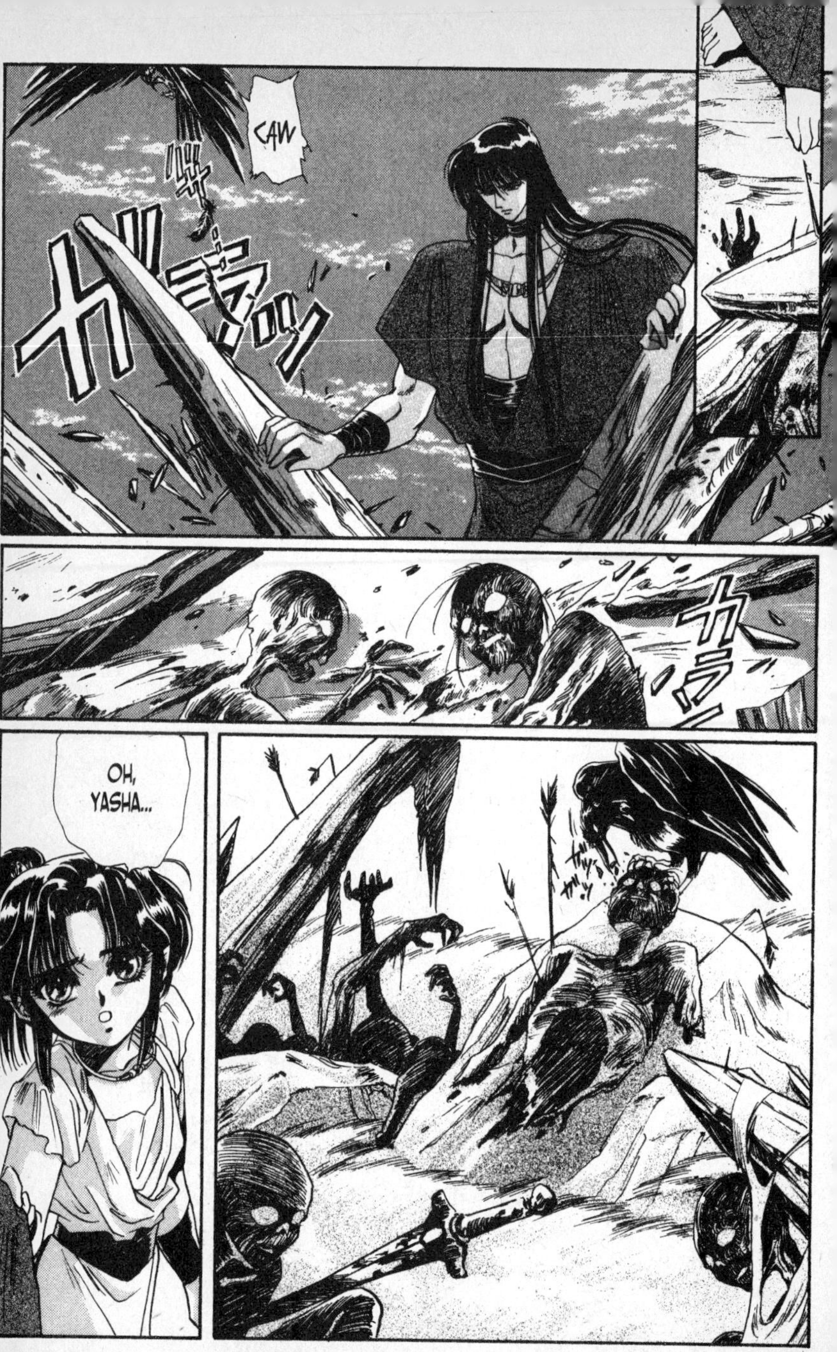
CAW
OH, YASHA...

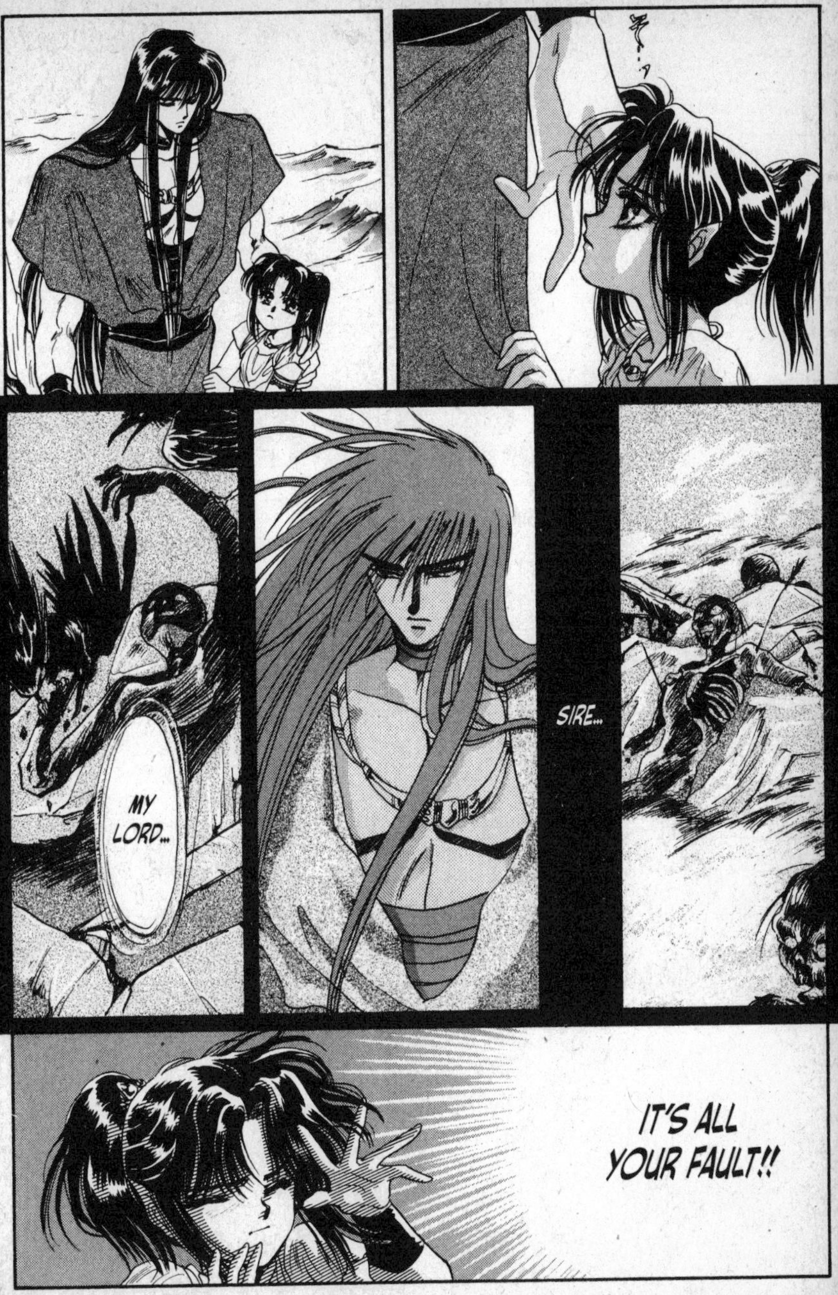
SIRE...
MY LORD...
IT'S ALL YOUR FAULT!!

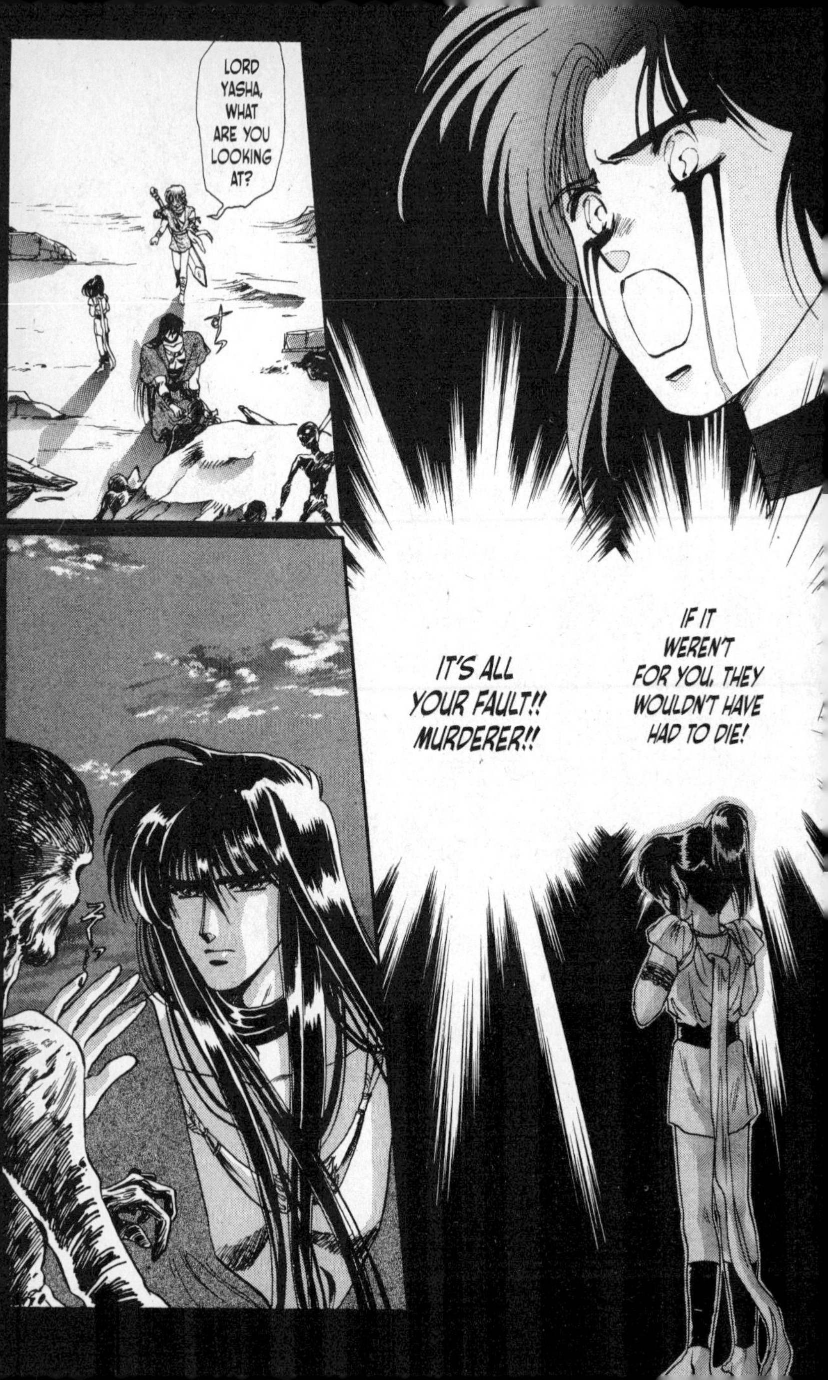
IT'S ALL YOUR FAULT!! MURDERER!!
IF IT WEREN'T FOR YOU, THEY WOULDN'T HAVE HAD TO DIE!
LORD YASHA, WHAT ARE YOU LOOKING AT?

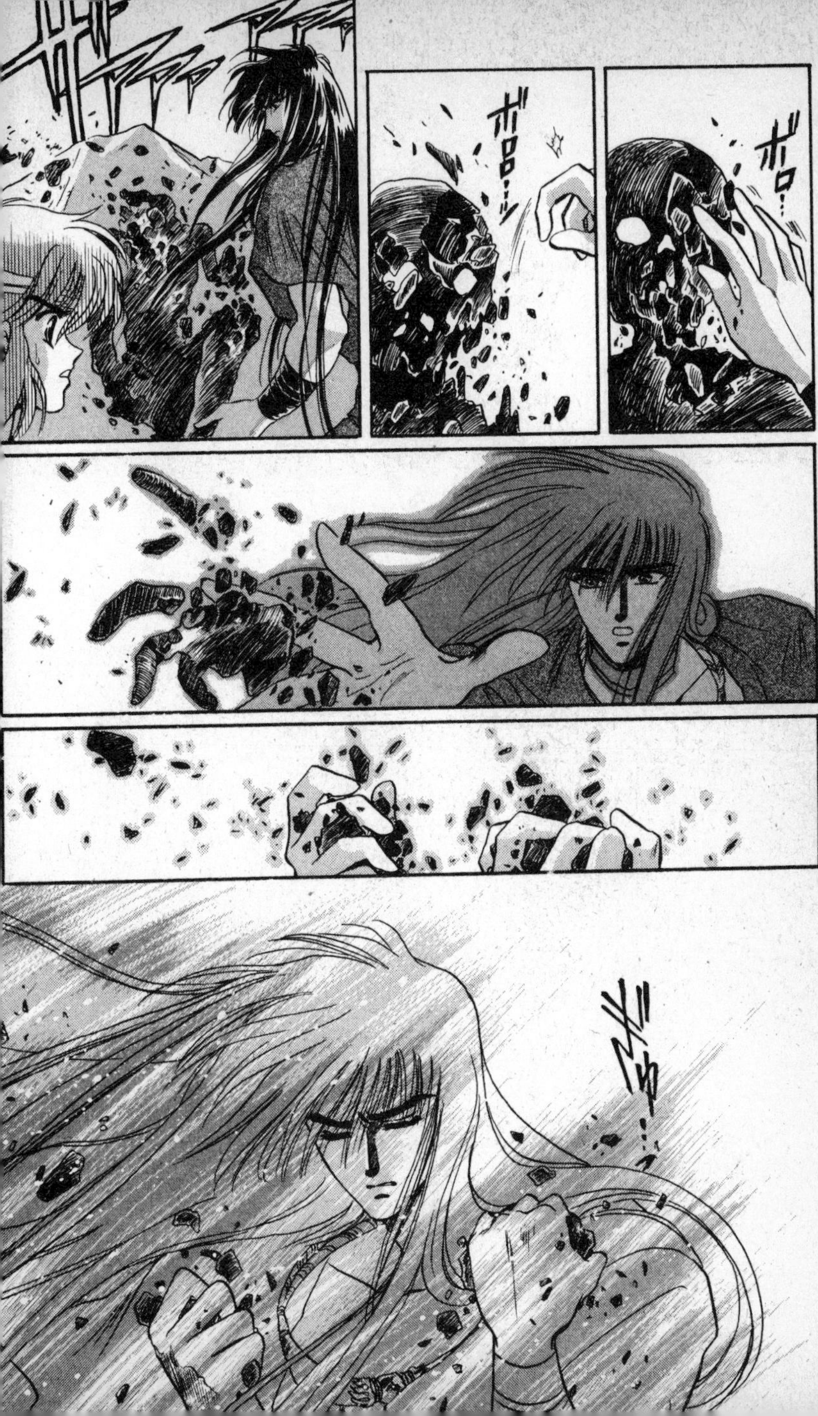

ボロ…
ボロ…ッ
ザアアアア
ギュッ…!

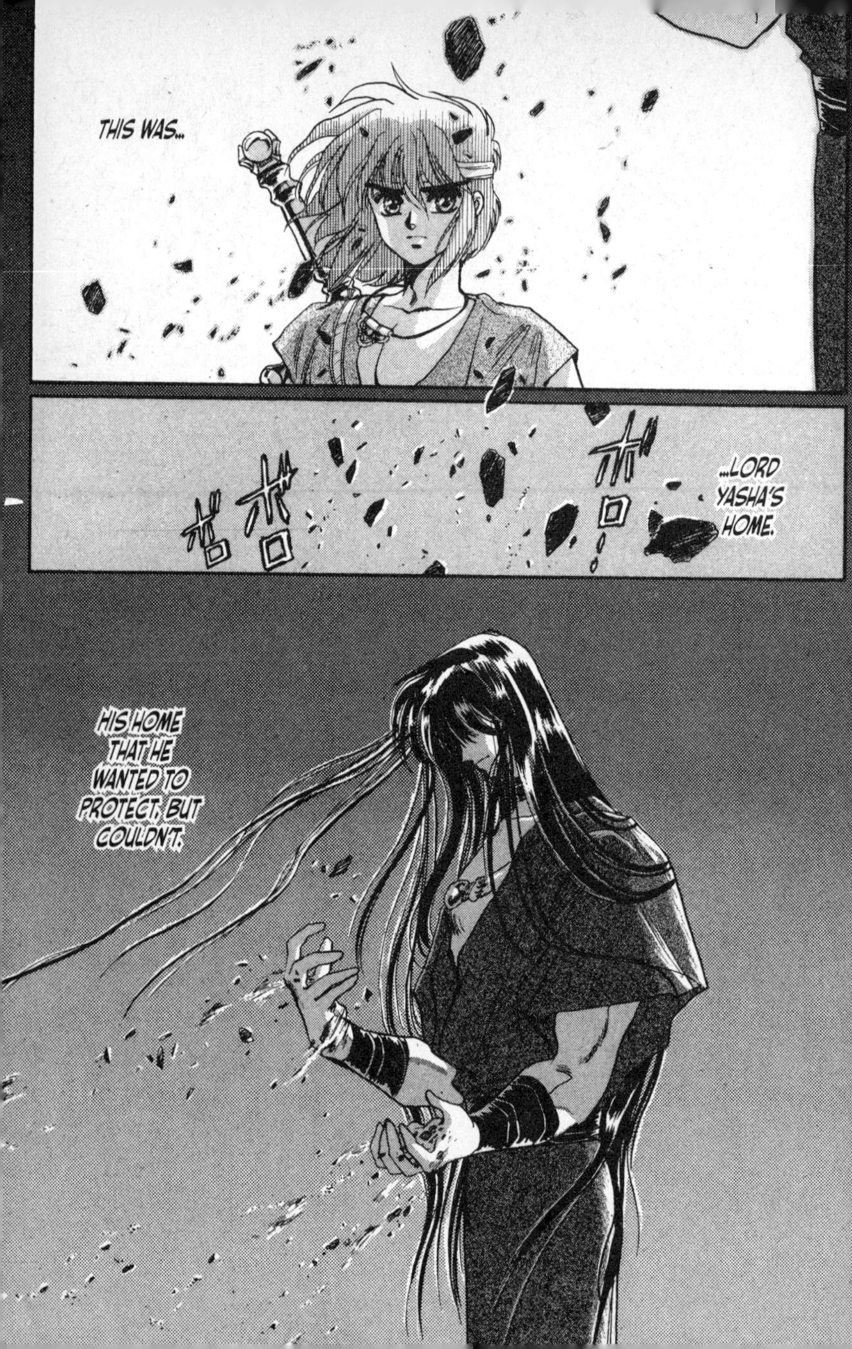
THIS WAS...
...LORD YASHA'S HOME.
HIS HOME THAT HE WANTED TO PROTECT, BUT COULDN'T.

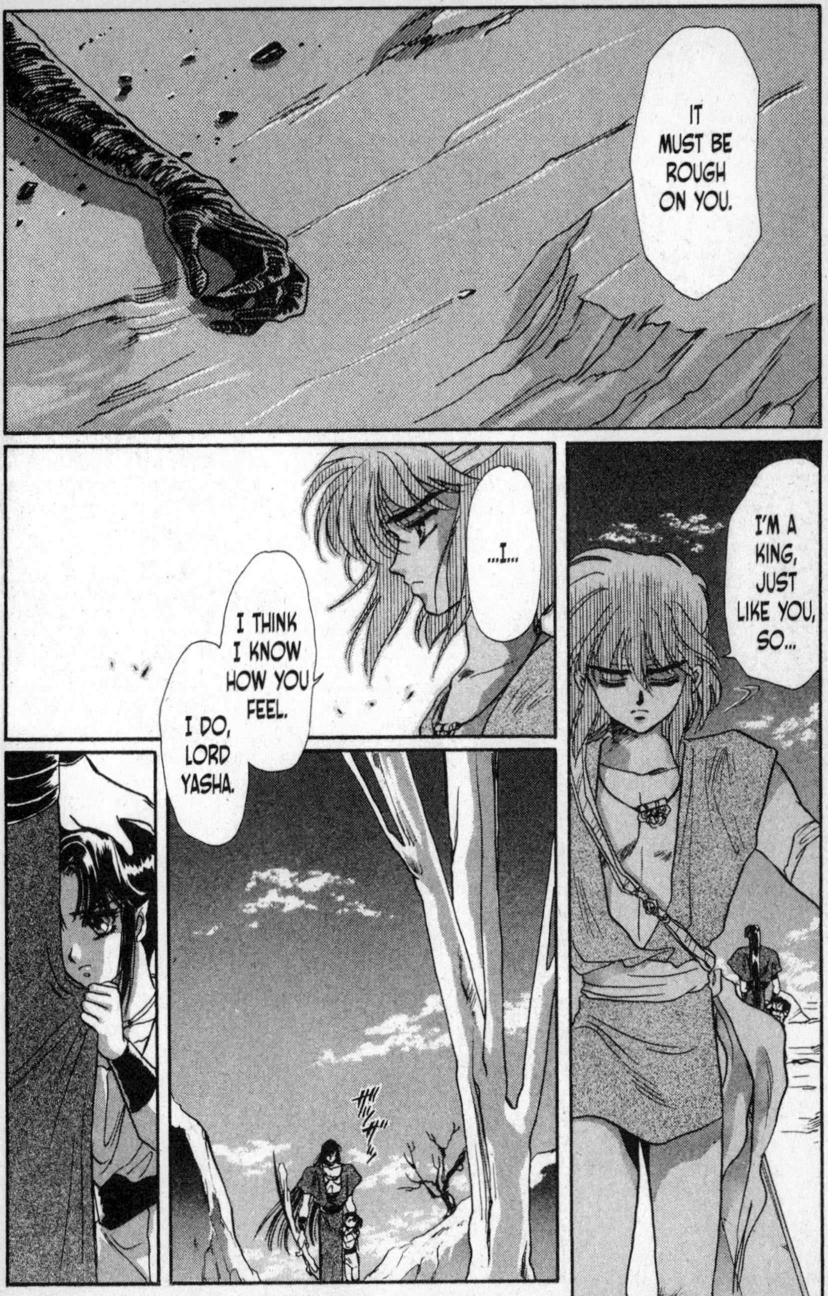
IT MUST BE ROUGH ON YOU.
I'M A KING, JUST LIKE YOU, SO...
...I...
I THINK I KNOW HOW YOU FEEL.
I DO, LORD YASHA.

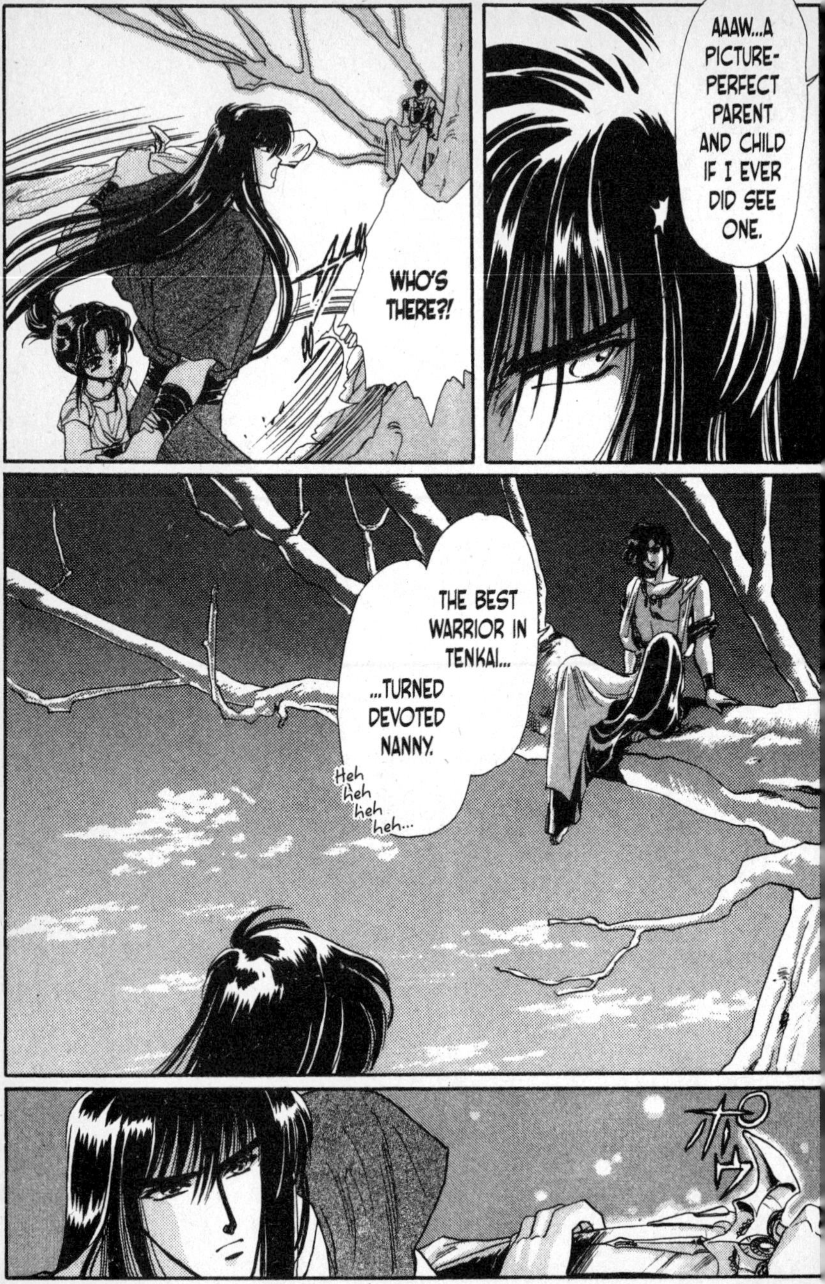
WHO'S THERE?!
AAAW...A PICTURE-PERFECT PARENT AND CHILD IF I EVER DID SEE ONE.
THE BEST WARRIOR IN TENKAI...
...TURNED DEVOTED NANNY.
Heh heh heh heh...

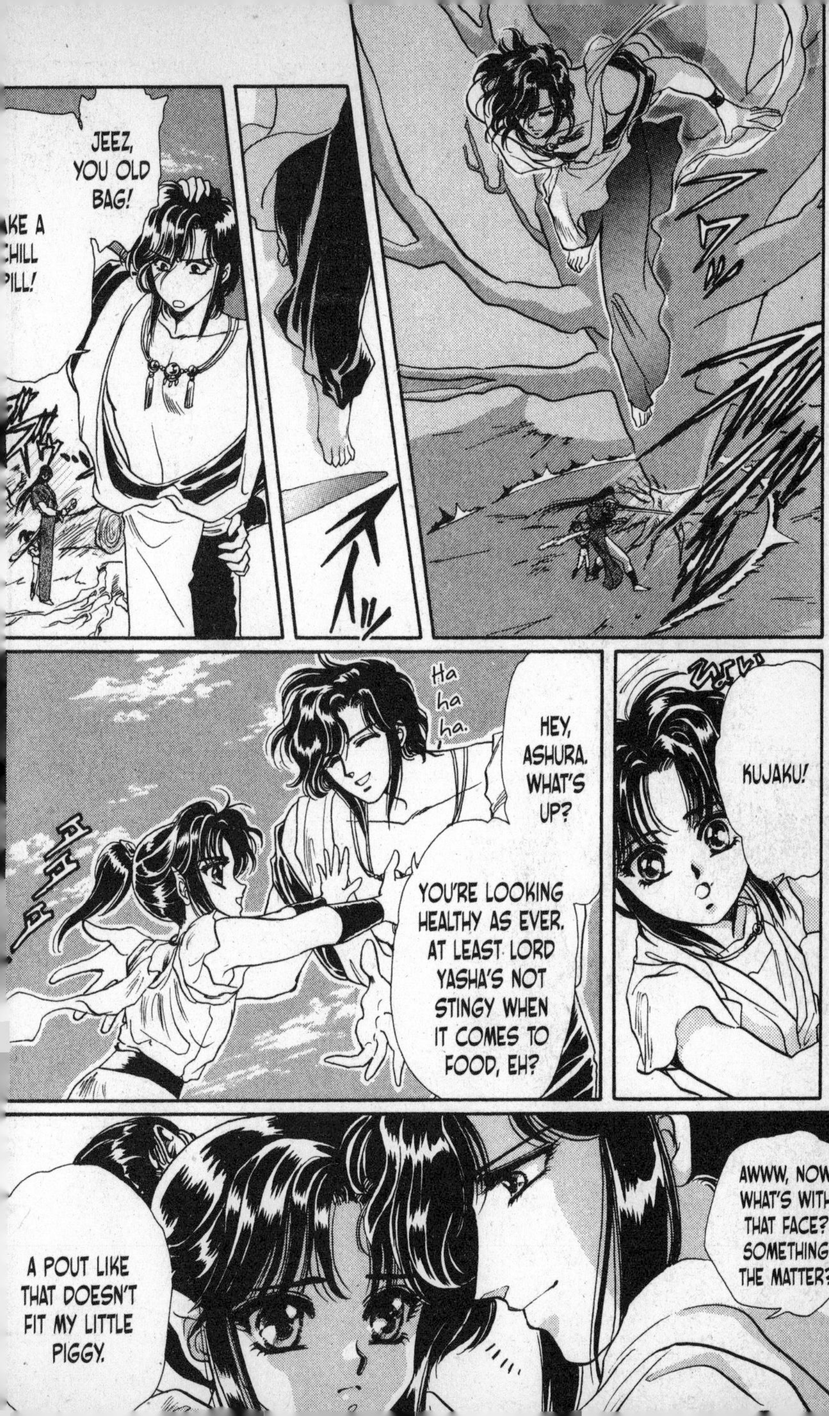
JEEZ, YOU OLD BAG!
KUJAKU!
Ha ha ha.
HEY, ASHURA. WHAT'S UP?
YOU'RE LOOKING HEALTHY AS EVER. AT LEAST LORD YASHA'S NOT STINGY WHEN IT COMES TO FOOD, EH?
AWWW, NOW WHAT'S WITH THAT FACE? SOMETHING THE MATTER?
A POUT LIKE THAT DOESN'T FIT MY LITTLE PIGGY.

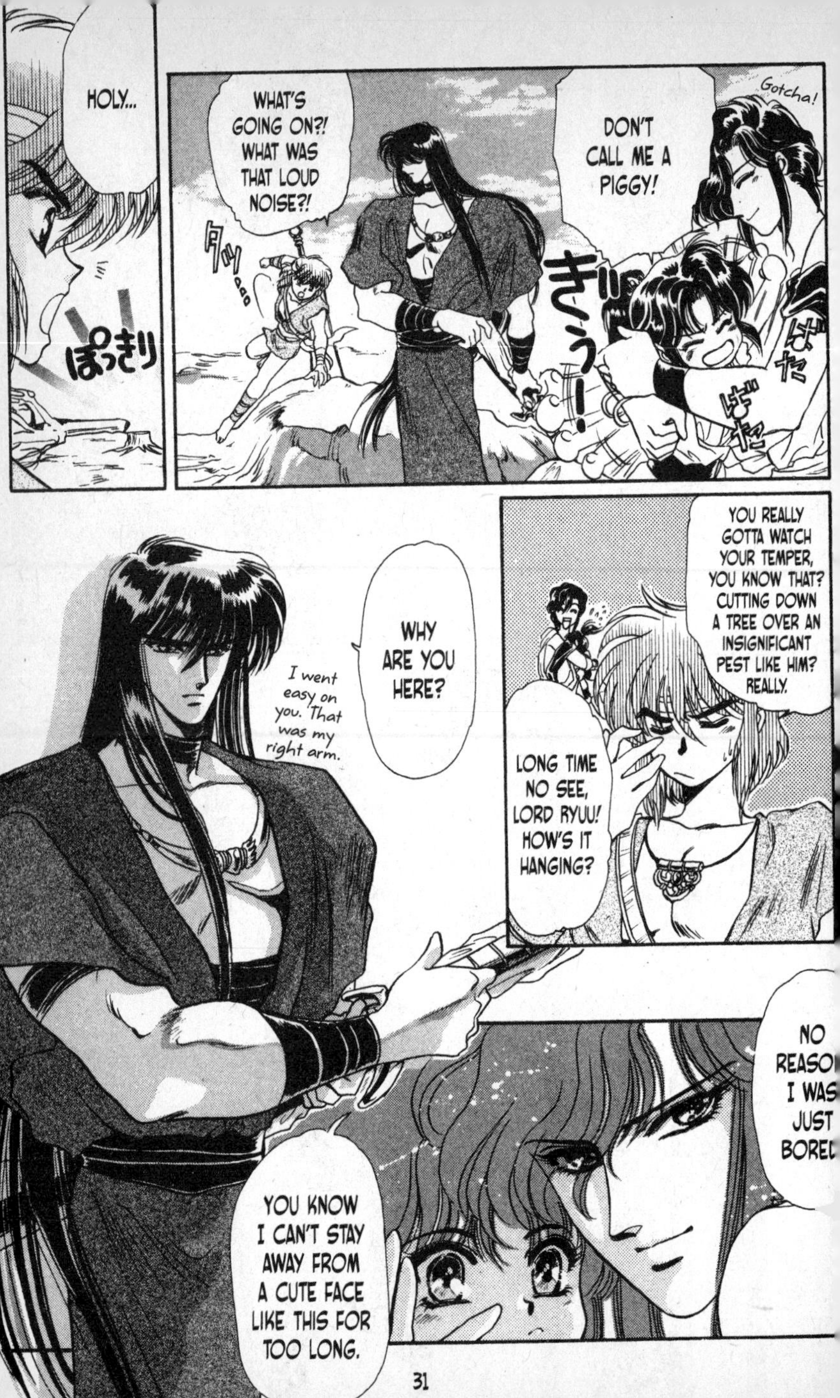
Gotcha!
DON'T CALL ME A PIGGY!
きゅうー!
ばたばた
WHAT'S GOING ON?! WHAT WAS THAT LOUD NOISE?!
タッ
HOLY...
ぽっきり
YOU REALLY GOTTA WATCH YOUR TEMPER, YOU KNOW THAT? CUTTING DOWN A TREE OVER AN INSIGNIFICANT PEST LIKE HIM? REALLY.
I went easy on you. That was my right arm.
LONG TIME NO SEE, LORD RYUU! HOW'S IT HANGING?
WHY ARE YOU HERE?
NO REASO I WAS JUST BORE
YOU KNOW I CAN'T STAY AWAY FROM A CUTE FACE LIKE THIS FOR TOO LONG.

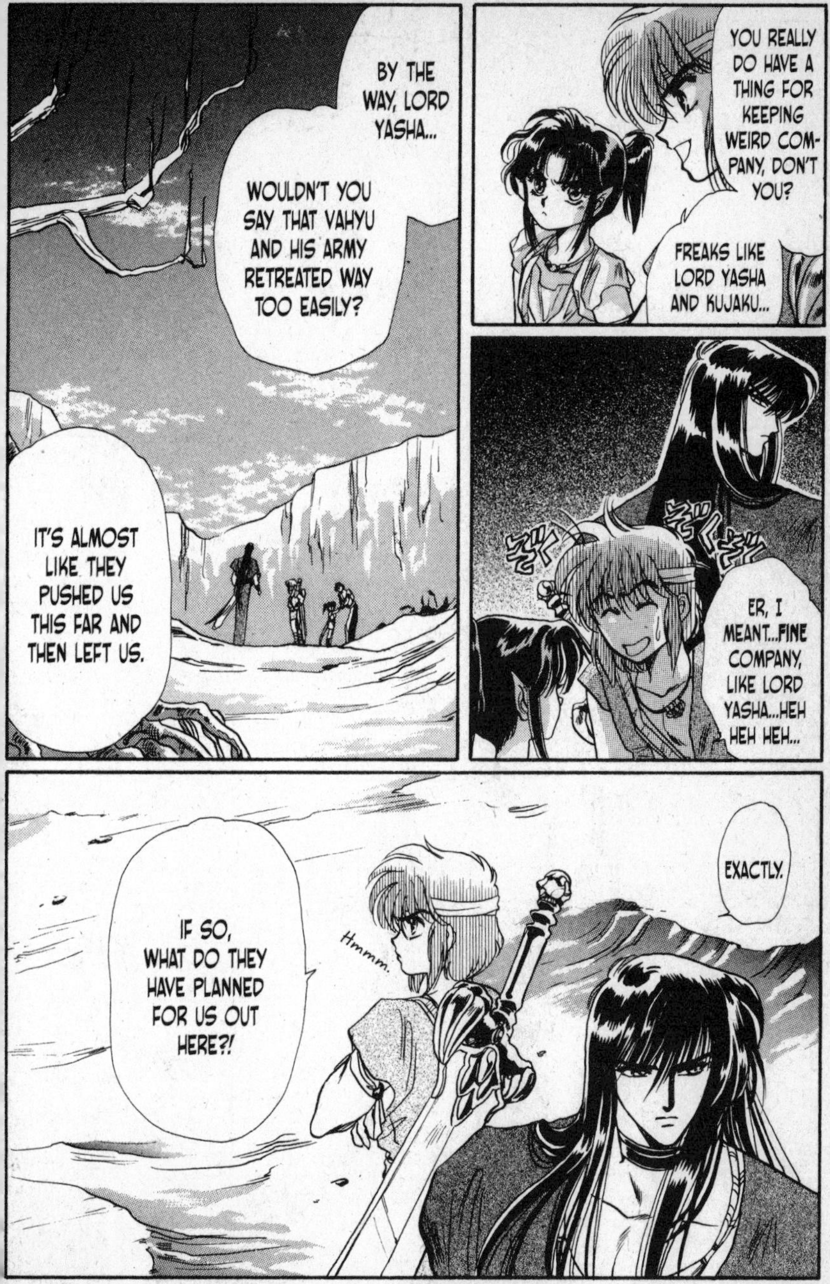
YOU REALLY DO HAVE A THING FOR KEEPING WEIRD COMPANY, DON'T YOU?
FREAKS LIKE LORD YASHA AND KUJAKU...
ER, I MEANT...FINE COMPANY, LIKE LORD YASHA...HEH HEH HEH...
BY THE WAY, LORD YASHA...
WOULDN'T YOU SAY THAT VAHYU AND HIS ARMY RETREATED WAY TOO EASILY?
IT'S ALMOST LIKE THEY PUSHED US THIS FAR AND THEN LEFT US.
EXACTLY.
Hmmm.
IF SO, WHAT DO THEY HAVE PLANNED FOR US OUT HERE?!

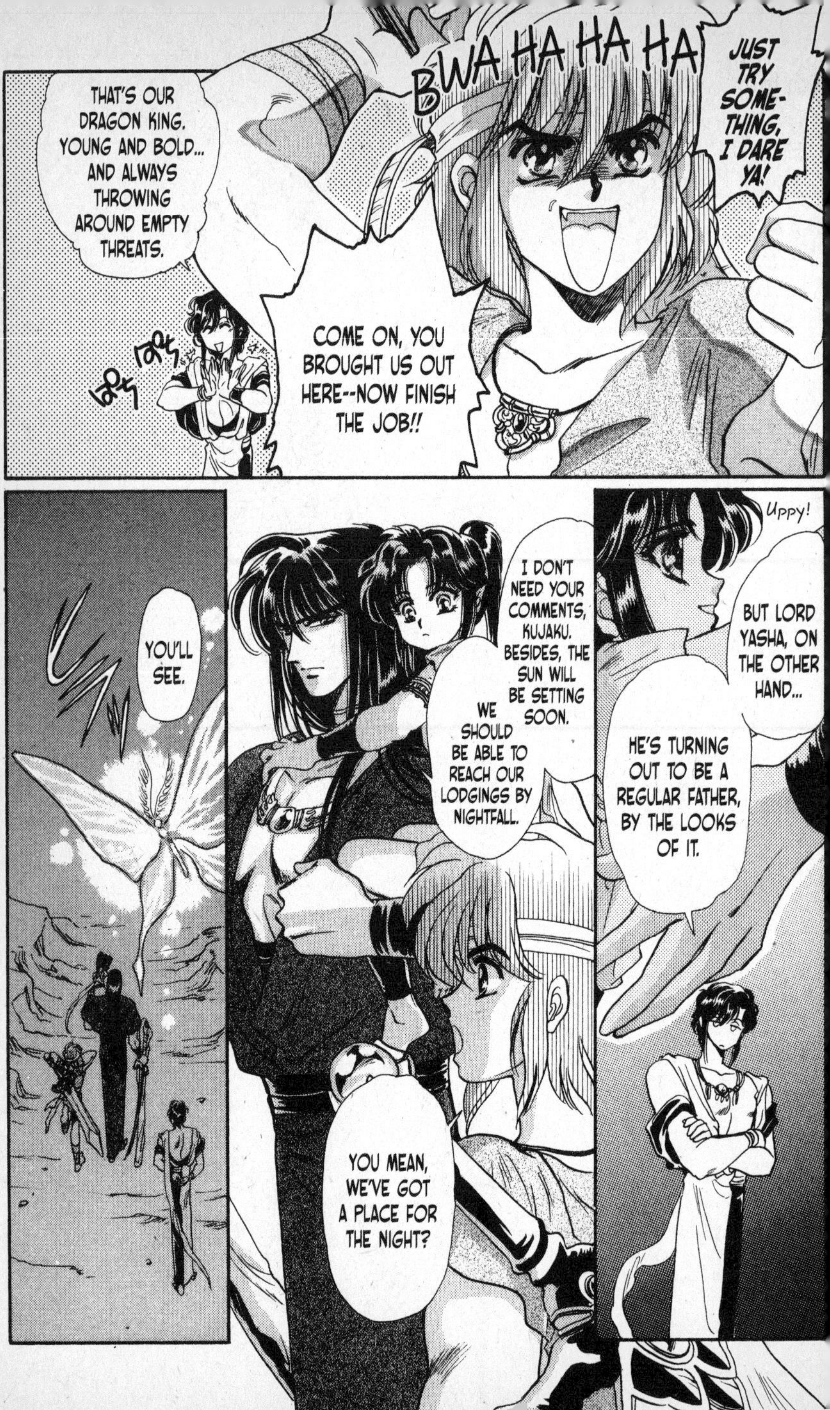
BWA HA HA HA
JUST TRY SOME-THING, I DARE YA!
COME ON, YOU BROUGHT US OUT HERE--NOW FINISH THE JOB!!
THAT'S OUR DRAGON KING. YOUNG AND BOLD... AND ALWAYS THROWING AROUND EMPTY THREATS.
ぱち ぱち
Uppy!
BUT LORD YASHA, ON THE OTHER HAND...
HE'S TURNING OUT TO BE A REGULAR FATHER, BY THE LOOKS OF IT.
I DON'T NEED YOUR COMMENTS, KUJAKU. BESIDES, THE SUN WILL BE SETTING SOON.
WE SHOULD BE ABLE TO REACH OUR LODGINGS BY NIGHTFALL.
YOU MEAN, WE'VE GOT A PLACE FOR THE NIGHT?
YOU'LL SEE.

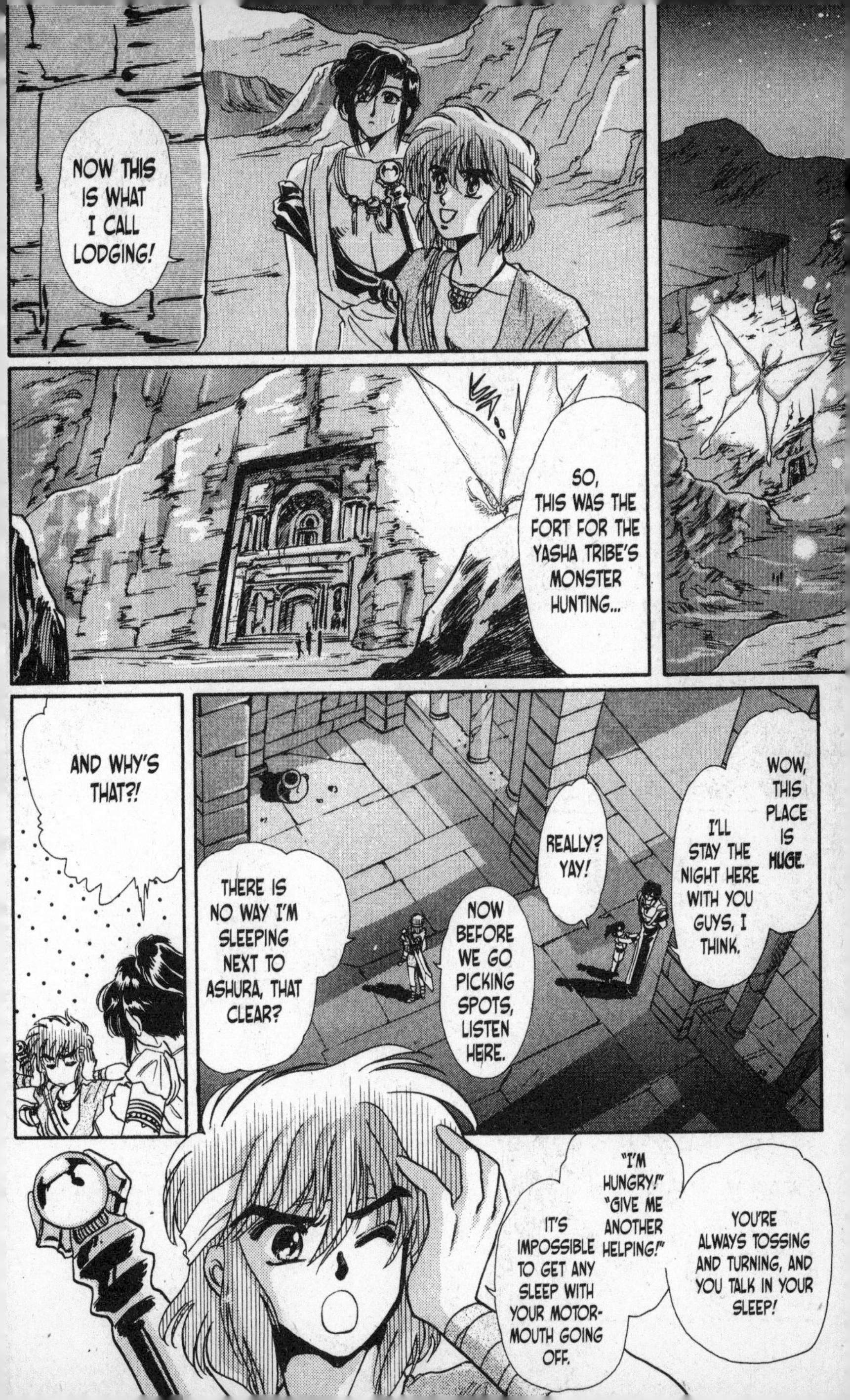
NOW THIS IS WHAT I CALL LODGING!
SO, THIS WAS THE FORT FOR THE YASHA TRIBE'S MONSTER HUNTING...
WOW, THIS PLACE IS HUGE.
I'LL STAY THE NIGHT HERE WITH YOU GUYS, I THINK.
REALLY? YAY!
NOW BEFORE WE GO PICKING SPOTS, LISTEN HERE.
THERE IS NO WAY I'M SLEEPING NEXT TO ASHURA, THAT CLEAR?
AND WHY'S THAT?!
YOU'RE ALWAYS TOSSING AND TURNING, AND YOU TALK IN YOUR SLEEP!
"I'M HUNGRY!" "GIVE ME ANOTHER HELPING!"
IT'S IMPOSSIBLE TO GET ANY SLEEP WITH YOUR MOTOR-MOUTH GOING OFF.

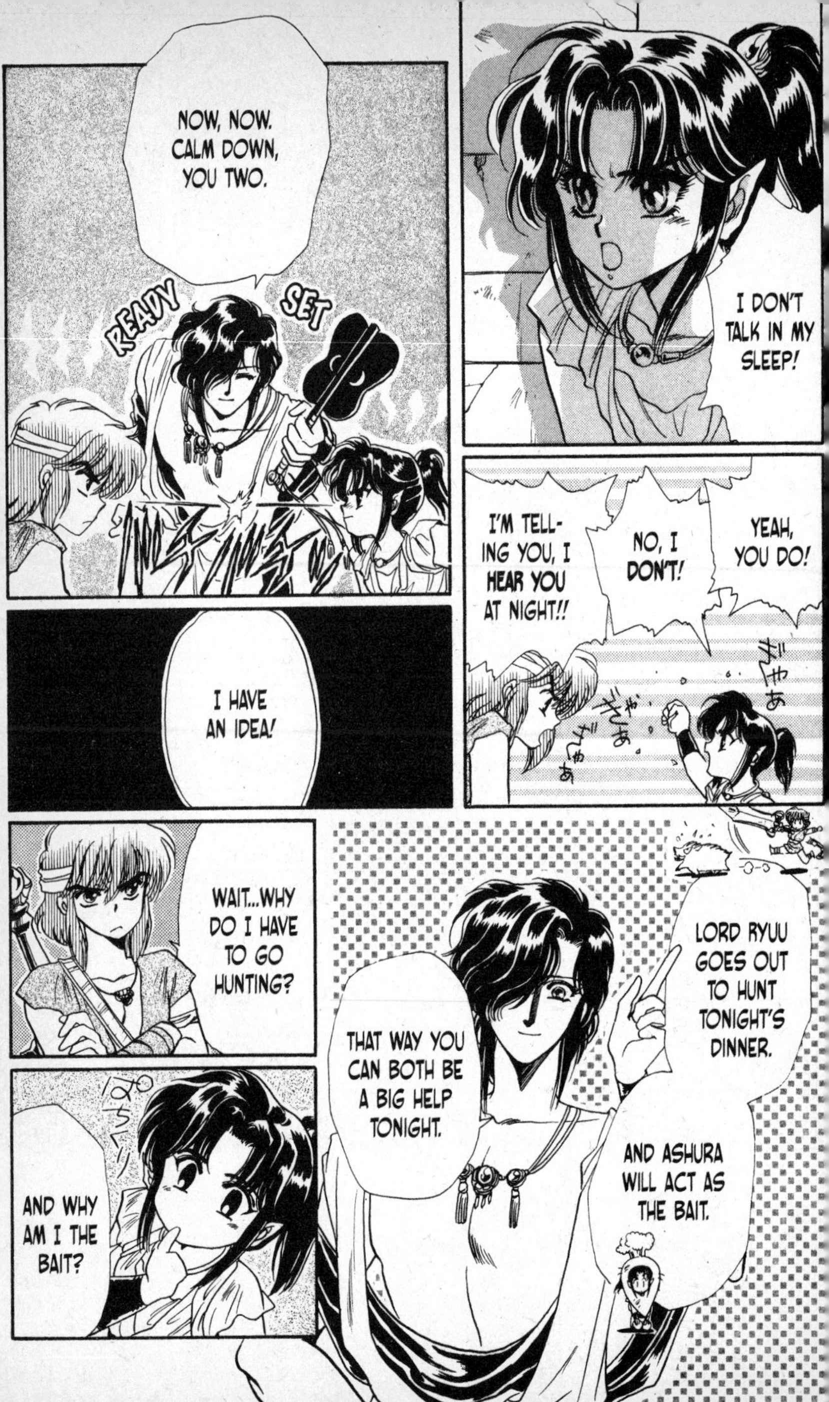
I DON'T TALK IN MY SLEEP!
I'M TELLING YOU, I HEAR YOU AT NIGHT!!
NO, I DON'T!
YEAH, YOU DO!
NOW, NOW. CALM DOWN, YOU TWO.
READY
SET
I HAVE AN IDEA!
LORD RYUU GOES OUT TO HUNT TONIGHT'S DINNER.
AND ASHURA WILL ACT AS THE BAIT.
THAT WAY YOU CAN BOTH BE A BIG HELP TONIGHT.
WAIT...WHY DO I HAVE TO GO HUNTING?
AND WHY AM I THE BAIT?

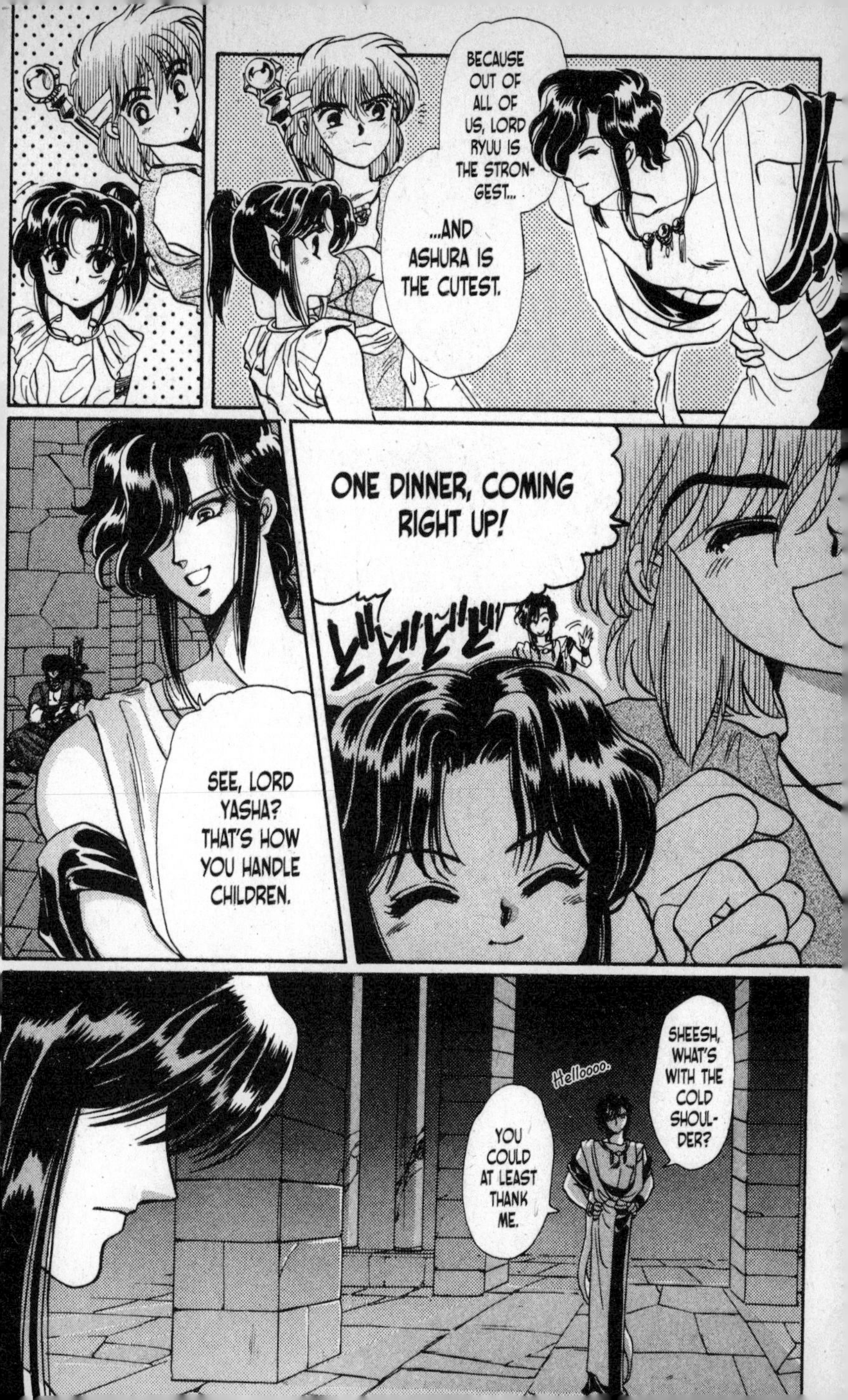
BECAUSE OUT OF ALL OF US, LORD RYUU IS THE STRONGEST...
...AND ASHURA IS THE CUTEST.
ONE DINNER, COMING RIGHT UP!
SEE, LORD YASHA? THAT'S HOW YOU HANDLE CHILDREN.
SHEESH, WHAT'S WITH THE COLD SHOULDER?
Helloooo.
YOU COULD AT LEAST THANK ME.

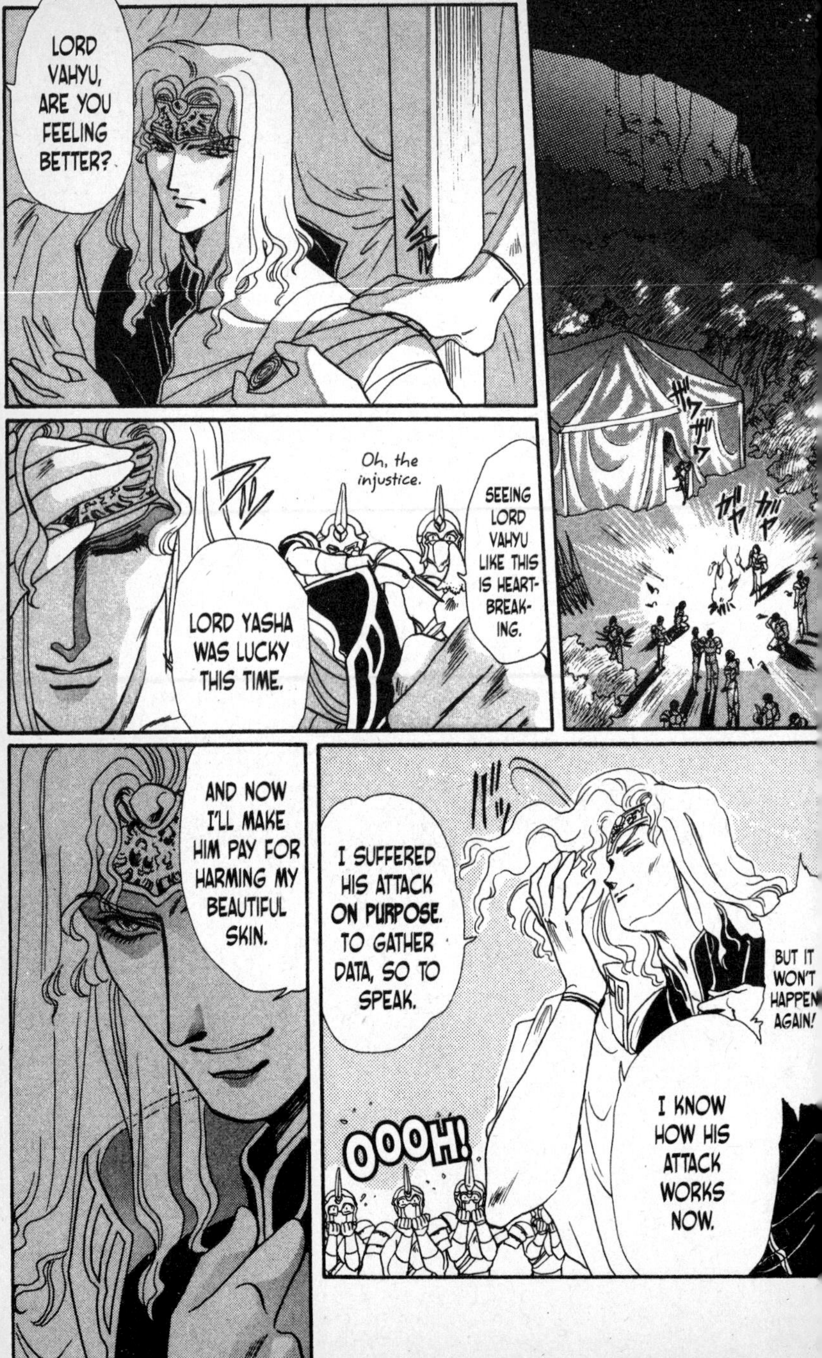
LORD VAHYU, ARE YOU FEELING BETTER?
Oh, the injustice.
SEEING LORD VAHYU LIKE THIS IS HEART-BREAK-ING.
LORD YASHA WAS LUCKY THIS TIME.
I SUFFERED HIS ATTACK ON PURPOSE. TO GATHER DATA, SO TO SPEAK.
OOOH!
I KNOW HOW HIS ATTACK WORKS NOW.
BUT IT WON'T HAPPEN AGAIN!
AND NOW I'LL MAKE HIM PAY FOR HARMING MY BEAUTIFUL SKIN.

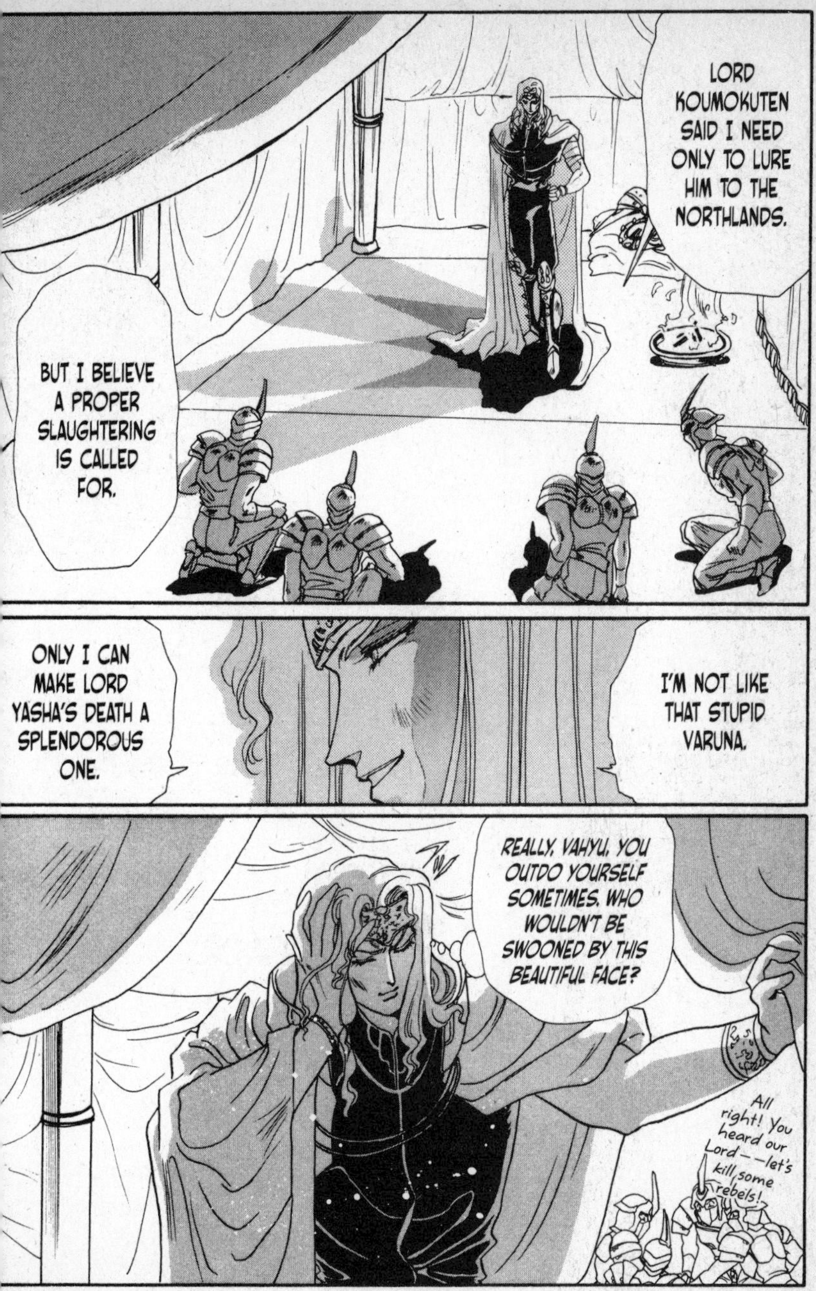
LORD KOUMOKUTEN SAID I NEED ONLY TO LURE HIM TO THE NORTHLANDS.
BUT I BELIEVE A PROPER SLAUGHTERING IS CALLED FOR.
I'M NOT LIKE THAT STUPID VARUNA.
ONLY I CAN MAKE LORD YASHA'S DEATH A SPLENDOROUS ONE.
REALLY, VAHYU, YOU OUTDO YOURSELF SOMETIMES. WHO WOULDN'T BE SWOONED BY THIS BEAUTIFUL FACE?
All right! You heard our Lord--let's kill some rebels!

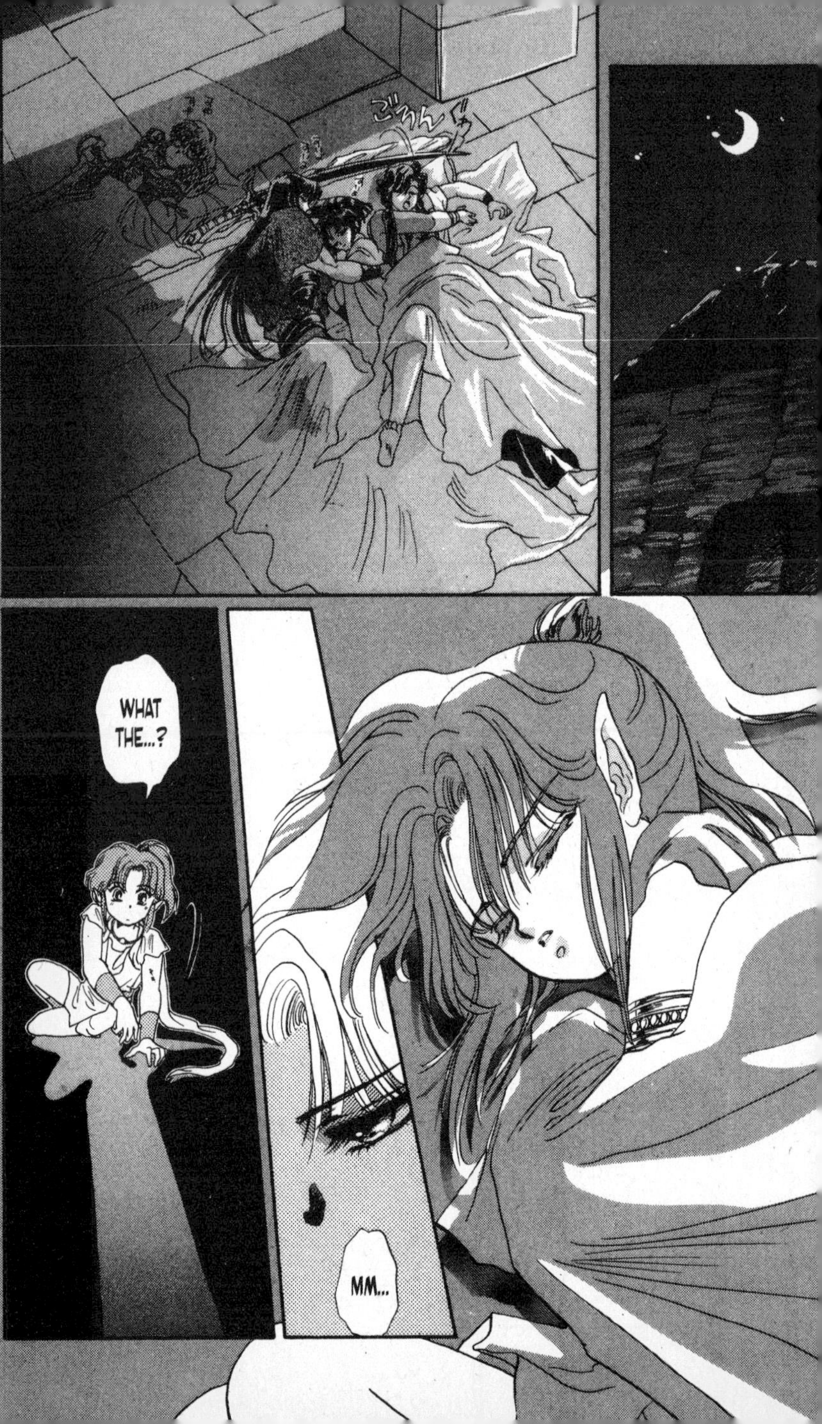
MM...
WHAT THE...?

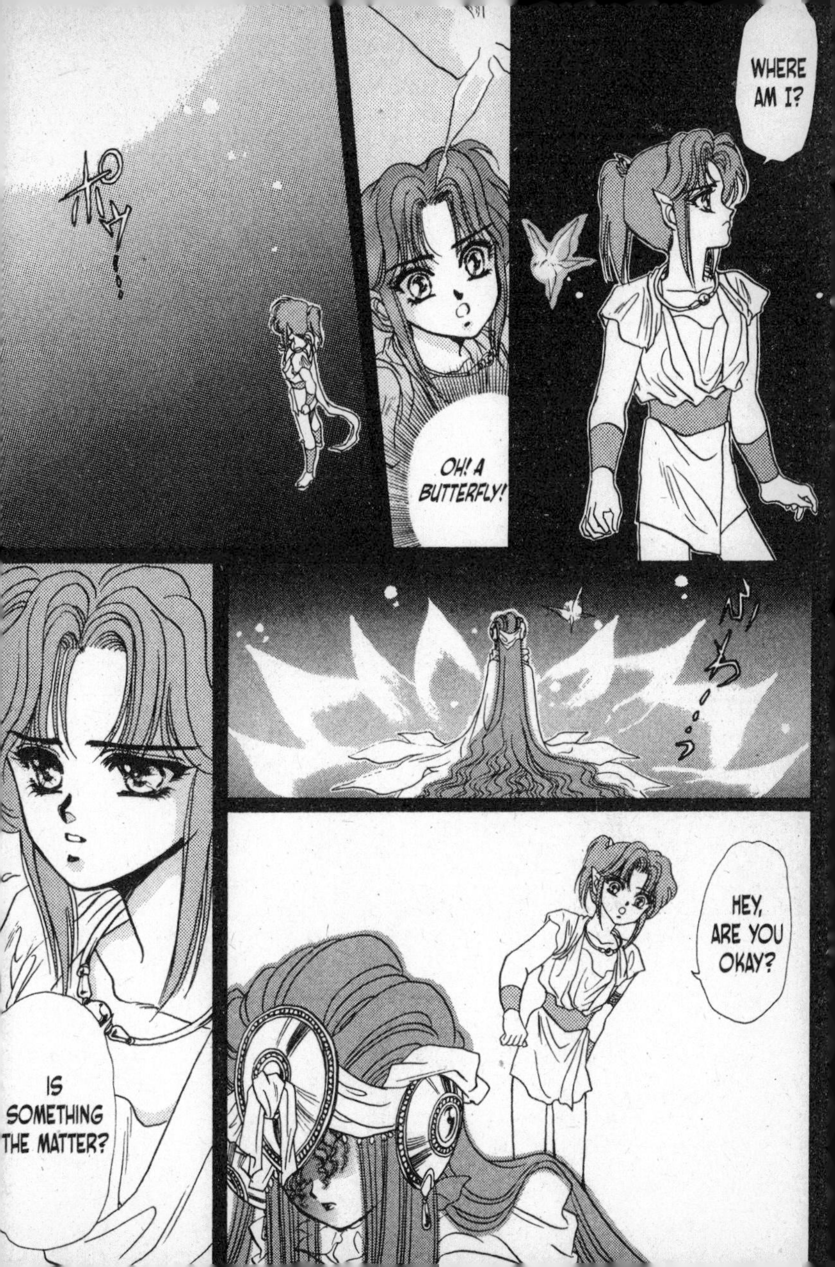
WHERE AM I?
OH! A BUTTERFLY!
HEY, ARE YOU OKAY?
IS SOMETHING THE MATTER?

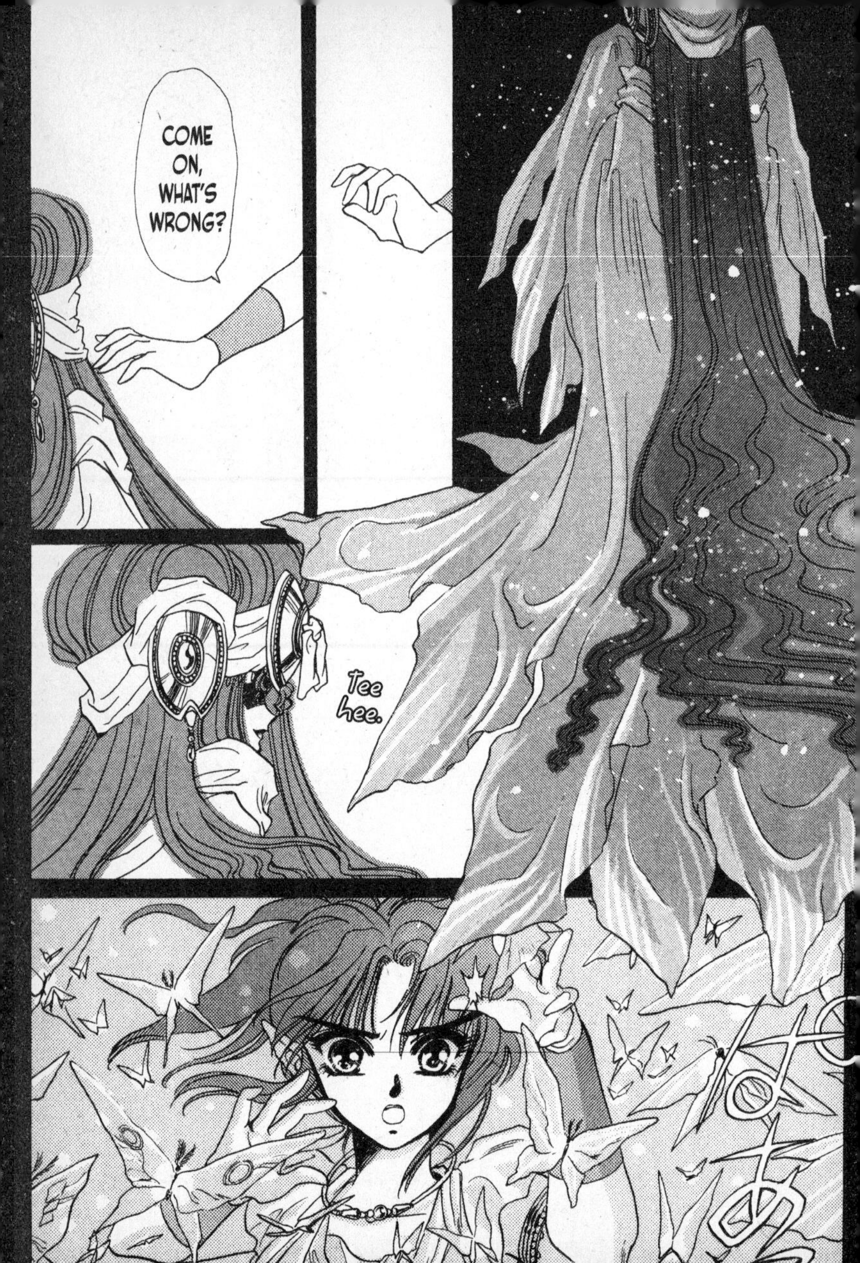
COME ON, WHAT'S WRONG?
Tee hee.

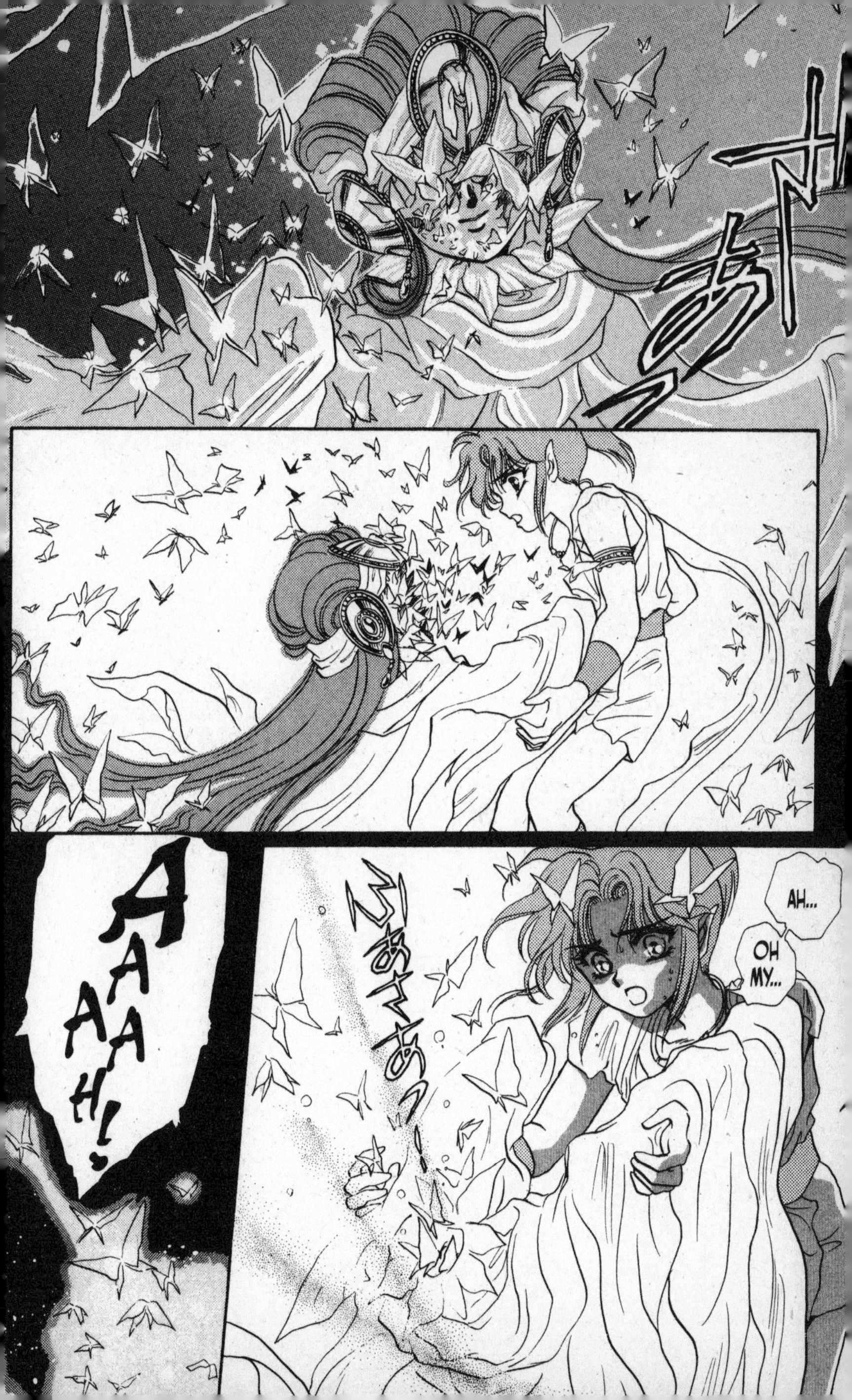
AH...
OH MY...
AAAAH!

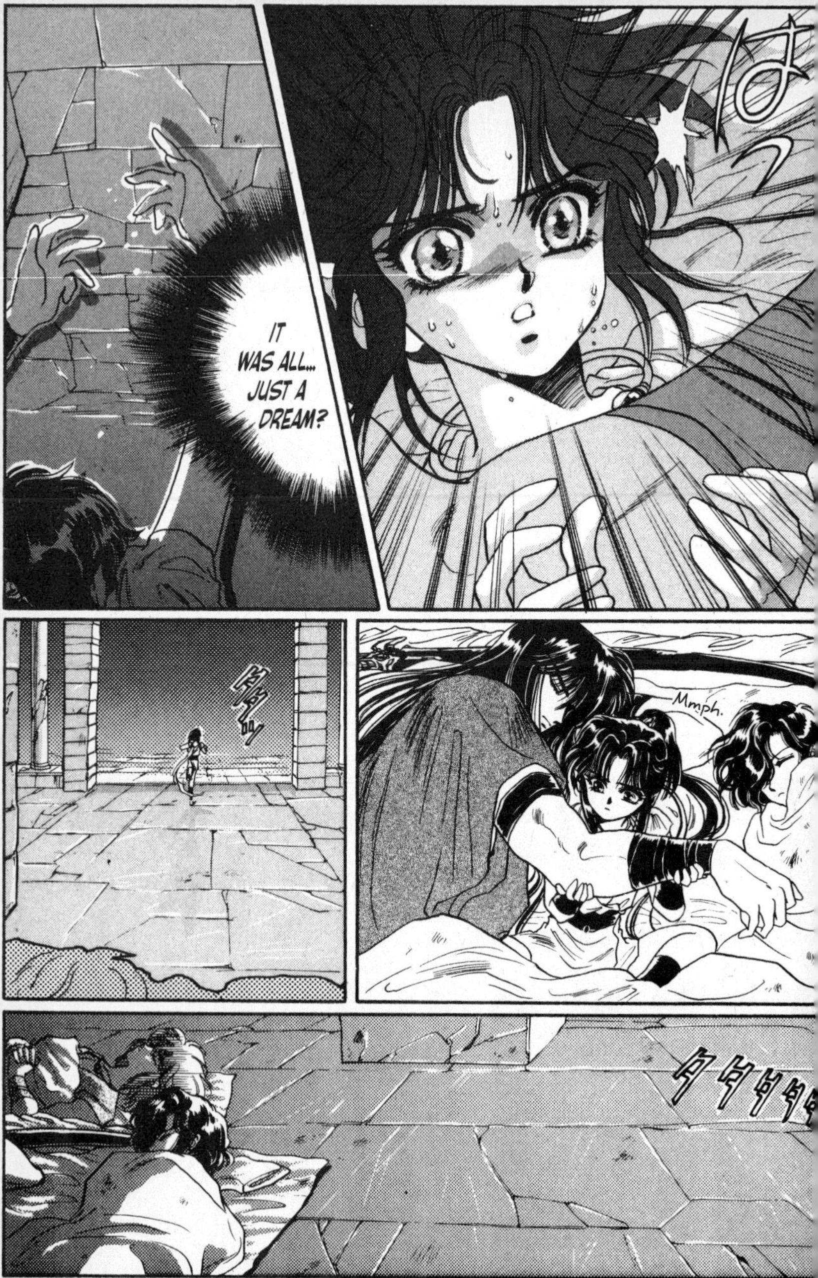
IT WAS ALL... JUST A DREAM?
Mmph.

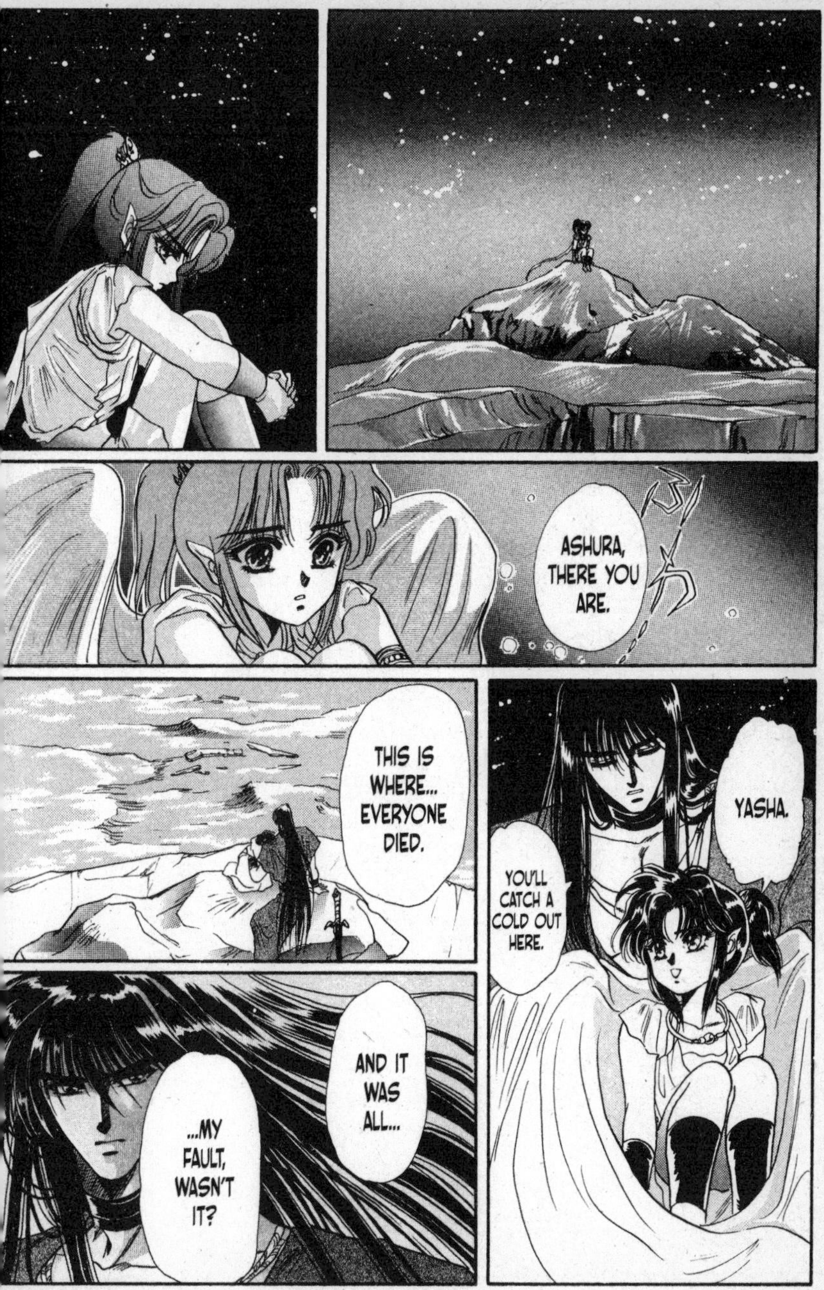
ASHURA, THERE YOU ARE.
YASHA.
YOU'LL CATCH A COLD OUT HERE.
THIS IS WHERE... EVERYONE DIED.
AND IT WAS ALL...
...MY FAULT, WASN'T IT?

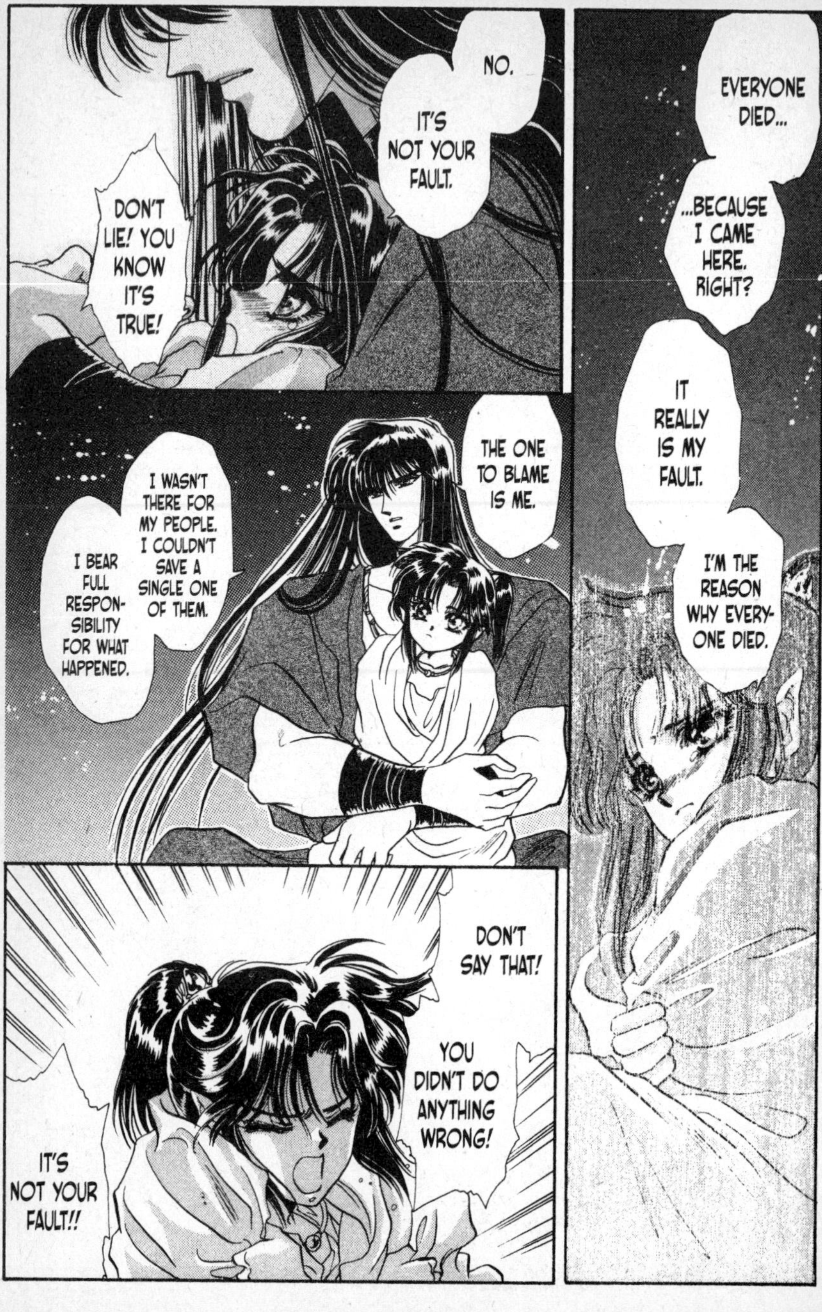
EVERYONE DIED...
...BECAUSE I CAME HERE. RIGHT?
IT REALLY IS MY FAULT.
I'M THE REASON WHY EVERY-ONE DIED.
NO.
IT'S NOT YOUR FAULT.
DON'T LIE! YOU KNOW IT'S TRUE!
THE ONE TO BLAME IS ME.
I WASN'T THERE FOR MY PEOPLE. I COULDN'T SAVE A SINGLE ONE OF THEM.
I BEAR FULL RESPON-SIBILITY FOR WHAT HAPPENED.
DON'T SAY THAT!
YOU DIDN'T DO ANYTHING WRONG!
IT'S NOT YOUR FAULT!!

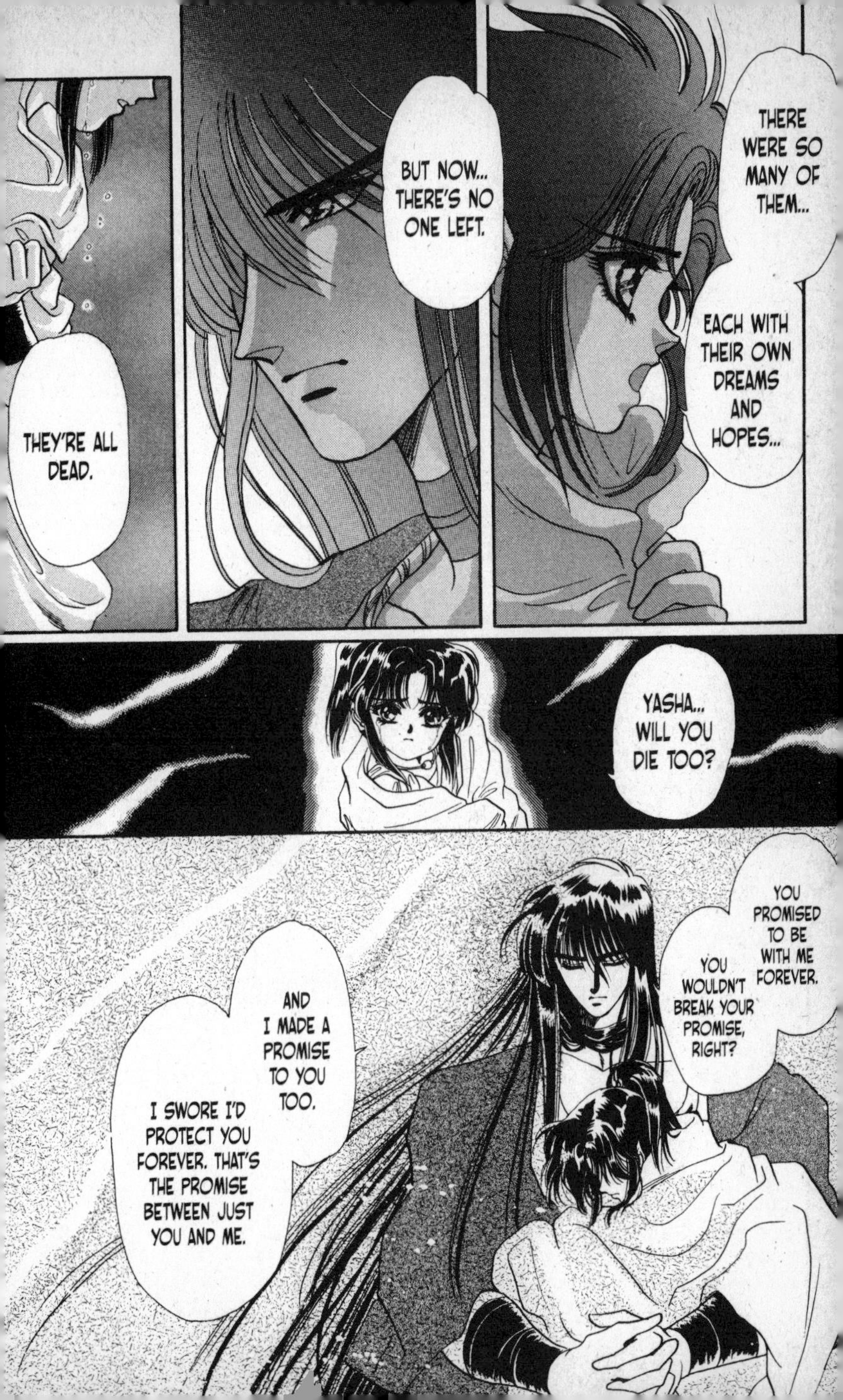
THERE WERE SO MANY OF THEM...
EACH WITH THEIR OWN DREAMS AND HOPES...
BUT NOW... THERE'S NO ONE LEFT.
THEY'RE ALL DEAD.
YASHA... WILL YOU DIE TOO?
YOU PROMISED TO BE WITH ME FOREVER.
YOU WOULDN'T BREAK YOUR PROMISE, RIGHT?
AND I MADE A PROMISE TO YOU TOO.
I SWORE I'D PROTECT YOU FOREVER. THAT'S THE PROMISE BETWEEN JUST YOU AND ME.

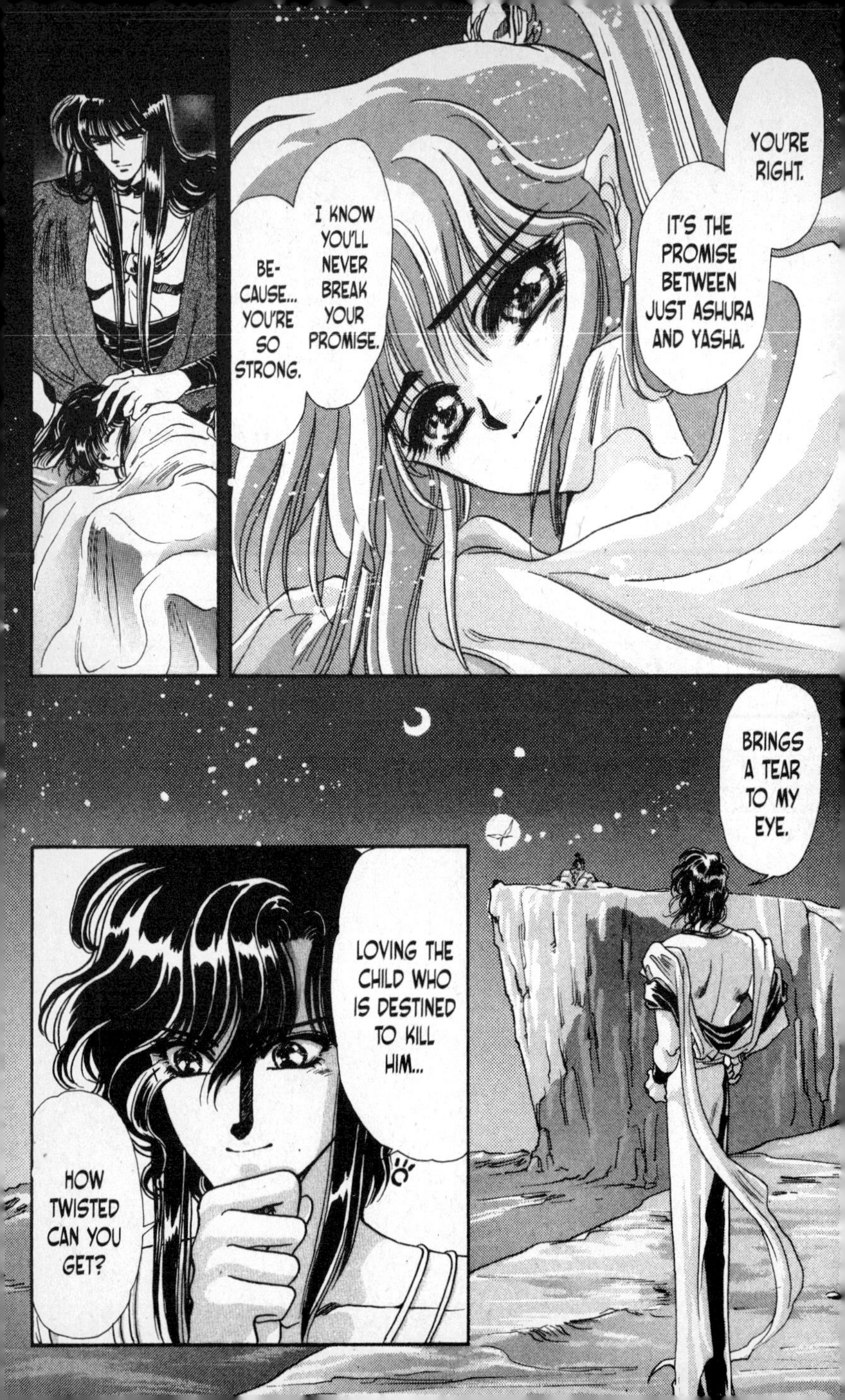
YOU'RE RIGHT.
IT'S THE PROMISE BETWEEN JUST ASHURA AND YASHA.
I KNOW YOU'LL NEVER BREAK YOUR PROMISE.
BE-CAUSE... YOU'RE SO STRONG.
BRINGS A TEAR TO MY EYE.
LOVING THE CHILD WHO IS DESTINED TO KILL HIM...
HOW TWISTED CAN YOU GET?

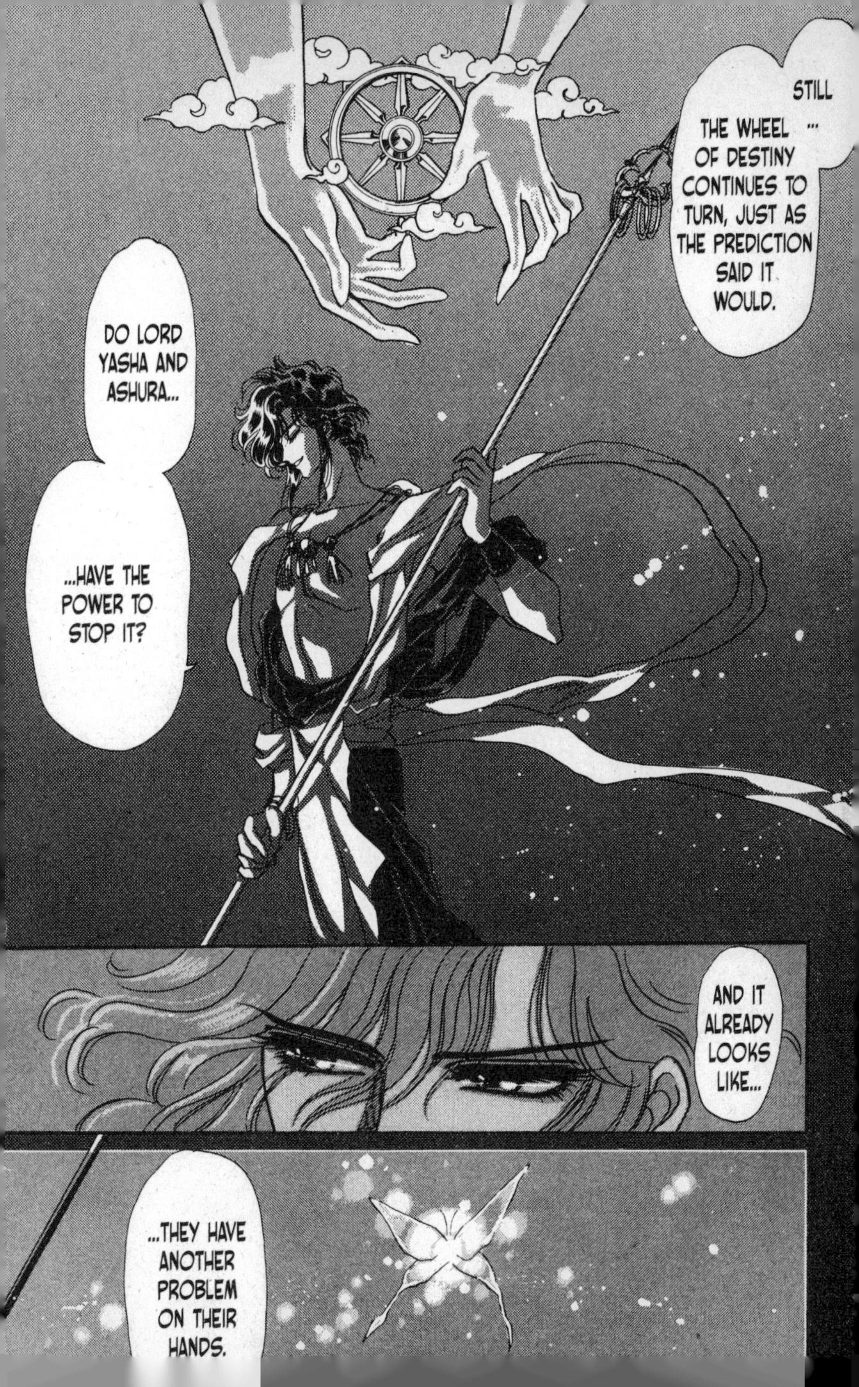
STILL THE WHEEL ... OF DESTINY CONTINUES TO TURN, JUST AS THE PREDICTION SAID IT WOULD.
DO LORD YASHA AND ASHURA...
...HAVE THE POWER TO STOP IT?
AND IT ALREADY LOOKS LIKE...
...THEY HAVE ANOTHER PROBLEM ON THEIR HANDS.

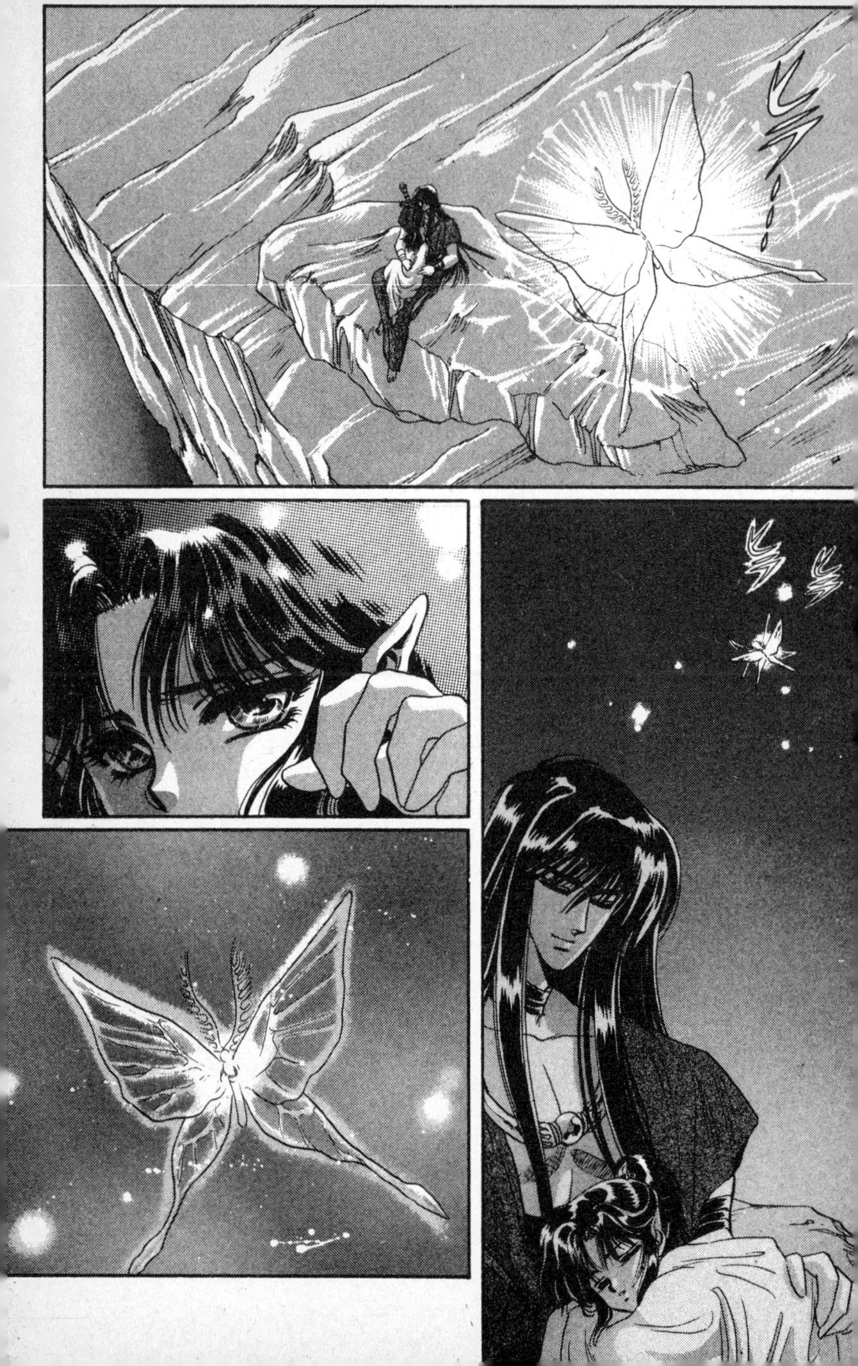

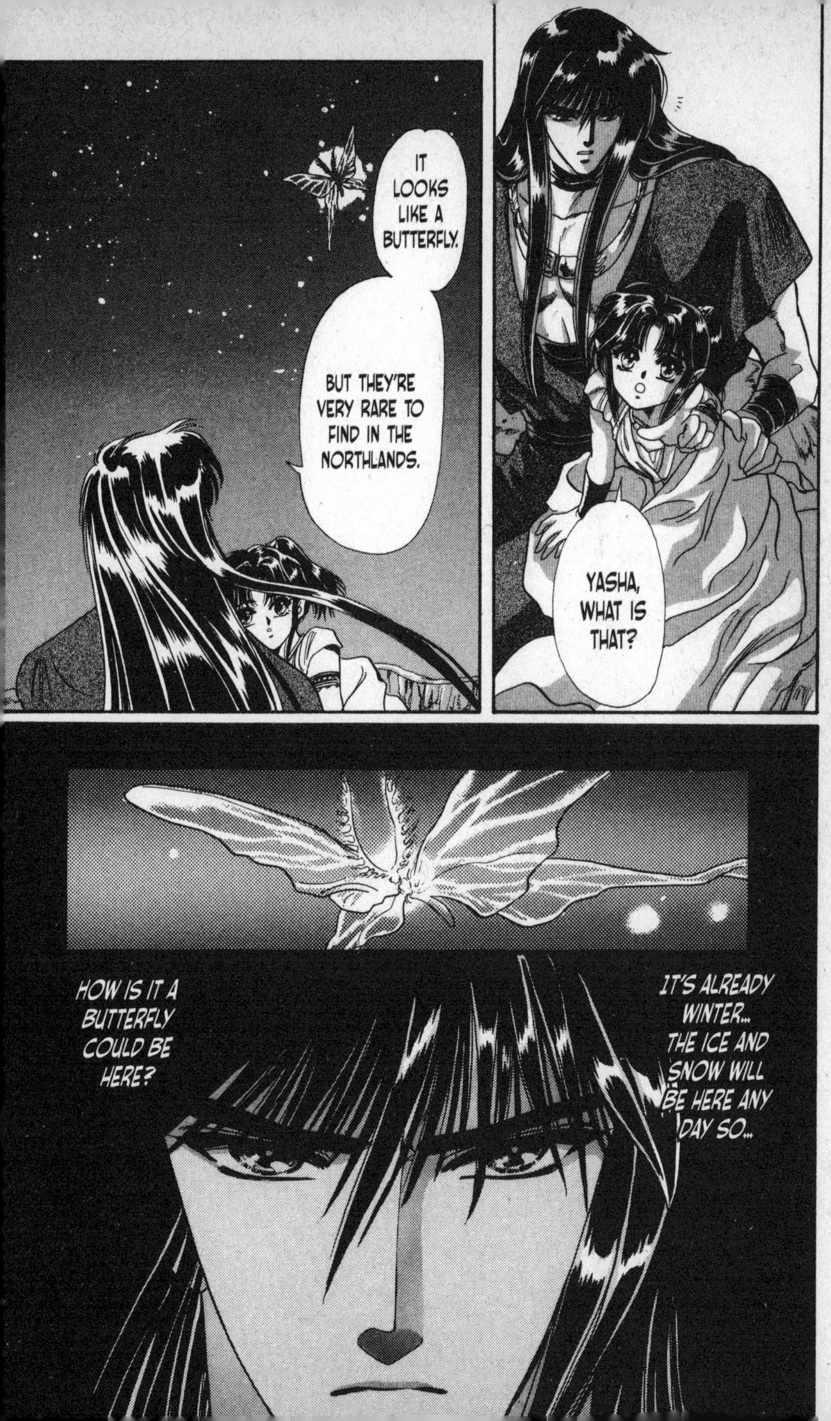
YASHA, WHAT IS THAT?
IT LOOKS LIKE A BUTTERFLY.
BUT THEY'RE VERY RARE TO FIND IN THE NORTHLANDS.
IT'S ALREADY WINTER... THE ICE AND SNOW WILL BE HERE ANY DAY SO...
HOW IS IT A BUTTERFLY COULD BE HERE?

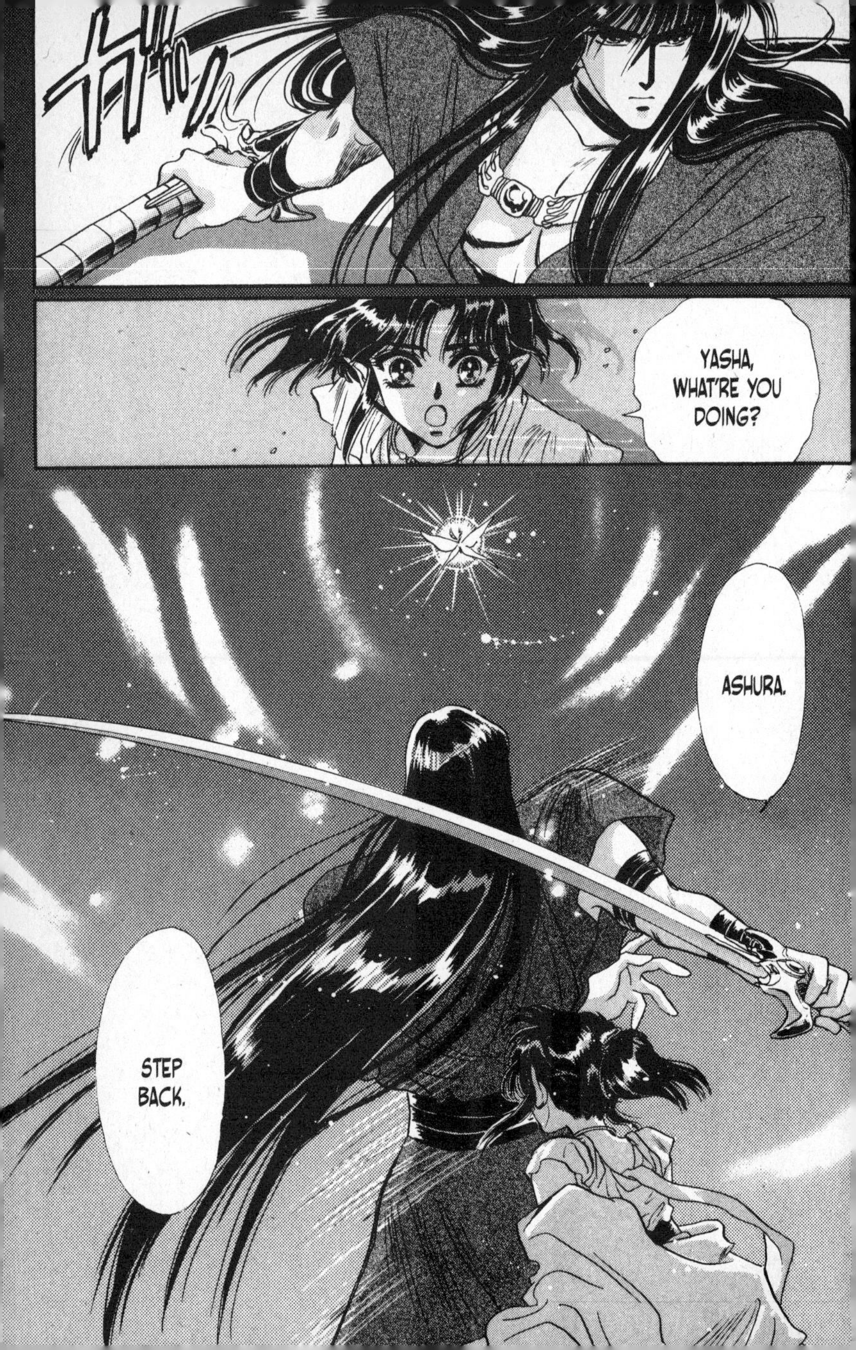
YASHA, WHAT'RE YOU DOING?
ASHURA.
STEP BACK.

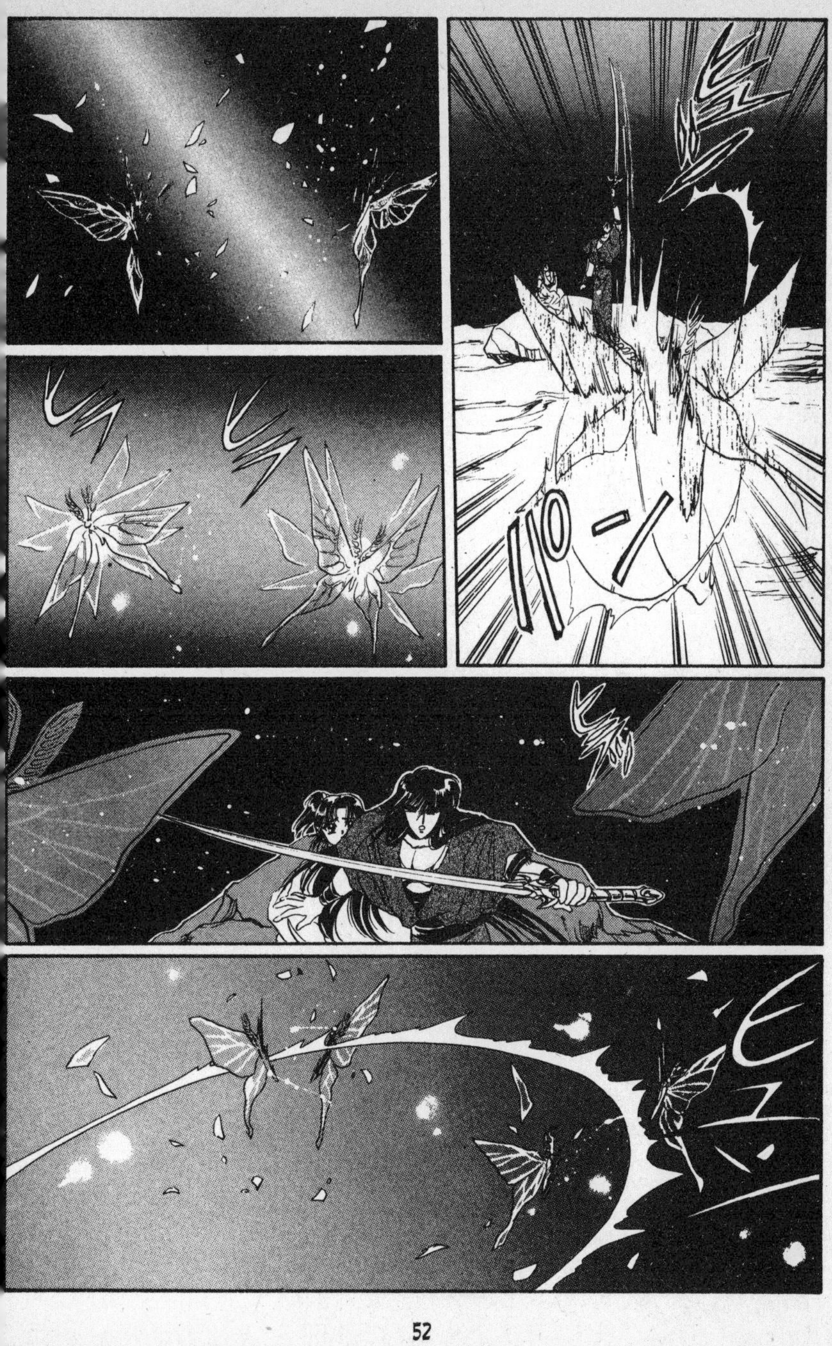
パーン

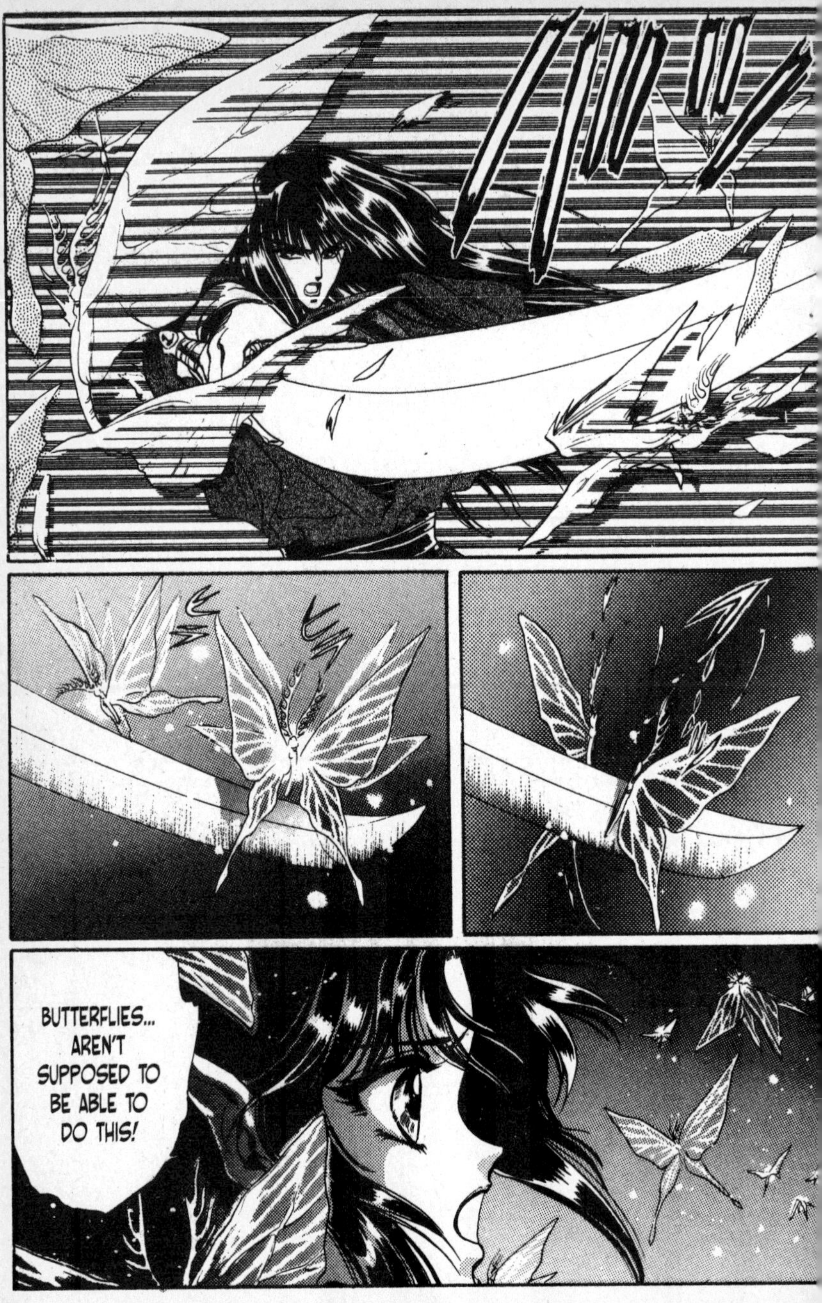
BUTTERFLIES... AREN'T SUPPOSED TO BE ABLE TO DO THIS!

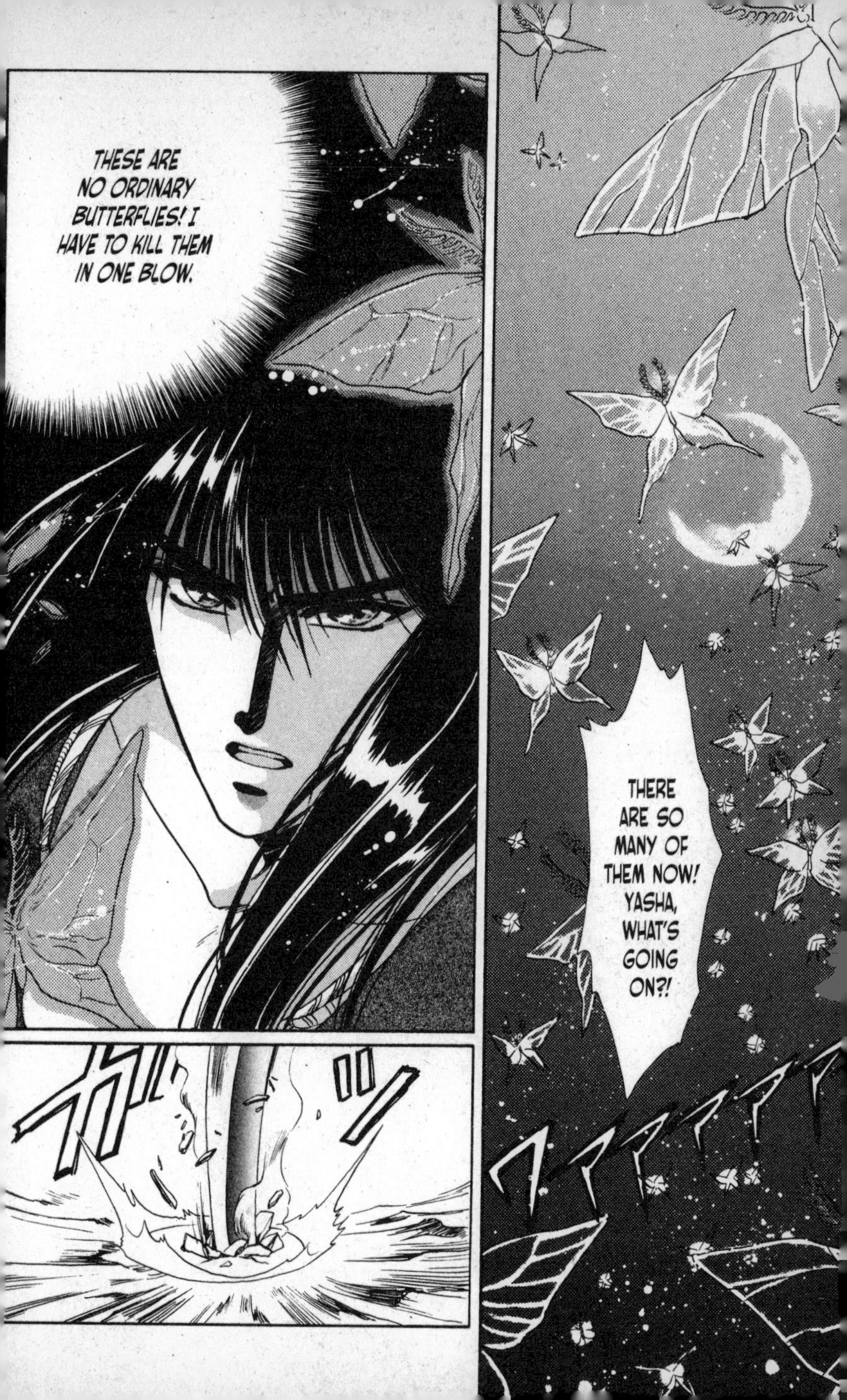
THERE ARE SO MANY OF THEM NOW! YASHA, WHAT'S GOING ON?!
THESE ARE NO ORDINARY BUTTERFLIES! I HAVE TO KILL THEM IN ONE BLOW.

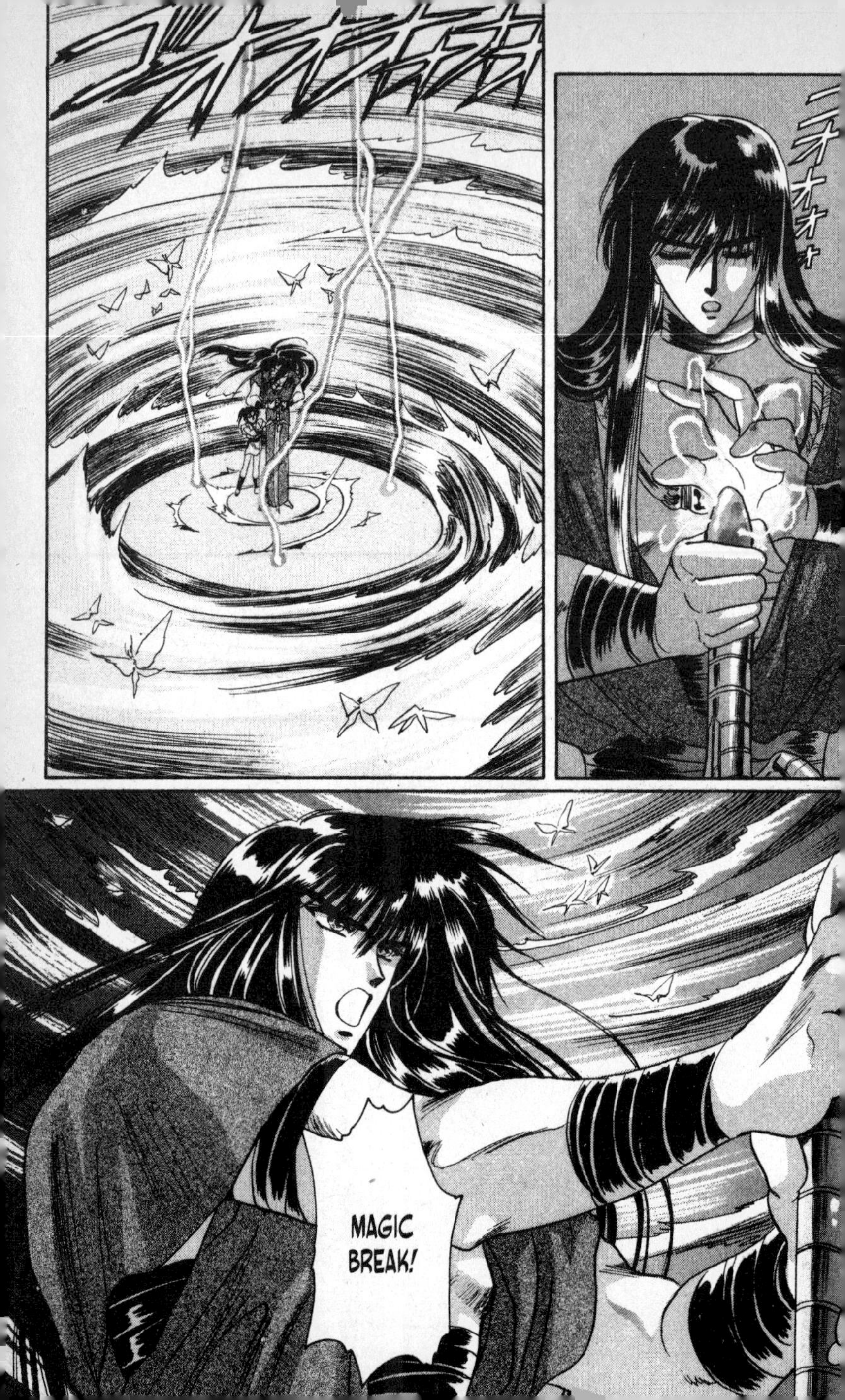
MAGIC BREAK!

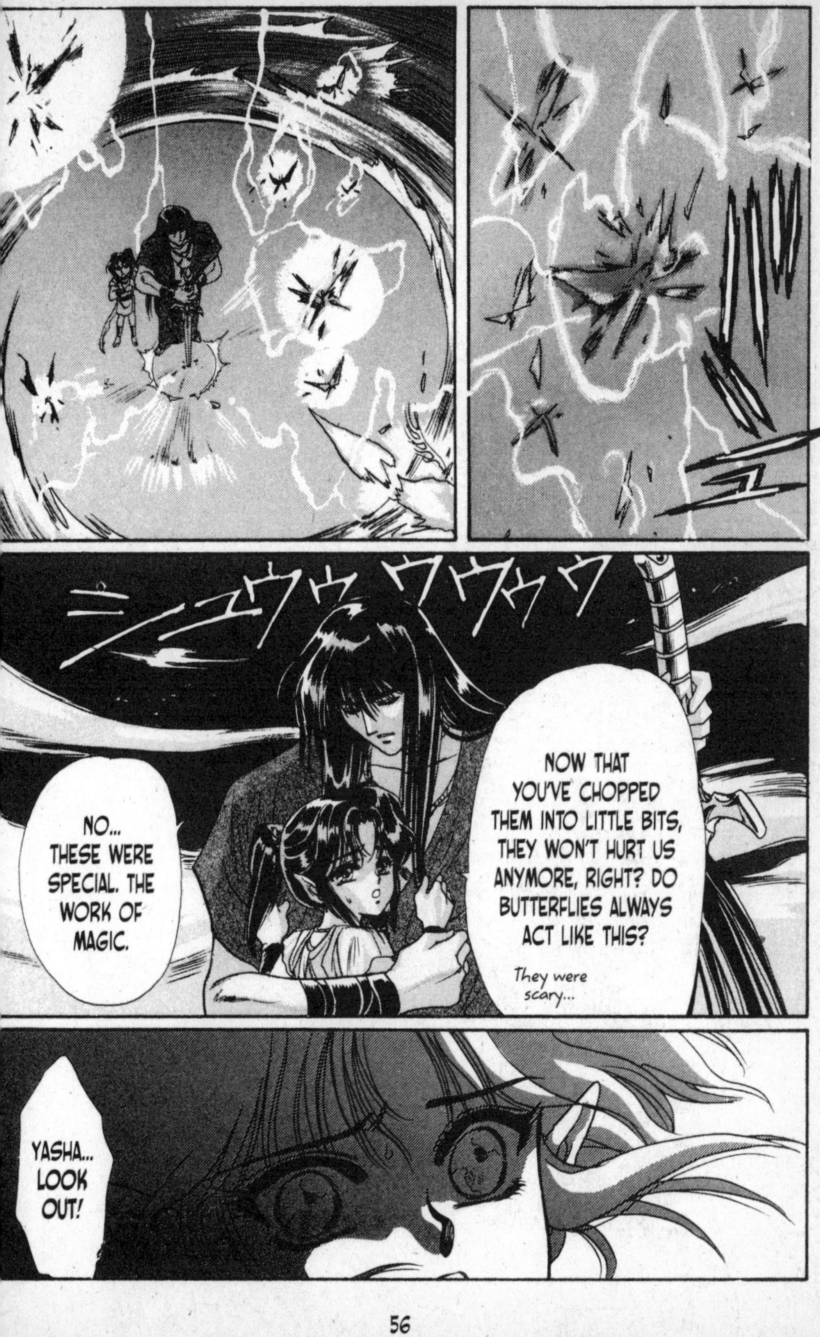
NOW THAT YOU'VE CHOPPED THEM INTO LITTLE BITS, THEY WON'T HURT US ANYMORE, RIGHT? DO BUTTERFLIES ALWAYS ACT LIKE THIS?
They were scary...
NO... THESE WERE SPECIAL. THE WORK OF MAGIC.
YASHA... LOOK OUT!

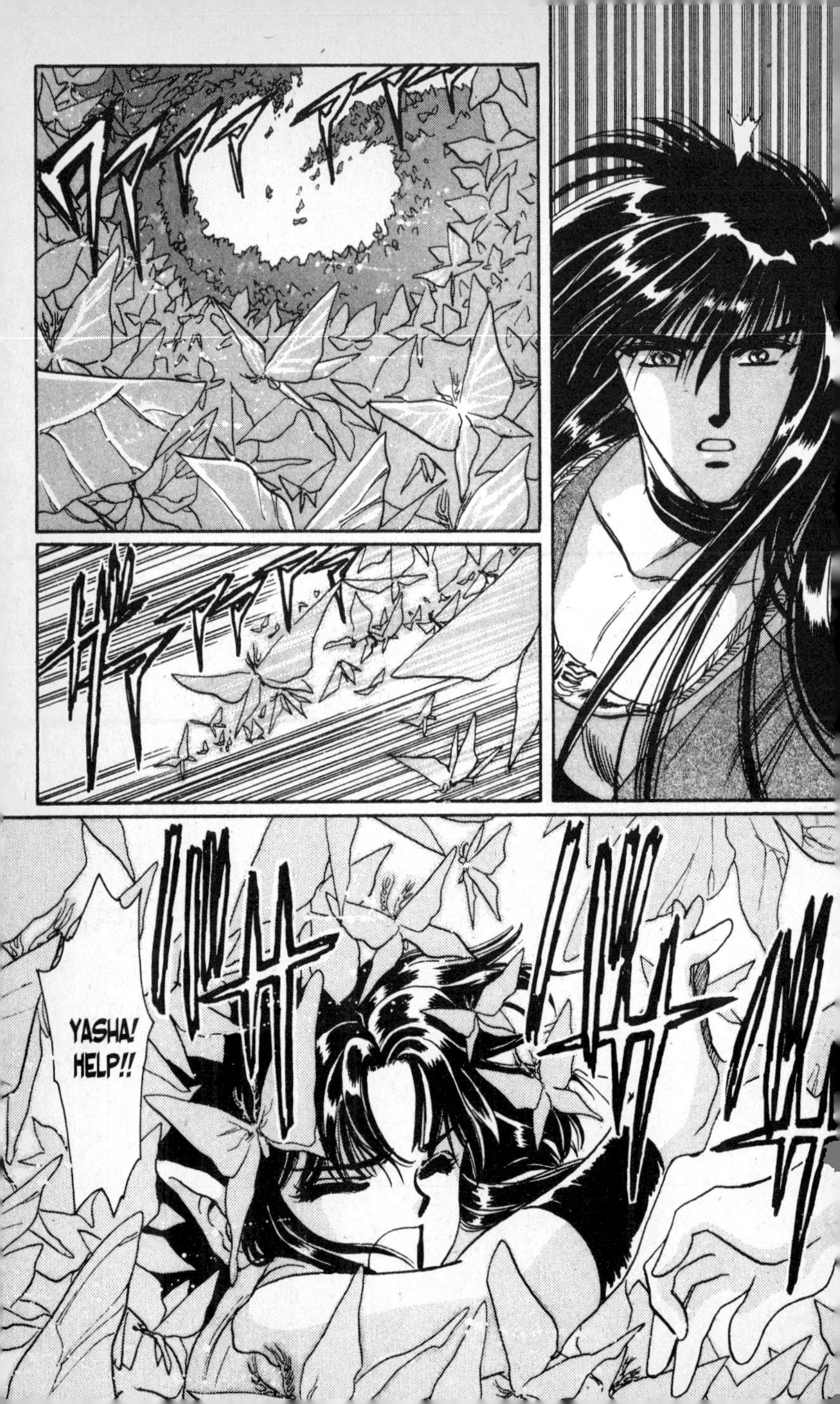
YASHA! HELP!!

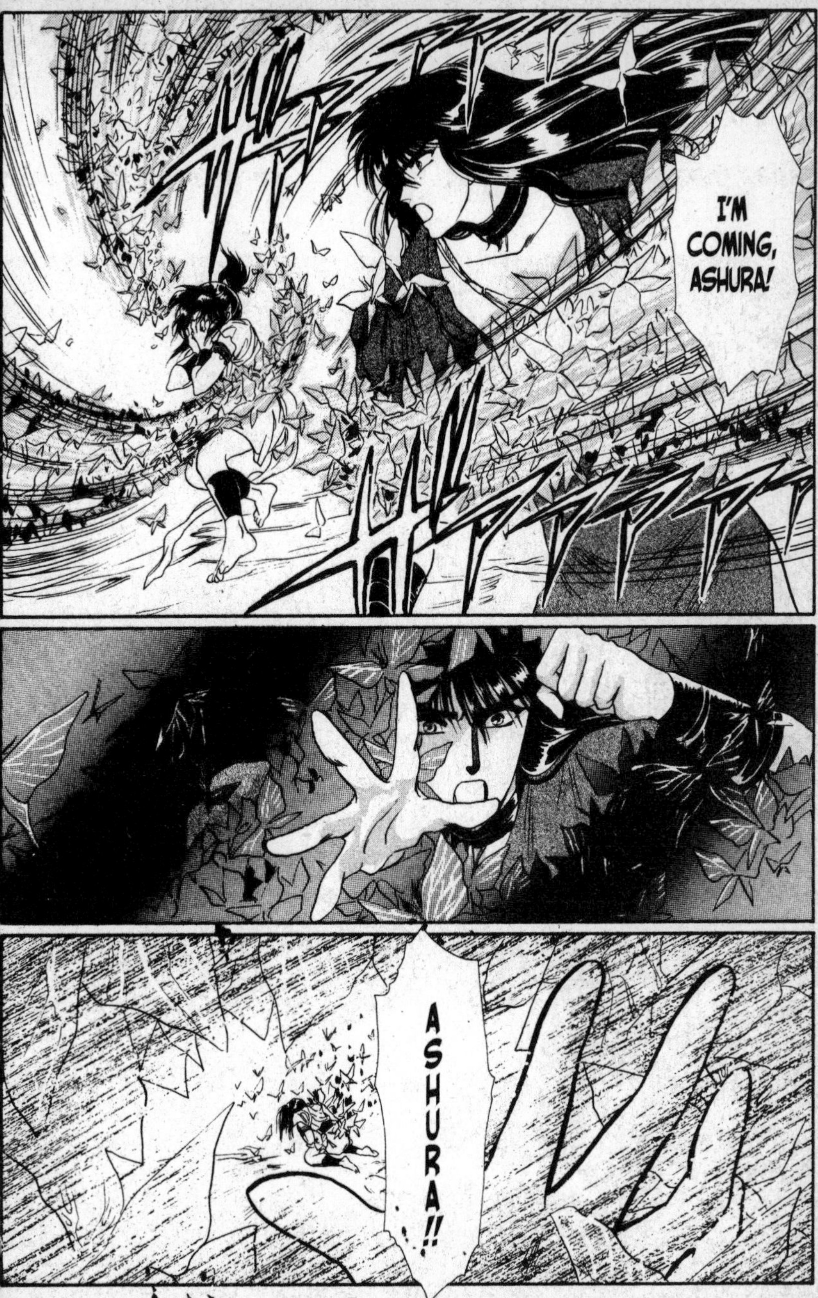
I'M COMING, ASHURA!
ASHURA!!

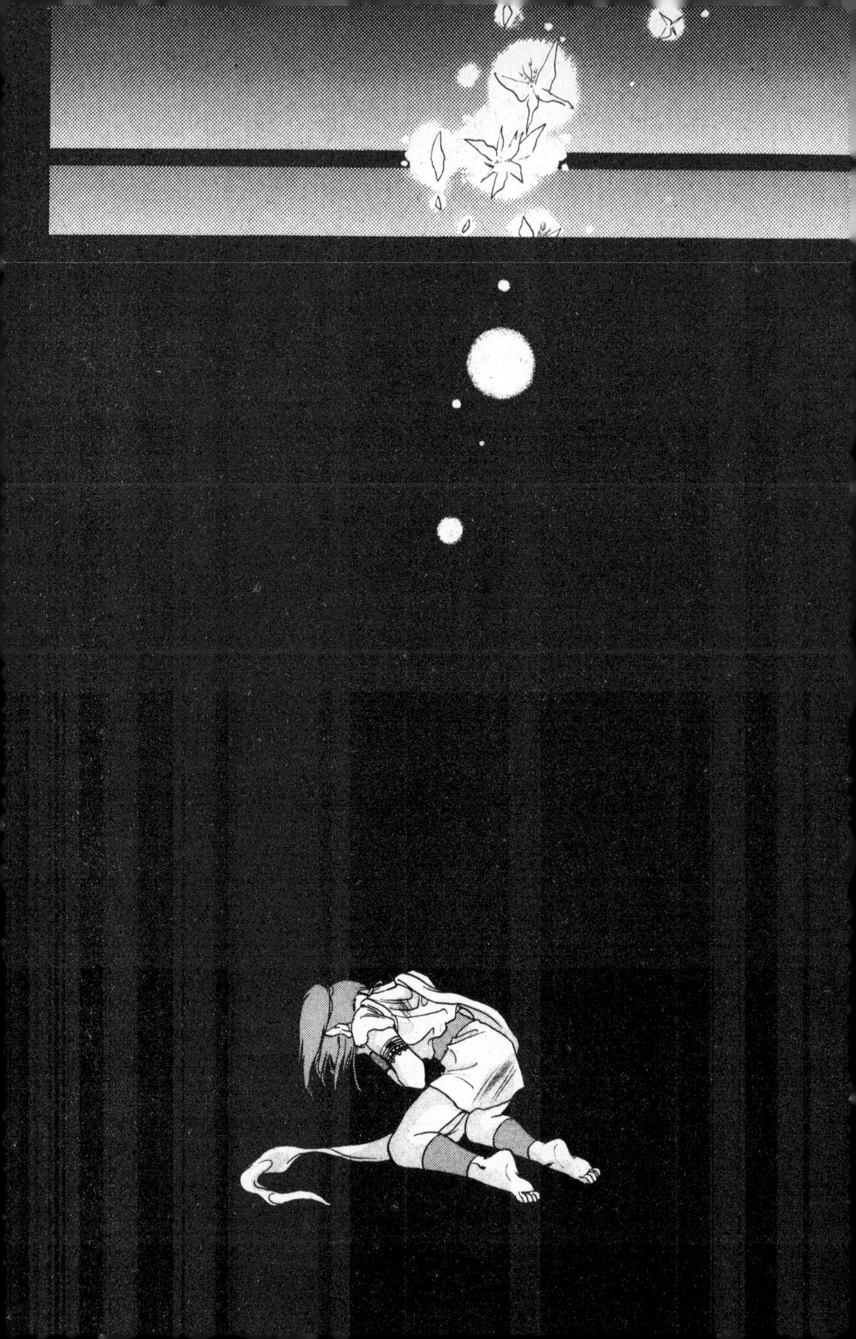

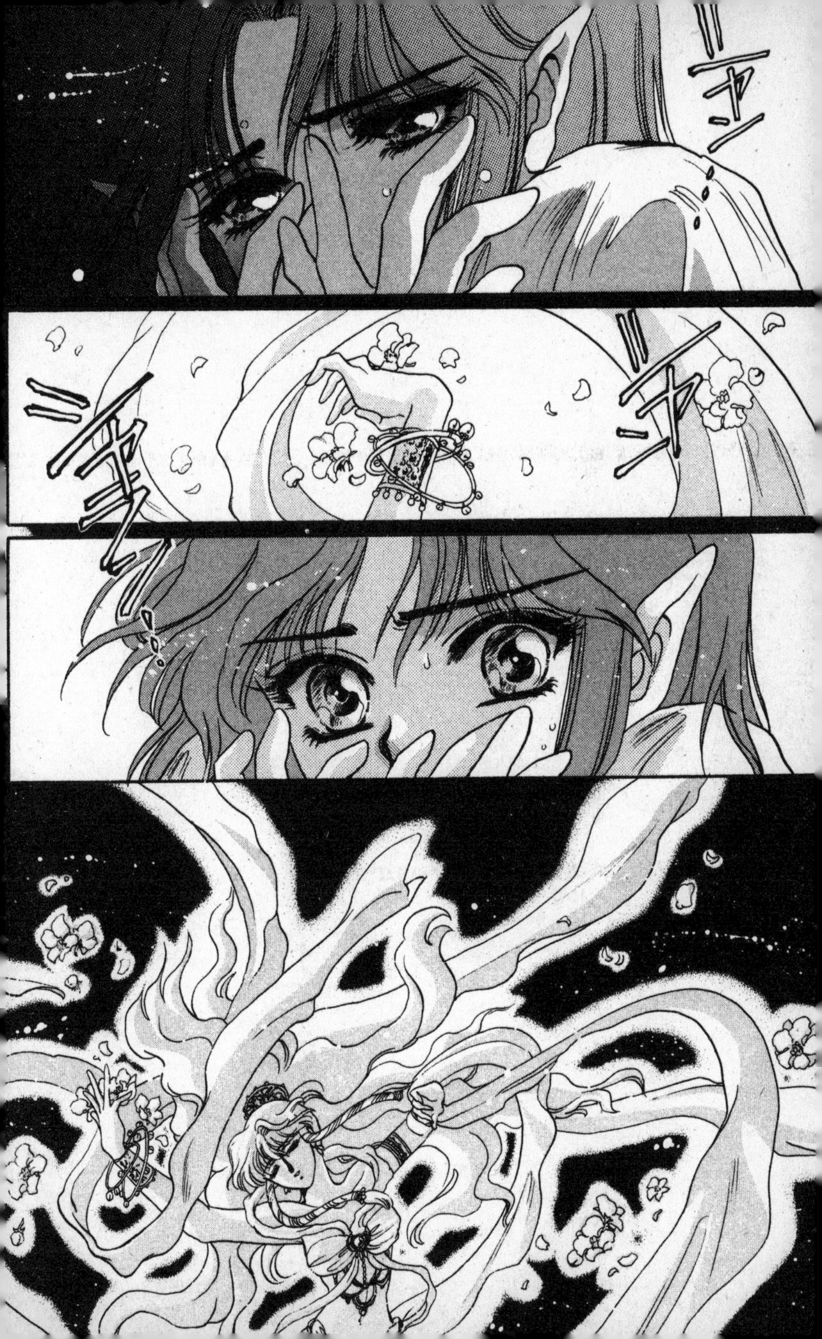
リャン…
リャン―

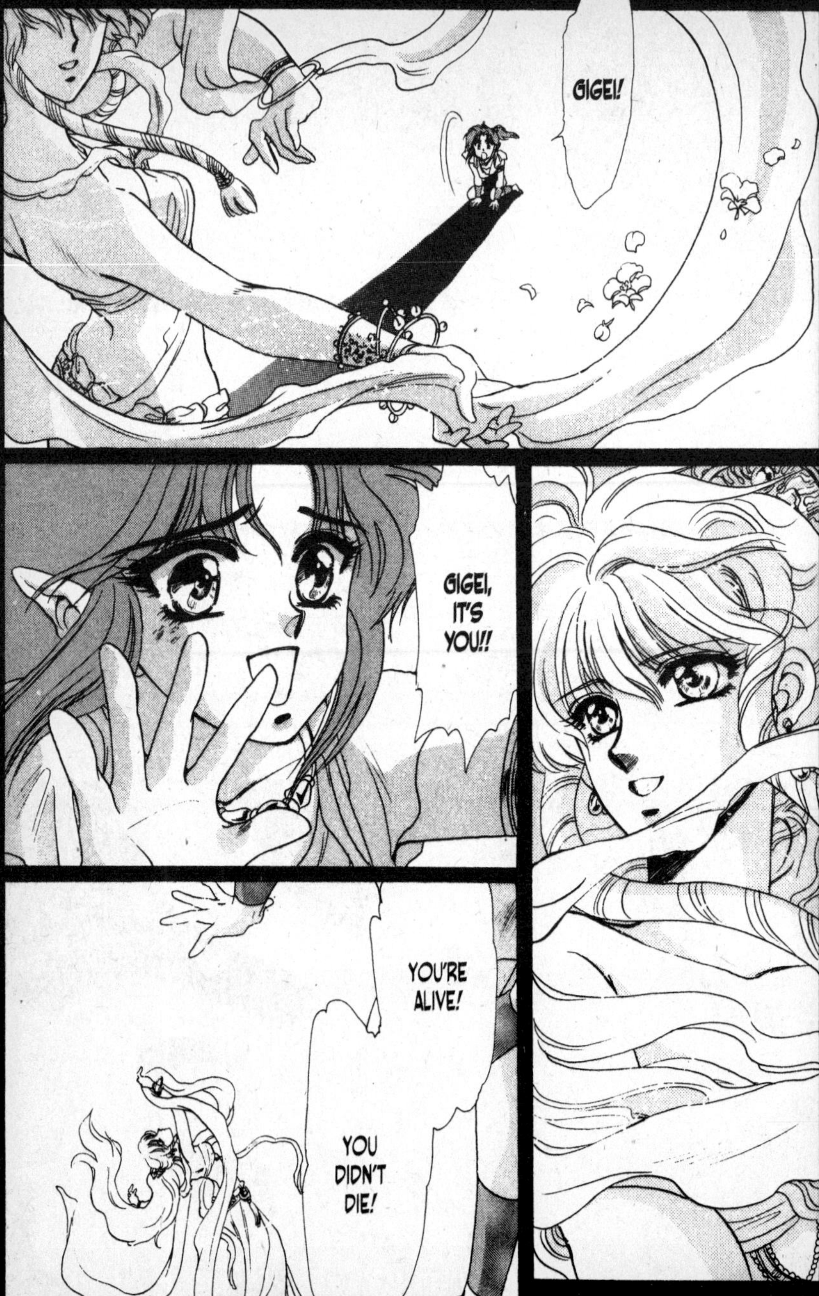
GIGEI!
GIGEI, IT'S YOU!!
YOU'RE ALIVE!
YOU DIDN'T DIE!

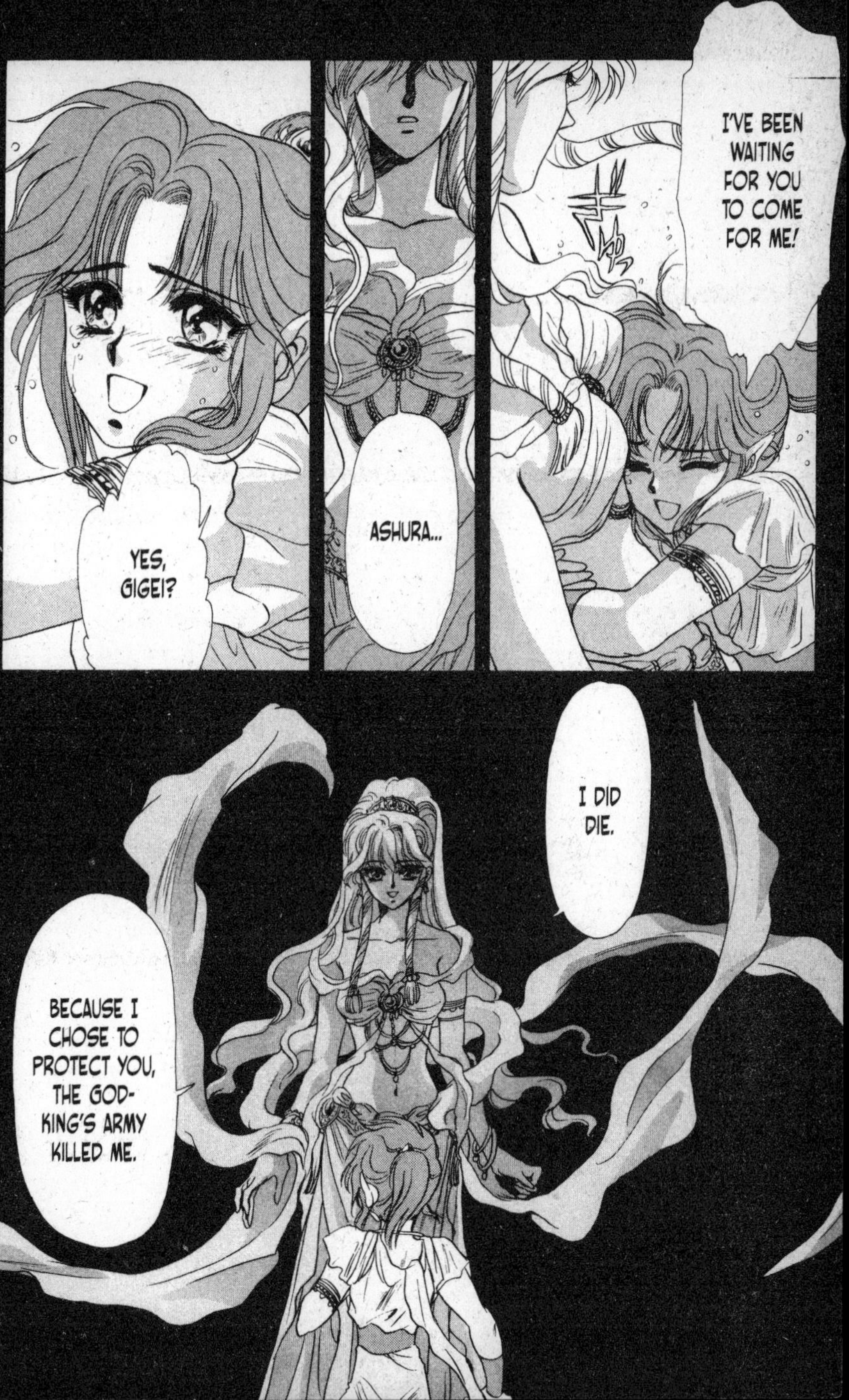
I'VE BEEN WAITING FOR YOU TO COME FOR ME!
ASHURA...
YES, GIGEI?
I DID DIE.
BECAUSE I CHOSE TO PROTECT YOU, THE GOD-KING'S ARMY KILLED ME.

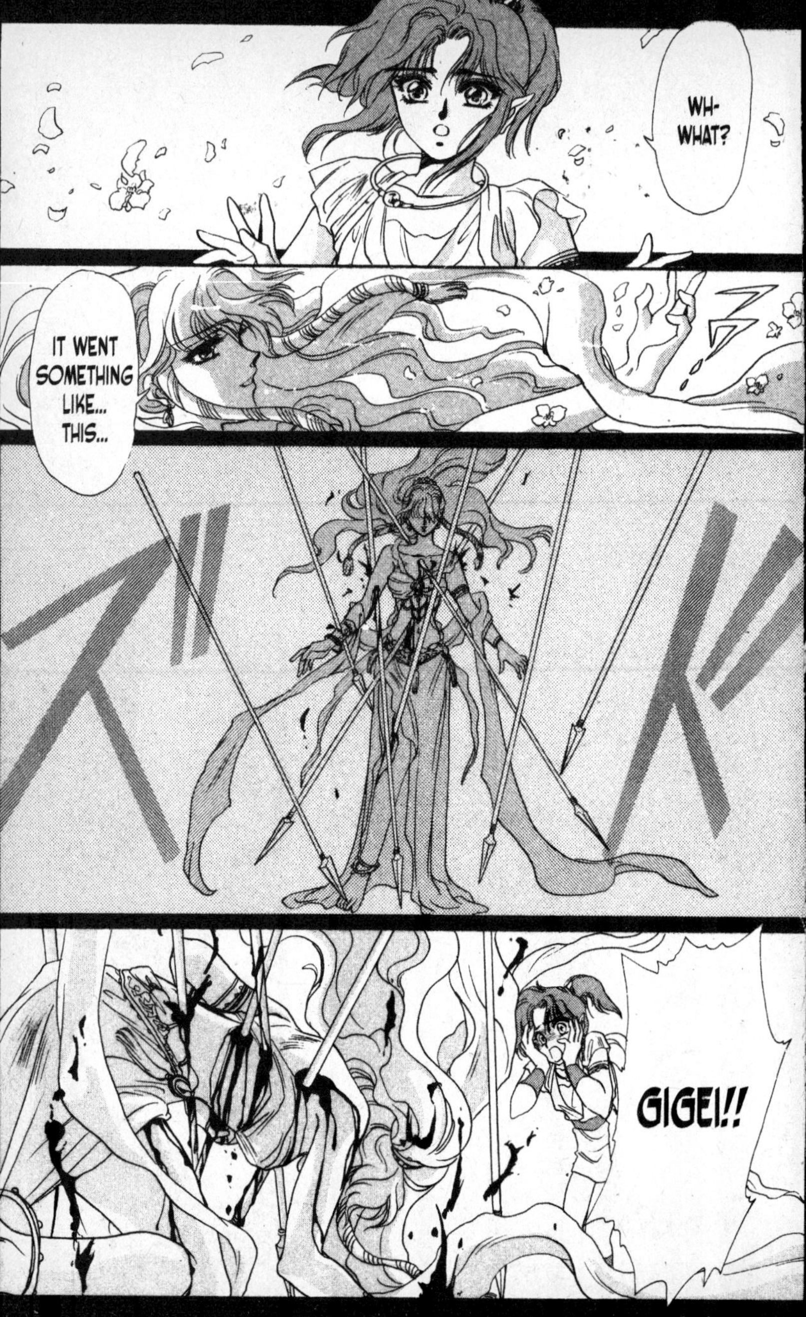
WH-
WHAT?
IT WENT SOMETHING LIKE... THIS...
GIGEI!!

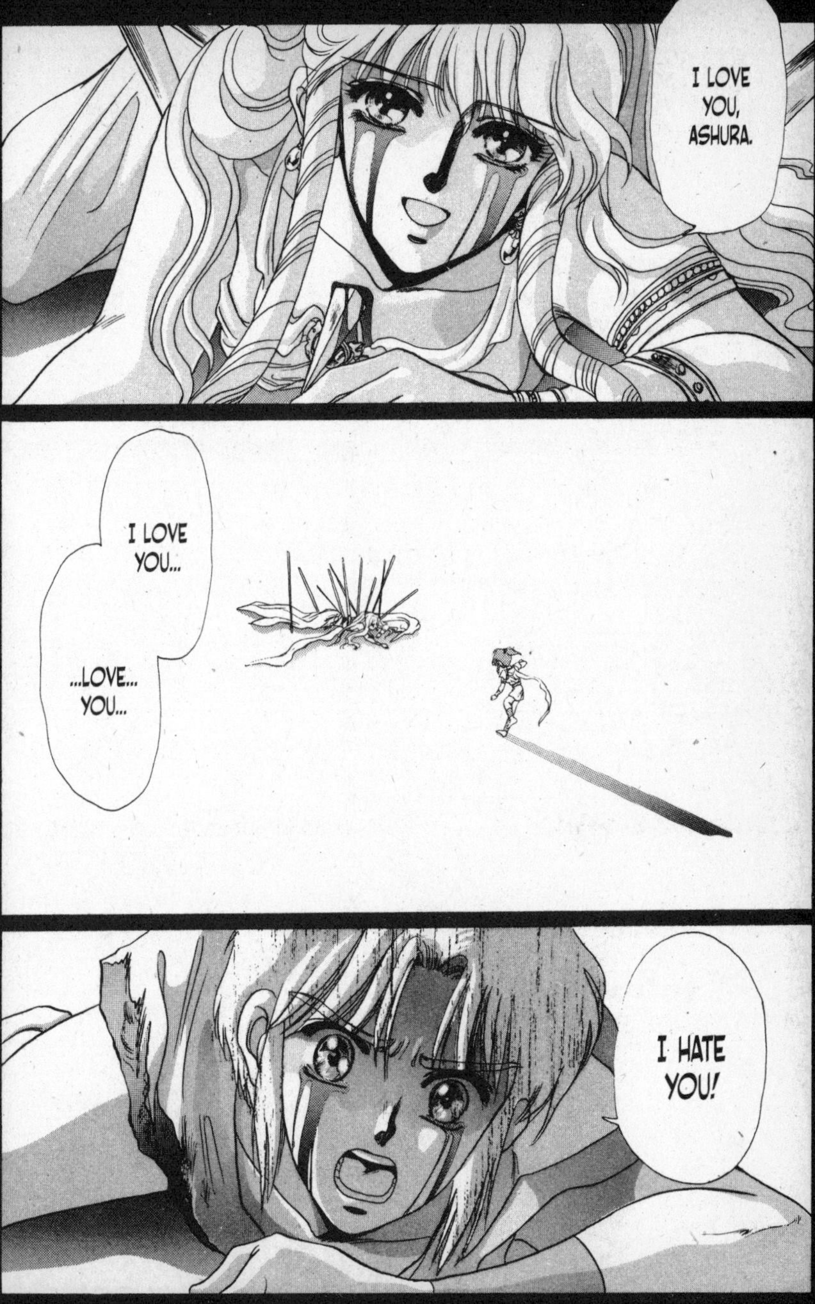
I LOVE YOU, ASHURA.
I LOVE YOU...
...LOVE... YOU...
I HATE YOU!

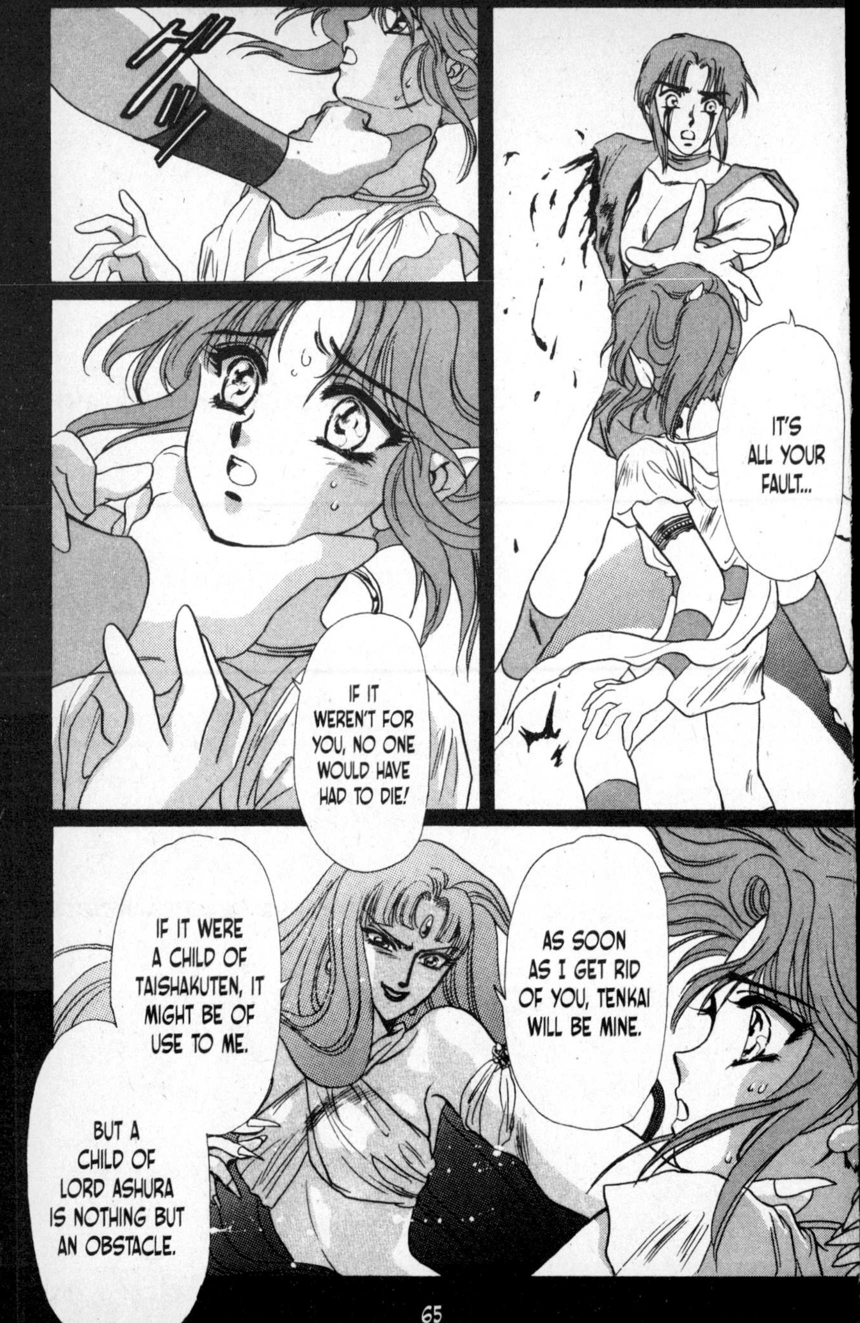
IT'S ALL YOUR FAULT...
IF IT WEREN'T FOR YOU, NO ONE WOULD HAVE HAD TO DIE!
AS SOON AS I GET RID OF YOU, TENKAI WILL BE MINE.
IF IT WERE A CHILD OF TAISHAKUTEN, IT MIGHT BE OF USE TO ME.
BUT A CHILD OF LORD ASHURA IS NOTHING BUT AN OBSTACLE.

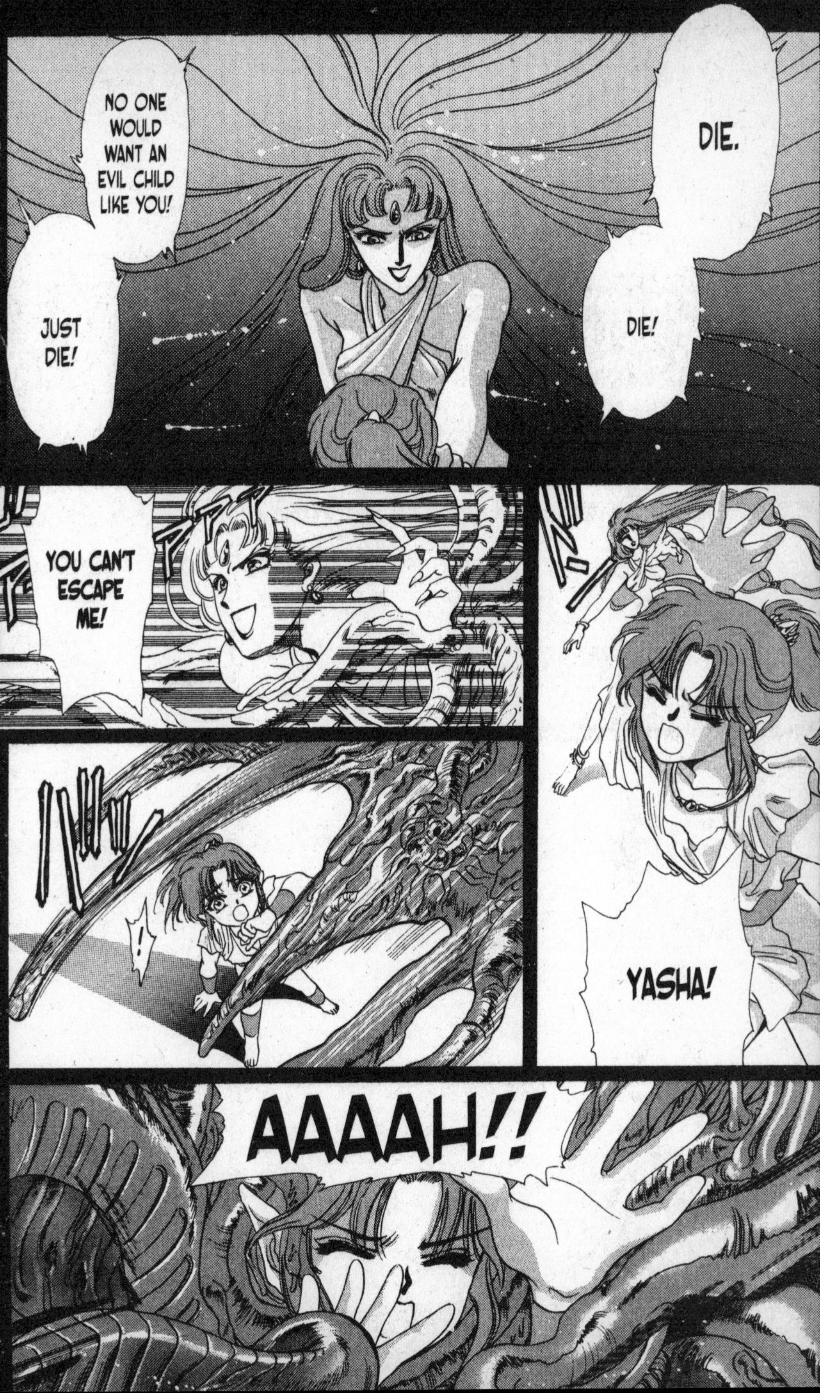
DIE.
NO ONE WOULD WANT AN EVIL CHILD LIKE YOU!
DIE!
JUST DIE!
YASHA!
YOU CAN'T ESCAPE ME!
!
AAAAH!!

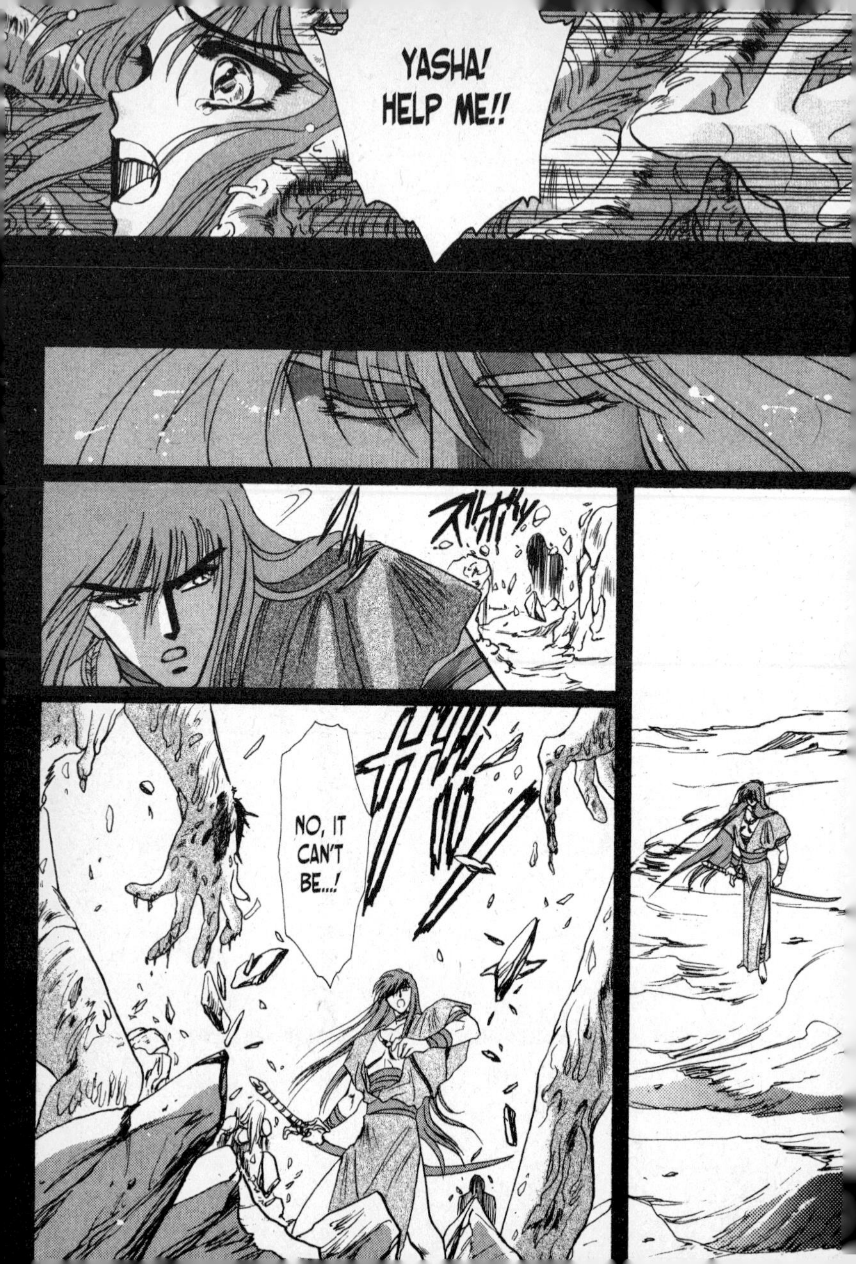
YASHA! HELP ME!!
NO, IT CAN'T BE...!

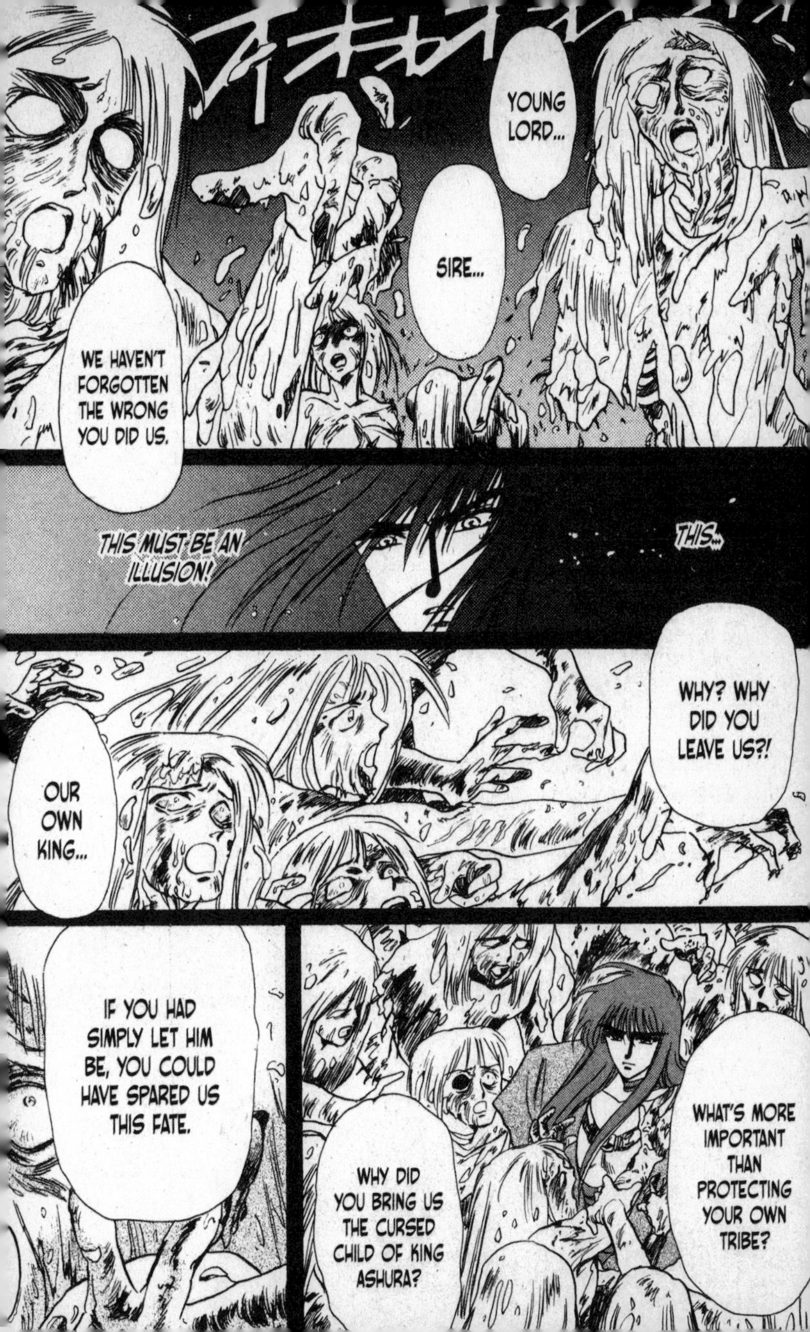
YOUNG LORD...
SIRE...
WE HAVEN'T FORGOTTEN THE WRONG YOU DID US.
THIS...
THIS MUST BE AN ILLUSION!
WHY? WHY DID YOU LEAVE US?!
OUR OWN KING...
WHAT'S MORE IMPORTANT THAN PROTECTING YOUR OWN TRIBE?
WHY DID YOU BRING US THE CURSED CHILD OF KING ASHURA?
IF YOU HAD SIMPLY LET HIM BE, YOU COULD HAVE SPARED US THIS FATE.

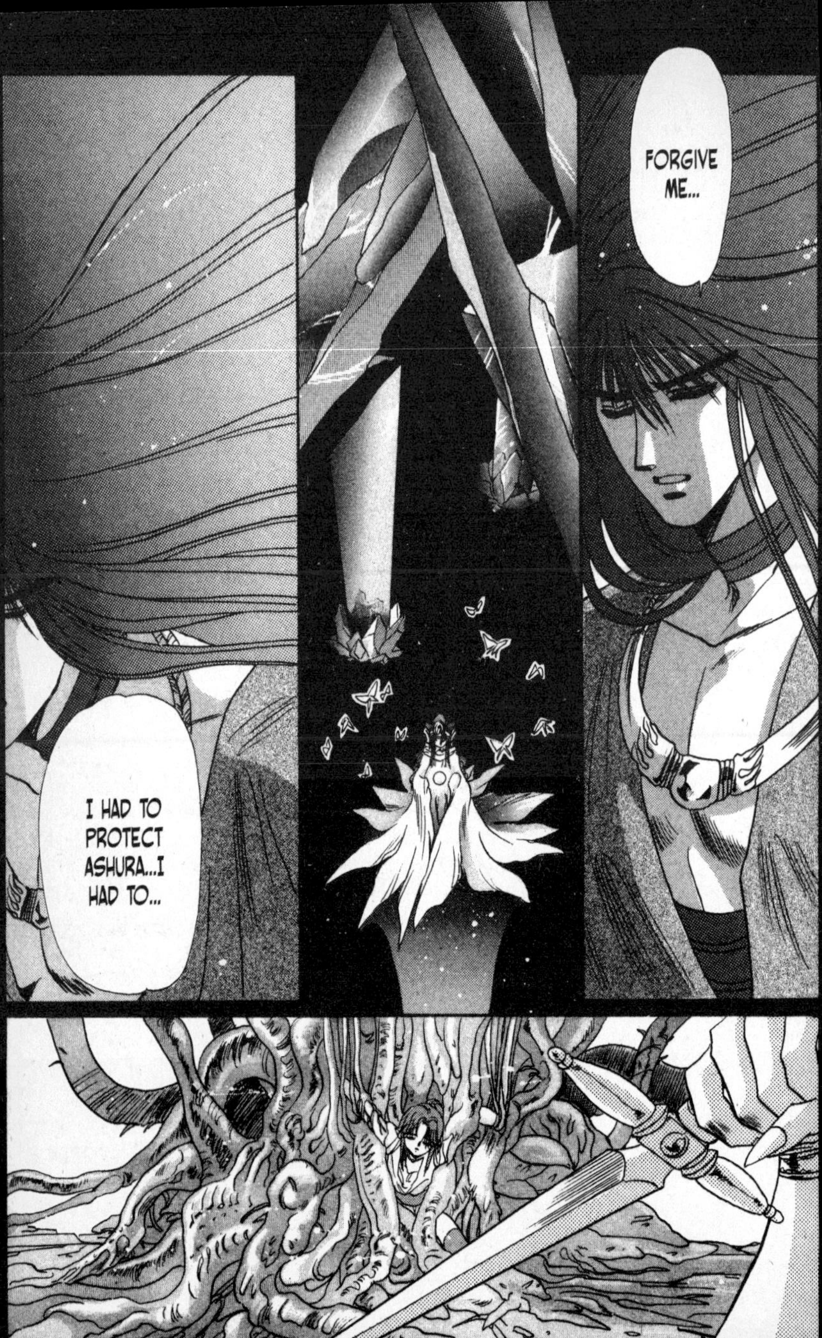
FORGIVE ME...
I HAD TO PROTECT ASHURA...I HAD TO...

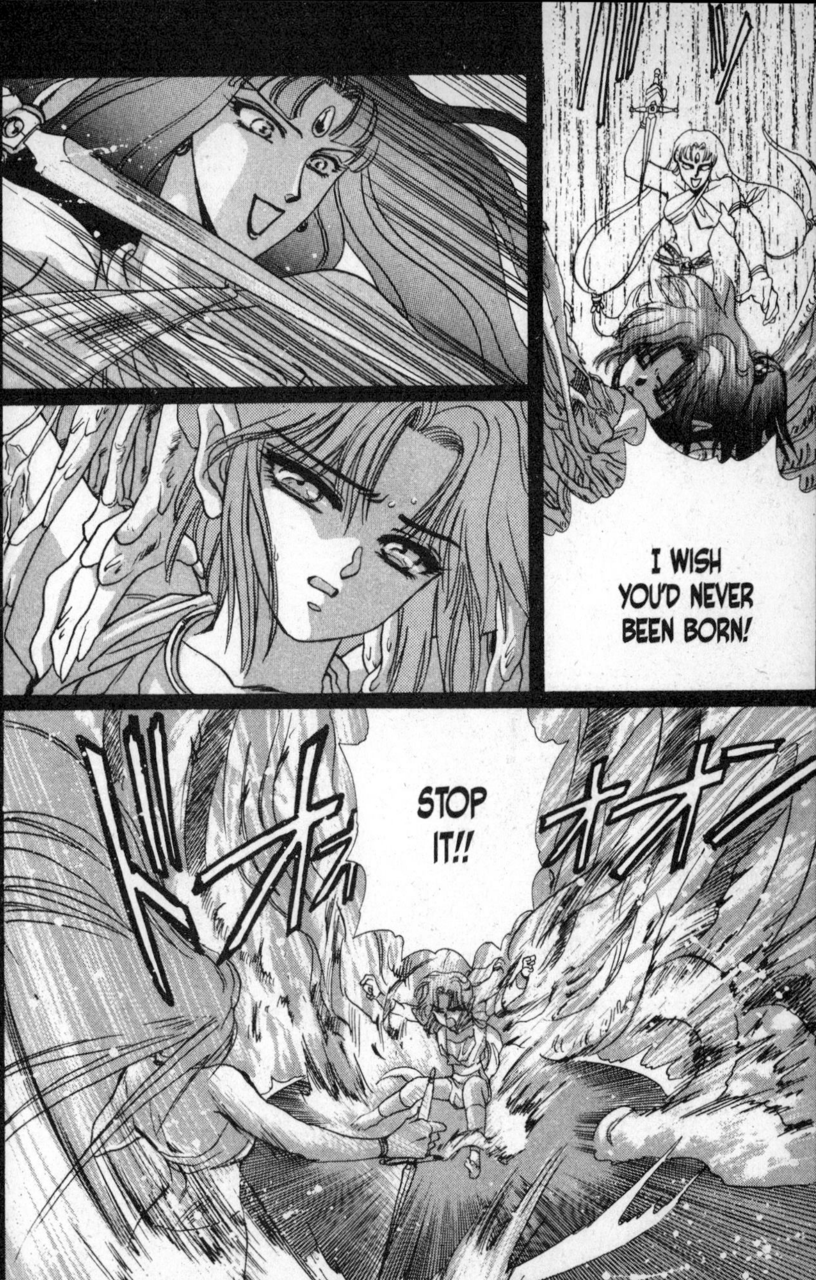
I WISH YOU'D NEVER BEEN BORN!
STOP IT!!

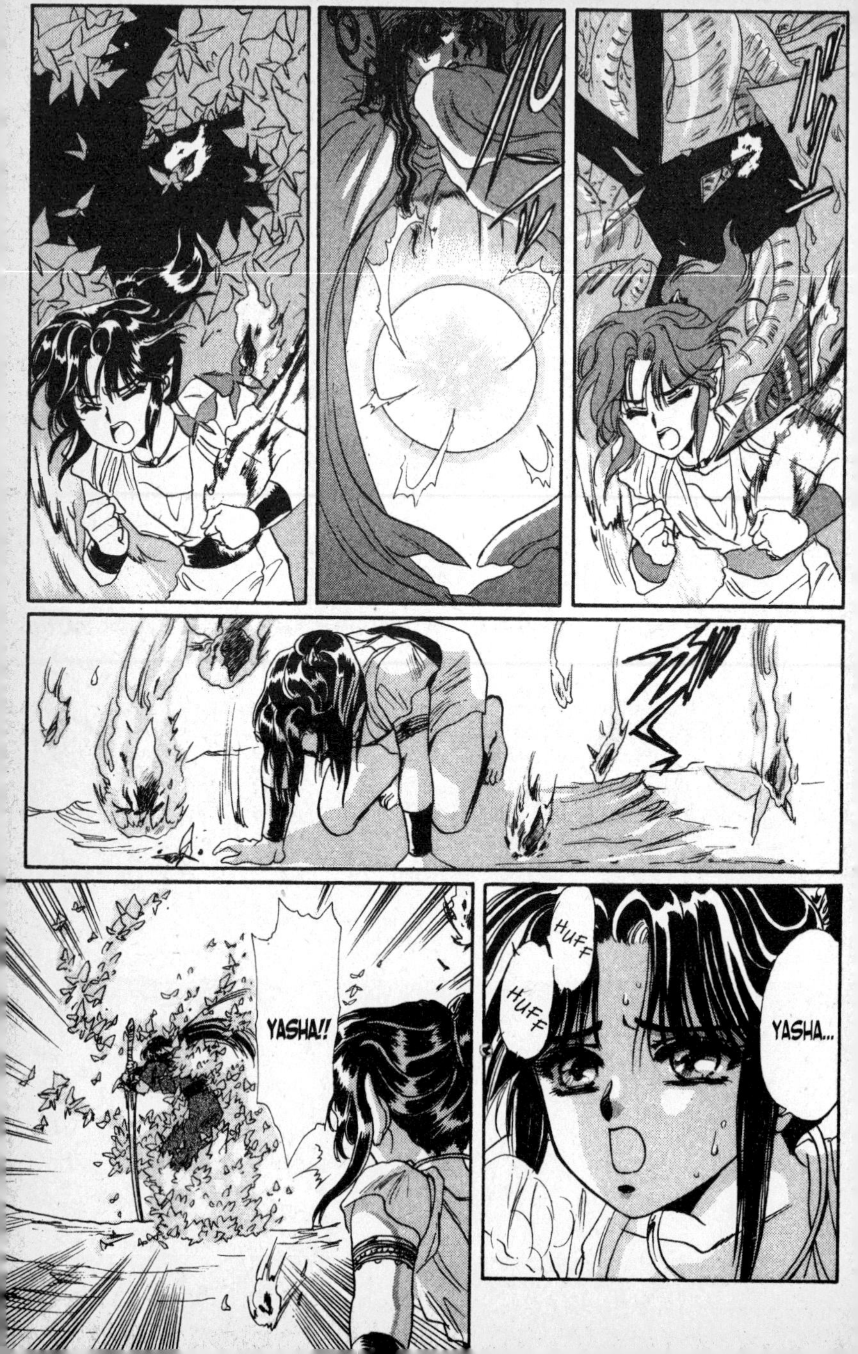
YASHA...
HUFF
HUFF
YASHA!!

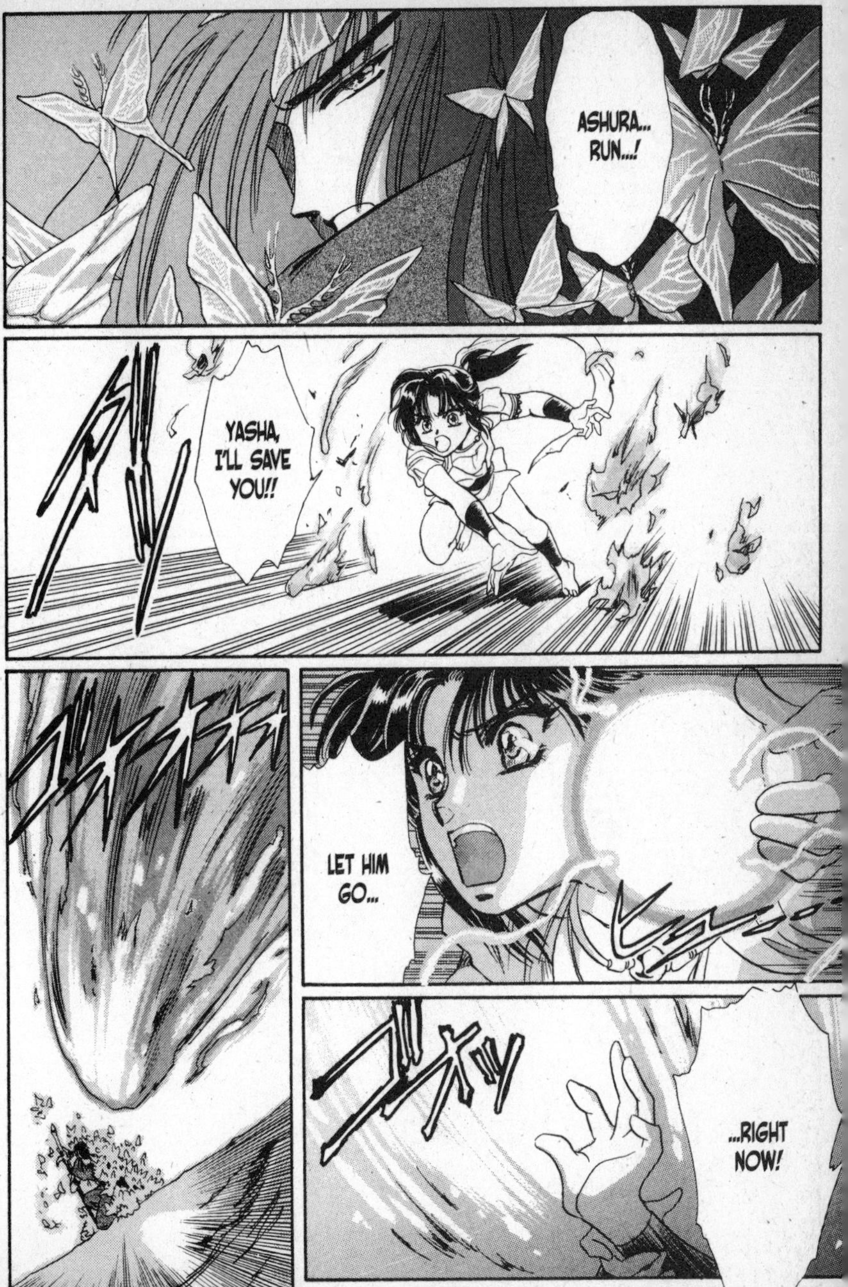
ASHURA... RUN...!
YASHA, I'LL SAVE YOU!!
LET HIM GO...
...RIGHT NOW!

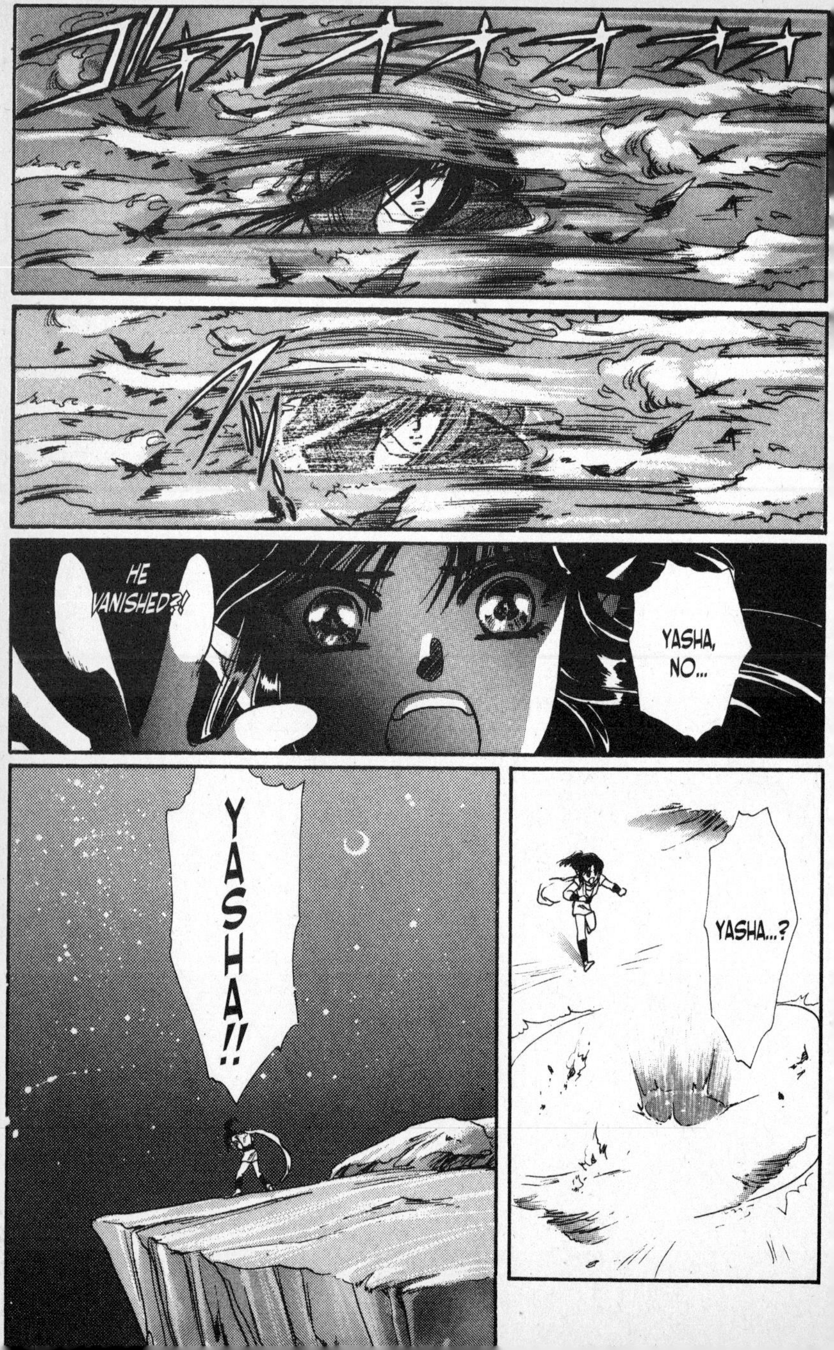
YASHA, NO...
HE VANISHED?!
YASHA...?
YASHA!!

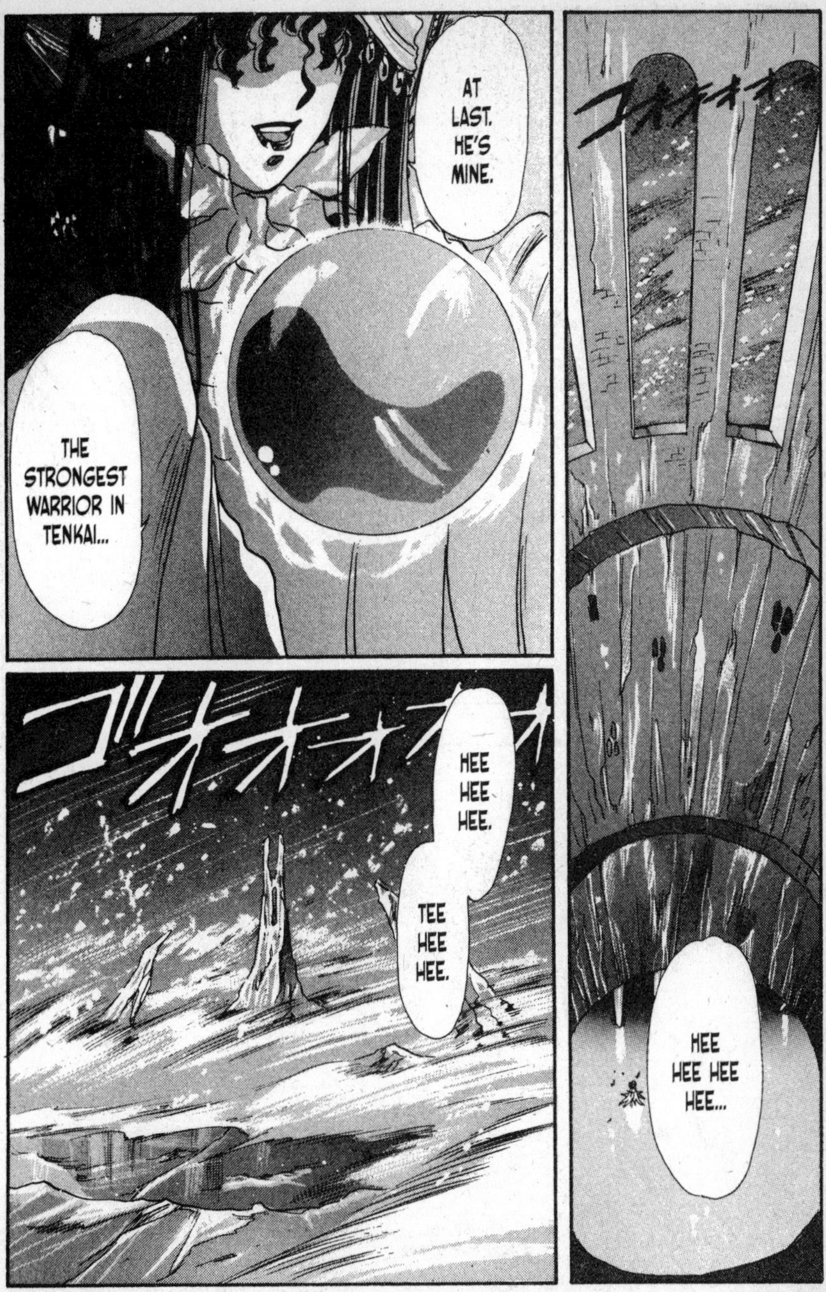

ゴオオオオ
HEE HEE HEE HEE...
AT LAST. HE'S MINE.
THE STRONGEST WARRIOR IN TENKAI...
ゴオオオオオ
HEE HEE HEE.
TEE HEE HEE.

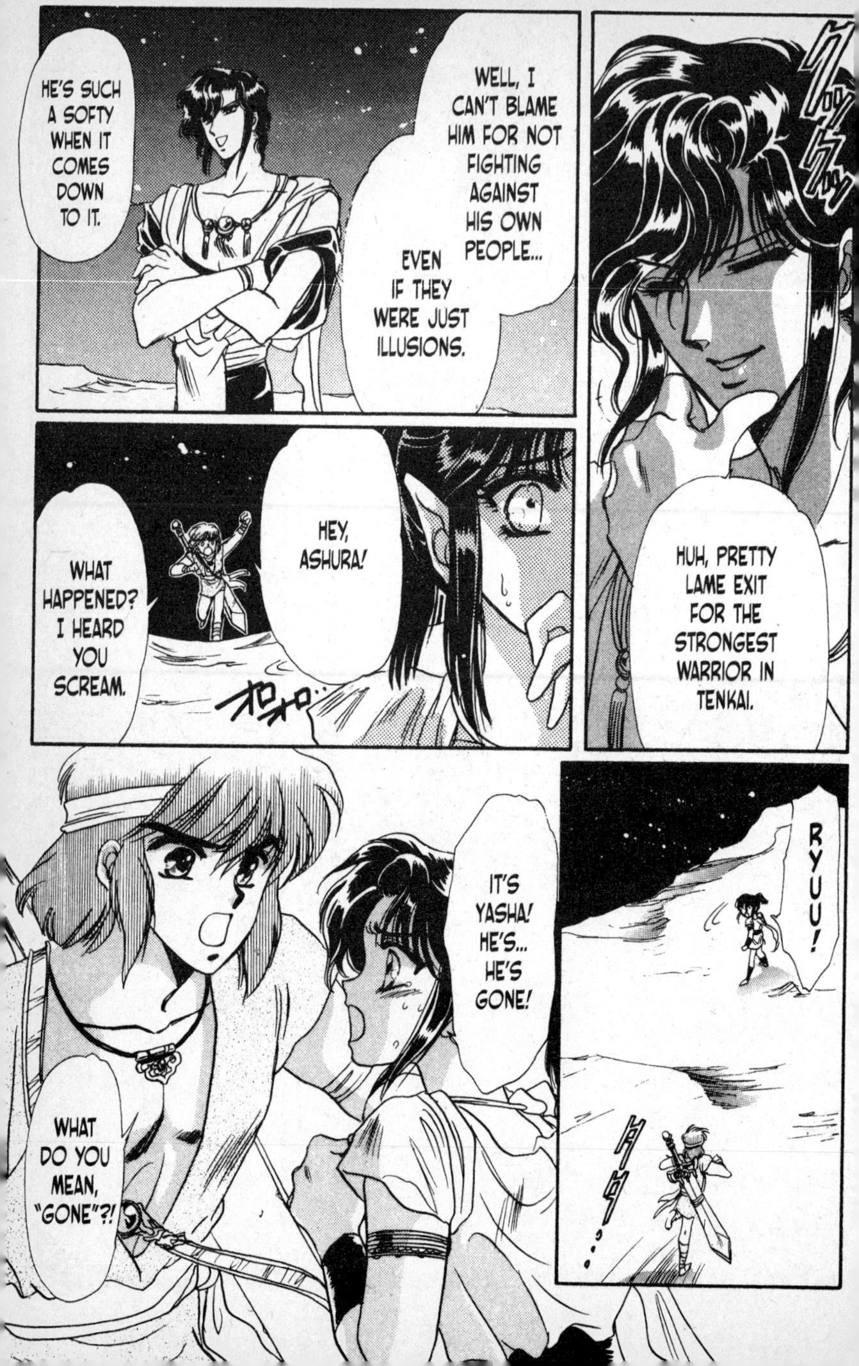
HUH, PRETTY LAME EXIT FOR THE STRONGEST WARRIOR IN TENKAI.
WELL, I CAN'T BLAME HIM FOR NOT FIGHTING AGAINST HIS OWN PEOPLE...
EVEN IF THEY WERE JUST ILLUSIONS.
HE'S SUCH A SOFTY WHEN IT COMES DOWN TO IT.
HEY, ASHURA!
WHAT HAPPENED? I HEARD YOU SCREAM.
オロオロ…
RYUU!
タッタッ…
IT'S YASHA! HE'S... HE'S GONE!
WHAT DO YOU MEAN, "GONE"?!

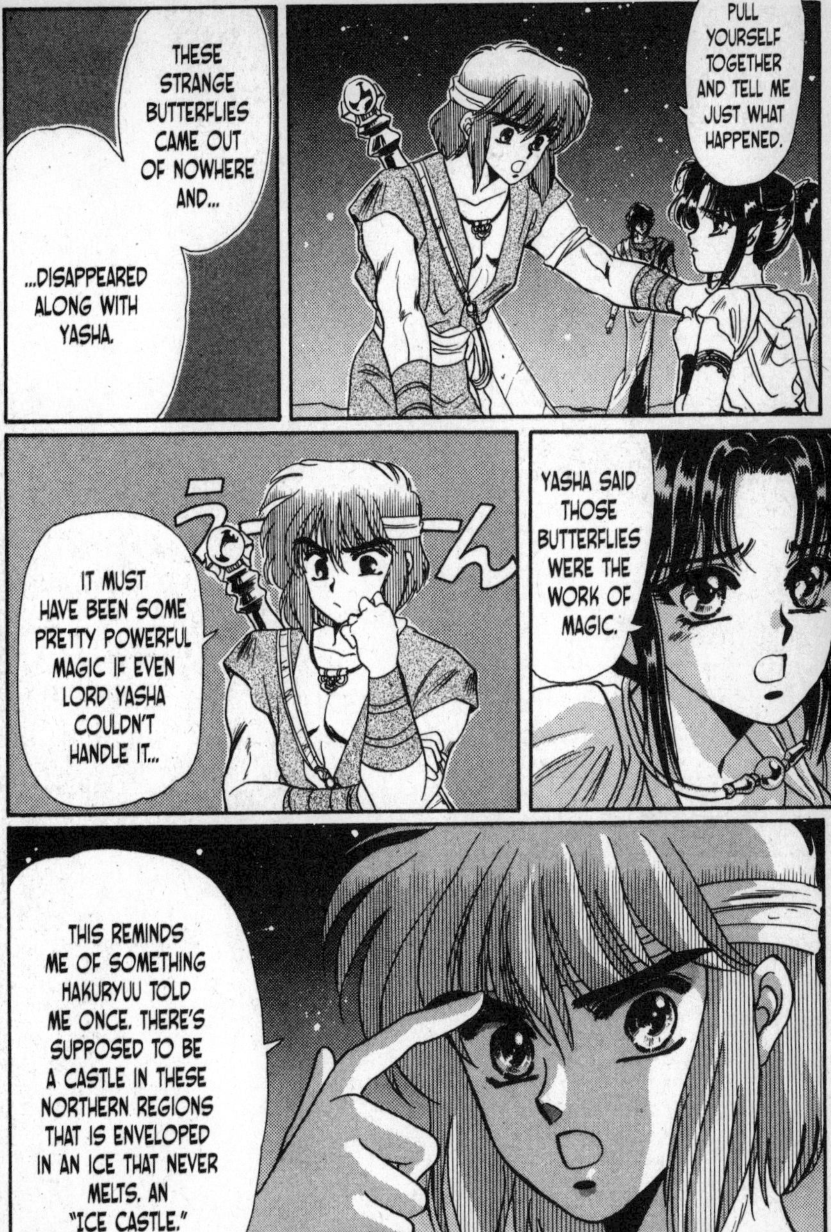
PULL YOURSELF TOGETHER AND TELL ME JUST WHAT HAPPENED.
THESE STRANGE BUTTERFLIES CAME OUT OF NOWHERE AND...
...DISAPPEARED ALONG WITH YASHA.
YASHA SAID THOSE BUTTERFLIES WERE THE WORK OF MAGIC.
うーん
IT MUST HAVE BEEN SOME PRETTY POWERFUL MAGIC IF EVEN LORD YASHA COULDN'T HANDLE IT...
THIS REMINDS ME OF SOMETHING HAKURYUU TOLD ME ONCE. THERE'S SUPPOSED TO BE A CASTLE IN THESE NORTHERN REGIONS THAT IS ENVELOPED IN AN ICE THAT NEVER MELTS. AN "ICE CASTLE."

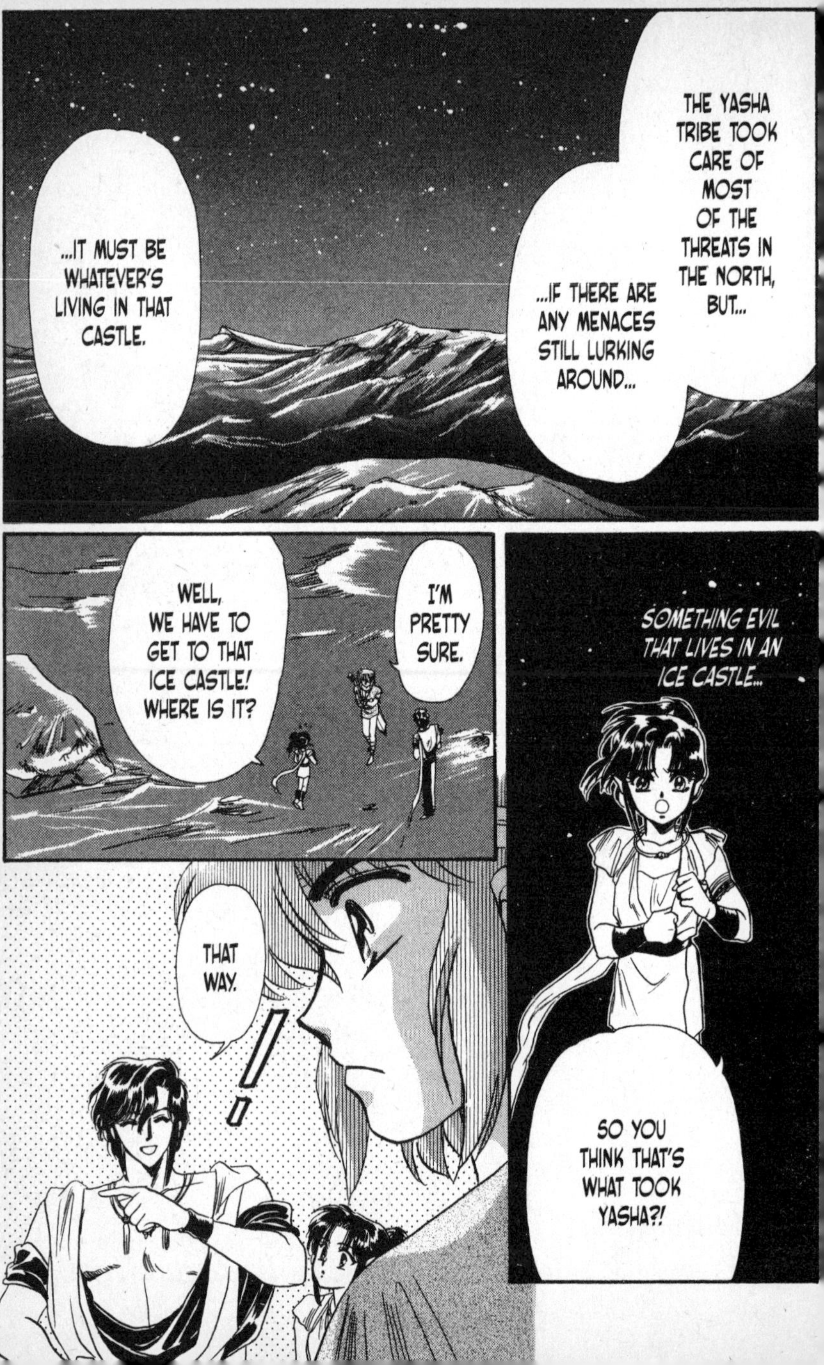
THE YASHA TRIBE TOOK CARE OF MOST OF THE THREATS IN THE NORTH, BUT...
...IF THERE ARE ANY MENACES STILL LURKING AROUND...
...IT MUST BE WHATEVER'S LIVING IN THAT CASTLE.
SOMETHING EVIL THAT LIVES IN AN ICE CASTLE...
SO YOU THINK THAT'S WHAT TOOK YASHA?!
I'M PRETTY SURE.
WELL, WE HAVE TO GET TO THAT ICE CASTLE! WHERE IS IT?
THAT WAY.

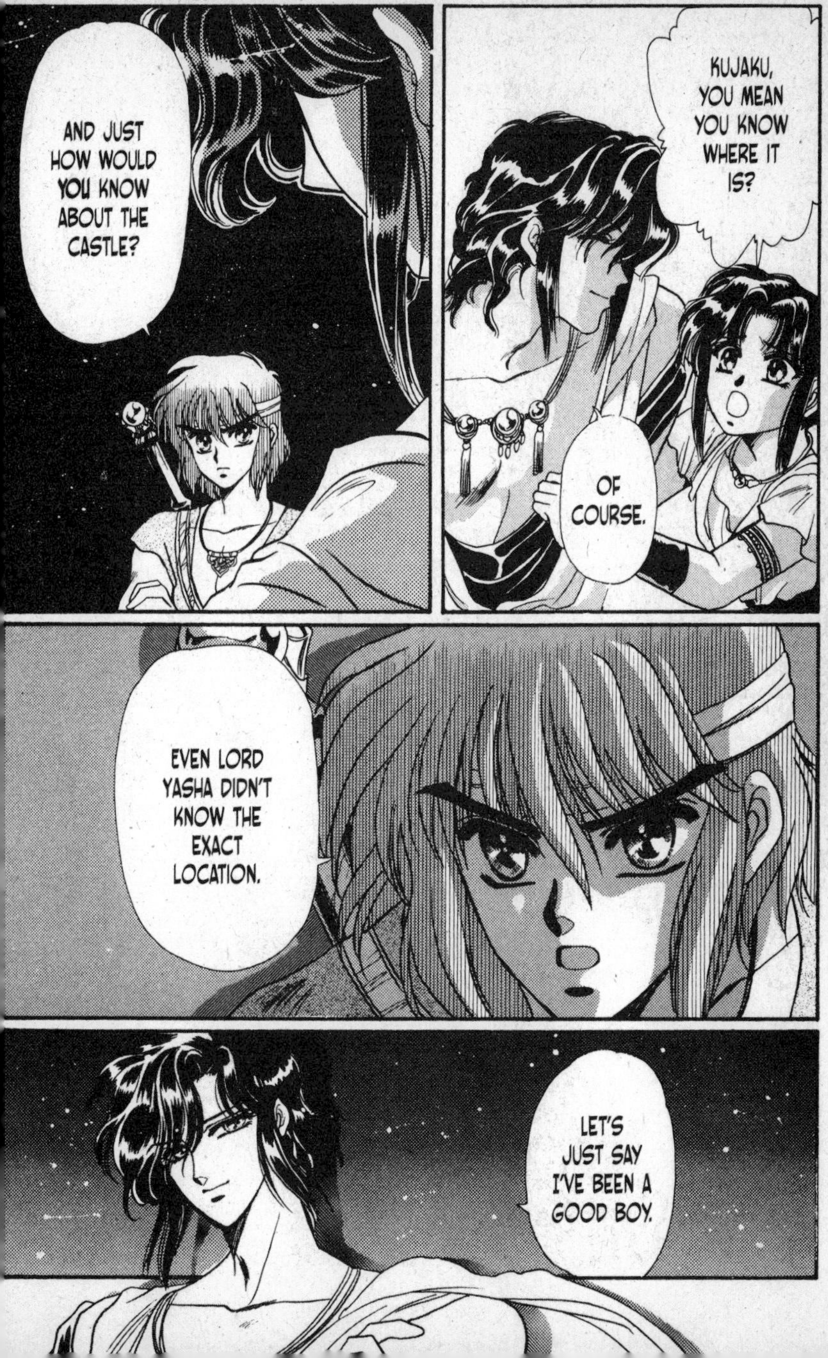
KUJAKU, YOU MEAN YOU KNOW WHERE IT IS?
OF COURSE.
AND JUST HOW WOULD YOU KNOW ABOUT THE CASTLE?
EVEN LORD YASHA DIDN'T KNOW THE EXACT LOCATION.
LET'S JUST SAY I'VE BEEN A GOOD BOY.

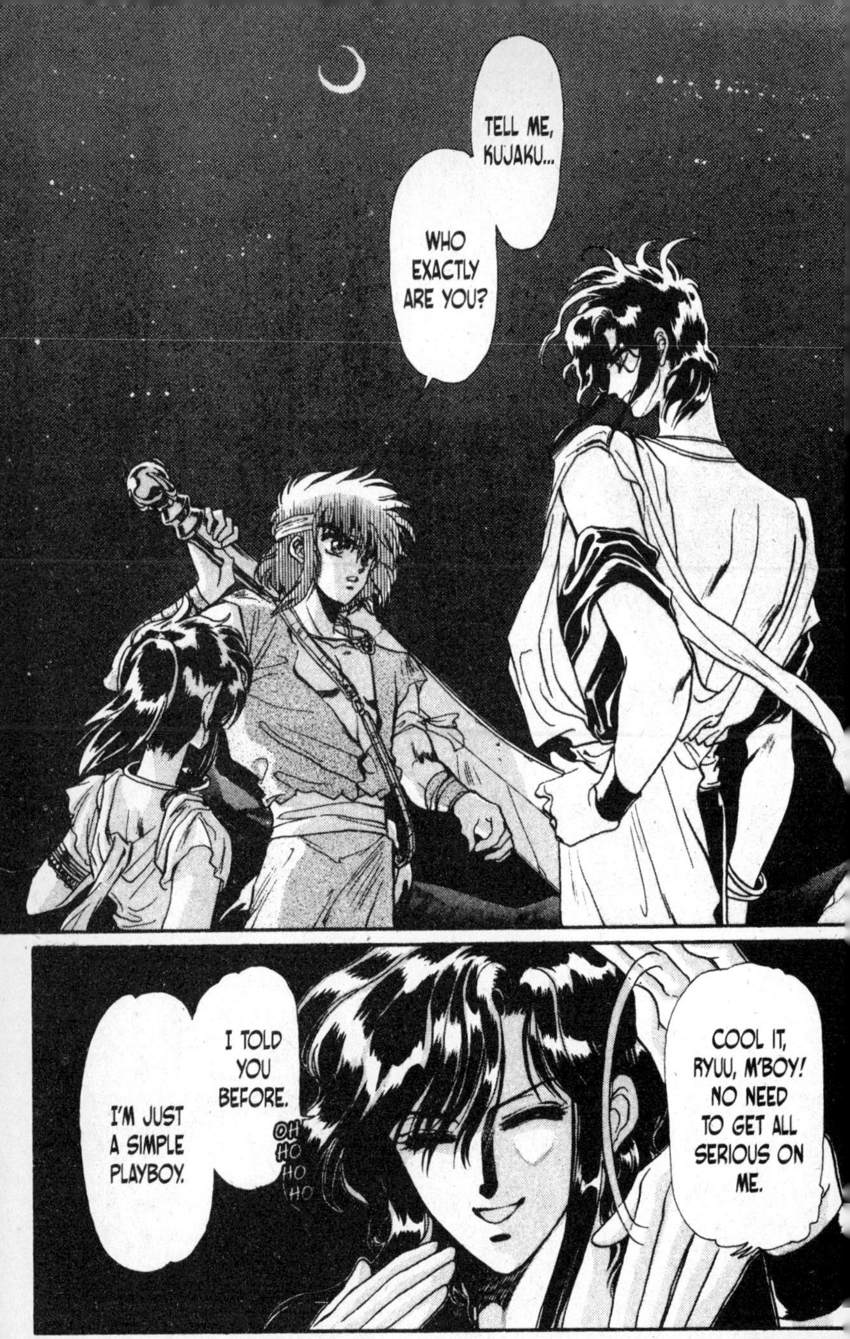
TELL ME, KUJAKU...
WHO EXACTLY ARE YOU?
COOL IT, RYUU, M'BOY! NO NEED TO GET ALL SERIOUS ON ME.
OH HO HO HO
I TOLD YOU BEFORE.
I'M JUST A SIMPLE PLAYBOY.

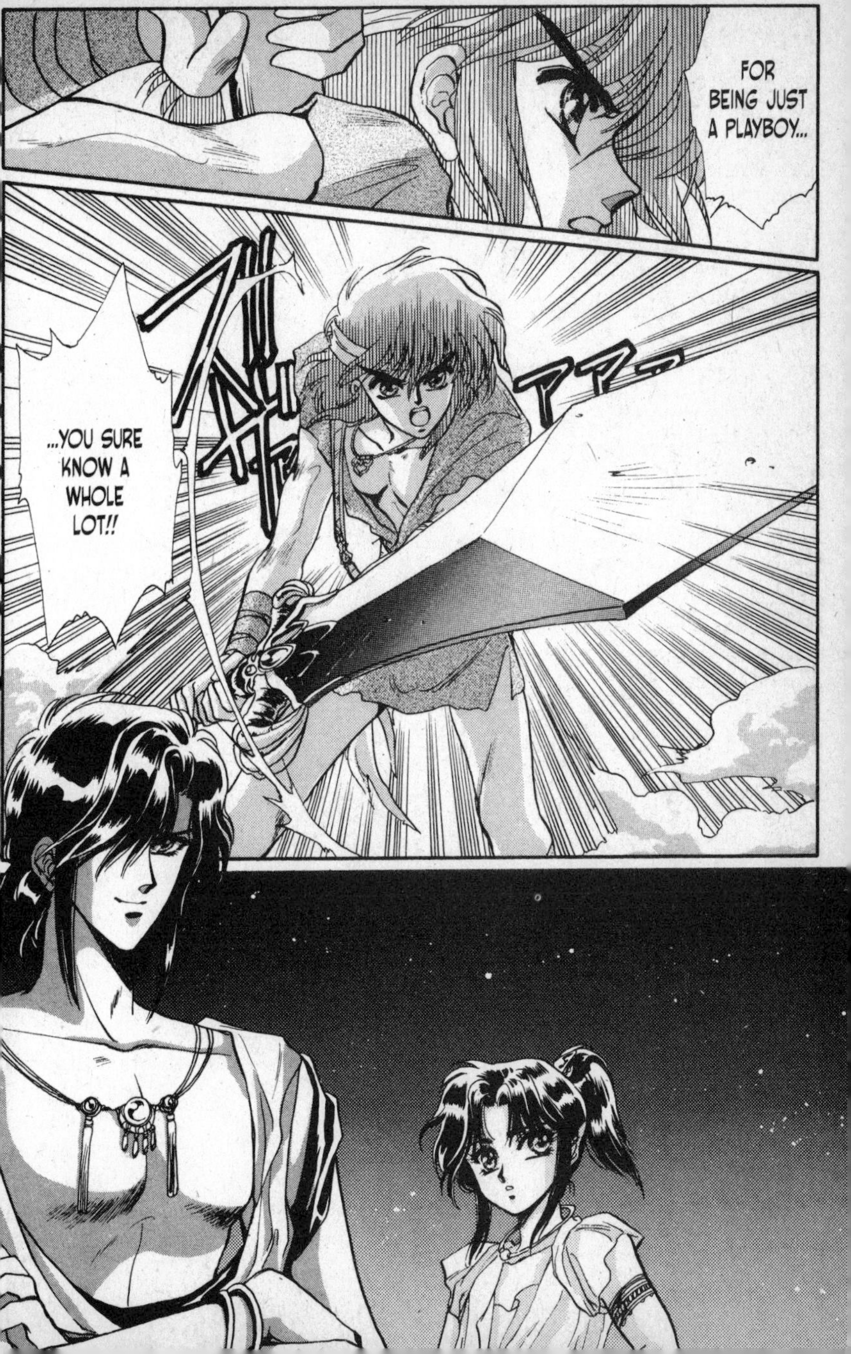
FOR BEING JUST A PLAYBOY...
...YOU SURE KNOW A WHOLE LOT!!

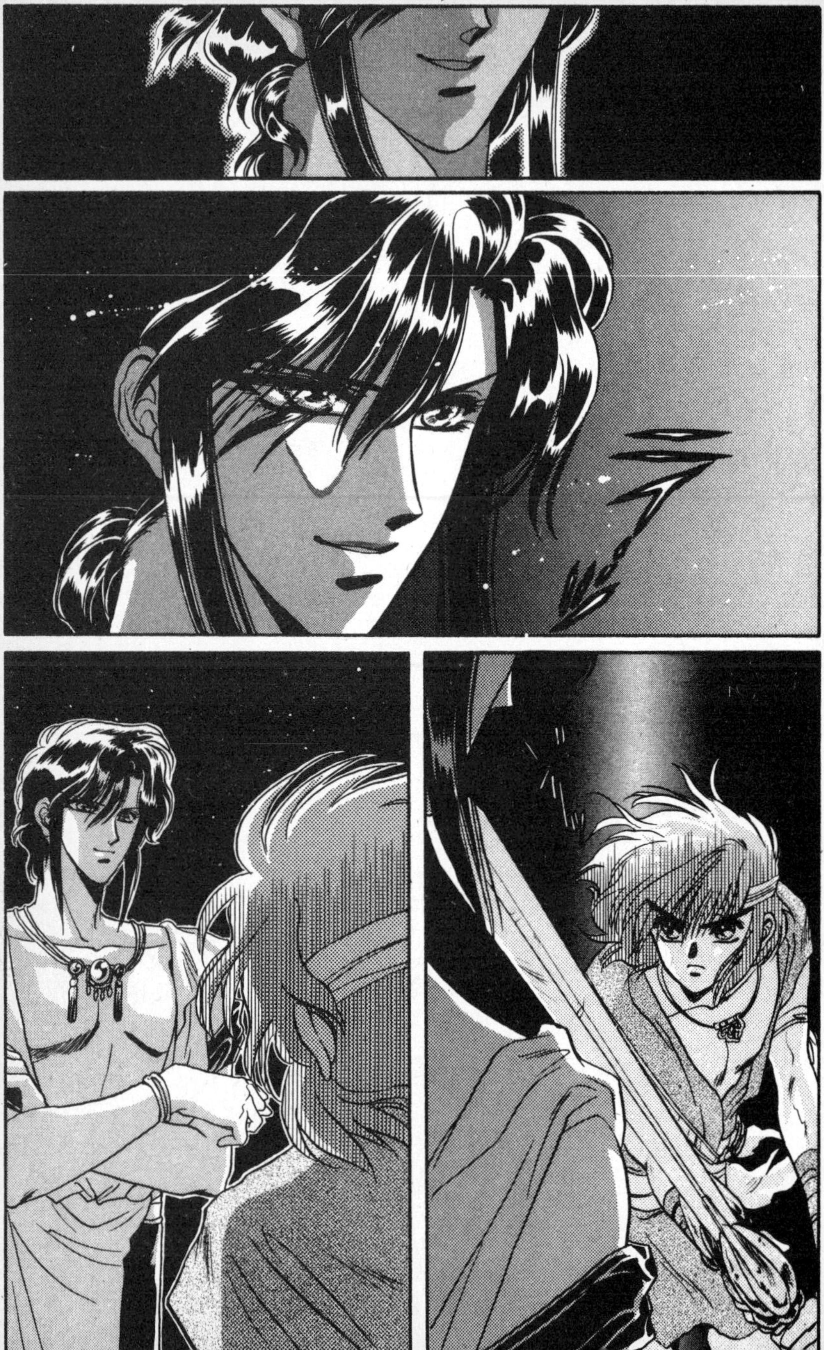

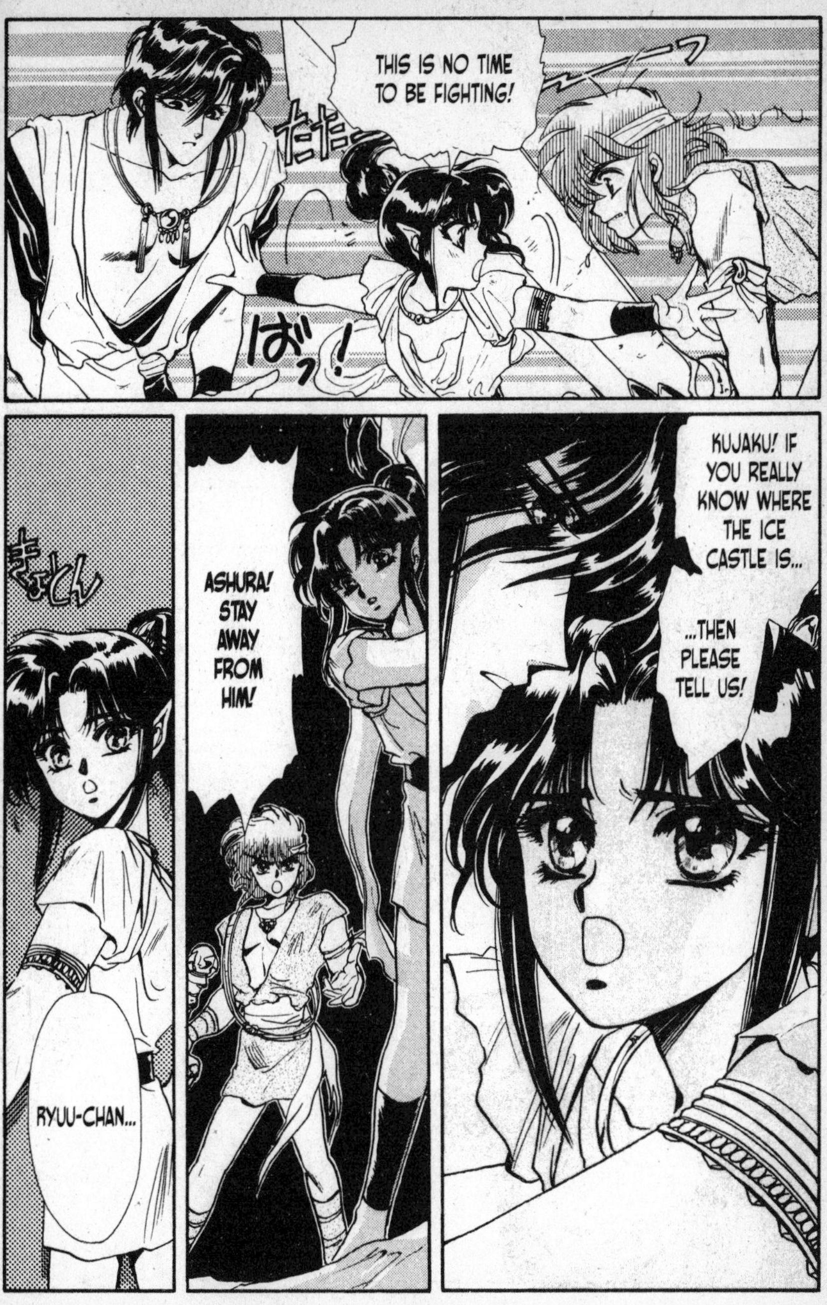
THIS IS NO TIME TO BE FIGHTING!
KUJAKU! IF YOU REALLY KNOW WHERE THE ICE CASTLE IS...
...THEN PLEASE TELL US!
ASHURA! STAY AWAY FROM HIM!
RYUU-CHAN...

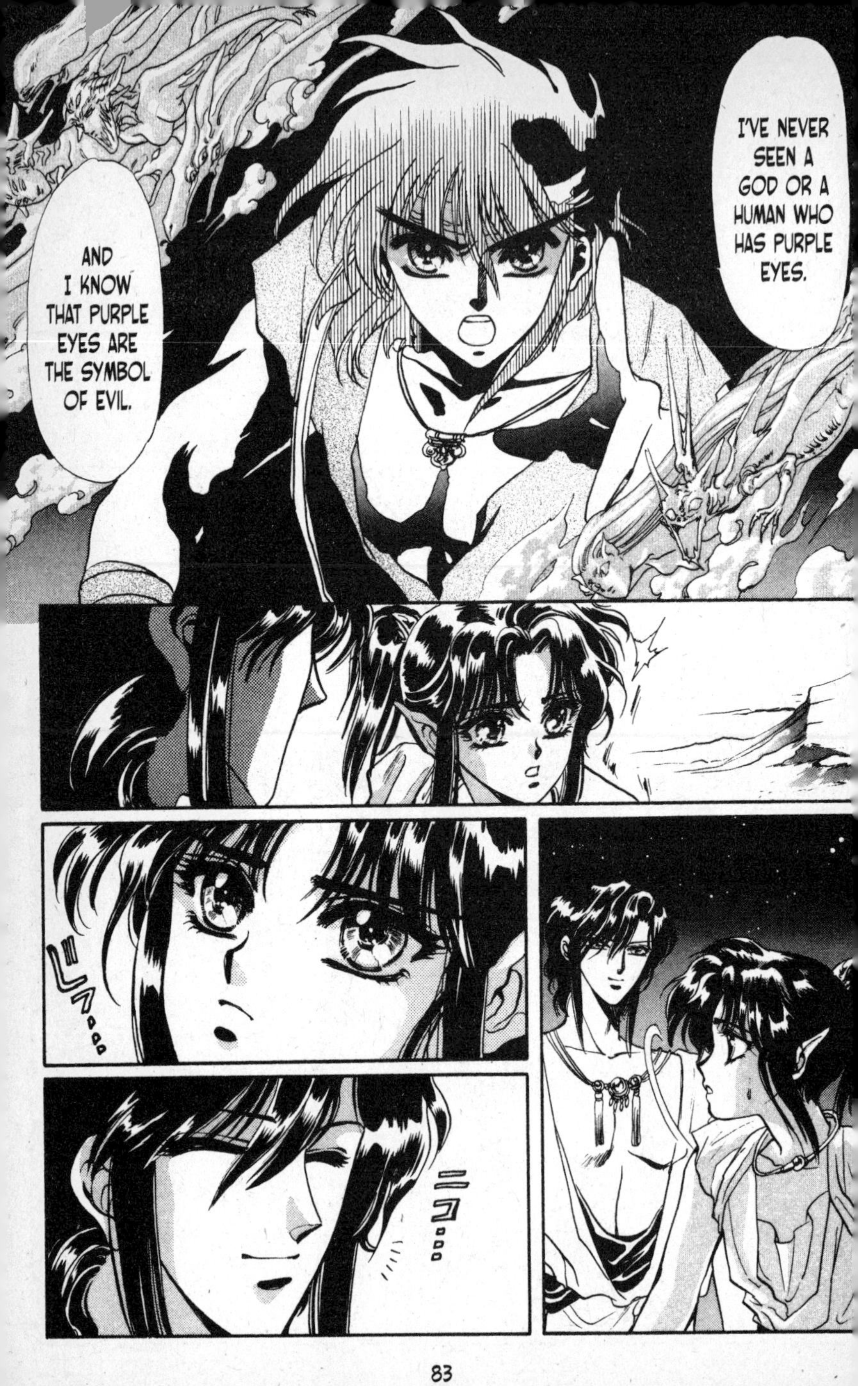

I'VE NEVER SEEN A GOD OR A HUMAN WHO HAS PURPLE EYES.
AND I KNOW THAT PURPLE EYES ARE THE SYMBOL OF EVIL.
ニコ…

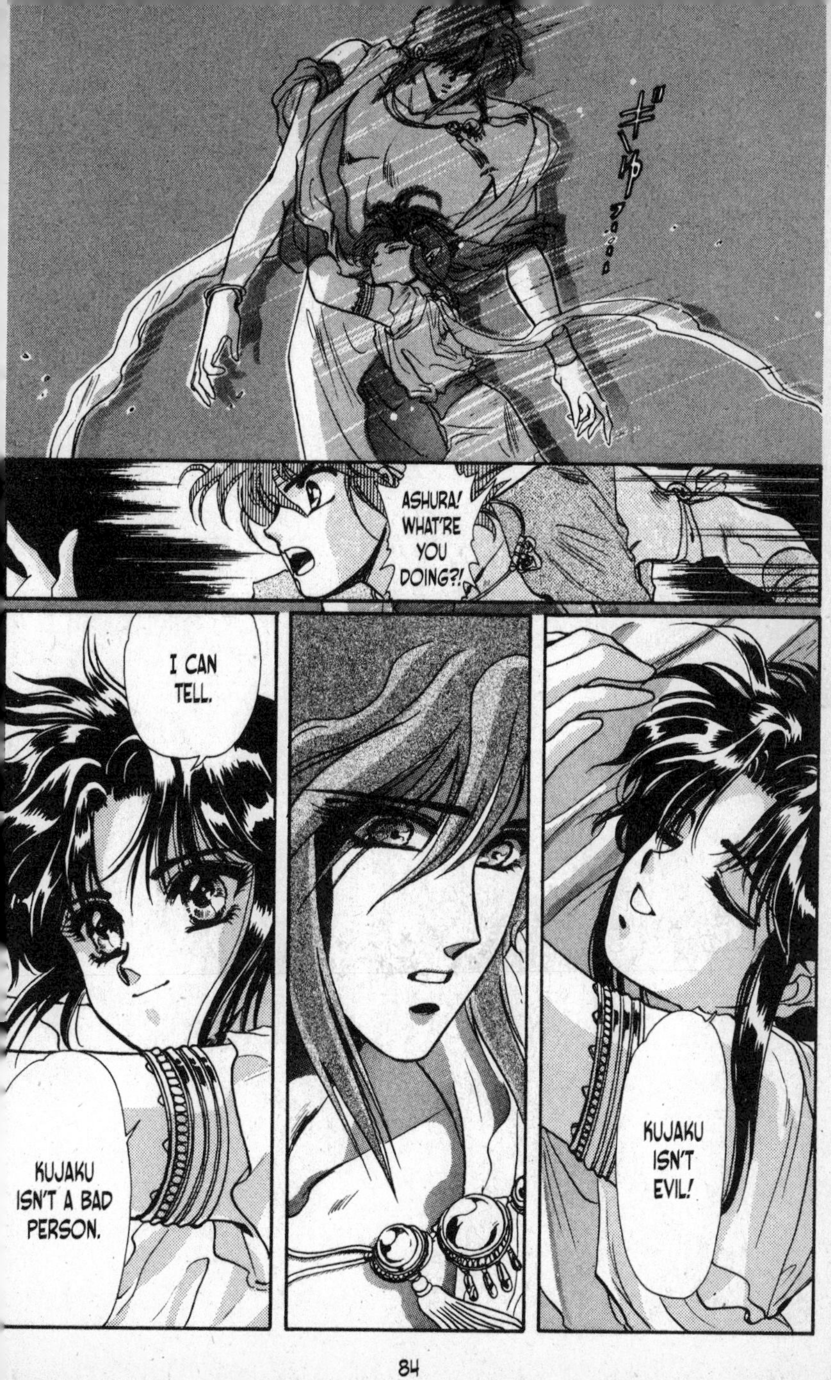
ASHURA! WHAT'RE YOU DOING?!
KUJAKU ISN'T EVIL!
I CAN TELL.
KUJAKU ISN'T A BAD PERSON.

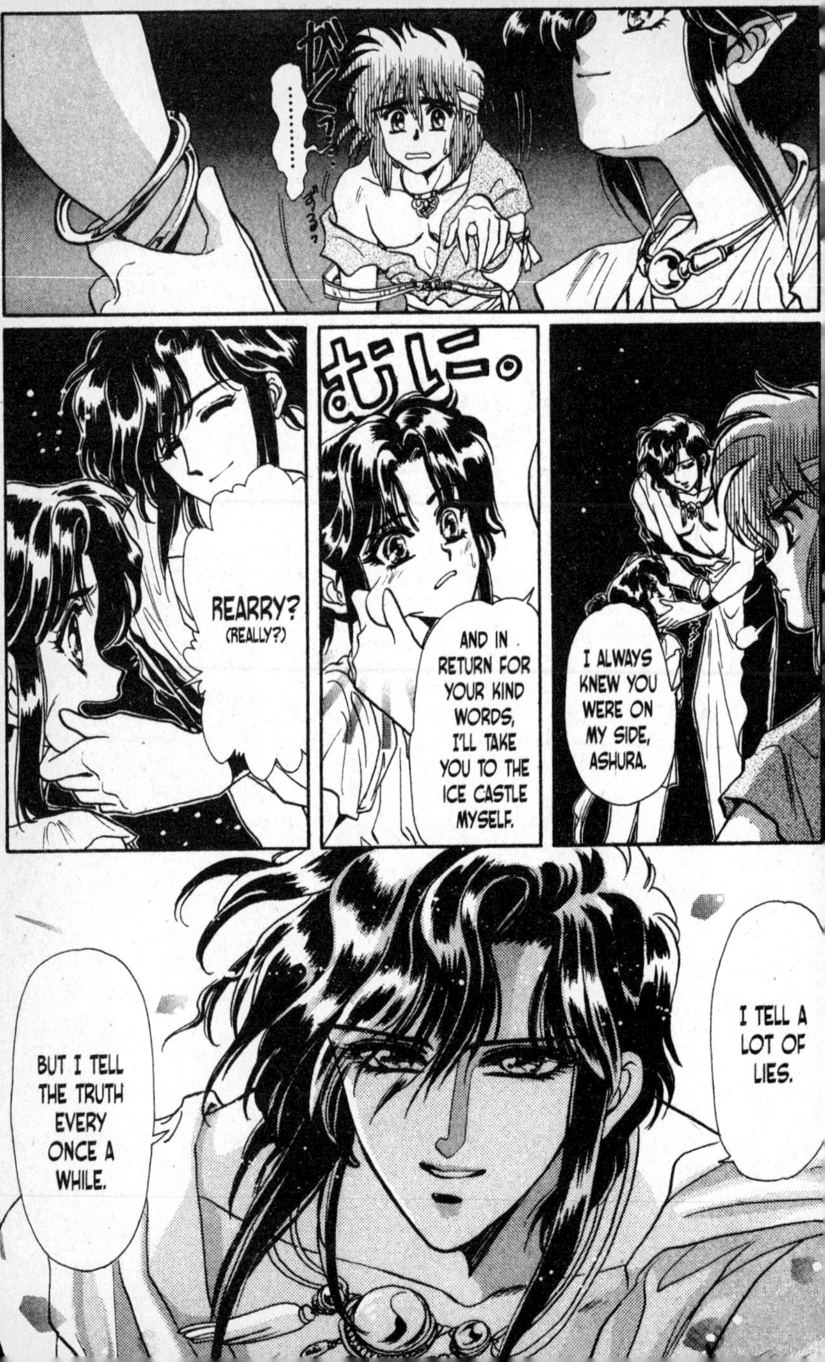
......
I ALWAYS KNEW YOU WERE ON MY SIDE, ASHURA.
むに。
AND IN RETURN FOR YOUR KIND WORDS, I'LL TAKE YOU TO THE ICE CASTLE MYSELF.
REARRY? (REALLY?)
I TELL A LOT OF LIES.
BUT I TELL THE TRUTH EVERY ONCE A WHILE.

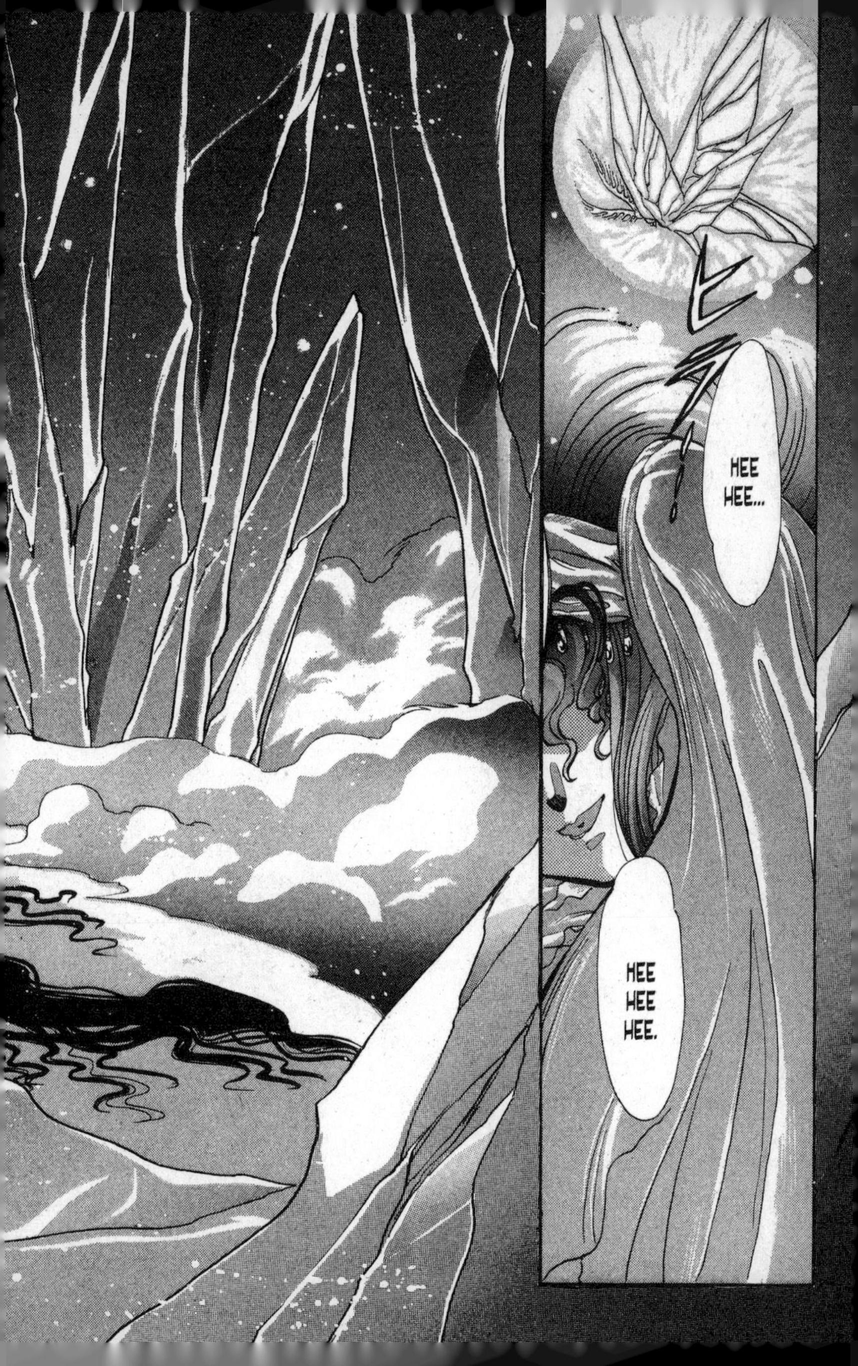
HEE HEE...
HEE HEE HEE.

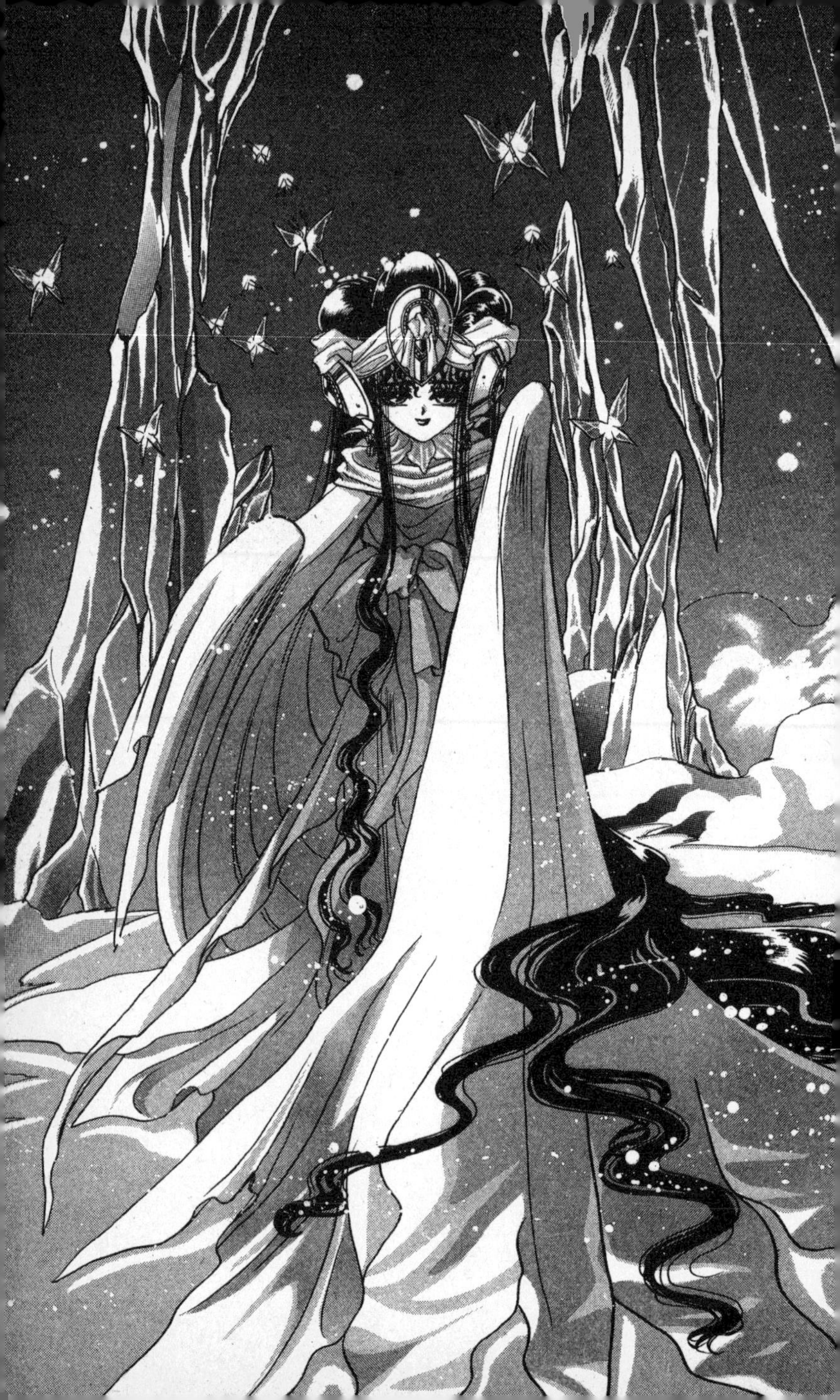

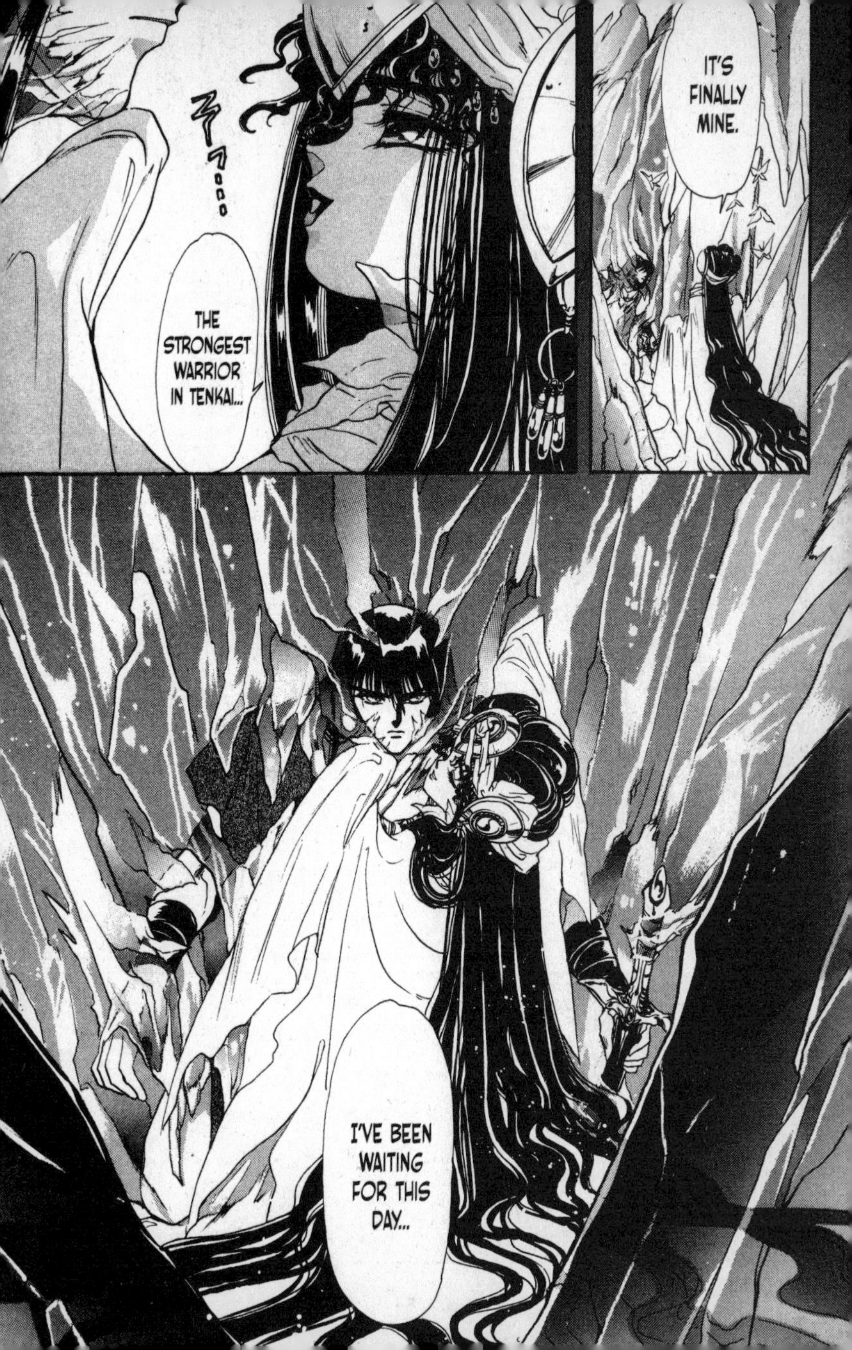
IT'S FINALLY MINE.
THE STRONGEST WARRIOR IN TENKAI...
I'VE BEEN WAITING FOR THIS DAY...

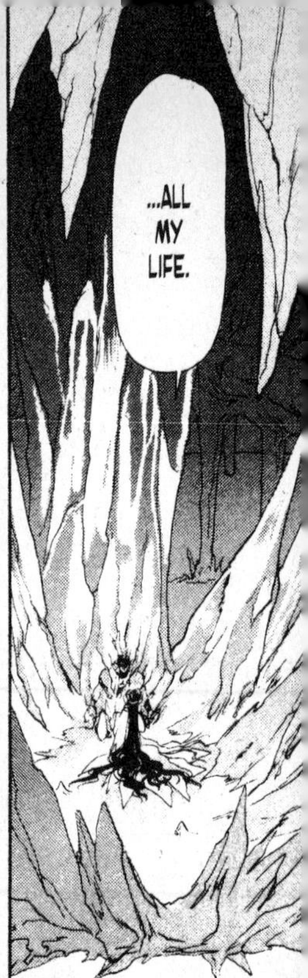
...ALL MY LIFE.

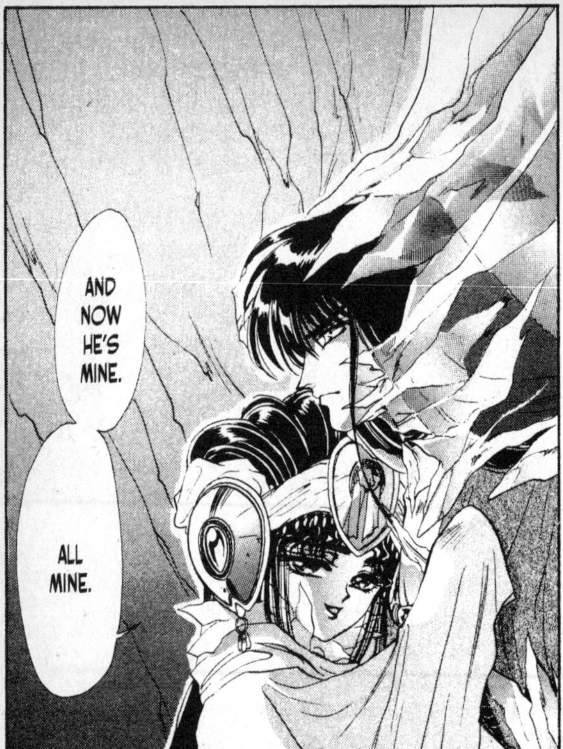
AND NOW HE'S MINE.
ALL MINE.

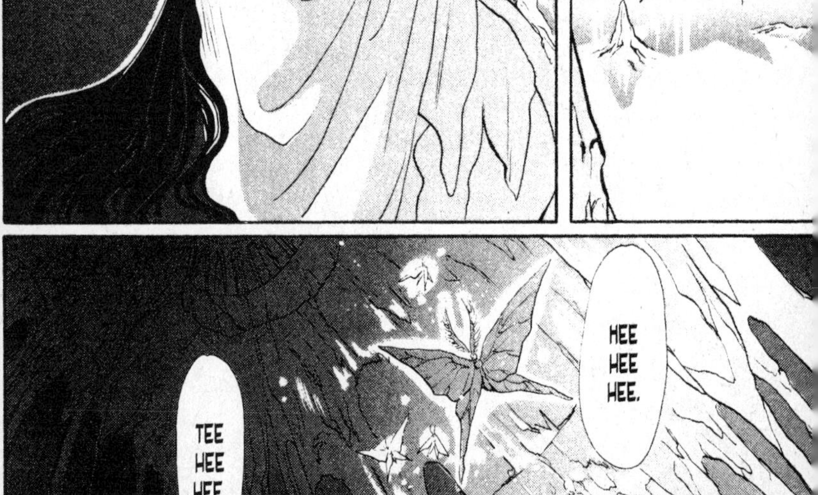
HEE HEE HEE.
TEE HEE HEE.

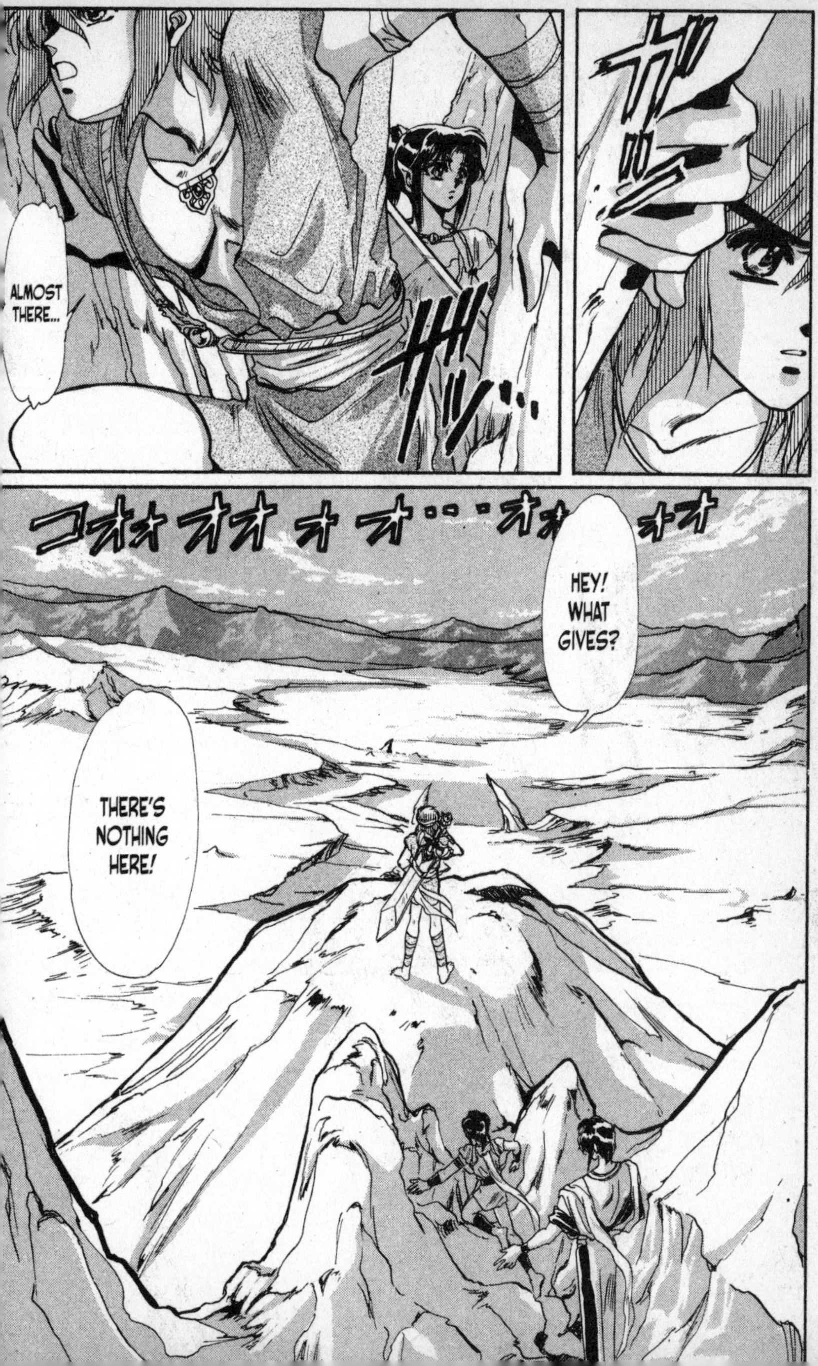
ALMOST THERE...
HEY! WHAT GIVES?
THERE'S NOTHING HERE!

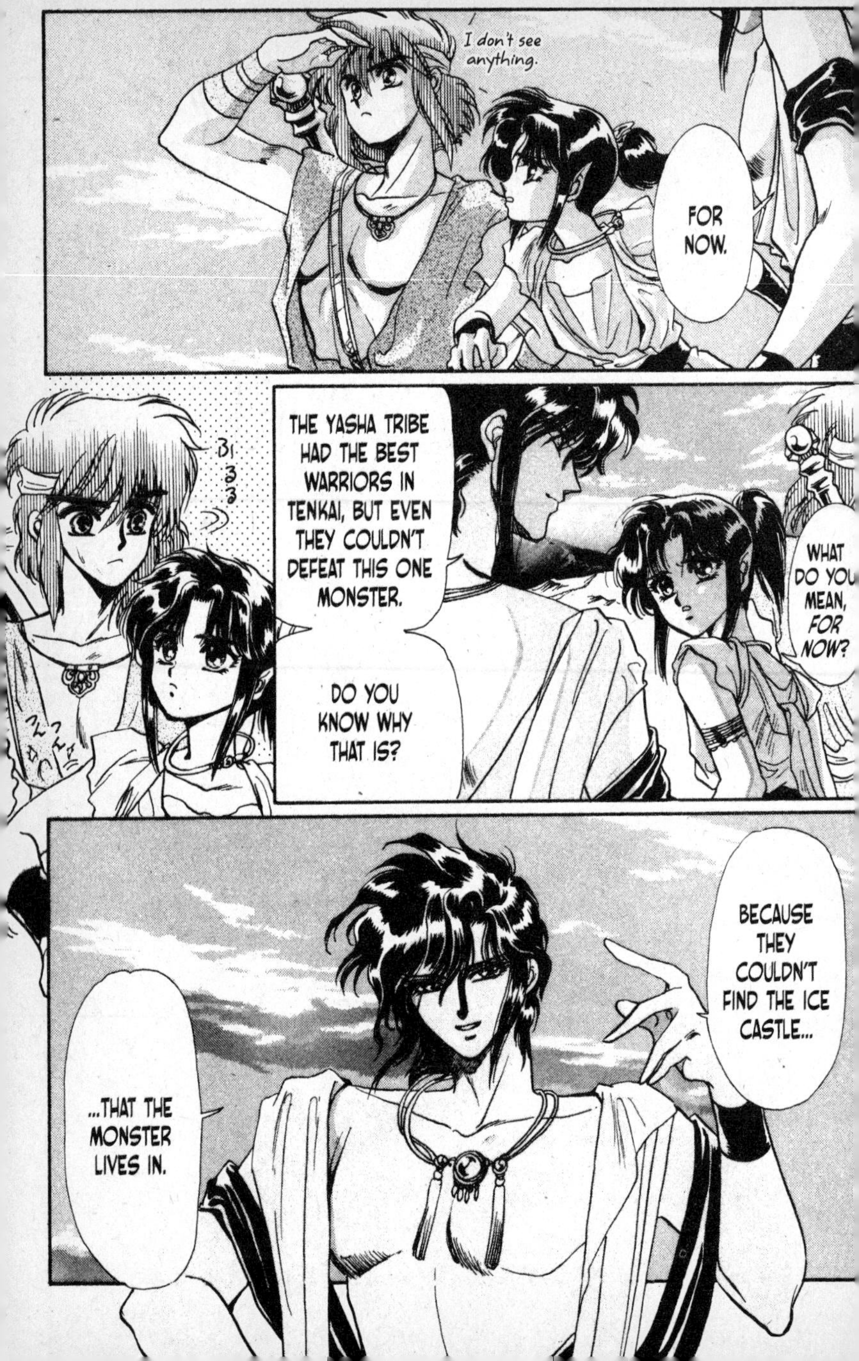
I don't see anything.
FOR NOW.
WHAT DO YOU MEAN, *FOR NOW*?
THE YASHA TRIBE HAD THE BEST WARRIORS IN TENKAI, BUT EVEN THEY COULDN'T DEFEAT THIS ONE MONSTER.
DO YOU KNOW WHY THAT IS?
BECAUSE THEY COULDN'T FIND THE ICE CASTLE...
...THAT THE MONSTER LIVES IN.

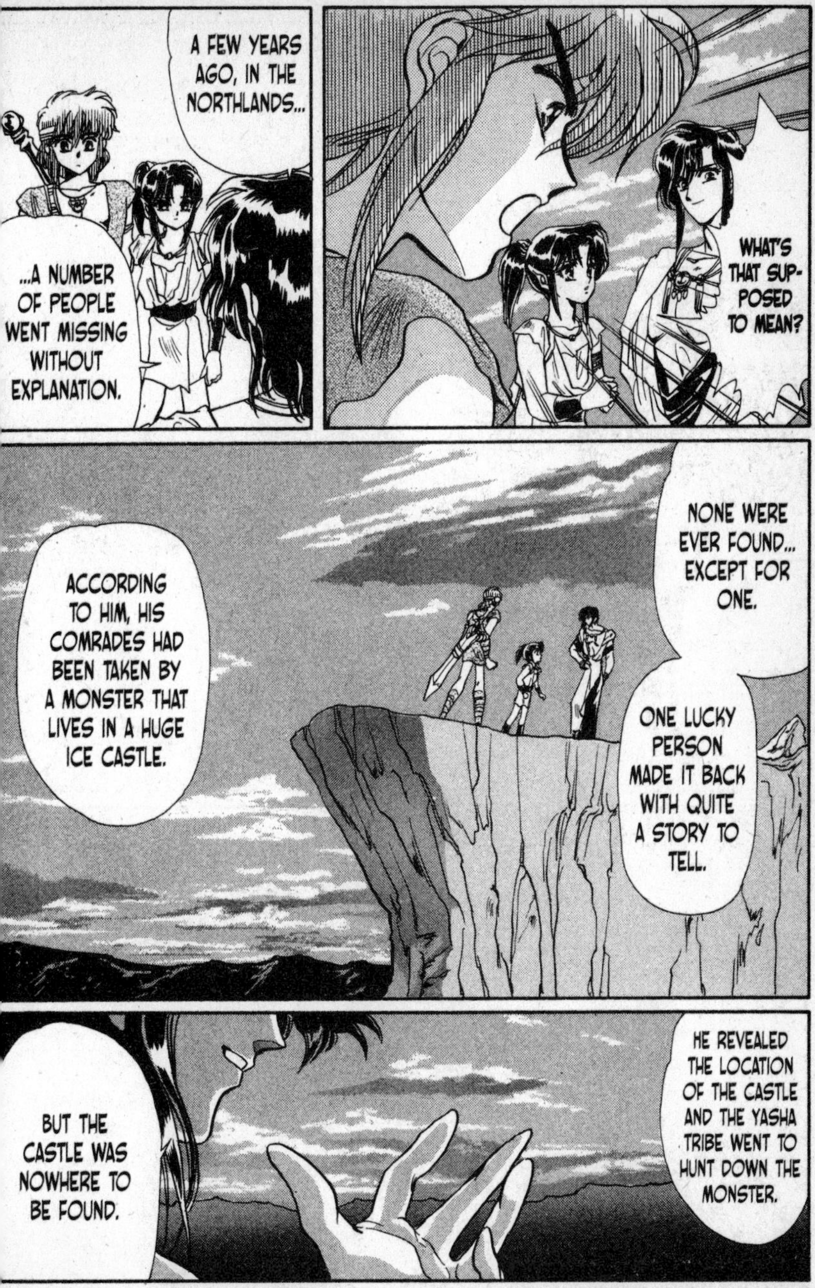
WHAT'S THAT SUP-POSED TO MEAN?
A FEW YEARS AGO, IN THE NORTHLANDS...
...A NUMBER OF PEOPLE WENT MISSING WITHOUT EXPLANATION.
NONE WERE EVER FOUND... EXCEPT FOR ONE.
ONE LUCKY PERSON MADE IT BACK WITH QUITE A STORY TO TELL.
ACCORDING TO HIM, HIS COMRADES HAD BEEN TAKEN BY A MONSTER THAT LIVES IN A HUGE ICE CASTLE.
HE REVEALED THE LOCATION OF THE CASTLE AND THE YASHA TRIBE WENT TO HUNT DOWN THE MONSTER.
BUT THE CASTLE WAS NOWHERE TO BE FOUND.

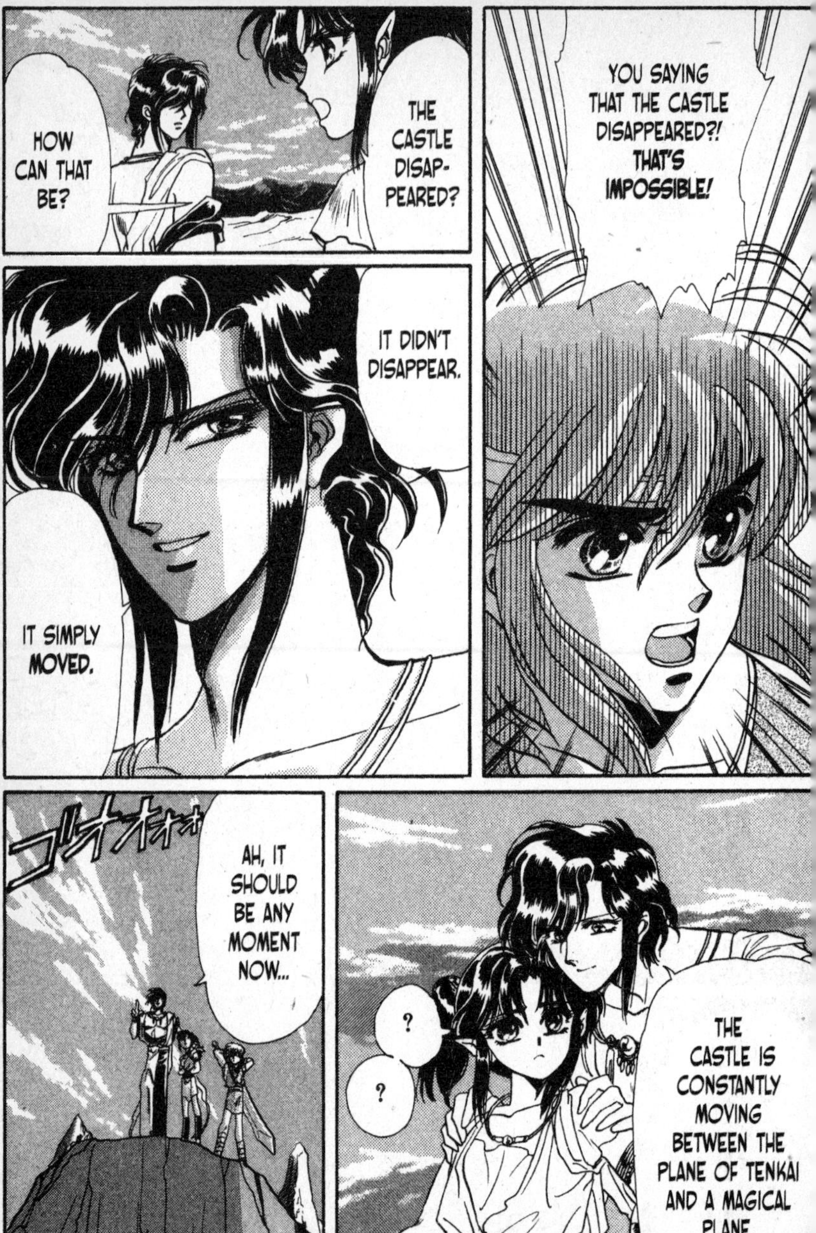
YOU SAYING THAT THE CASTLE DISAPPEARED?! THAT'S IMPOSSIBLE!
THE CASTLE DISAP-PEARED?
HOW CAN THAT BE?
IT DIDN'T DISAPPEAR.
IT SIMPLY MOVED.
THE CASTLE IS CONSTANTLY MOVING BETWEEN THE PLANE OF TENKAI AND A MAGICAL PLANE.
?
?
AH, IT SHOULD BE ANY MOMENT NOW...

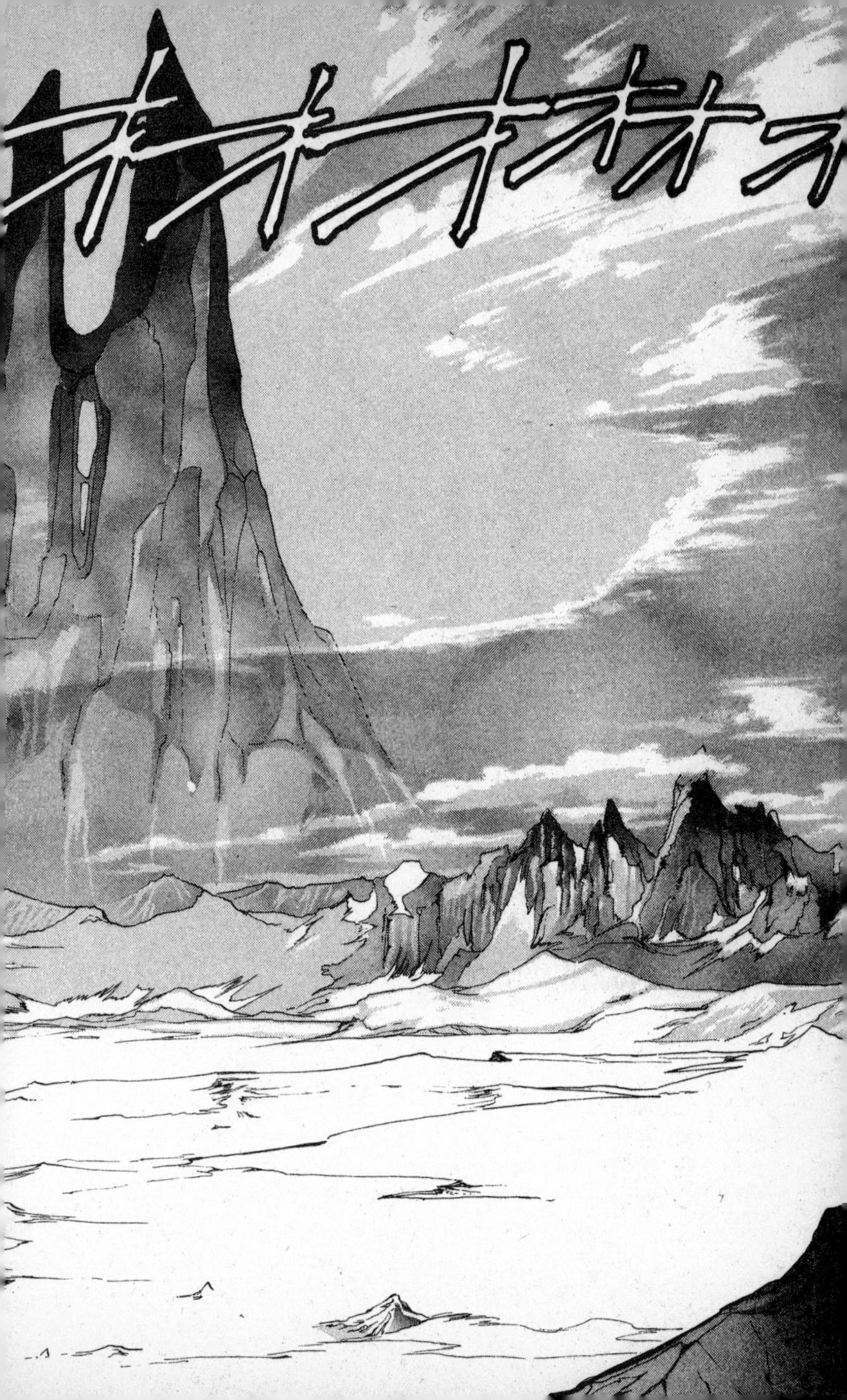
オオオオオオ

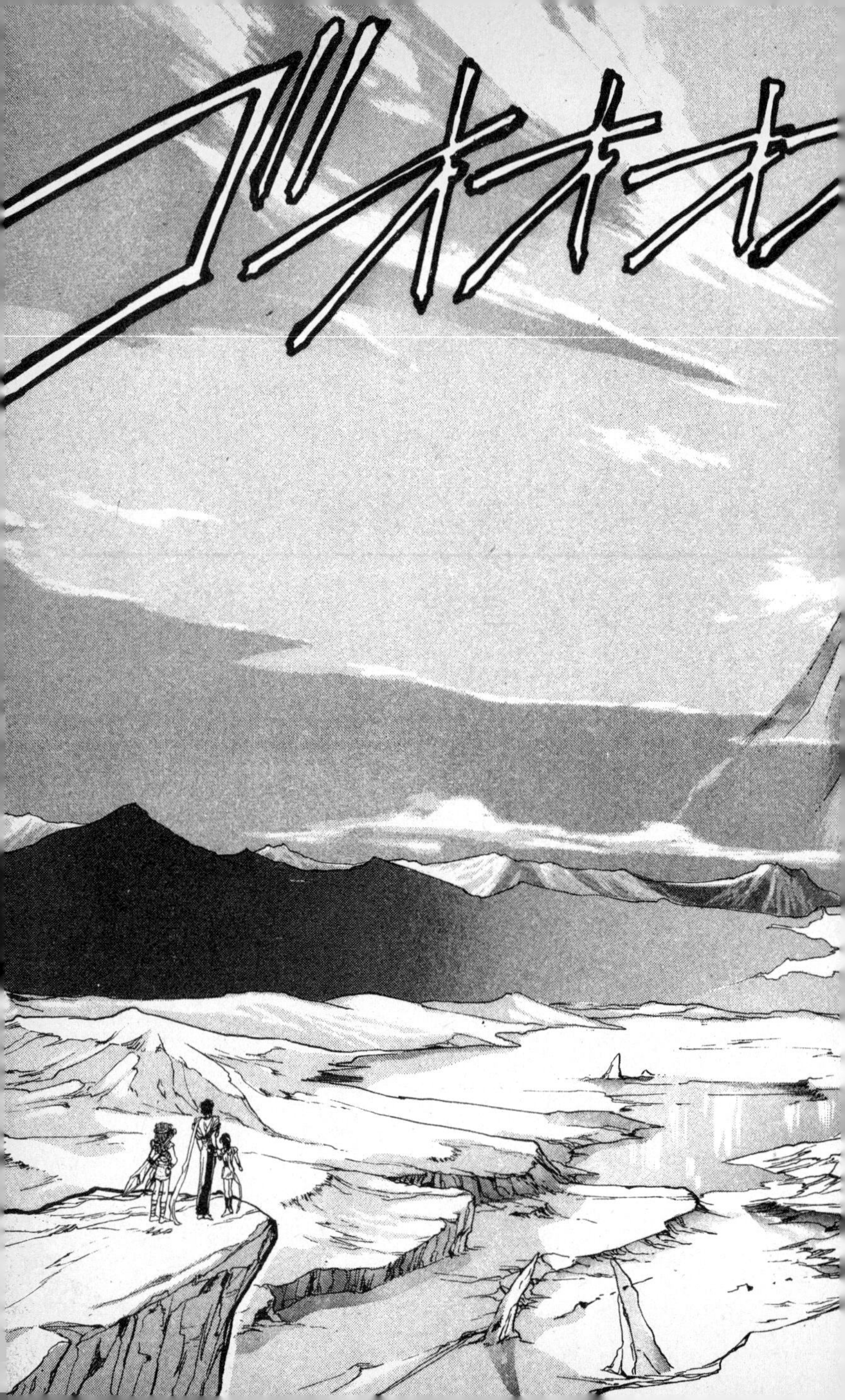
ゴオオオ

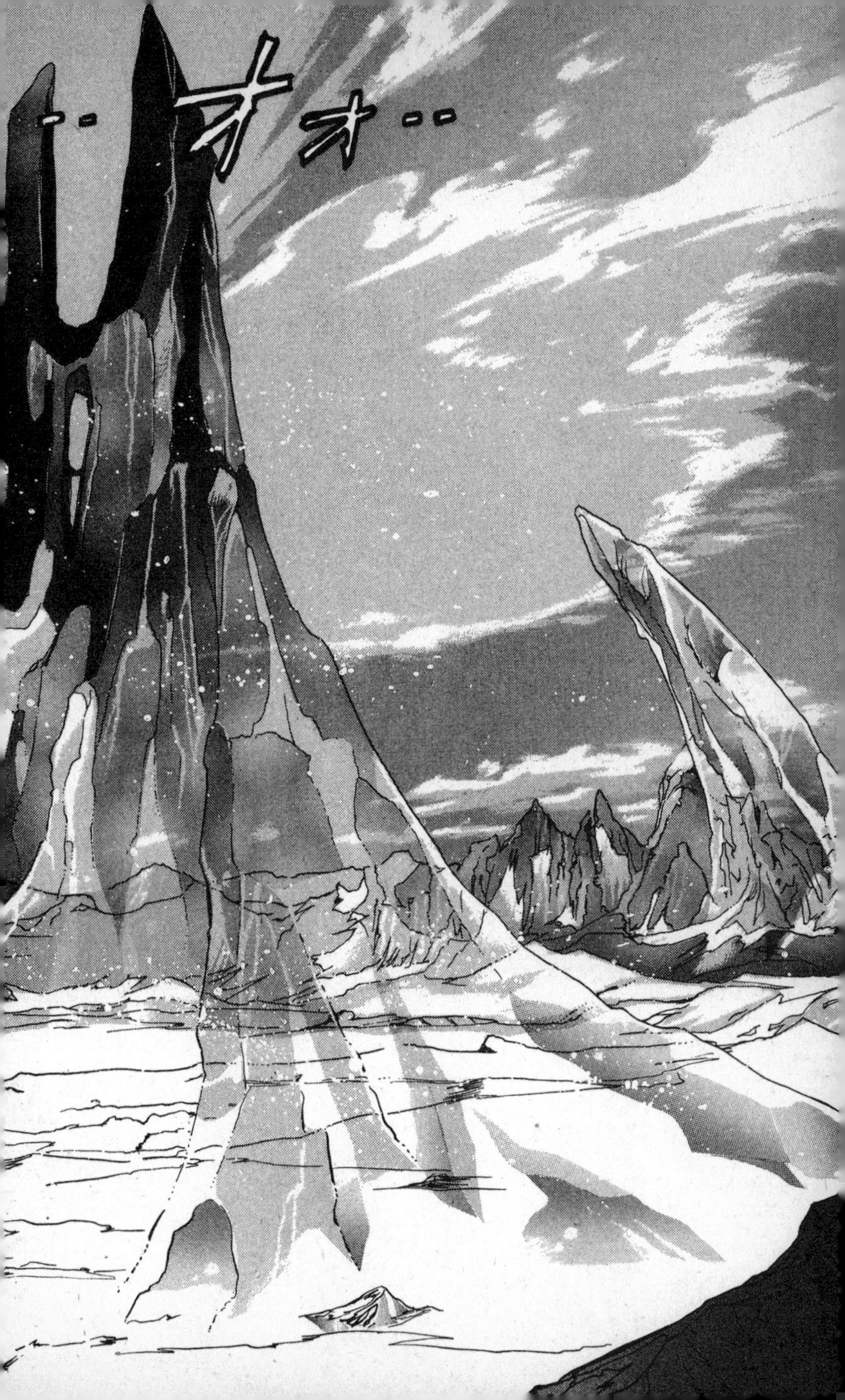
ーーオオーー

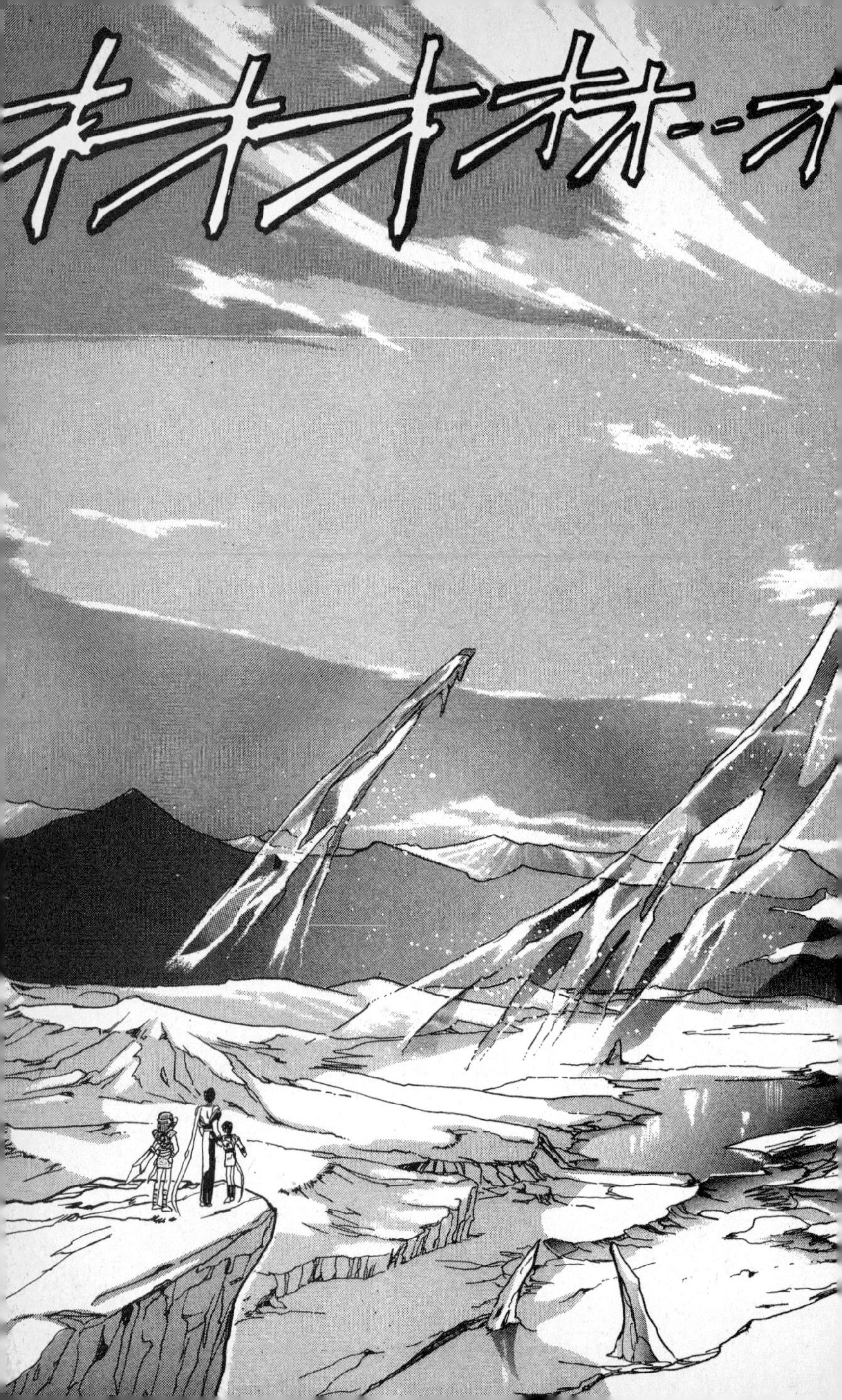
オオオオオオ－－オ

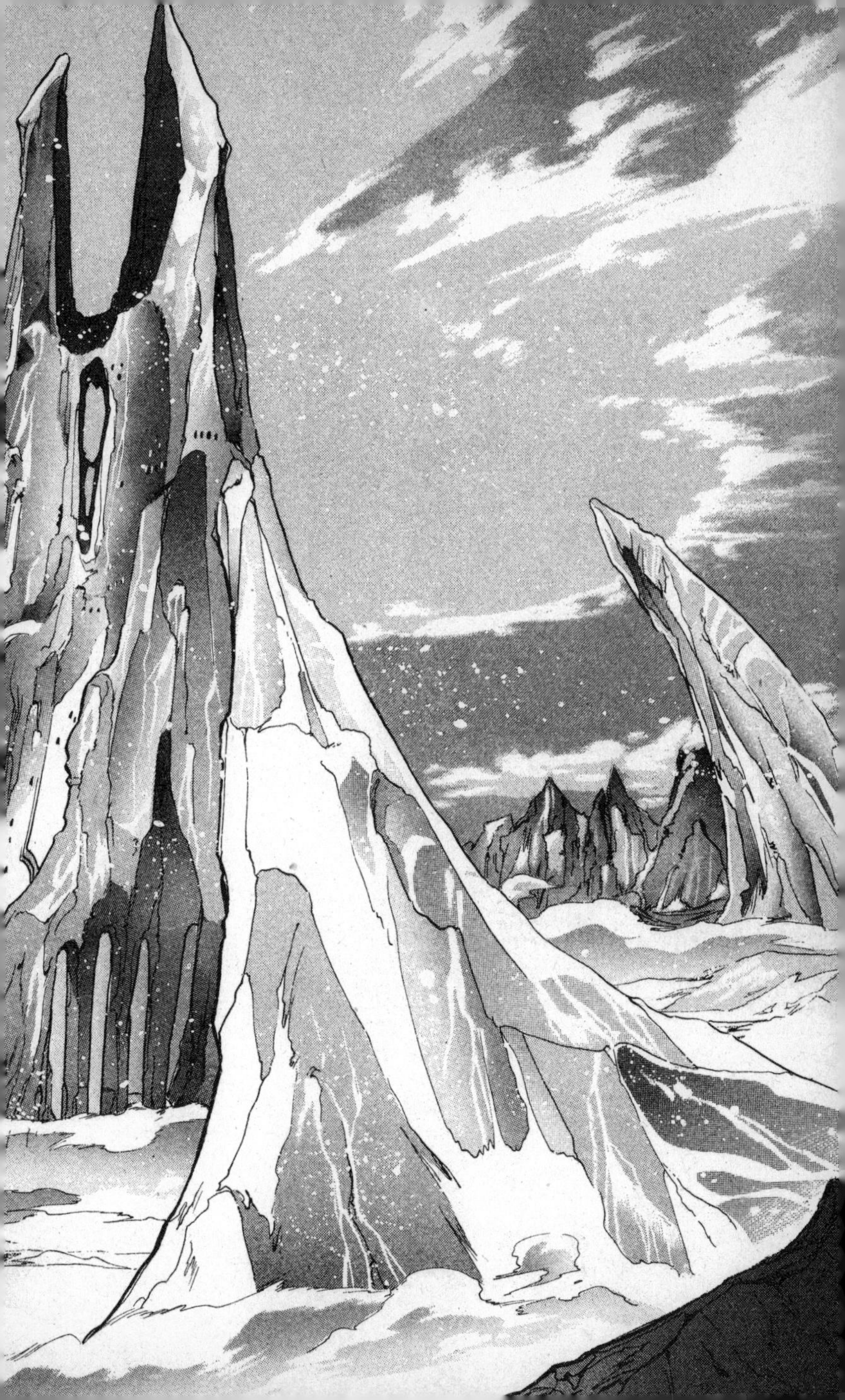

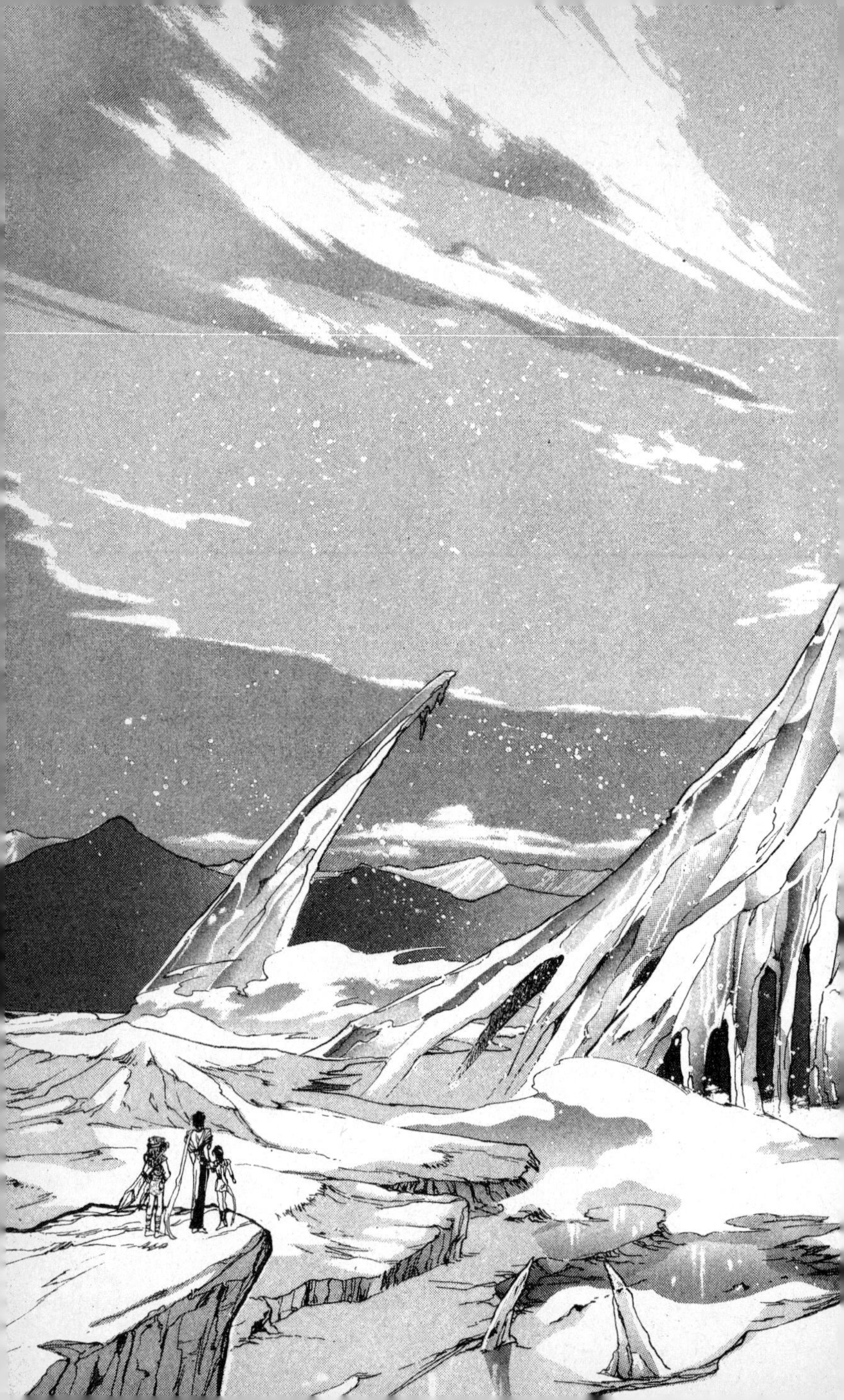

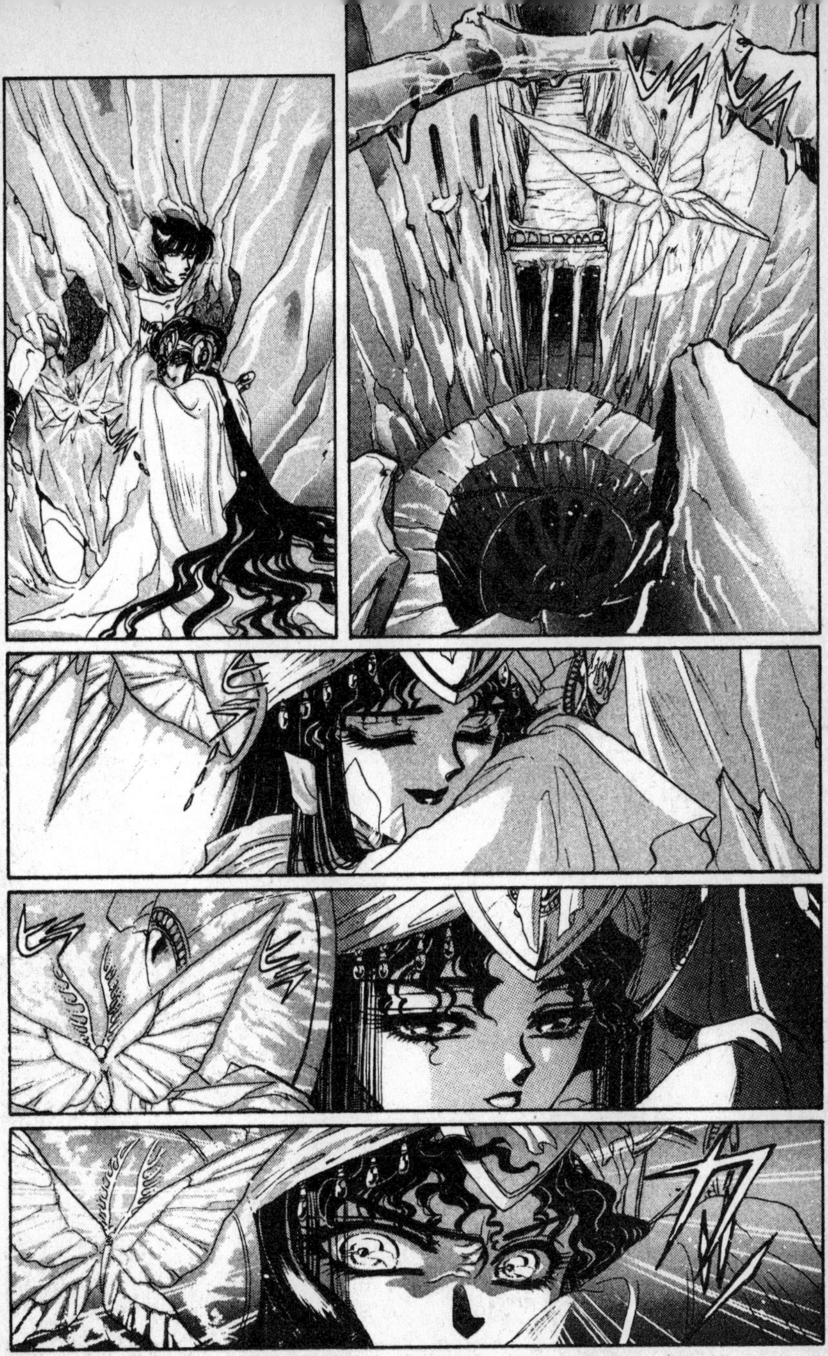

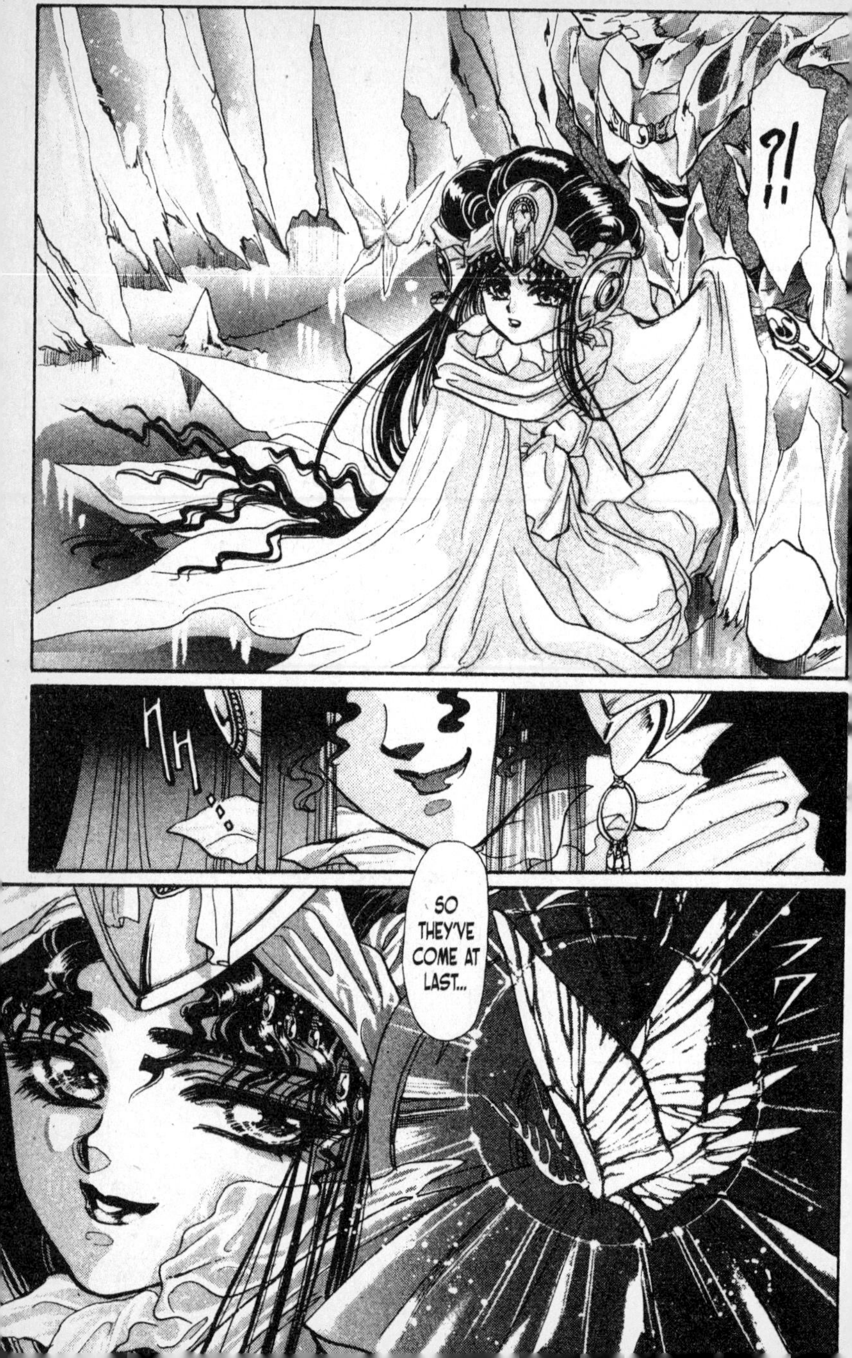
?!
SO THEY'VE COME AT LAST...

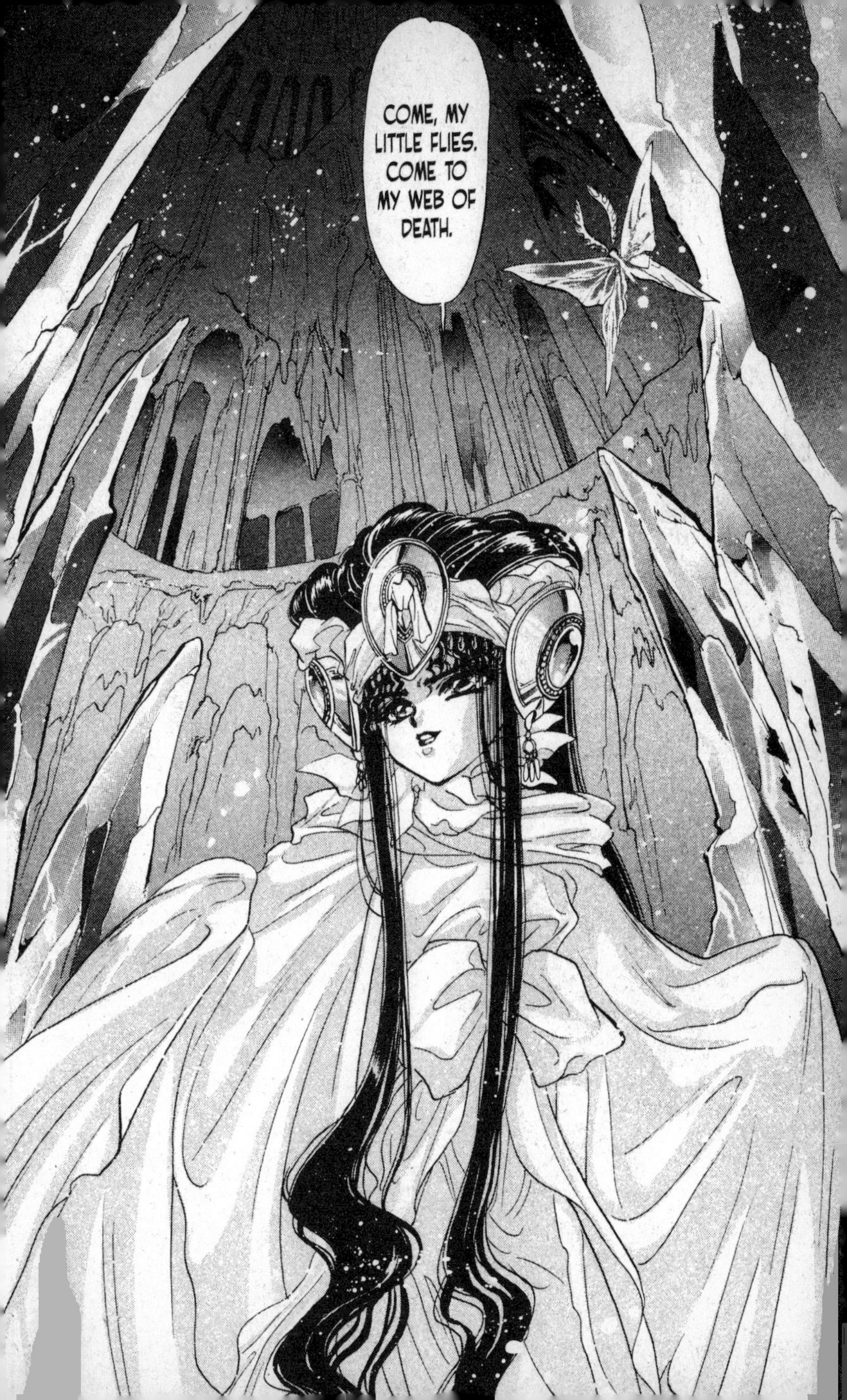
COME, MY LITTLE FLIES. COME TO MY WEB OF DEATH.

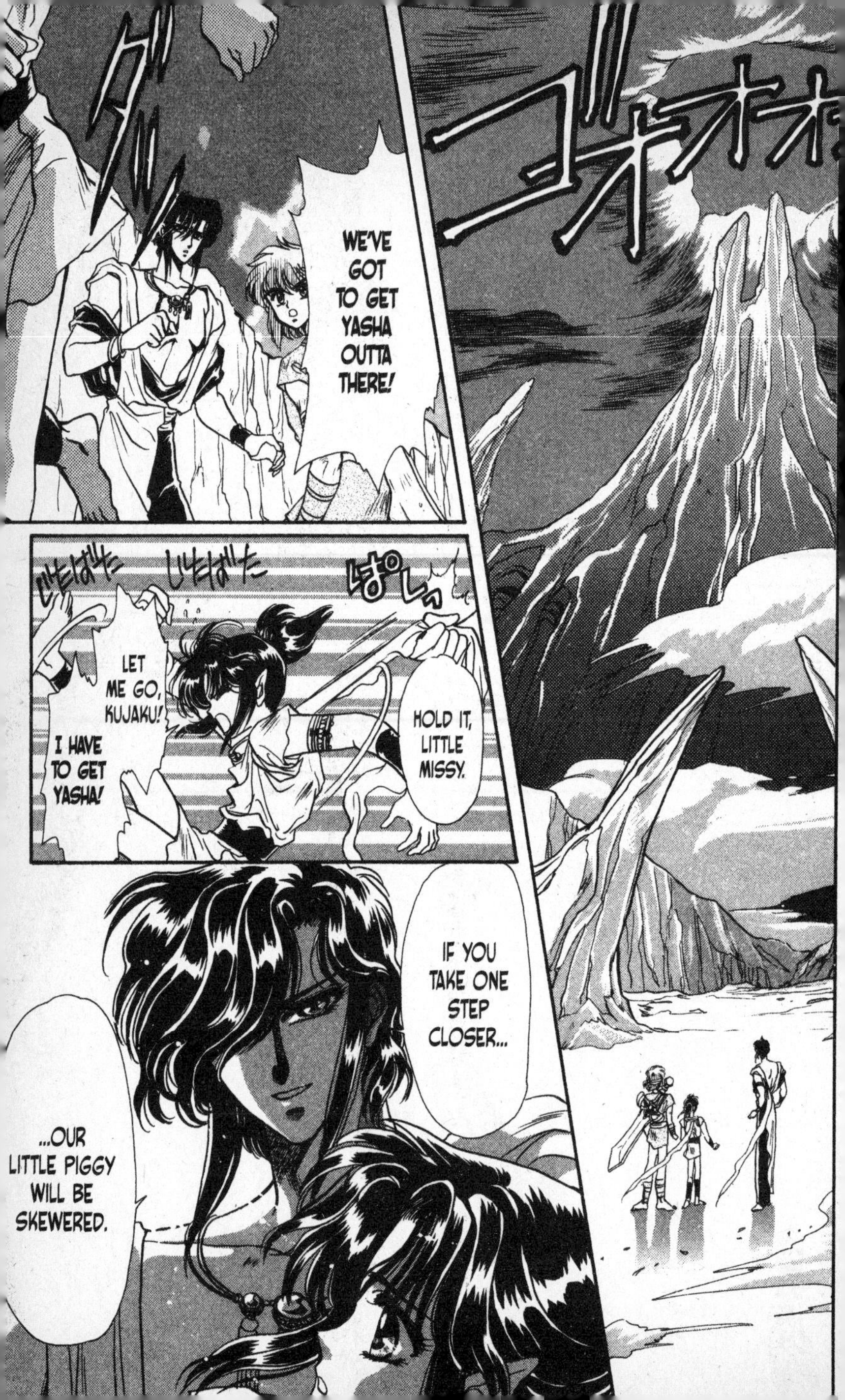
ダッ
WE'VE GOT TO GET YASHA OUTTA THERE!
じたばた
じたばた
ぱしっ
HOLD IT, LITTLE MISSY.
LET ME GO, KUJAKU!
I HAVE TO GET YASHA!
IF YOU TAKE ONE STEP CLOSER...
...OUR LITTLE PIGGY WILL BE SKEWERED.

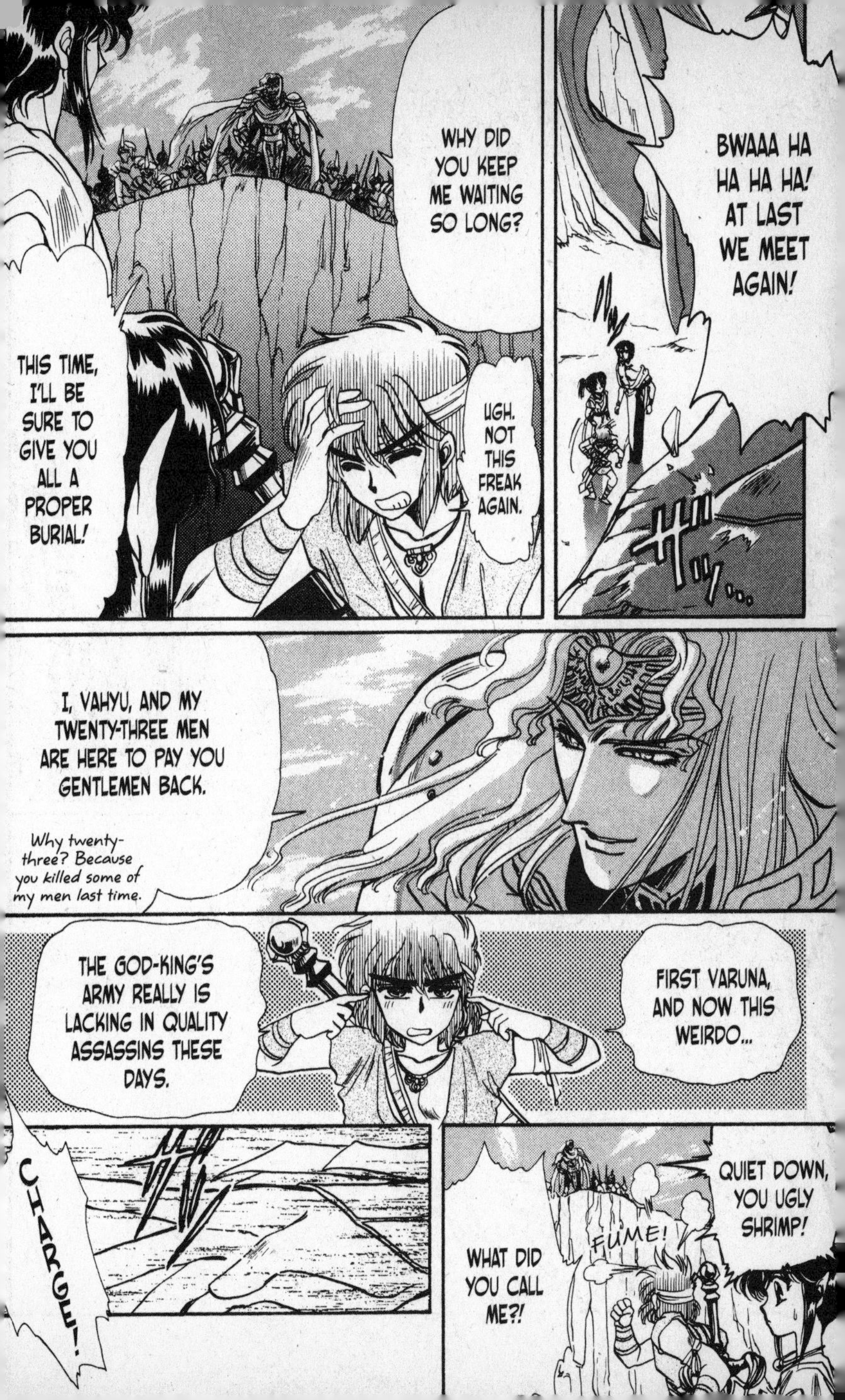
BWAAA HA HA HA HA! AT LAST WE MEET AGAIN!
WHY DID YOU KEEP ME WAITING SO LONG?
UGH. NOT THIS FREAK AGAIN.
THIS TIME, I'LL BE SURE TO GIVE YOU ALL A PROPER BURIAL!
I, VAHYU, AND MY TWENTY-THREE MEN ARE HERE TO PAY YOU GENTLEMEN BACK.
Why twenty-three? Because you killed some of my men last time.
FIRST VARUNA, AND NOW THIS WEIRDO...
THE GOD-KING'S ARMY REALLY IS LACKING IN QUALITY ASSASSINS THESE DAYS.
QUIET DOWN, YOU UGLY SHRIMP!
FUME!
WHAT DID YOU CALL ME?!
CHARGE!

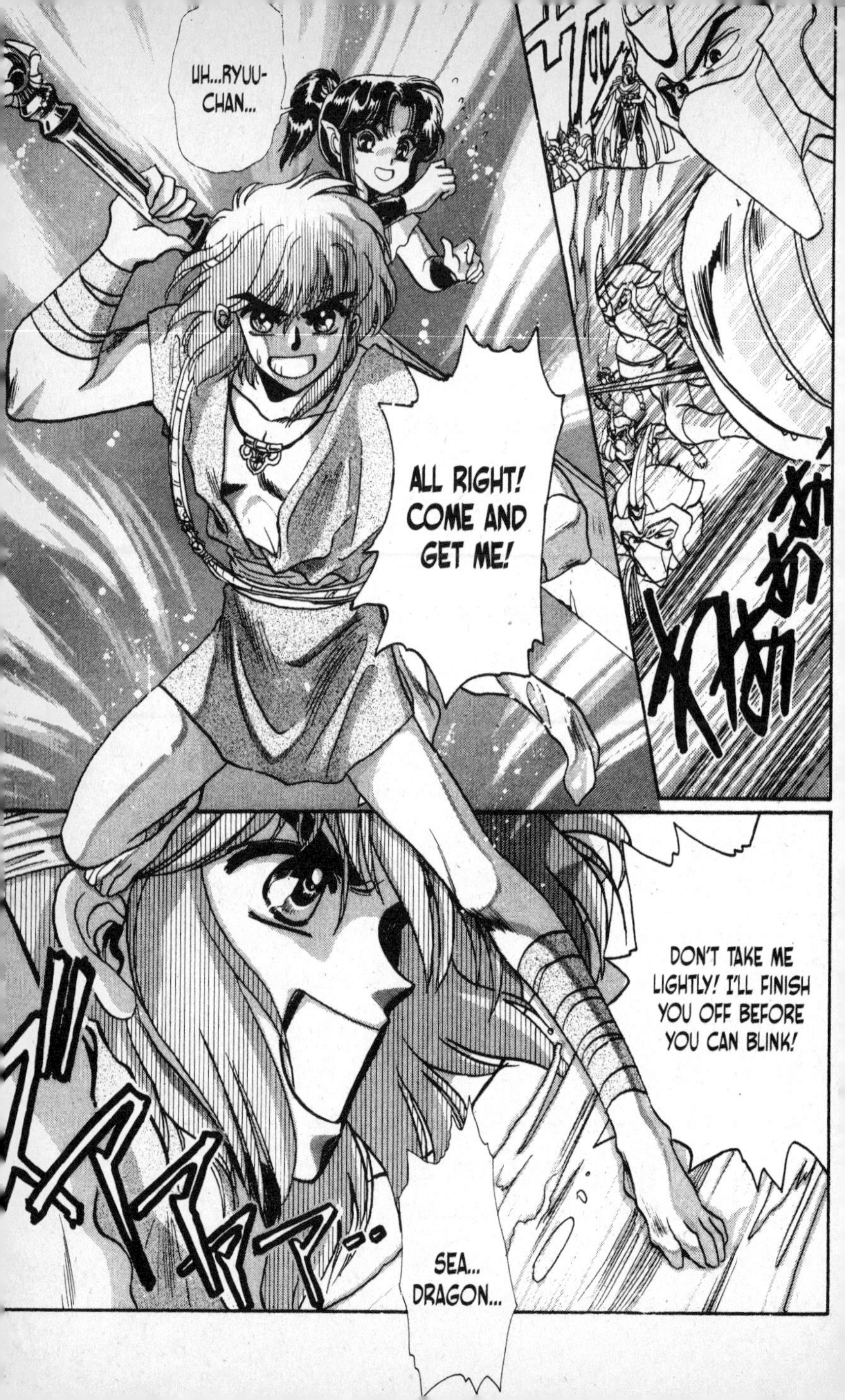
UH...RYUU-CHAN...
ALL RIGHT! COME AND GET ME!
DON'T TAKE ME LIGHTLY! I'LL FINISH YOU OFF BEFORE YOU CAN BLINK!
SEA... DRAGON...

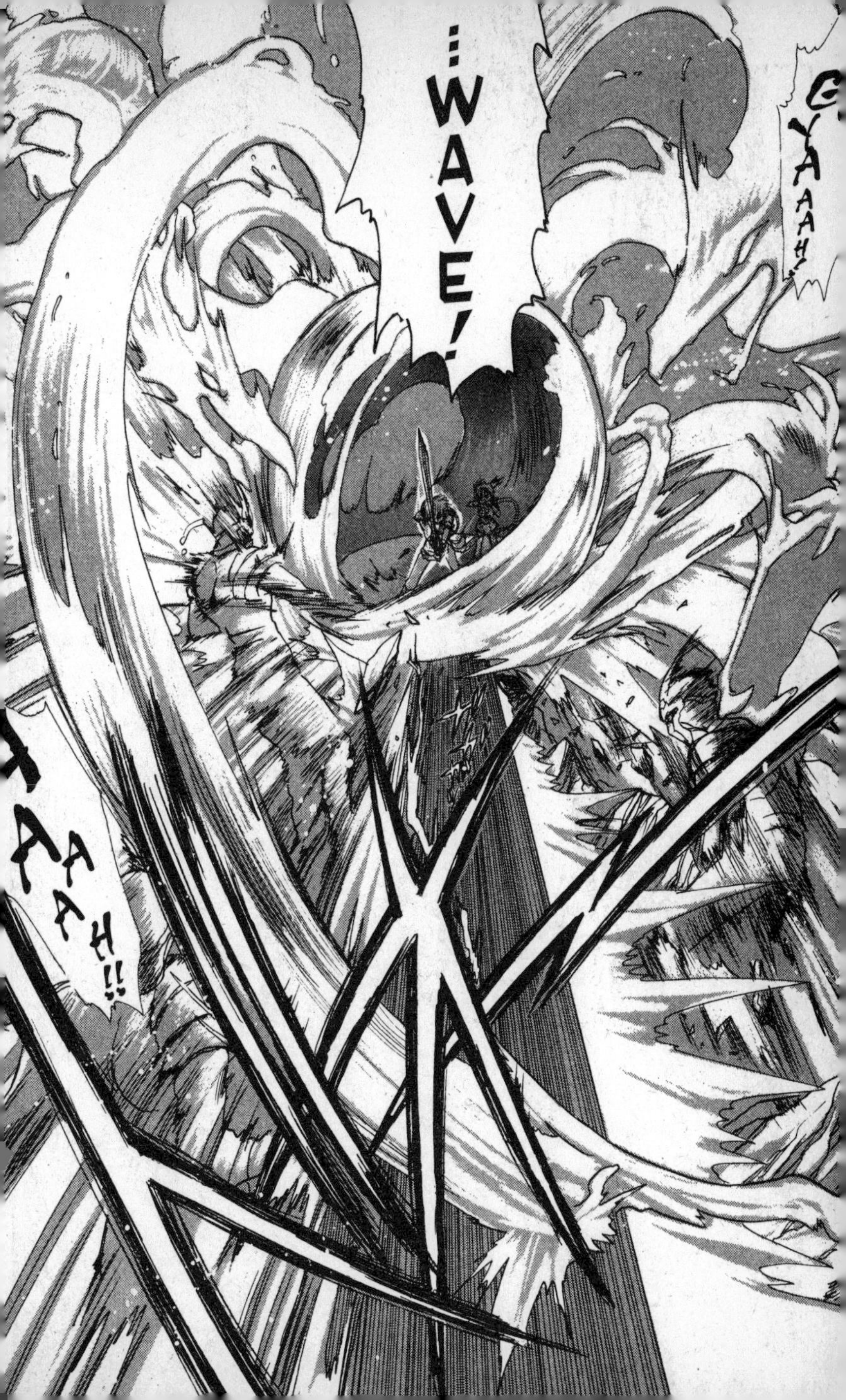
GYAAAH!
...WAVE!!
AAAH!!

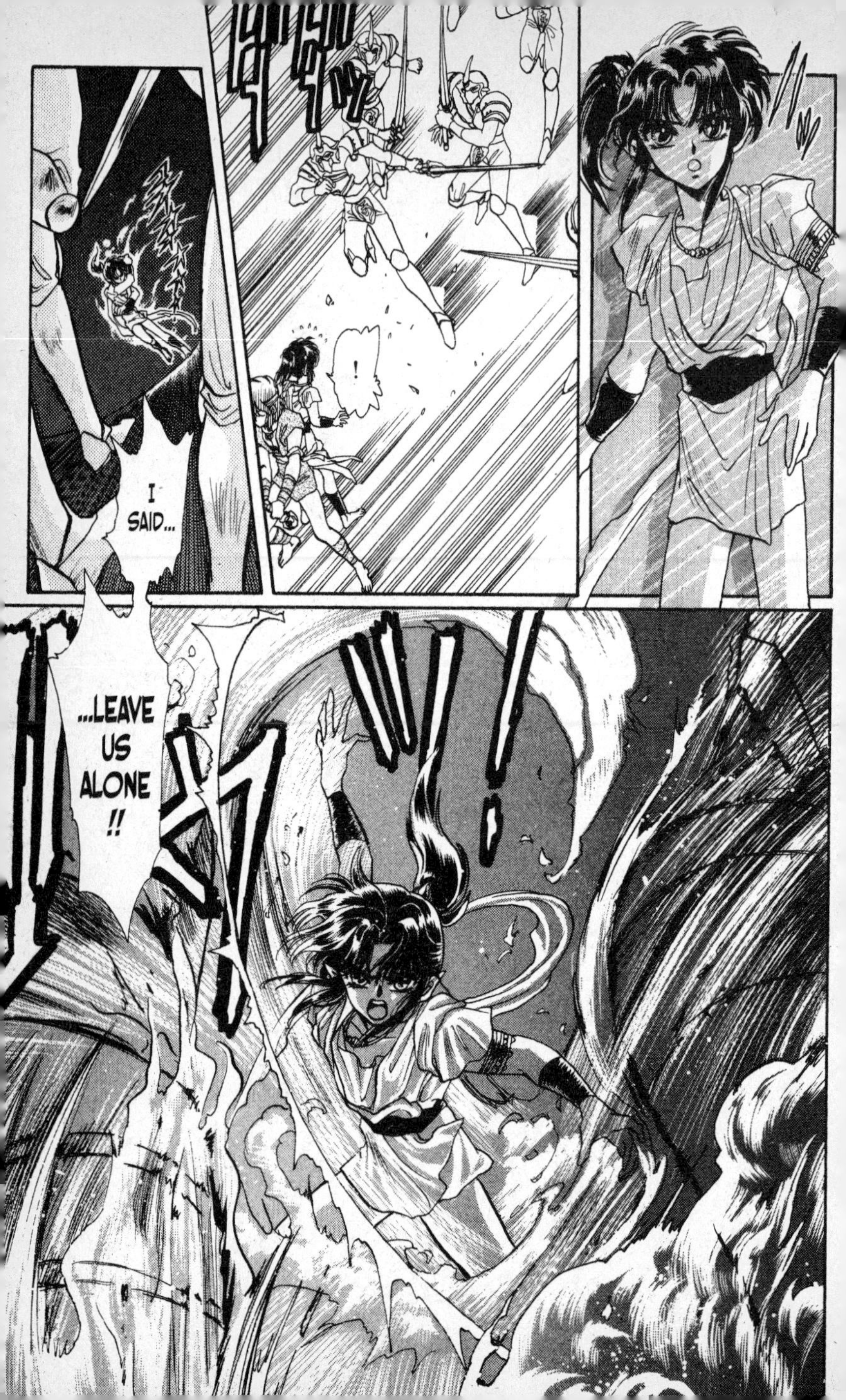
!
I SAID...
...LEAVE US ALONE !!

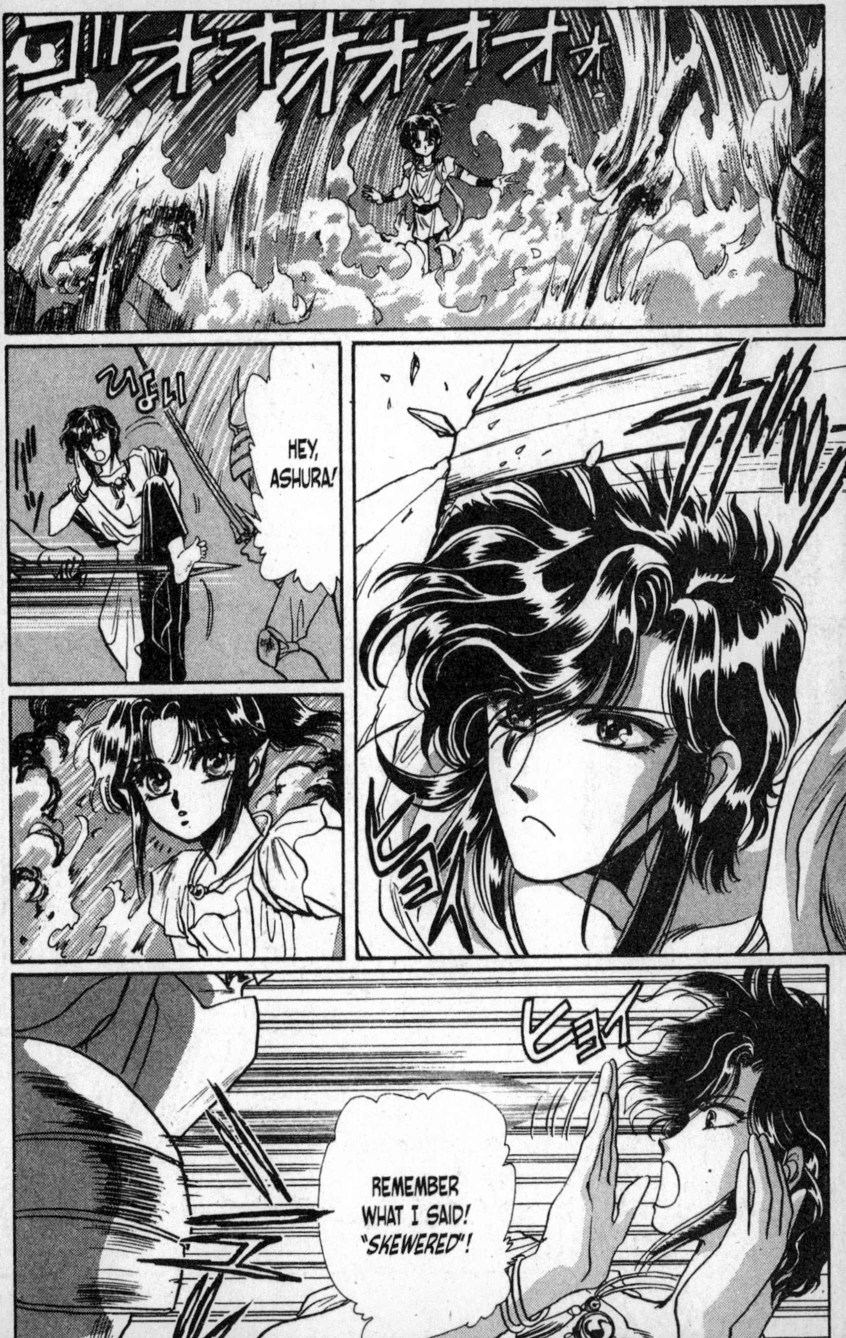
HEY, ASHURA!
REMEMBER WHAT I SAID! "SKEWERED"!

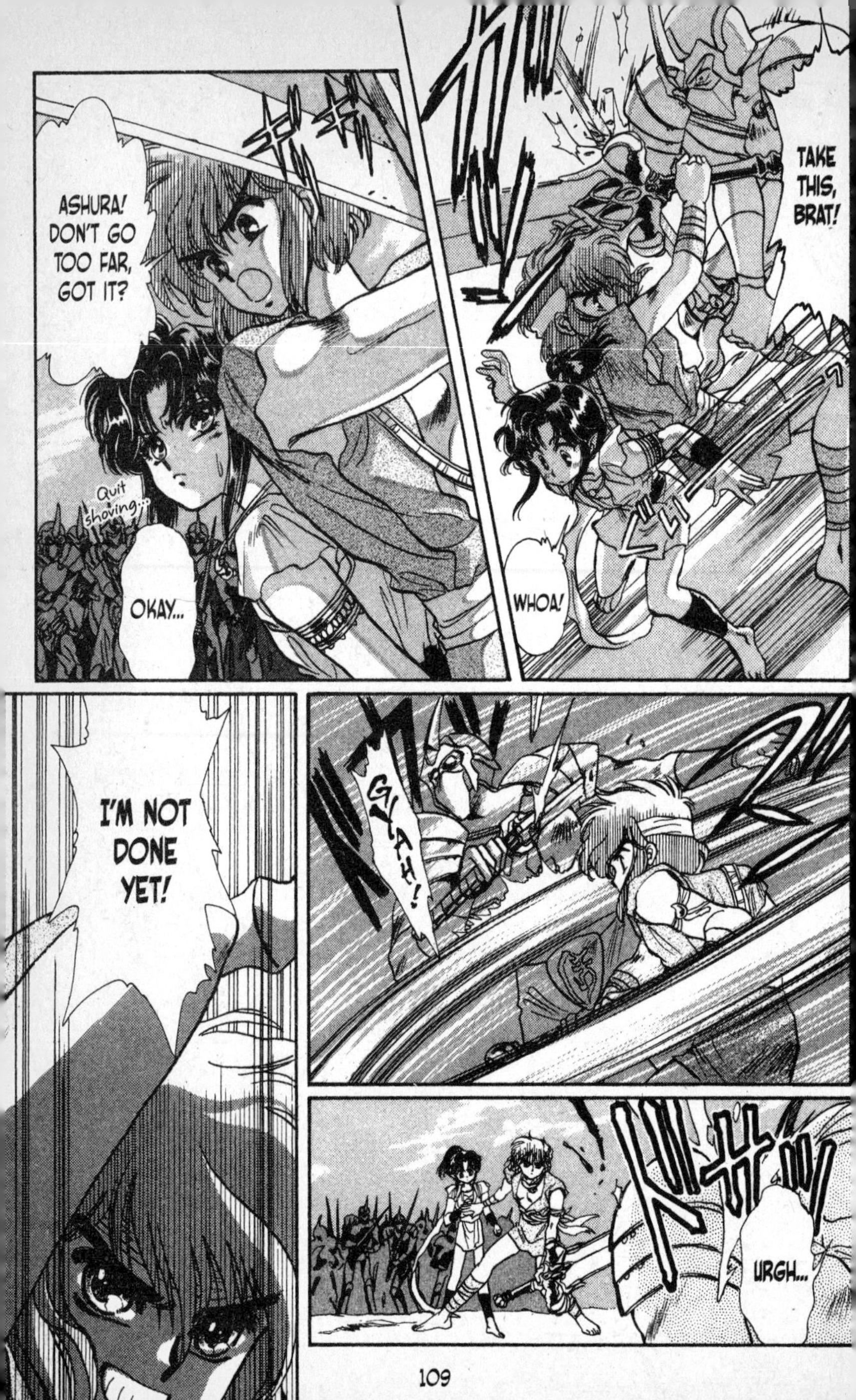
TAKE THIS, BRAT!
WHOA!
ASHURA! DON'T GO TOO FAR, GOT IT?
Quit shoving...
OKAY...
GYAH!
URGH...
I'M NOT DONE YET!

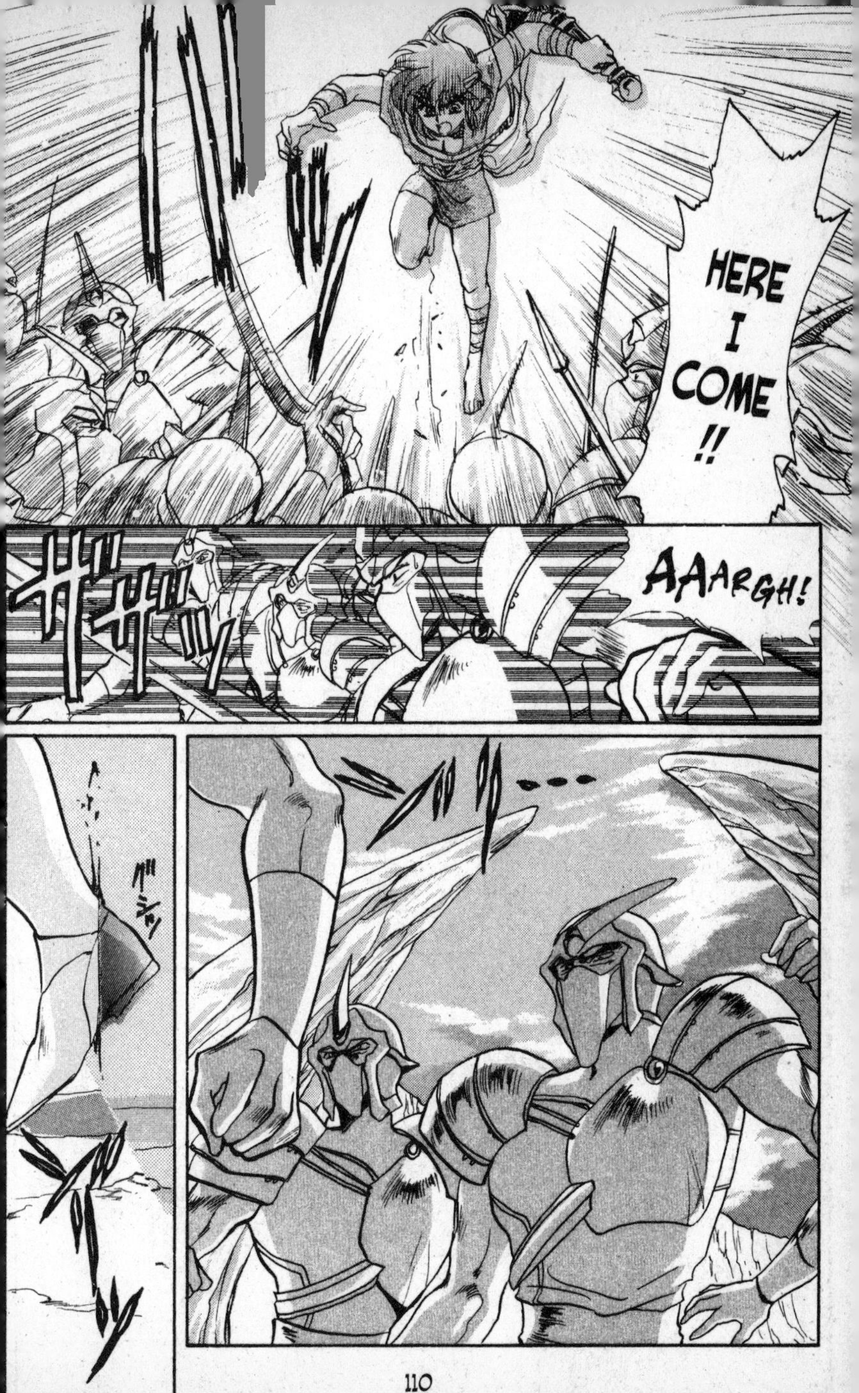
HERE I COME !!
AAARGH!

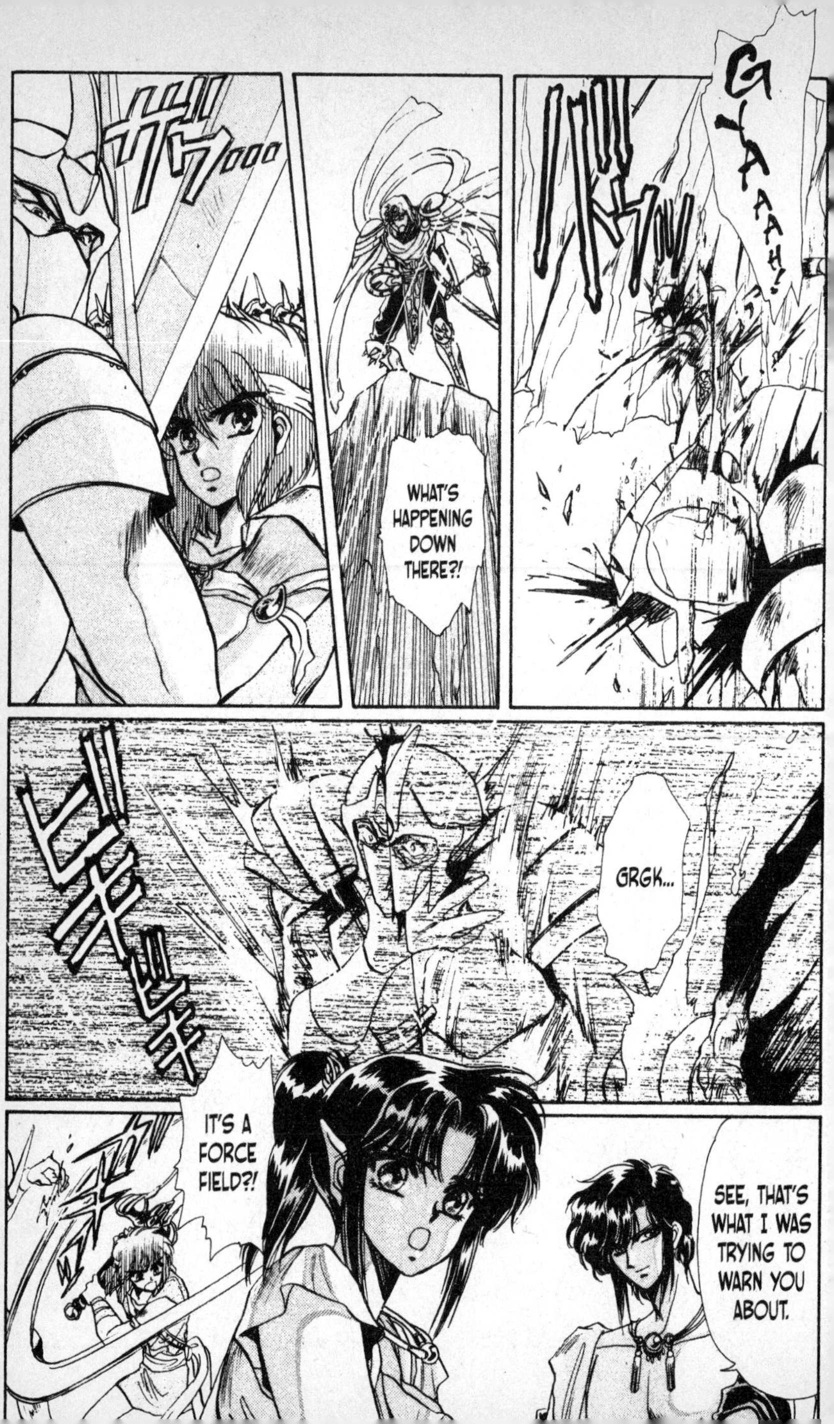
GYAAAAH!
WHAT'S HAPPENING DOWN THERE?!
GRGK...
IT'S A FORCE FIELD?!
SEE, THAT'S WHAT I WAS TRYING TO WARN YOU ABOUT.

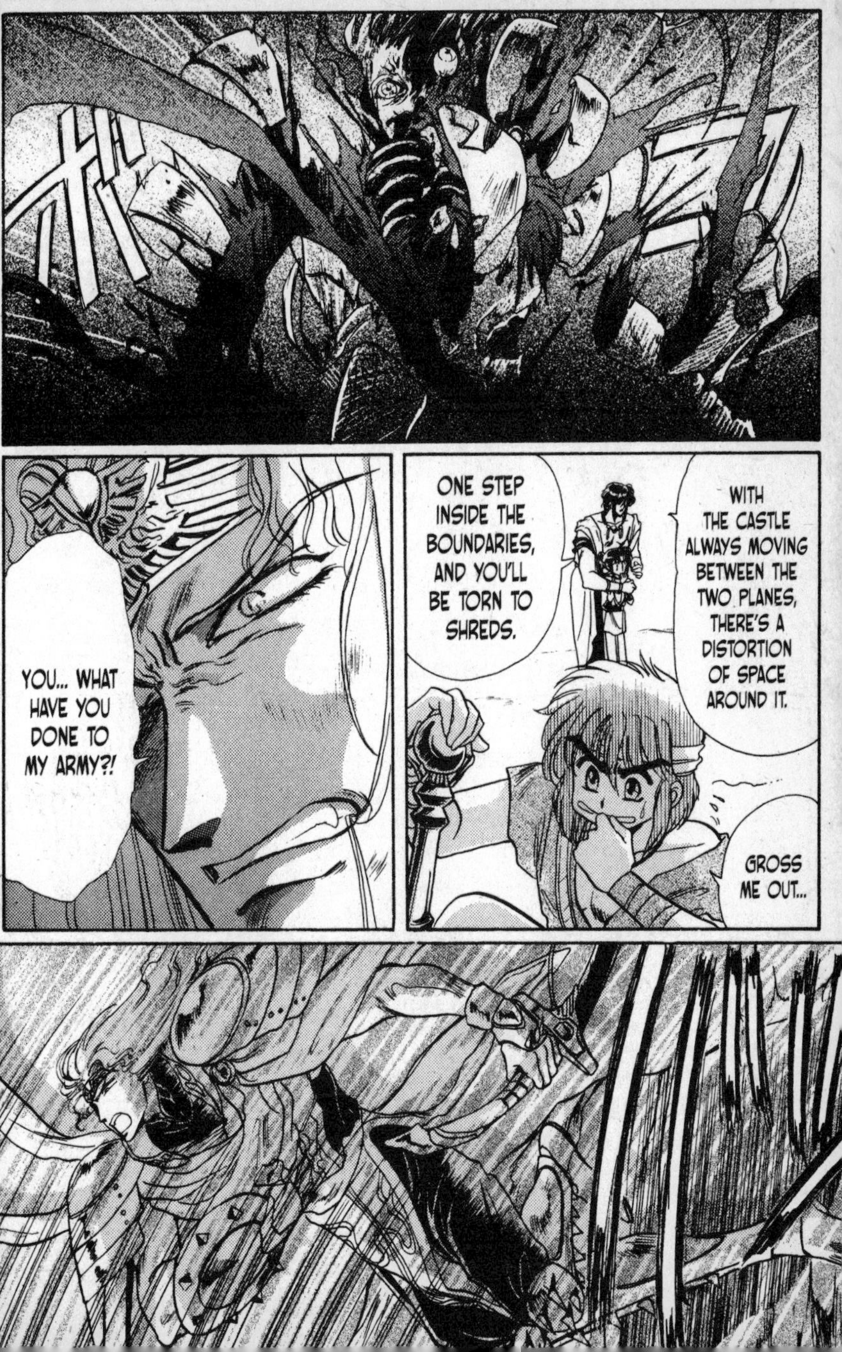
WITH THE CASTLE ALWAYS MOVING BETWEEN THE TWO PLANES, THERE'S A DISTORTION OF SPACE AROUND IT.
ONE STEP INSIDE THE BOUNDARIES, AND YOU'LL BE TORN TO SHREDS.
GROSS ME OUT...
YOU... WHAT HAVE YOU DONE TO MY ARMY?!

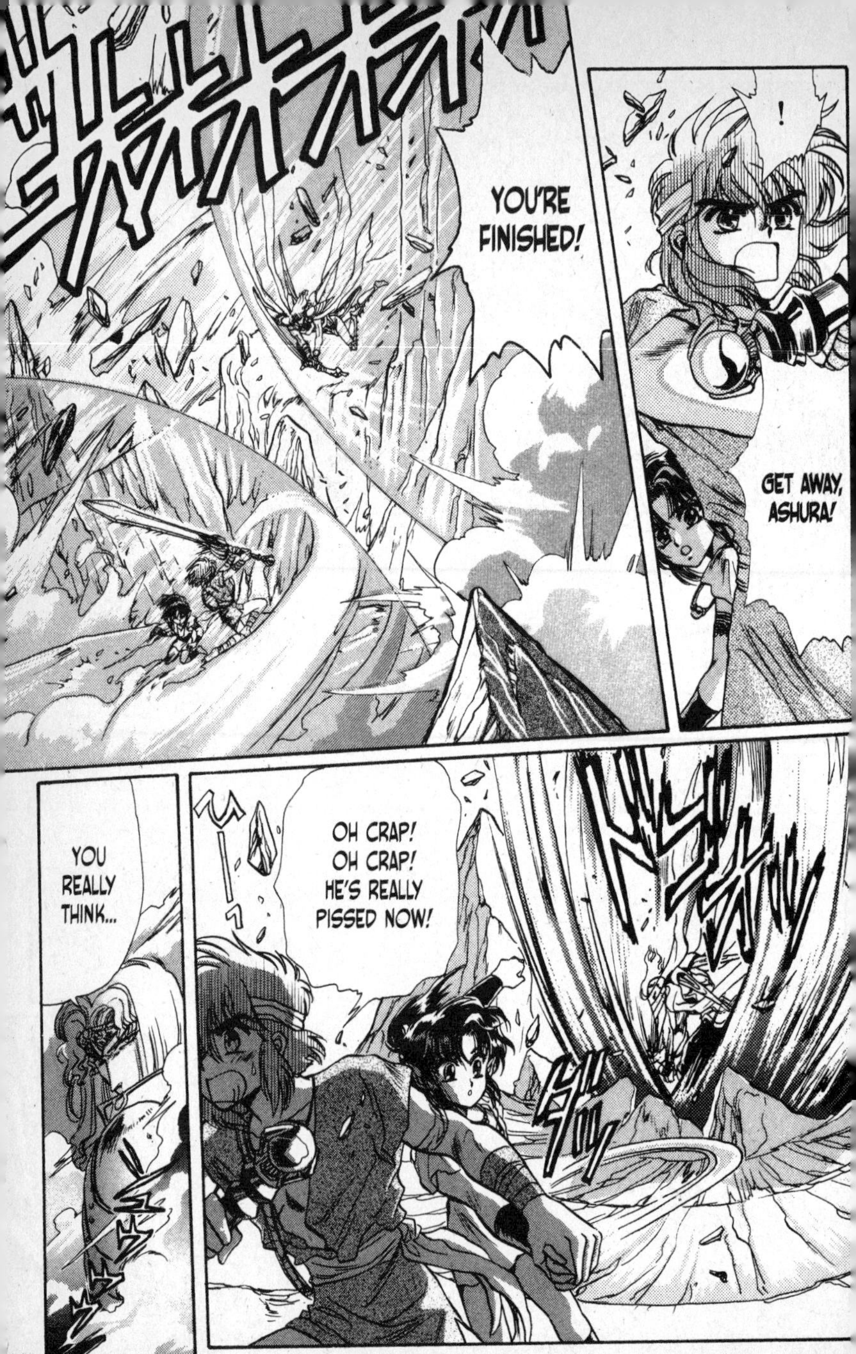
YOU'RE FINISHED!
!
GET AWAY, ASHURA!
OH CRAP! OH CRAP! HE'S REALLY PISSED NOW!
YOU REALLY THINK...

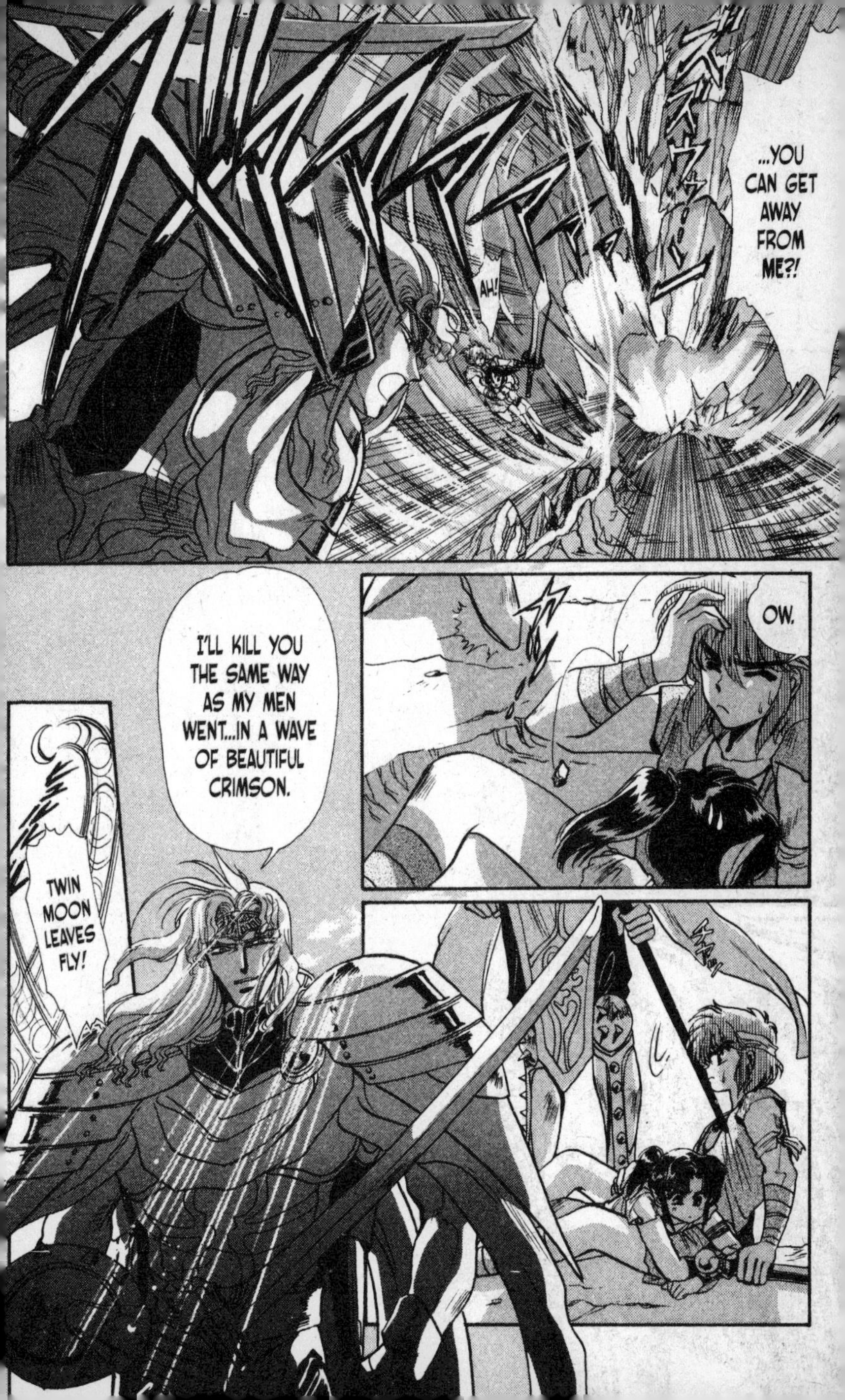
...YOU CAN GET AWAY FROM ME?!
AH!
OW.
I'LL KILL YOU THE SAME WAY AS MY MEN WENT...IN A WAVE OF BEAUTIFUL CRIMSON.
TWIN MOON LEAVES FLY!

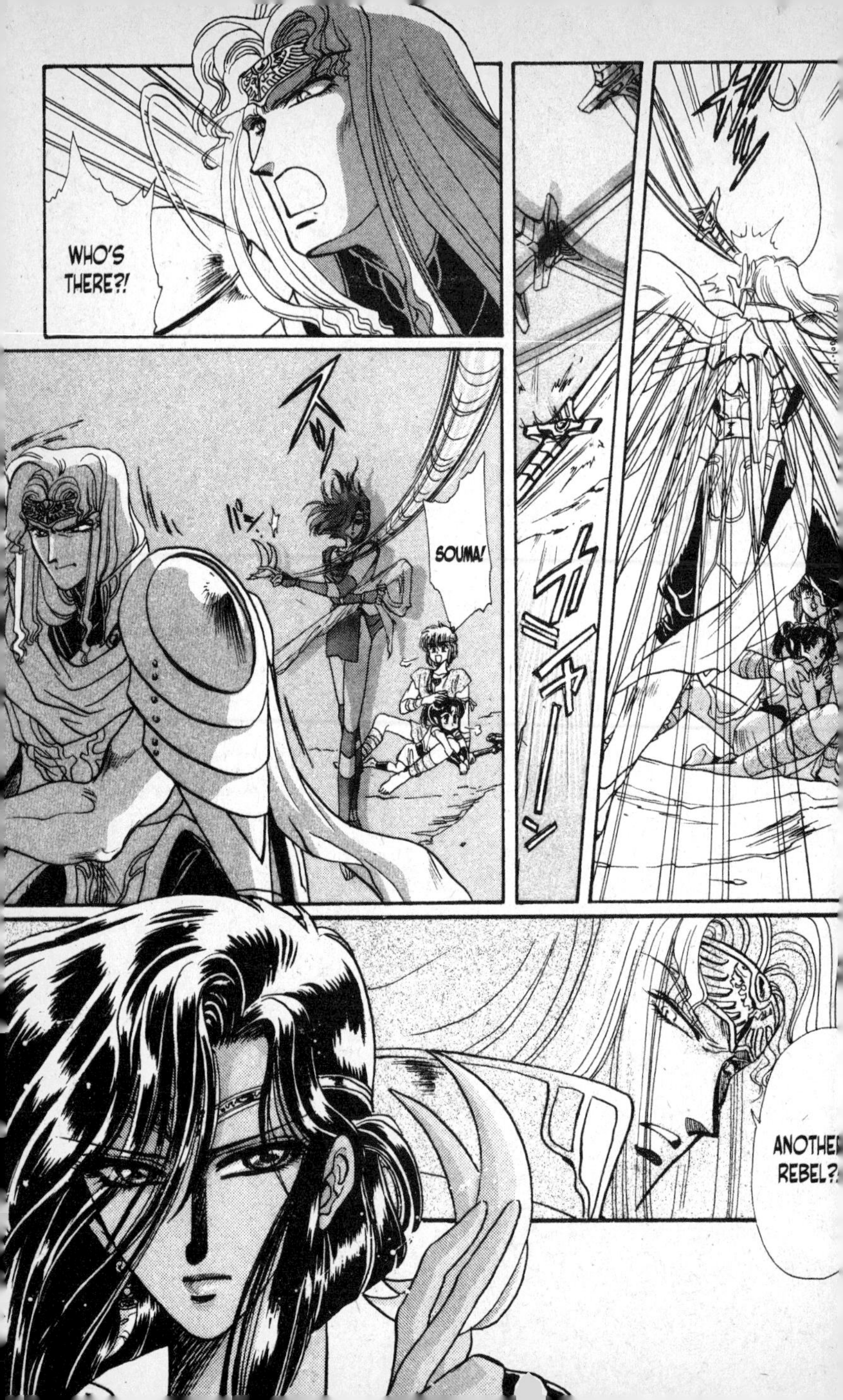
WHO'S THERE?!
SOUMA!
ANOTHE
REBEL?

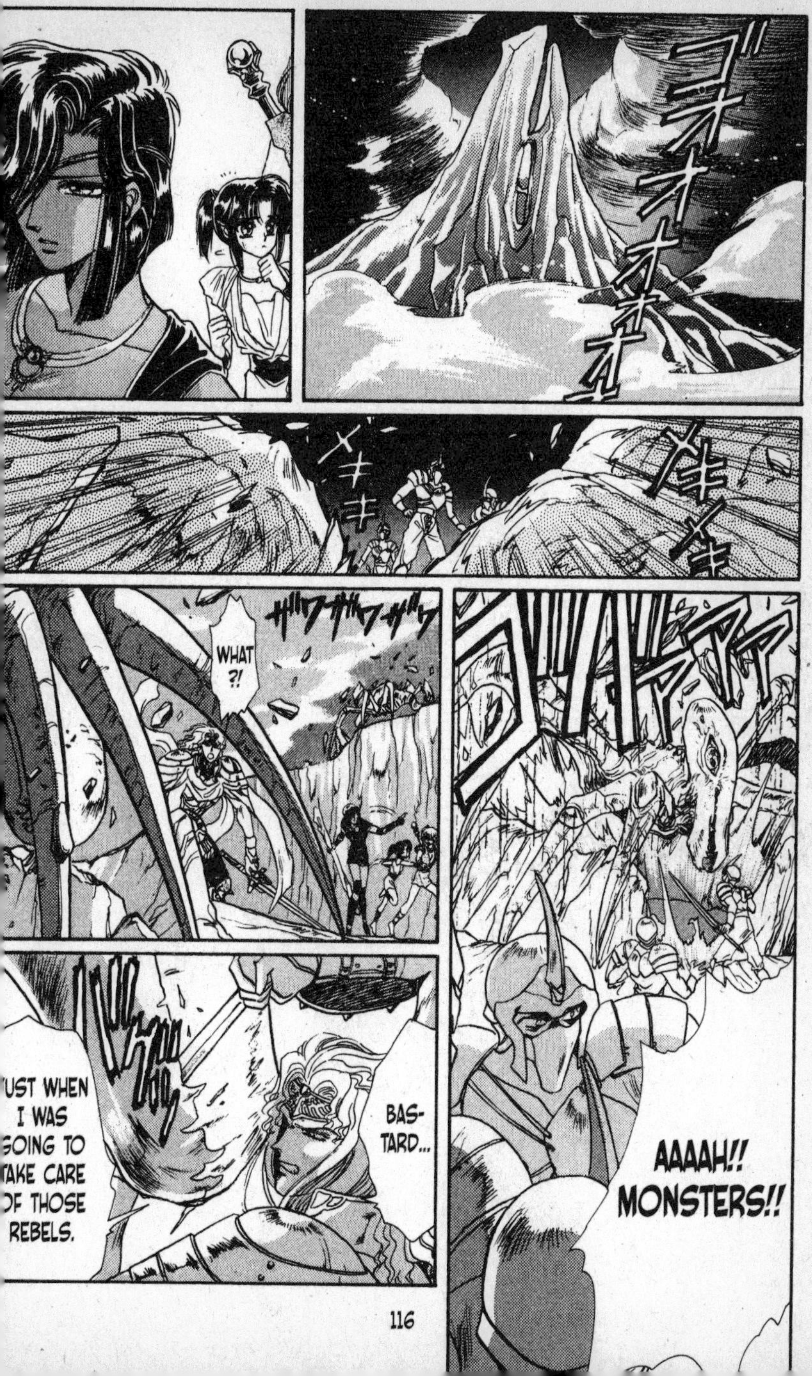
AAAAH!! MONSTERS!!
WHAT ?!
BASTARD...
JUST WHEN I WAS GOING TO TAKE CARE OF THOSE REBELS.

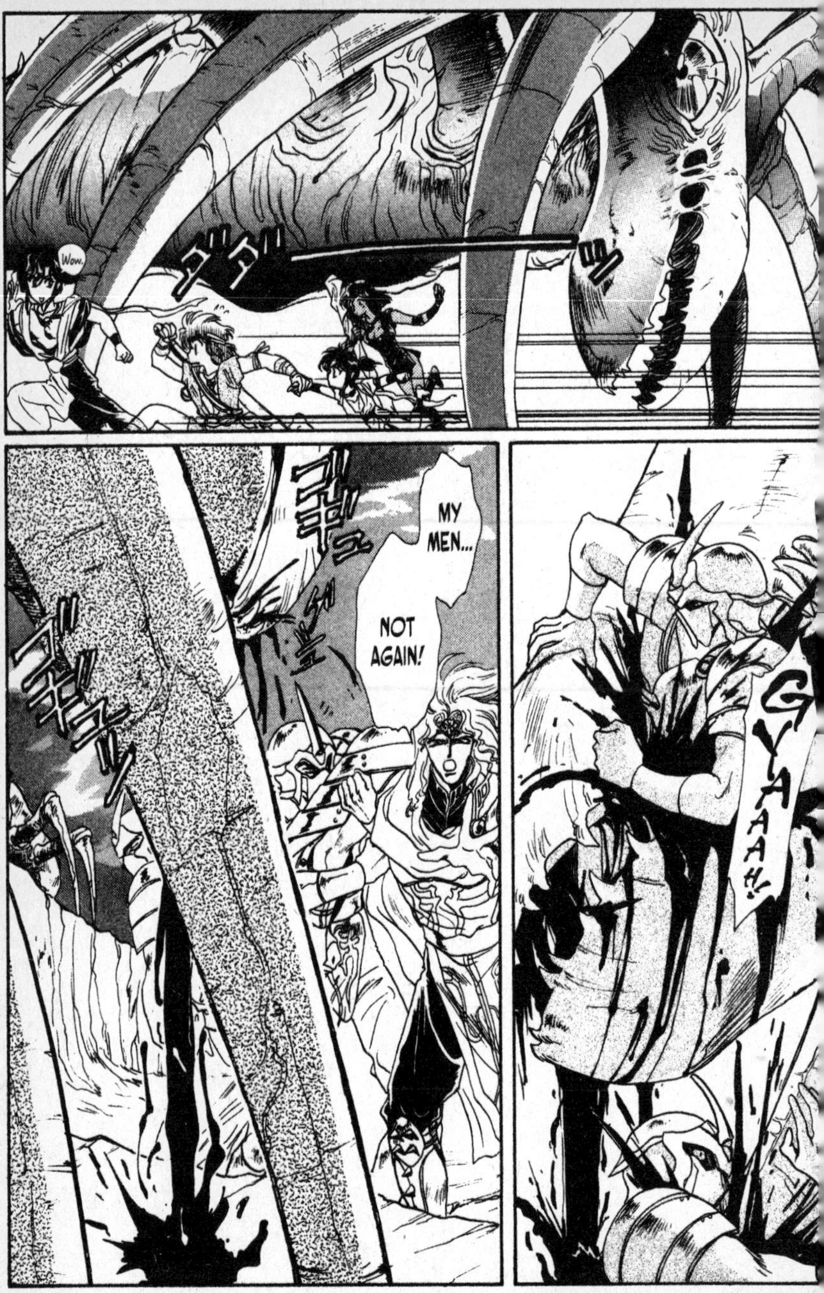
Wow.
GYAAAH!!
MY MEN...
NOT AGAIN!

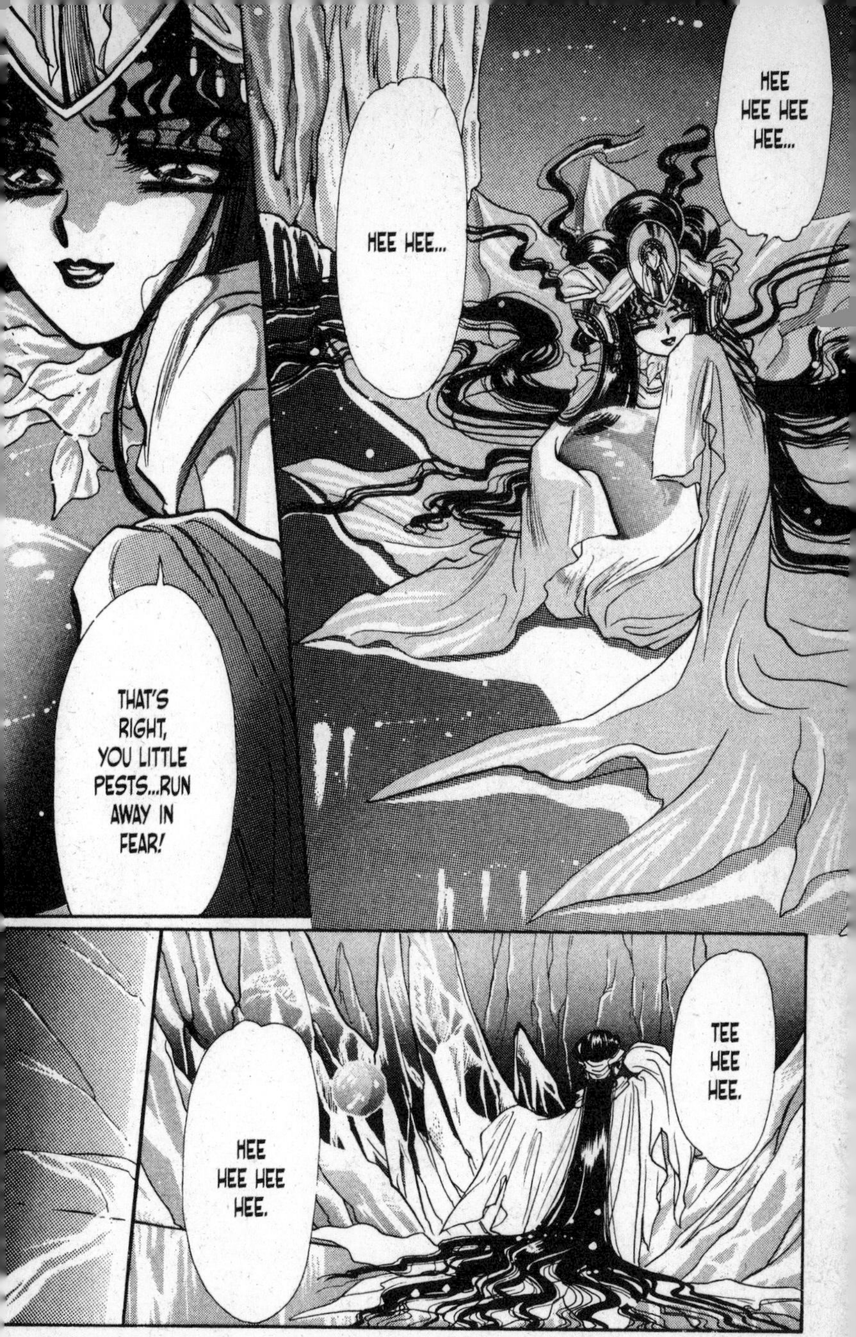
HEE HEE HEE HEE...
HEE HEE...
THAT'S RIGHT, YOU LITTLE PESTS...RUN AWAY IN FEAR!
TEE HEE HEE.
HEE HEE HEE HEE.

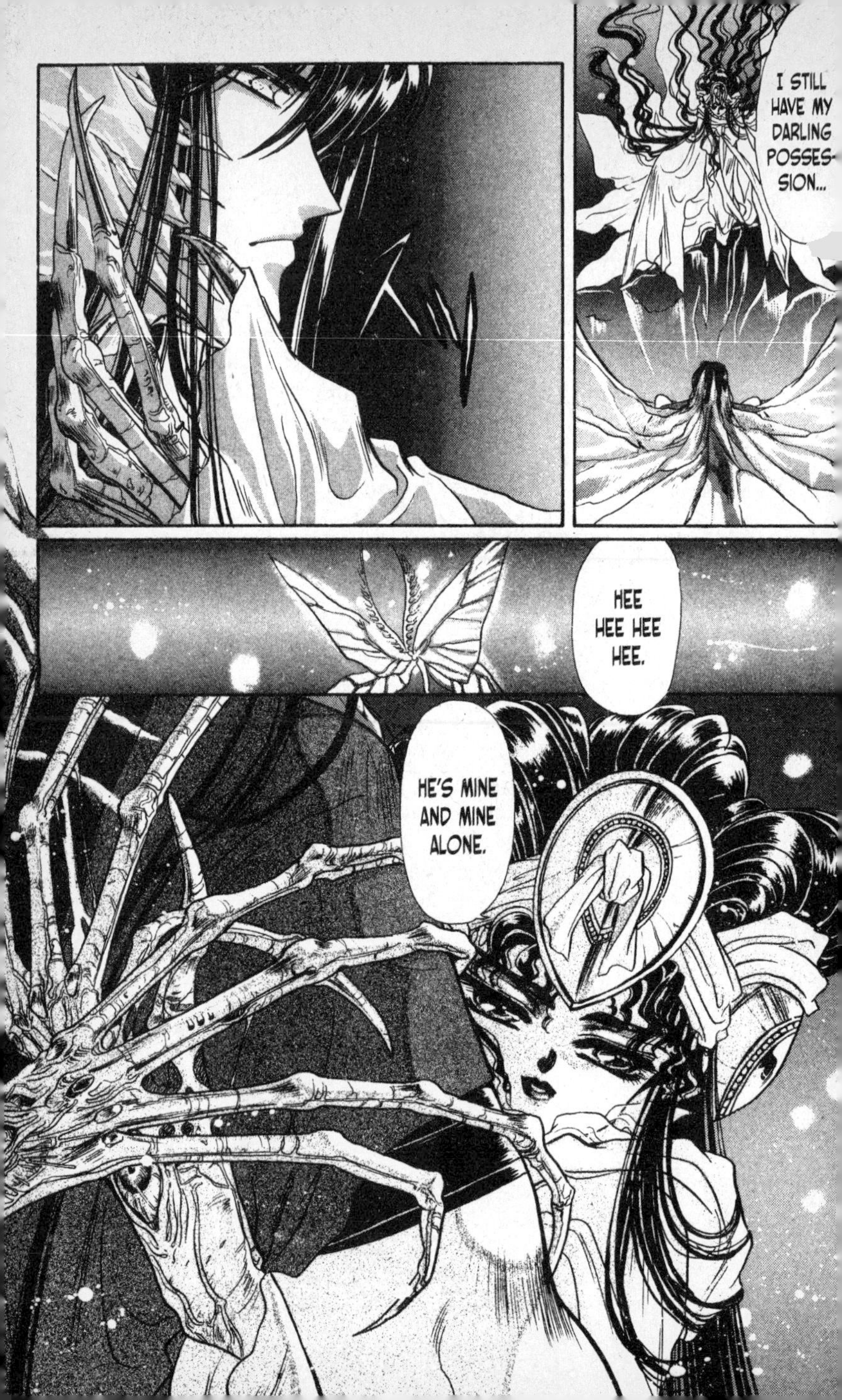
I STILL HAVE MY DARLING POSSES-SION...
HEE HEE HEE HEE.
HE'S MINE AND MINE ALONE.

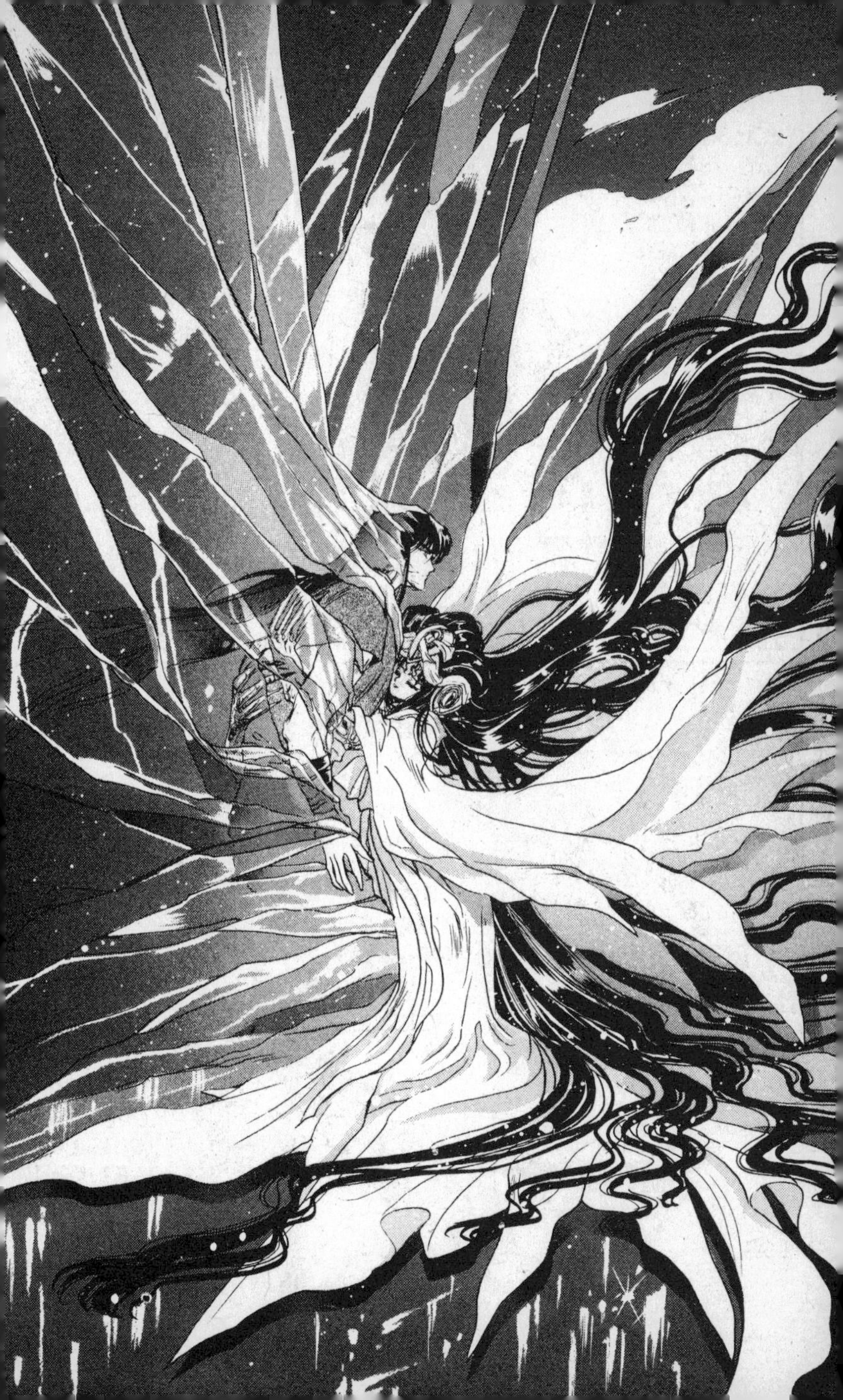

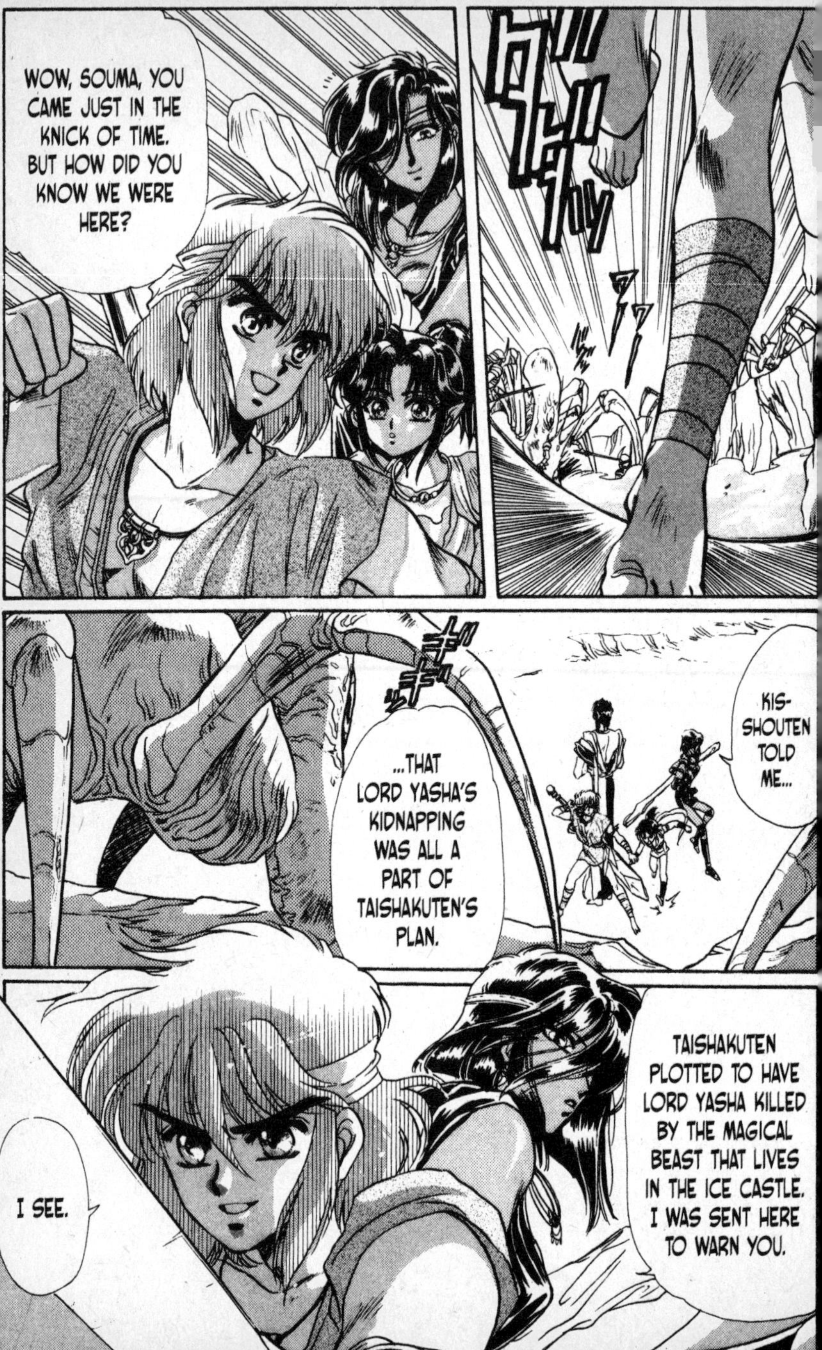
WOW, SOUMA, YOU CAME JUST IN THE KNICK OF TIME. BUT HOW DID YOU KNOW WE WERE HERE?
KIS-SHOUTEN TOLD ME...
...THAT LORD YASHA'S KIDNAPPING WAS ALL A PART OF TAISHAKUTEN'S PLAN.
TAISHAKUTEN PLOTTED TO HAVE LORD YASHA KILLED BY THE MAGICAL BEAST THAT LIVES IN THE ICE CASTLE. I WAS SENT HERE TO WARN YOU.
I SEE.

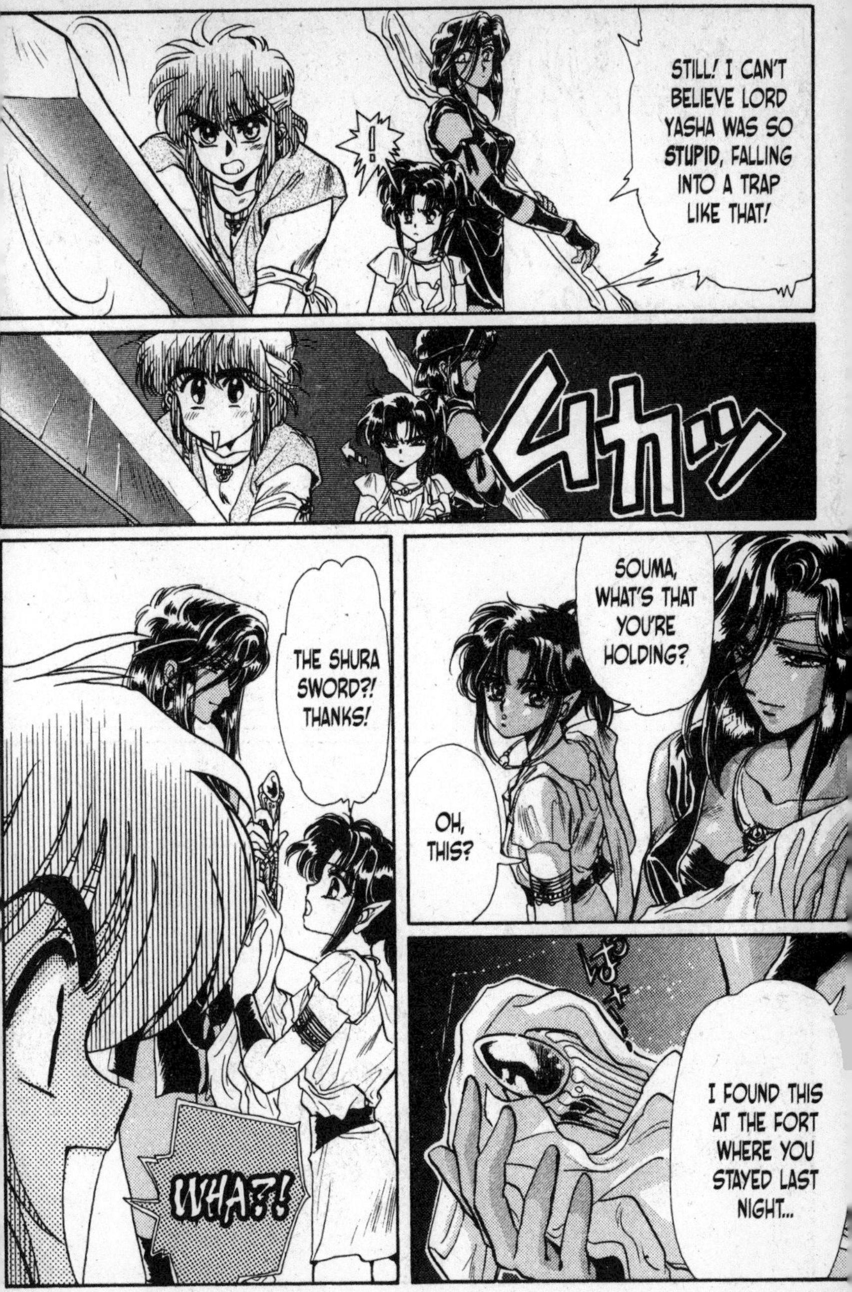
STILL! I CAN'T BELIEVE LORD YASHA WAS SO STUPID, FALLING INTO A TRAP LIKE THAT!
!
ムカッ
SOUMA, WHAT'S THAT YOU'RE HOLDING?
OH, THIS?
I FOUND THIS AT THE FORT WHERE YOU STAYED LAST NIGHT...
THE SHURA SWORD?! THANKS!
WHA?!

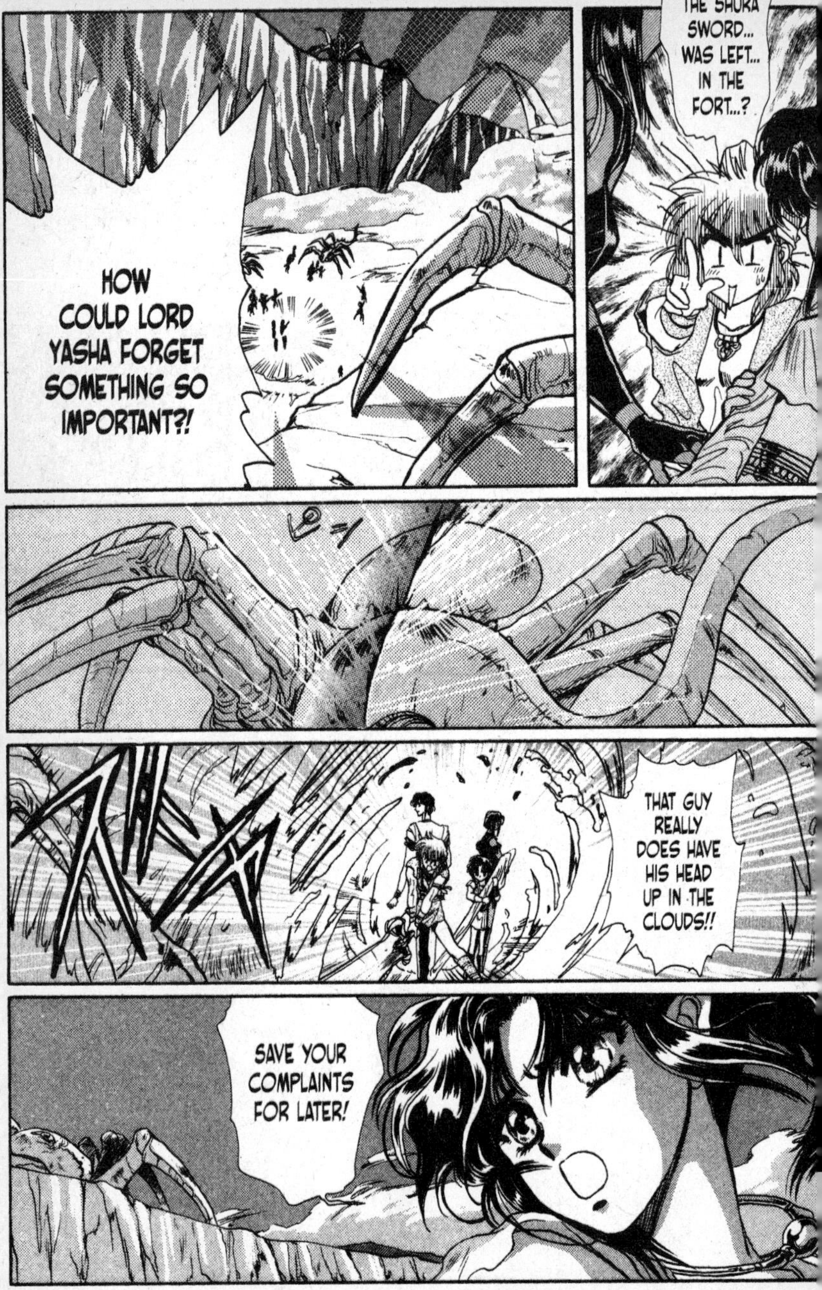

THE SHURA SWORD... WAS LEFT... IN THE FORT...?
HOW COULD LORD YASHA FORGET SOMETHING SO IMPORTANT?!
THAT GUY REALLY DOES HAVE HIS HEAD UP IN THE CLOUDS!!
SAVE YOUR COMPLAINTS FOR LATER!

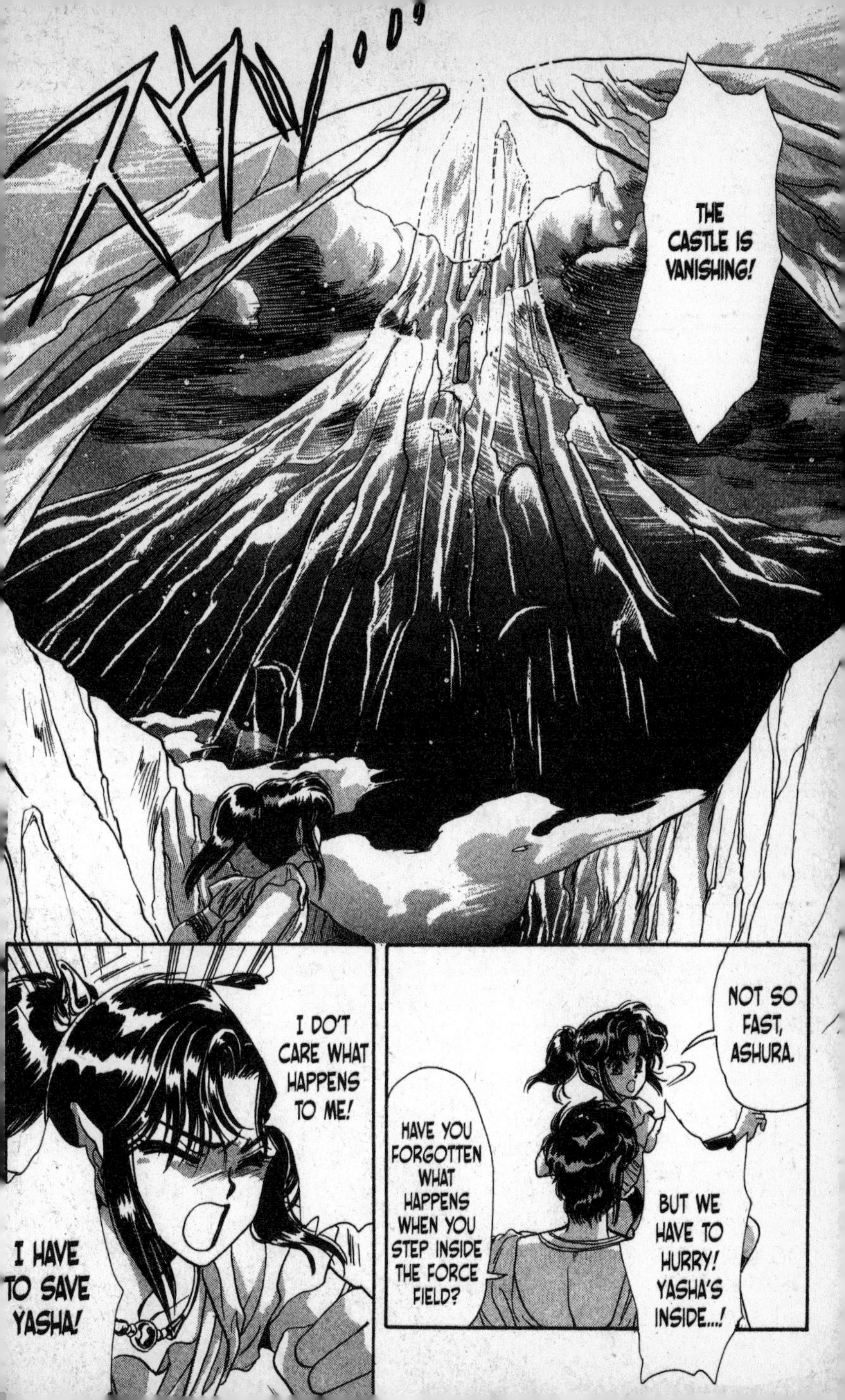
THE CASTLE IS VANISHING!
NOT SO FAST, ASHURA.
BUT WE HAVE TO HURRY! YASHA'S INSIDE...!
HAVE YOU FORGOTTEN WHAT HAPPENS WHEN YOU STEP INSIDE THE FORCE FIELD?
I DON'T CARE WHAT HAPPENS TO ME!
I HAVE TO SAVE YASHA!

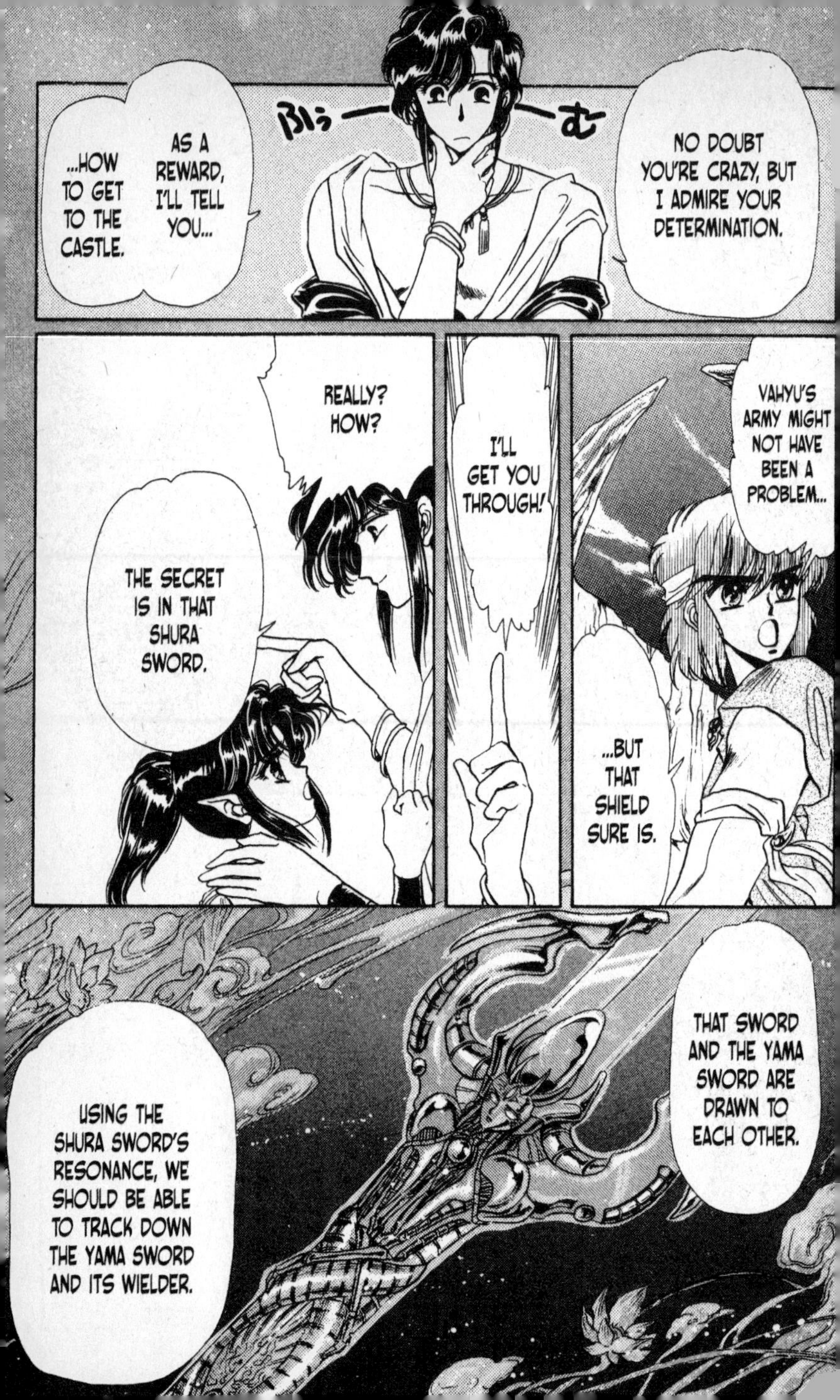
NO DOUBT YOU'RE CRAZY, BUT I ADMIRE YOUR DETERMINATION.
ふぅーーむ
AS A REWARD, I'LL TELL YOU...
...HOW TO GET TO THE CASTLE.
VAHYU'S ARMY MIGHT NOT HAVE BEEN A PROBLEM...
...BUT THAT SHIELD SURE IS.
I'LL GET YOU THROUGH!
REALLY? HOW?
THE SECRET IS IN THAT SHURA SWORD.
THAT SWORD AND THE YAMA SWORD ARE DRAWN TO EACH OTHER.
USING THE SHURA SWORD'S RESONANCE, WE SHOULD BE ABLE TO TRACK DOWN THE YAMA SWORD AND ITS WIELDER.

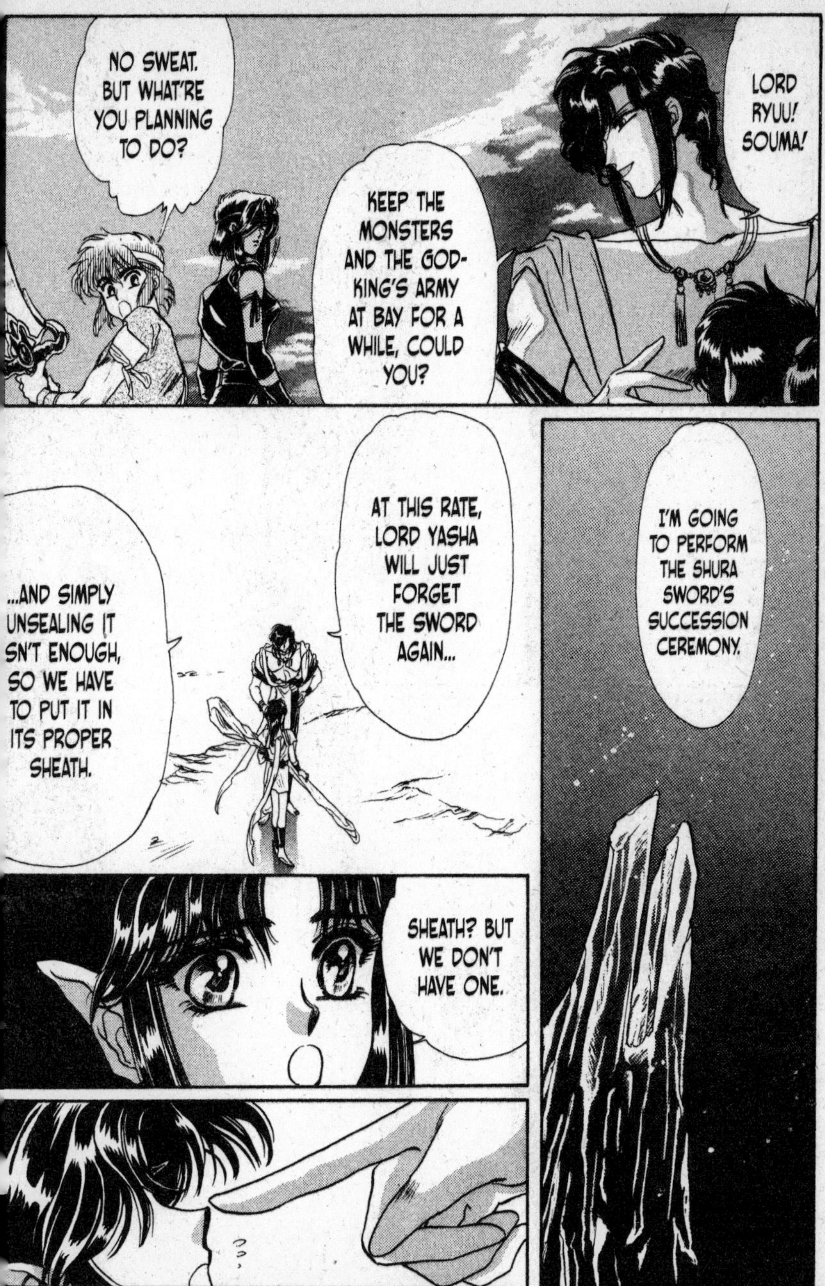

LORD RYUU! SOUMA!
KEEP THE MONSTERS AND THE GOD-KING'S ARMY AT BAY FOR A WHILE, COULD YOU?
NO SWEAT. BUT WHAT'RE YOU PLANNING TO DO?
I'M GOING TO PERFORM THE SHURA SWORD'S SUCCESSION CEREMONY.
AT THIS RATE, LORD YASHA WILL JUST FORGET THE SWORD AGAIN...
...AND SIMPLY UNSEALING IT SN'T ENOUGH, SO WE HAVE TO PUT IT IN ITS PROPER SHEATH.
SHEATH? BUT WE DON'T HAVE ONE.

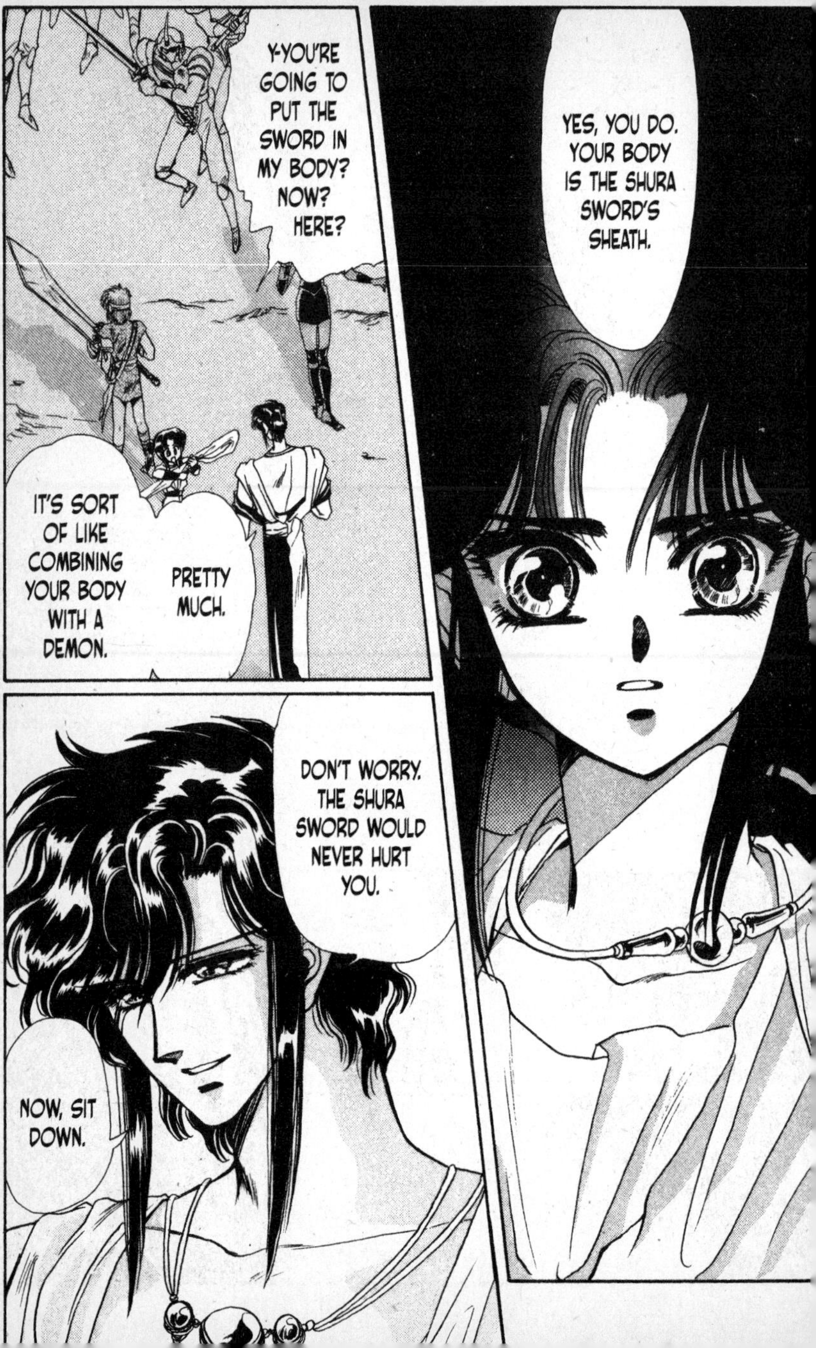
YES, YOU DO. YOUR BODY IS THE SHURA SWORD'S SHEATH.
Y-YOU'RE GOING TO PUT THE SWORD IN MY BODY? NOW? HERE?
IT'S SORT OF LIKE COMBINING YOUR BODY WITH A DEMON.
PRETTY MUCH.
DON'T WORRY. THE SHURA SWORD WOULD NEVER HURT YOU.
NOW, SIT DOWN.

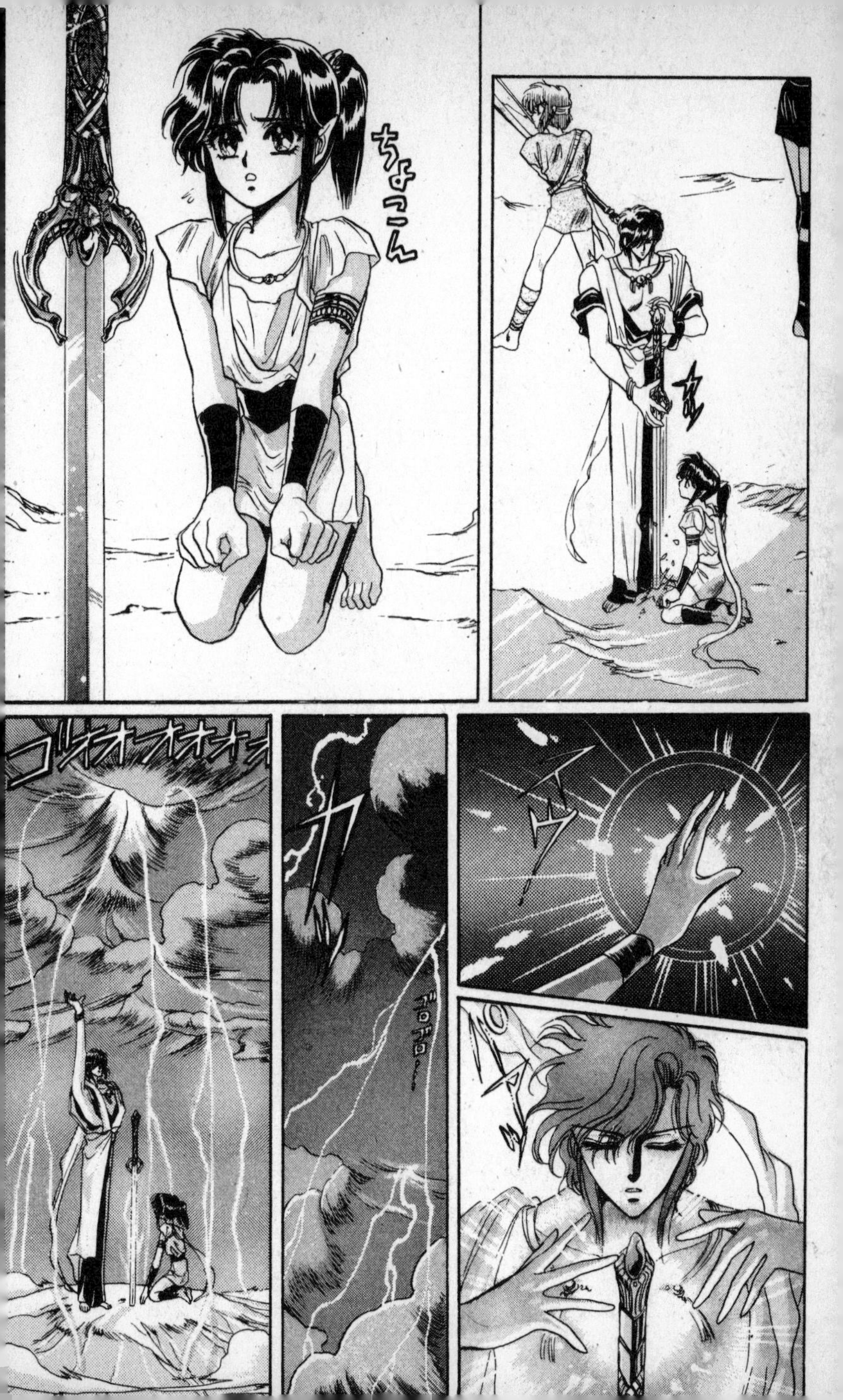
ちょこん
ゴロゴロ…
コルオオオオオ

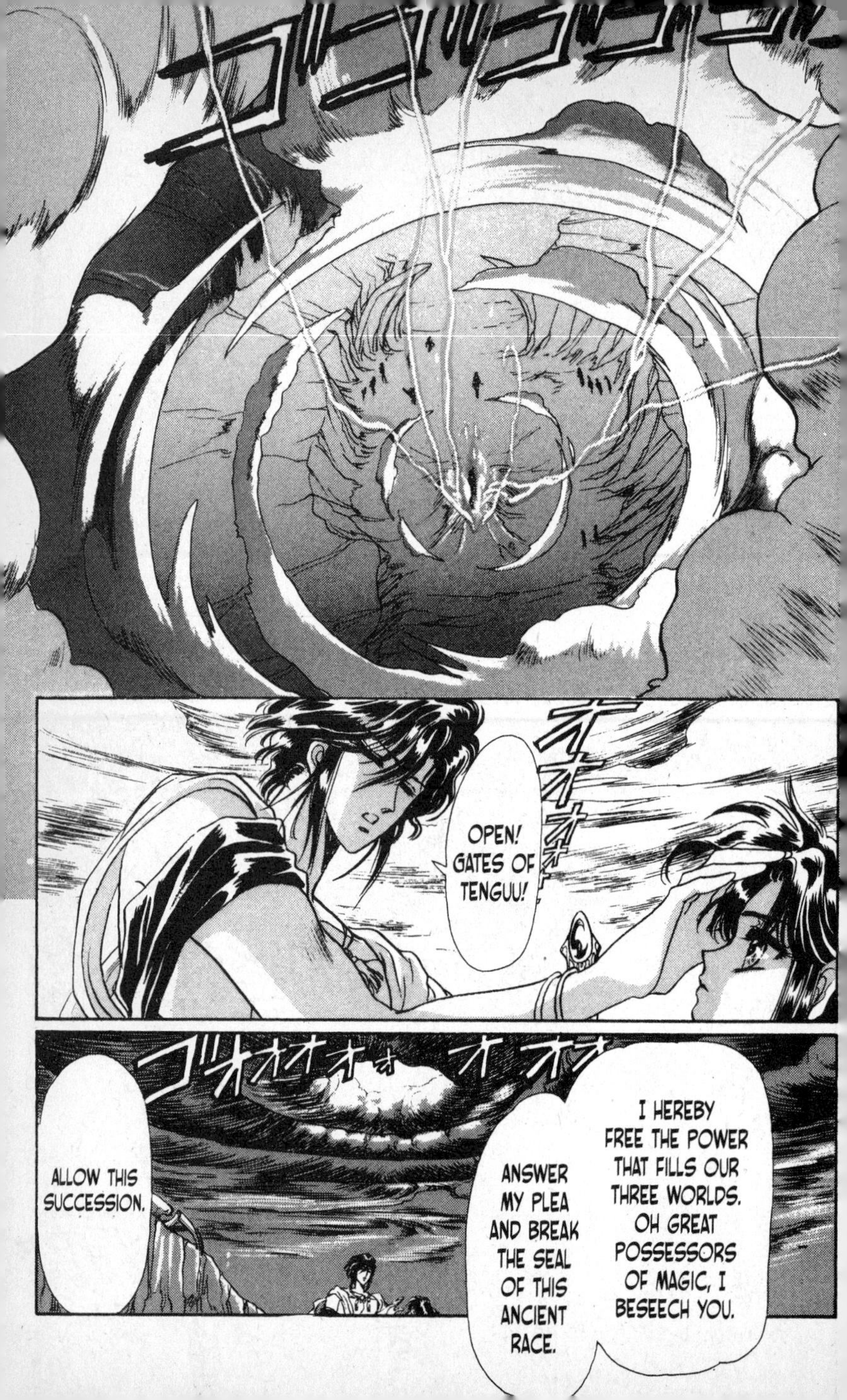
OPEN! GATES OF TENGUU!
I HEREBY FREE THE POWER THAT FILLS OUR THREE WORLDS. OH GREAT POSSESSORS OF MAGIC, I BESEECH YOU.
ANSWER MY PLEA AND BREAK THE SEAL OF THIS ANCIENT RACE.
ALLOW THIS SUCCESSION.

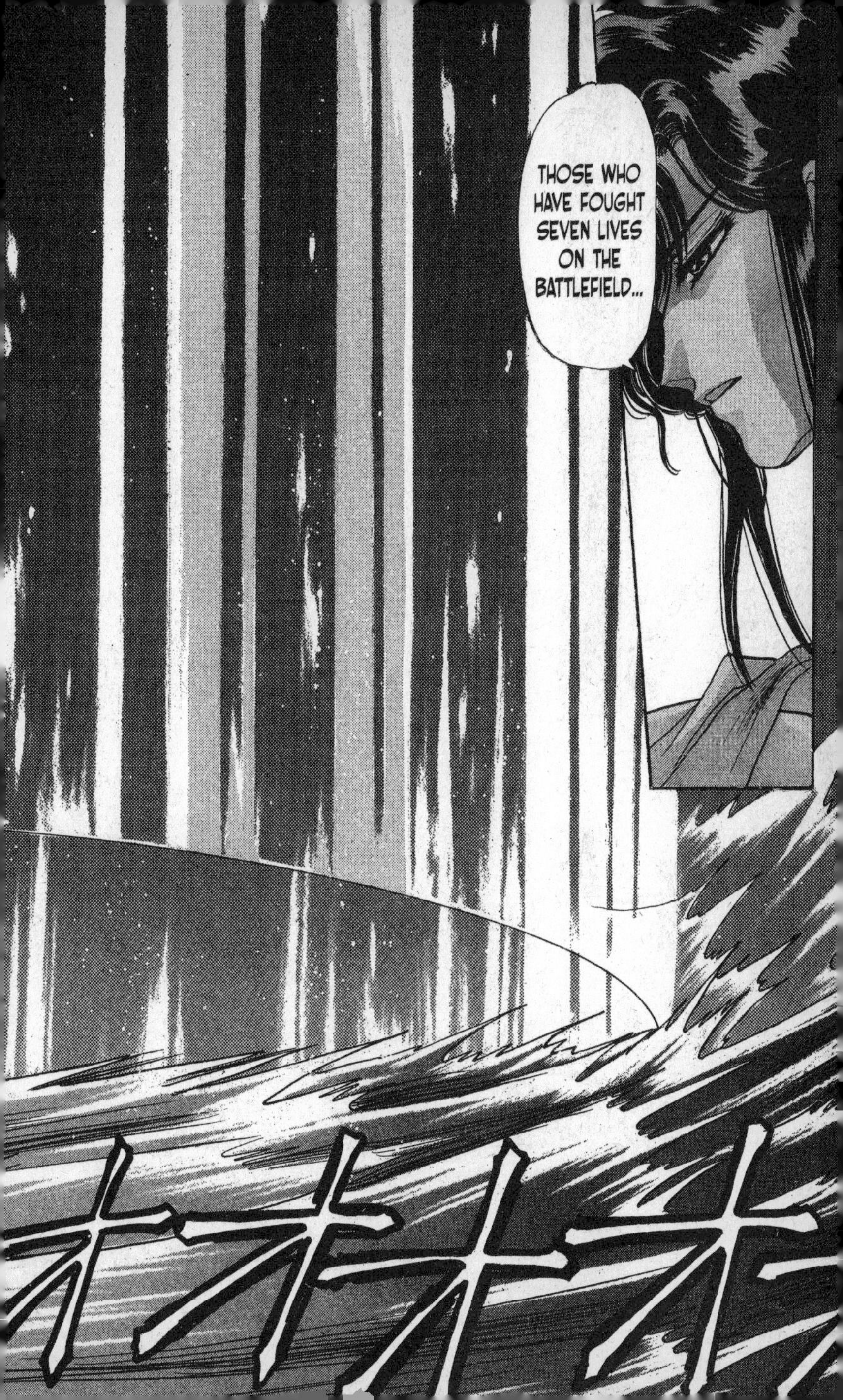
THOSE WHO HAVE FOUGHT SEVEN LIVES ON THE BATTLEFIELD...

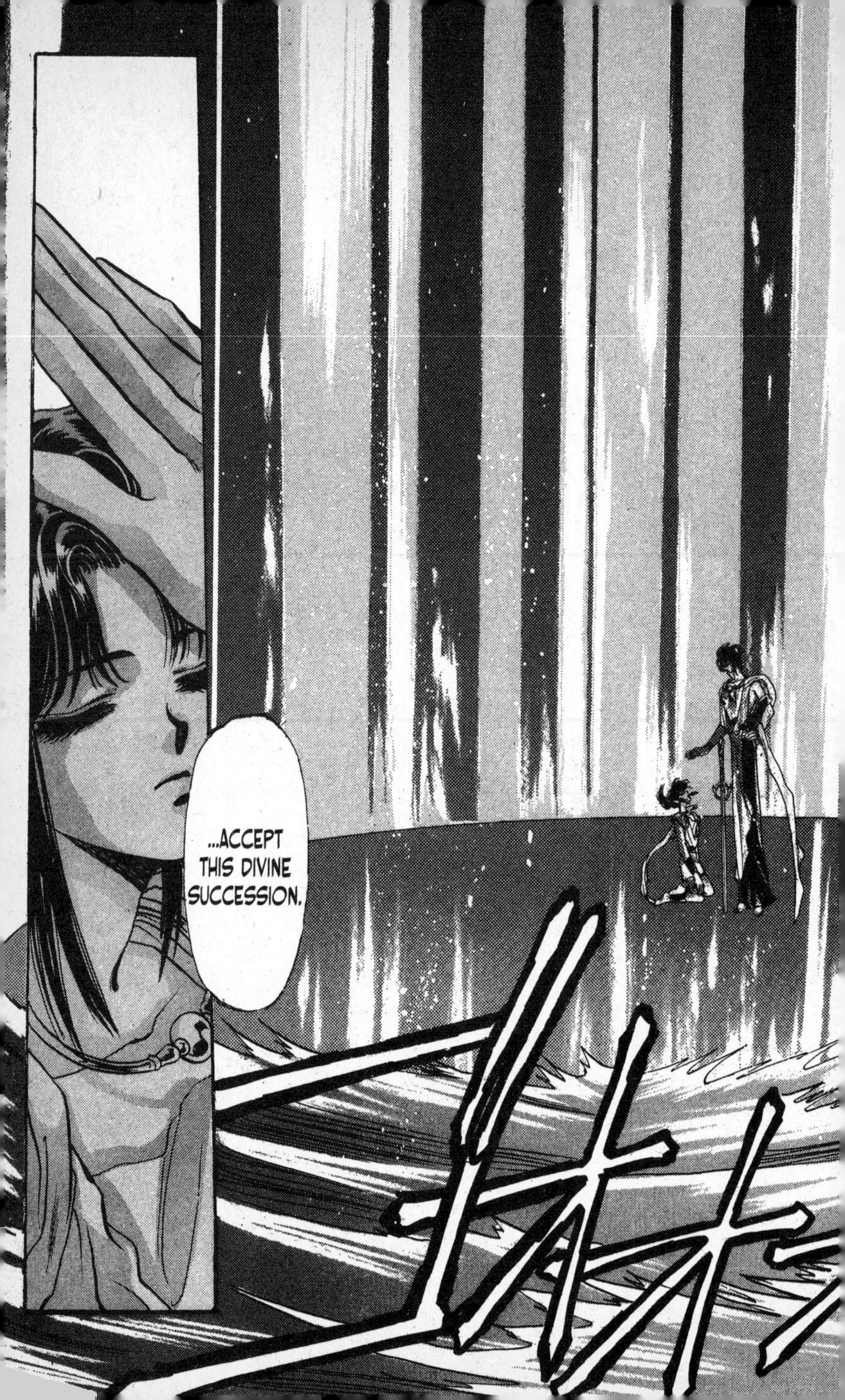
...ACCEPT THIS DIVINE SUCCESSION.

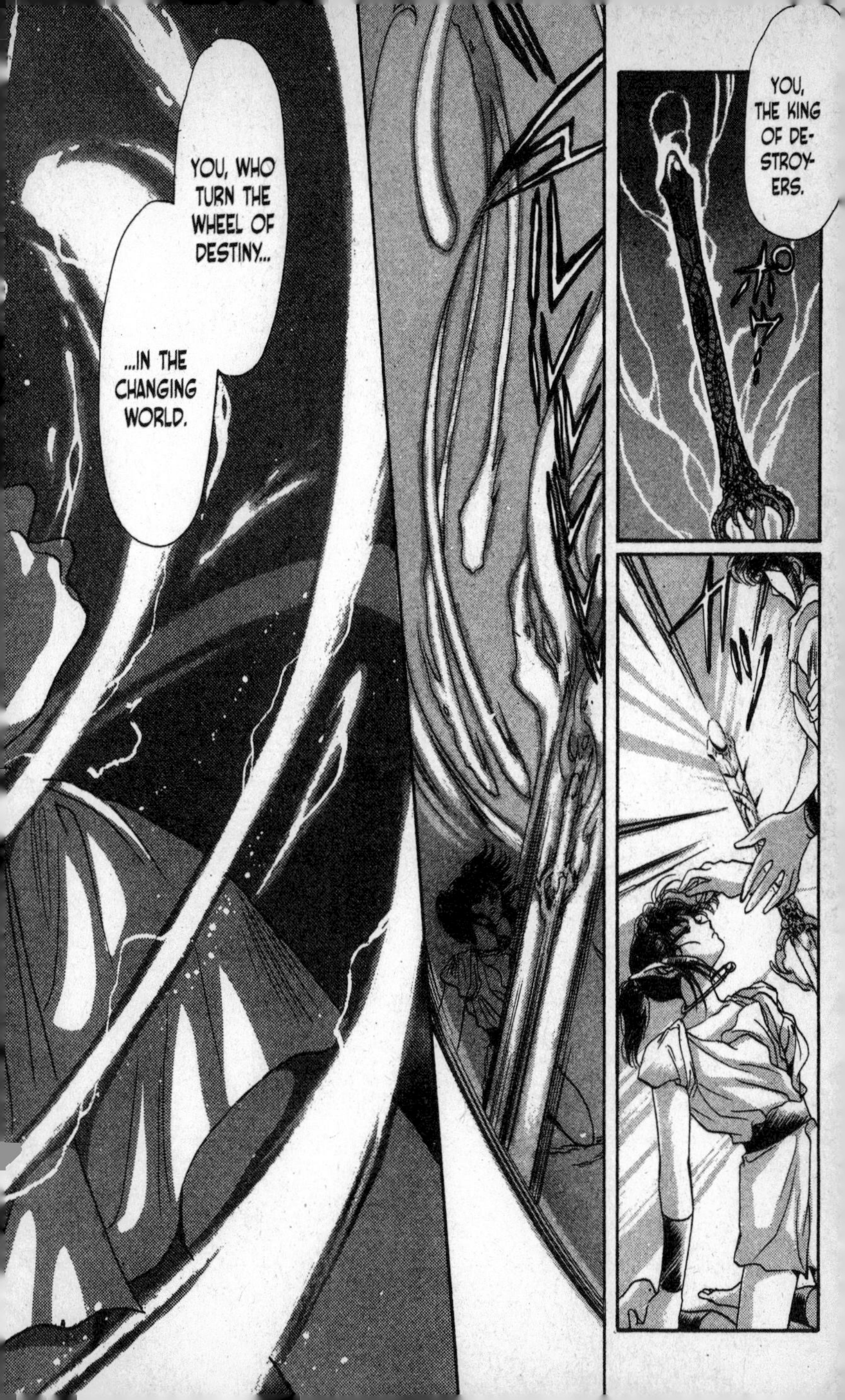
YOU, THE KING OF DE-STROYERS.
YOU, WHO TURN THE WHEEL OF DESTINY...
...IN THE CHANGING WORLD.

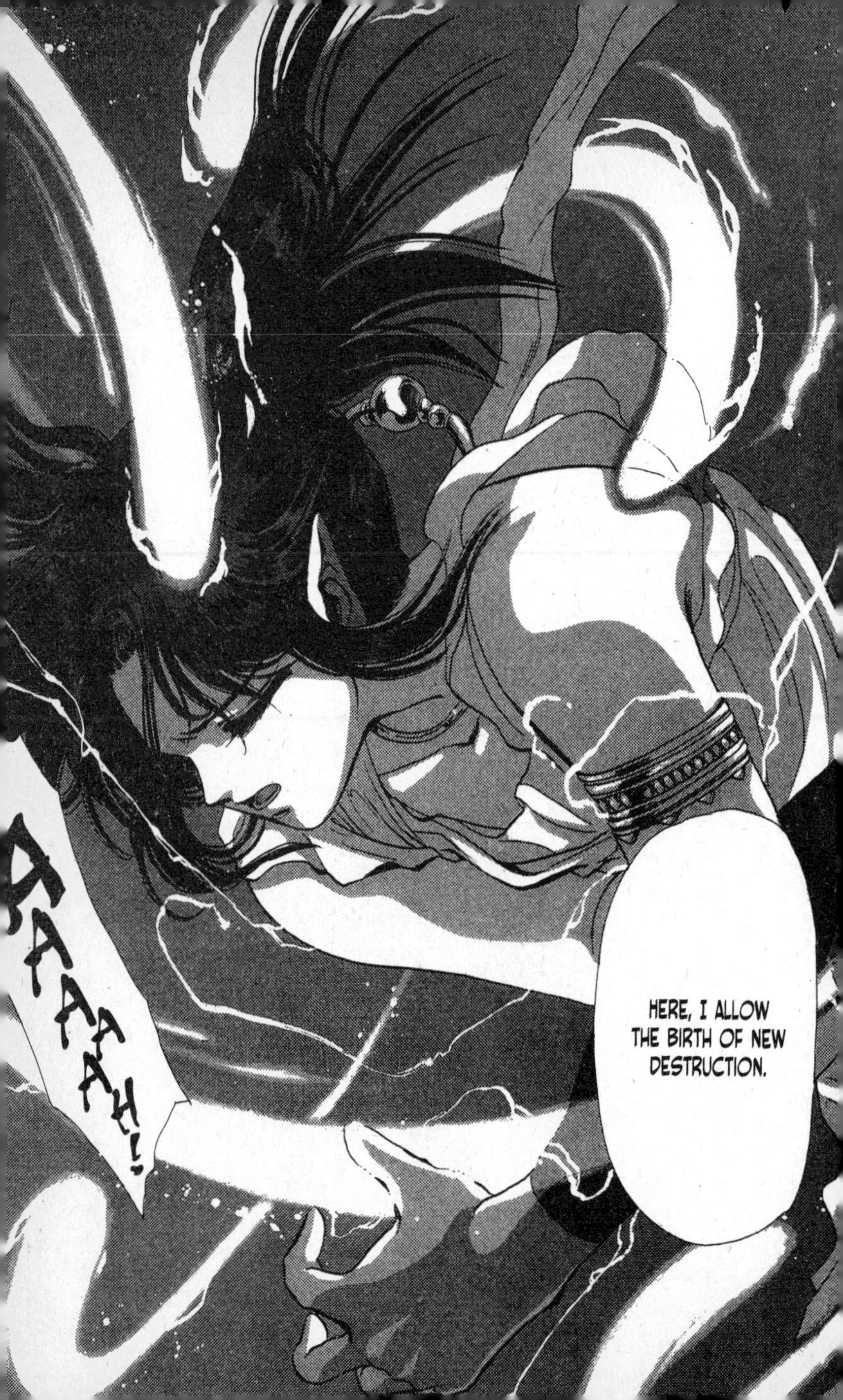
HERE, I ALLOW THE BIRTH OF NEW DESTRUCTION.
AAAAAH!

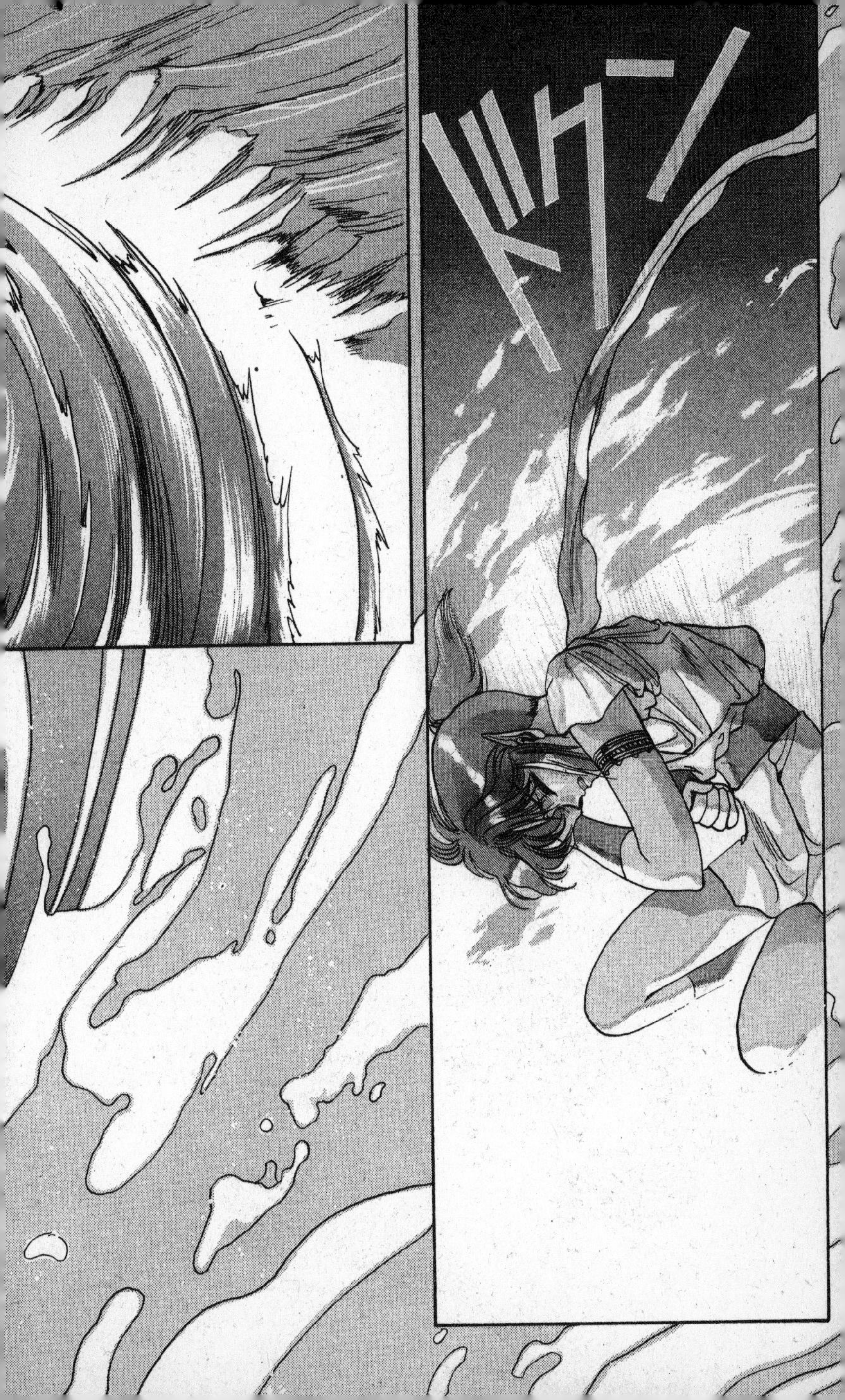
ドゥーン

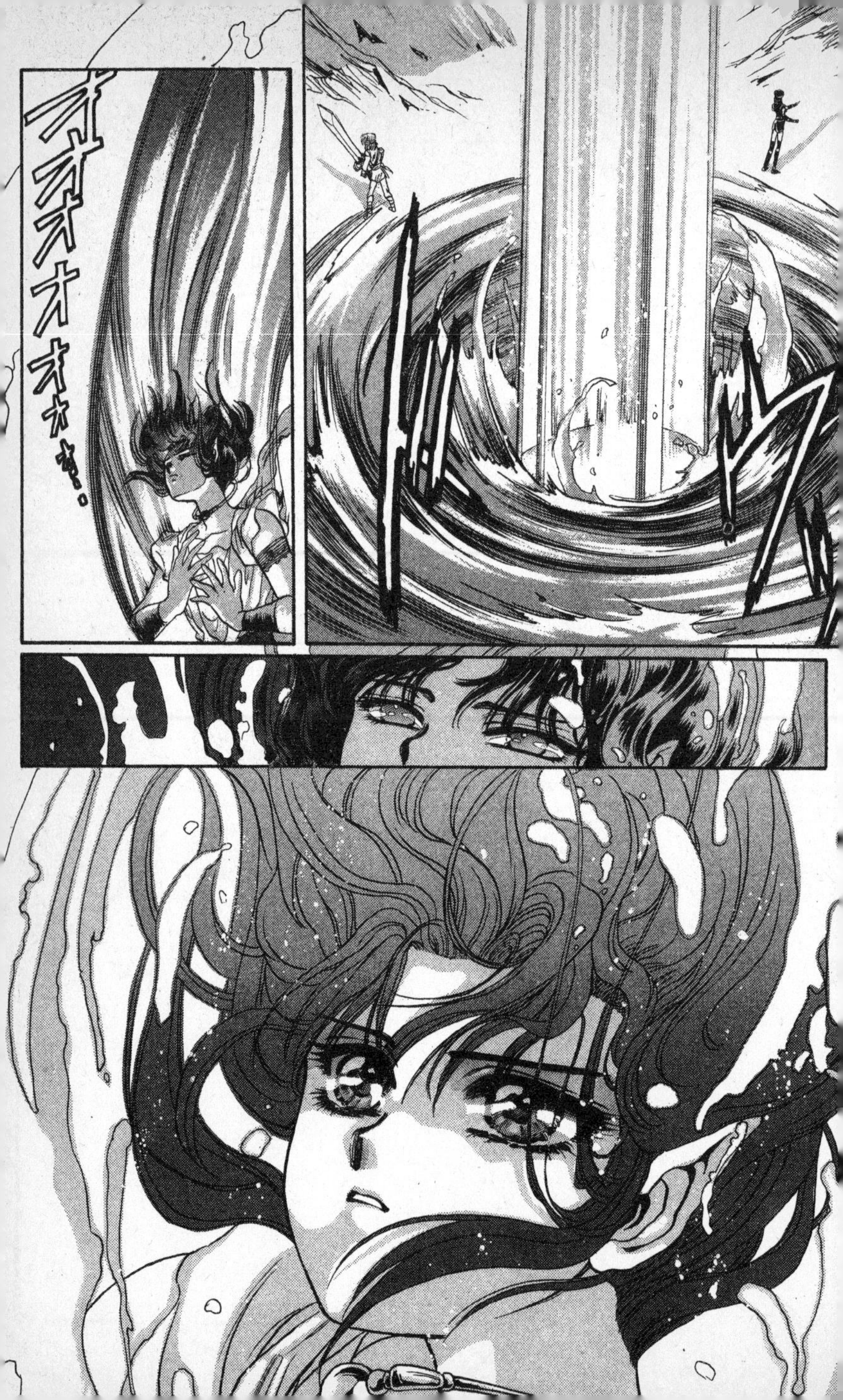
オオオオオォォ。

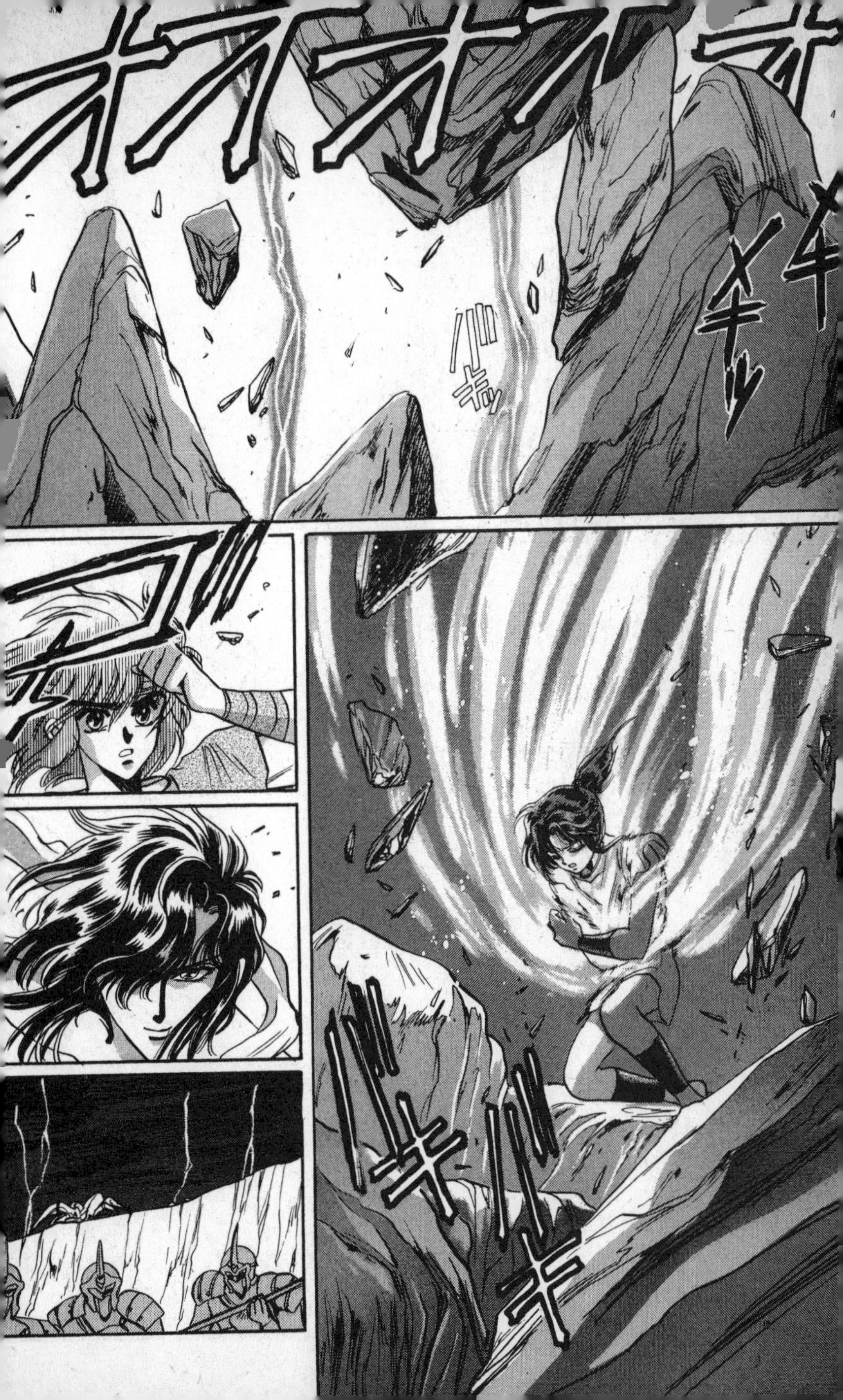
オオオオオオ
メキメキッ
バキッ
バキバキ
ゴォ

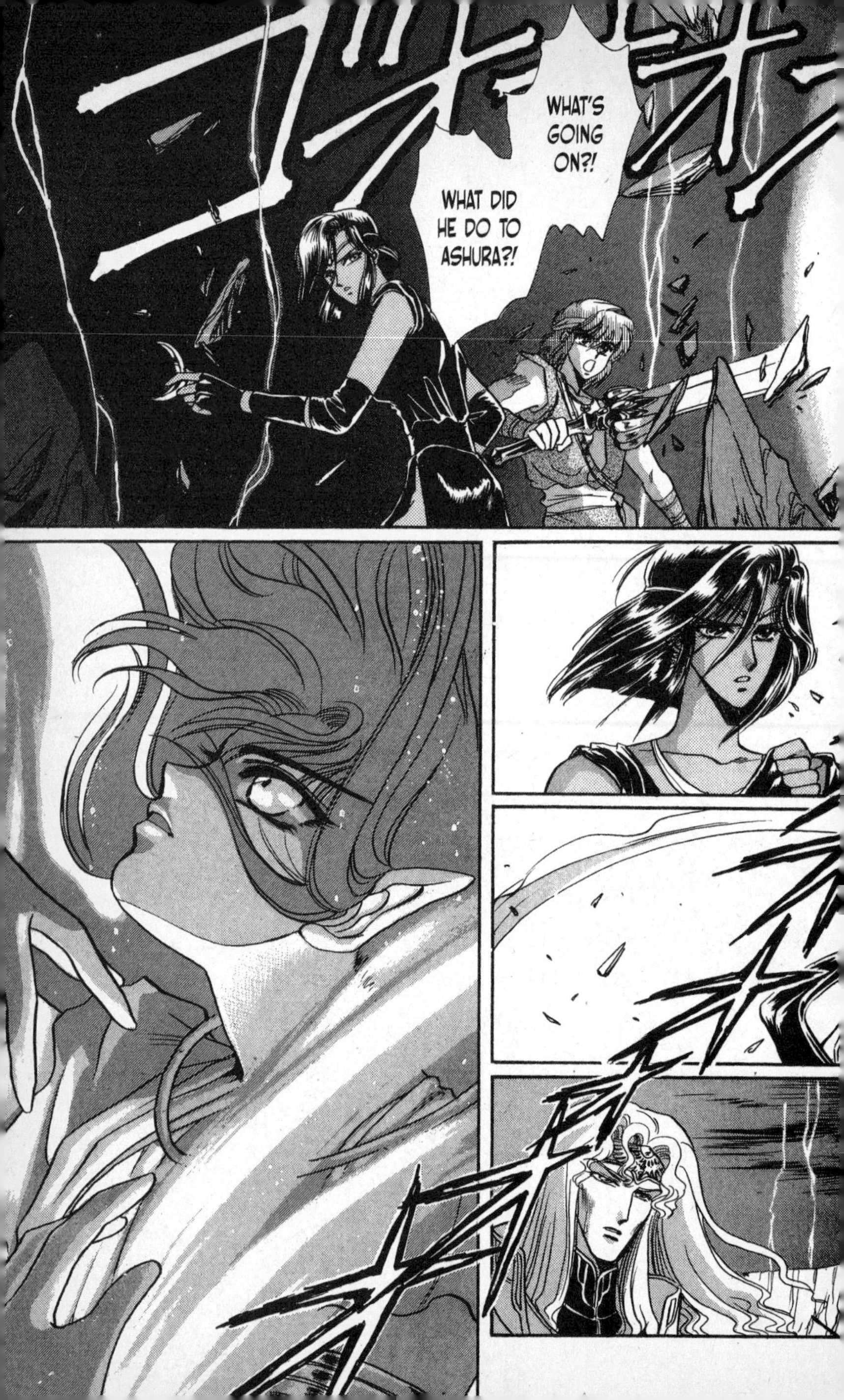
WHAT'S GOING ON?!
WHAT DID HE DO TO ASHURA?!

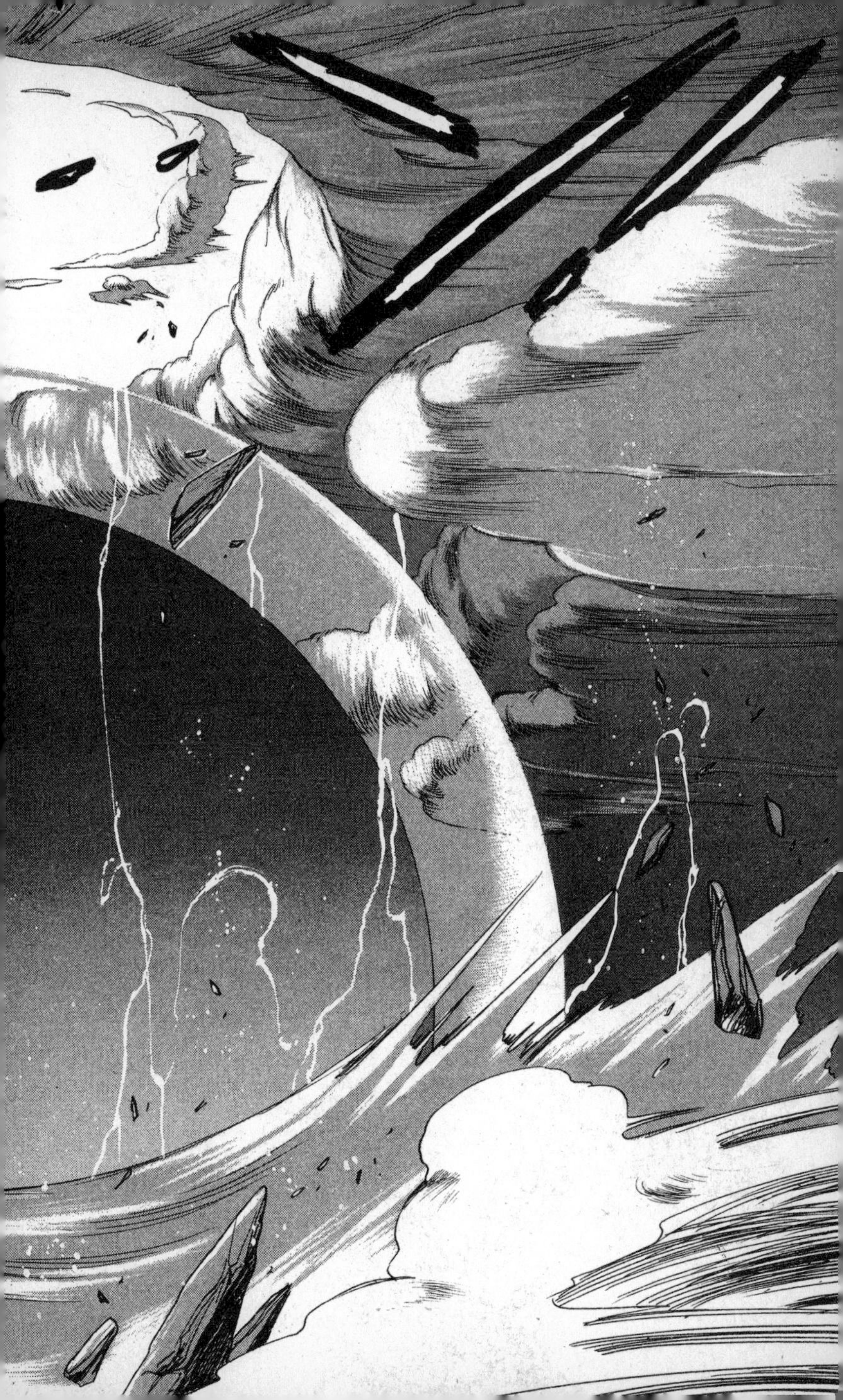

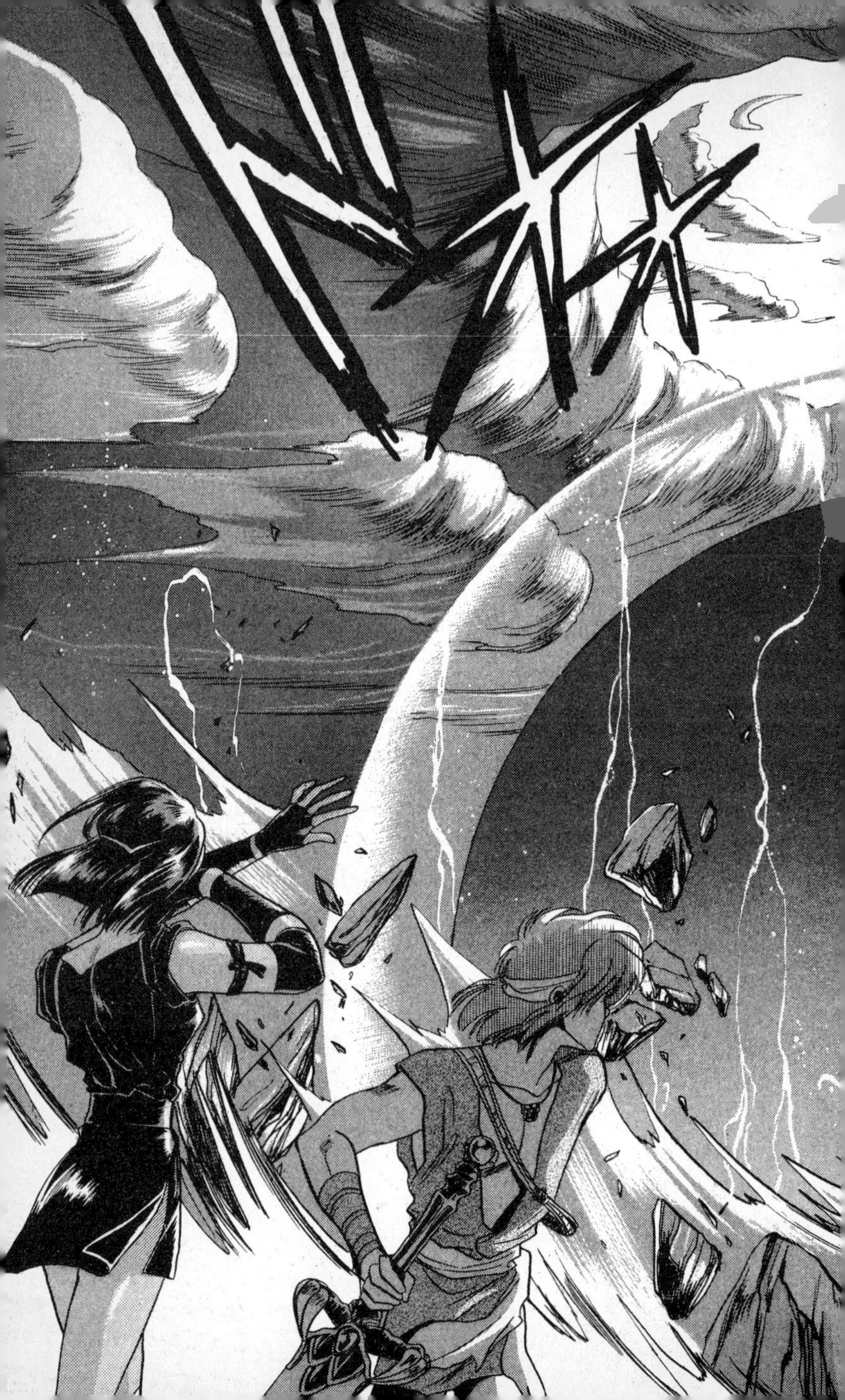

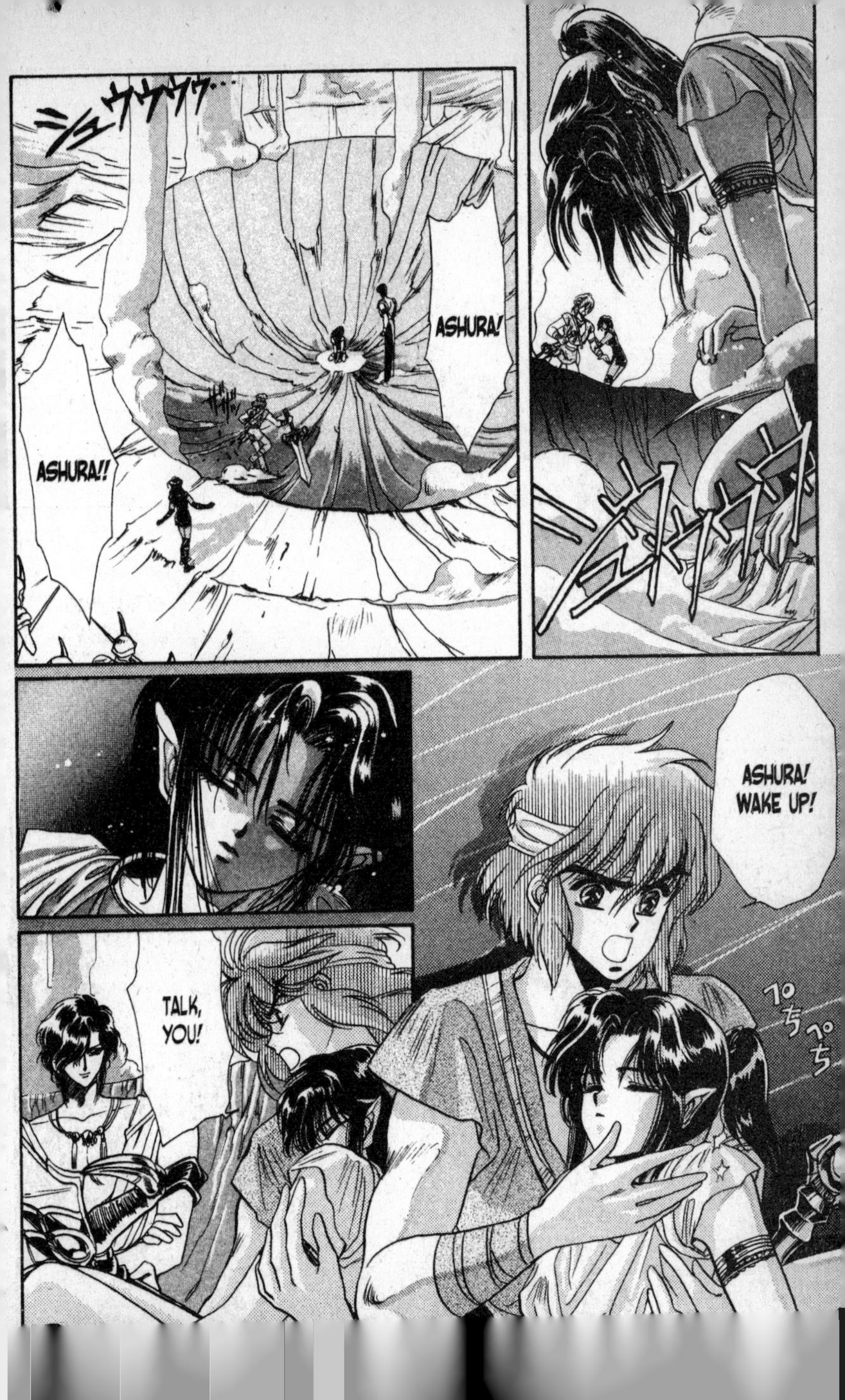
シュウウウウ…
ASHURA!
ASHURA!!
ASHURA! WAKE UP!
ぺちぺち
TALK, YOU!

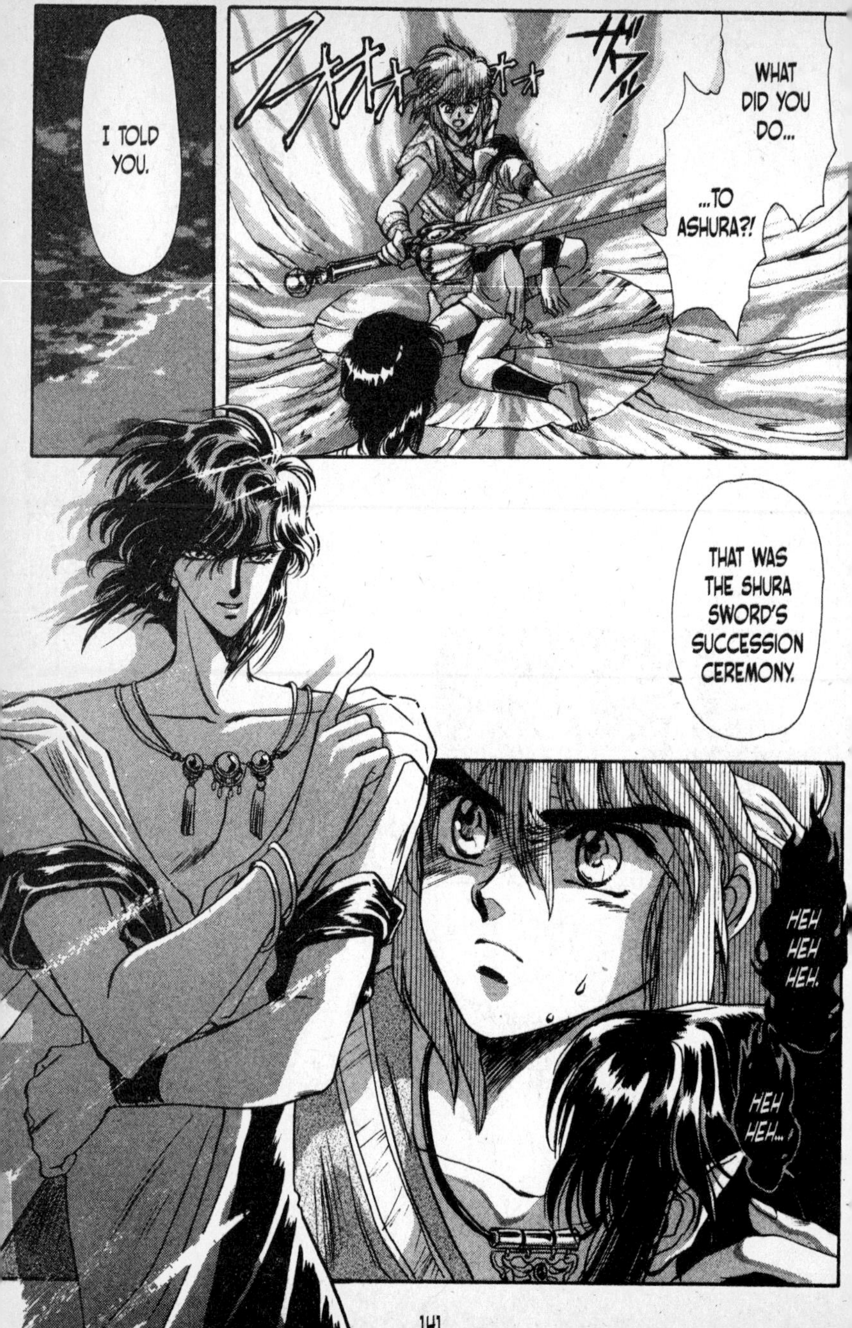
WHAT DID YOU DO...
...TO ASHURA?!
I TOLD YOU.
THAT WAS THE SHURA SWORD'S SUCCESSION CEREMONY.
HEH HEH HEH.
HEH HEH...

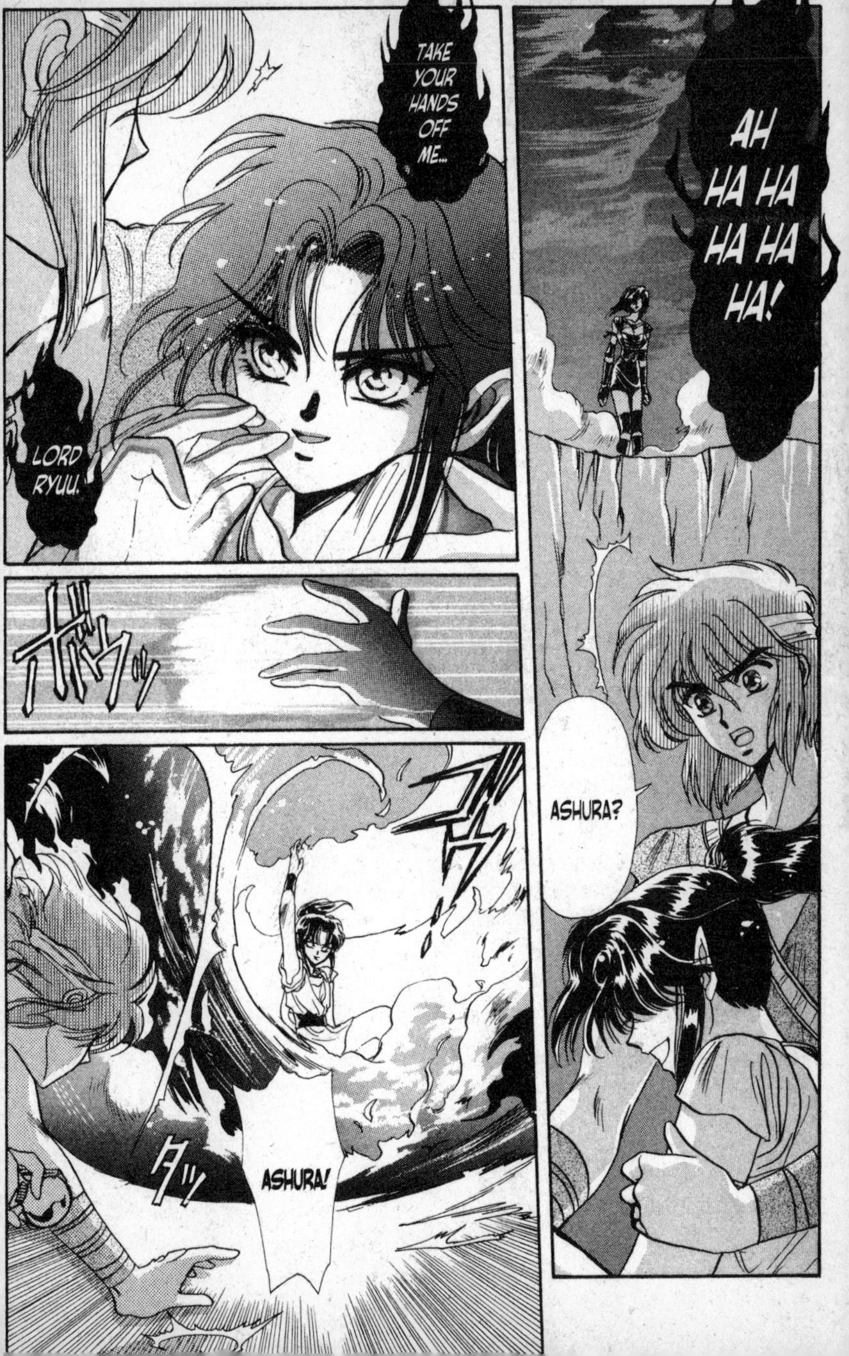
AH HA HA HA HA HA!
TAKE YOUR HANDS OFF ME...
LORD RYUU.
ASHURA?
ASHURA!

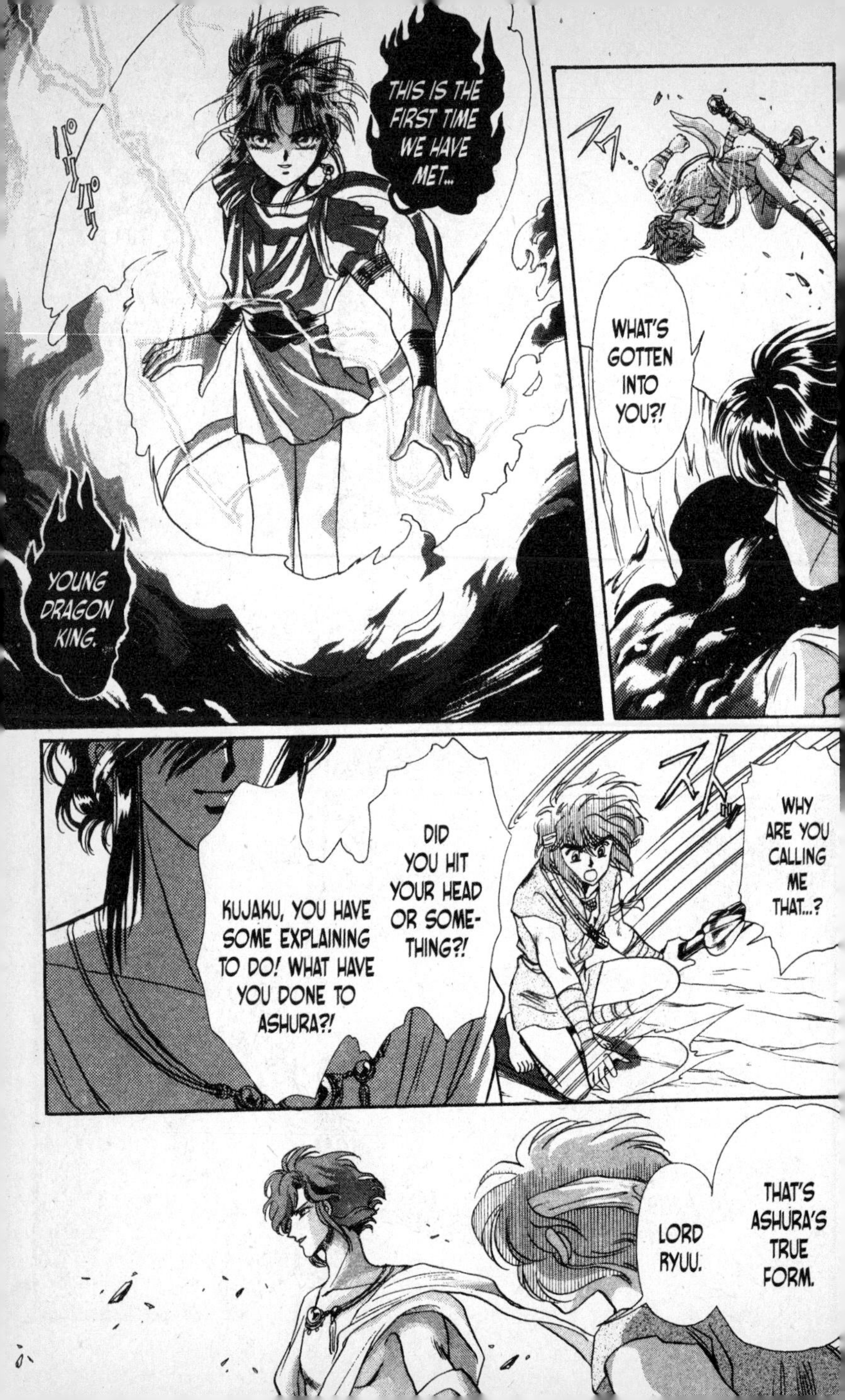
WHAT'S GOTTEN INTO YOU?!
THIS IS THE FIRST TIME WE HAVE MET...
YOUNG DRAGON KING.
WHY ARE YOU CALLING ME THAT...?
DID YOU HIT YOUR HEAD OR SOME-THING?!
KUJAKU, YOU HAVE SOME EXPLAINING TO DO! WHAT HAVE YOU DONE TO ASHURA?!
THAT'S ASHURA'S TRUE FORM.
LORD RYUU.

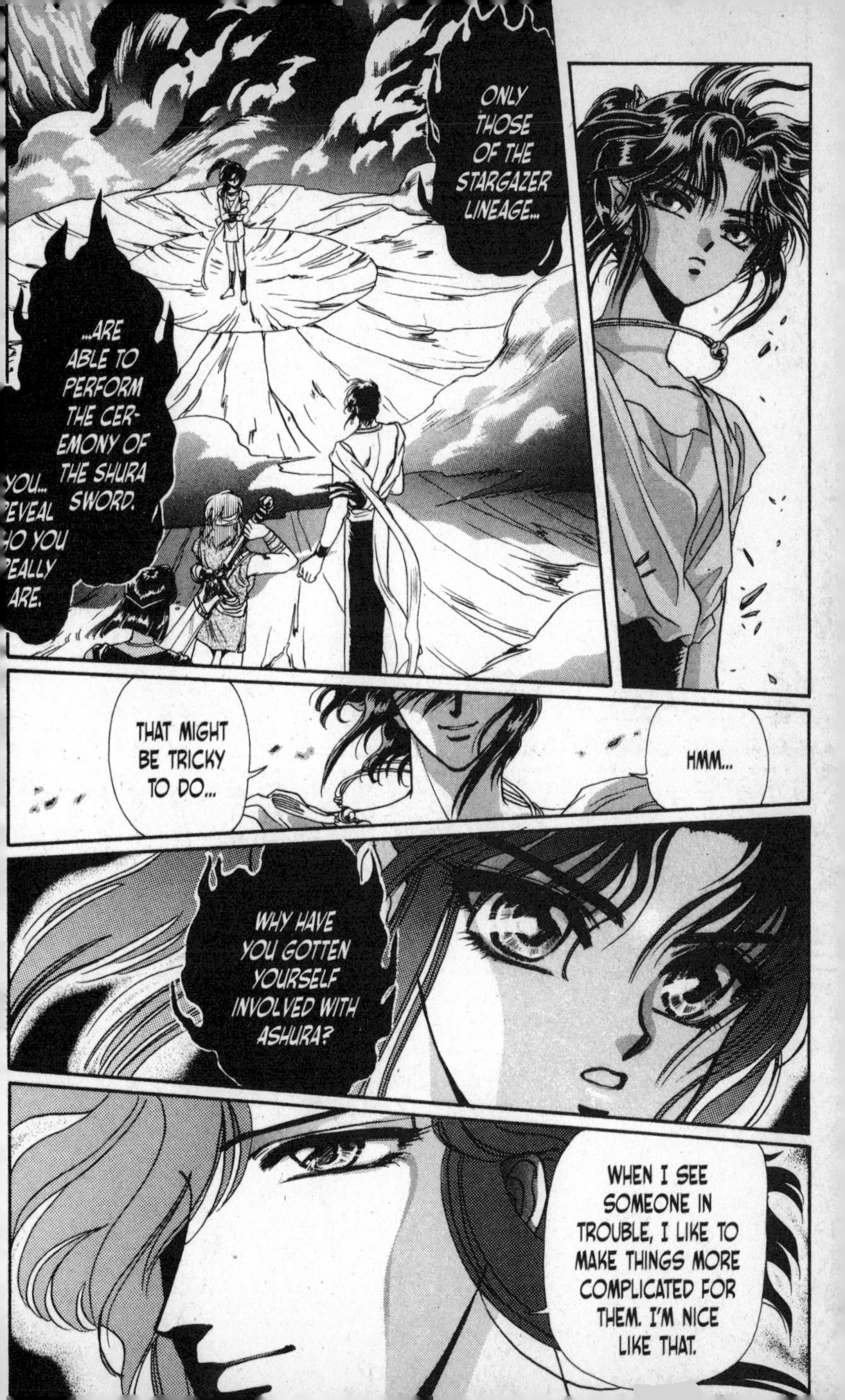
ONLY THOSE OF THE STARGAZER LINEAGE...
...ARE ABLE TO PERFORM THE CER-EMONY OF THE SHURA SWORD.
YOU... EVEAL HO YOU EALLY ARE.
HMM...
THAT MIGHT BE TRICKY TO DO...
WHY HAVE YOU GOTTEN YOURSELF INVOLVED WITH ASHURA?
WHEN I SEE SOMEONE IN TROUBLE, I LIKE TO MAKE THINGS MORE COMPLICATED FOR THEM. I'M NICE LIKE THAT.

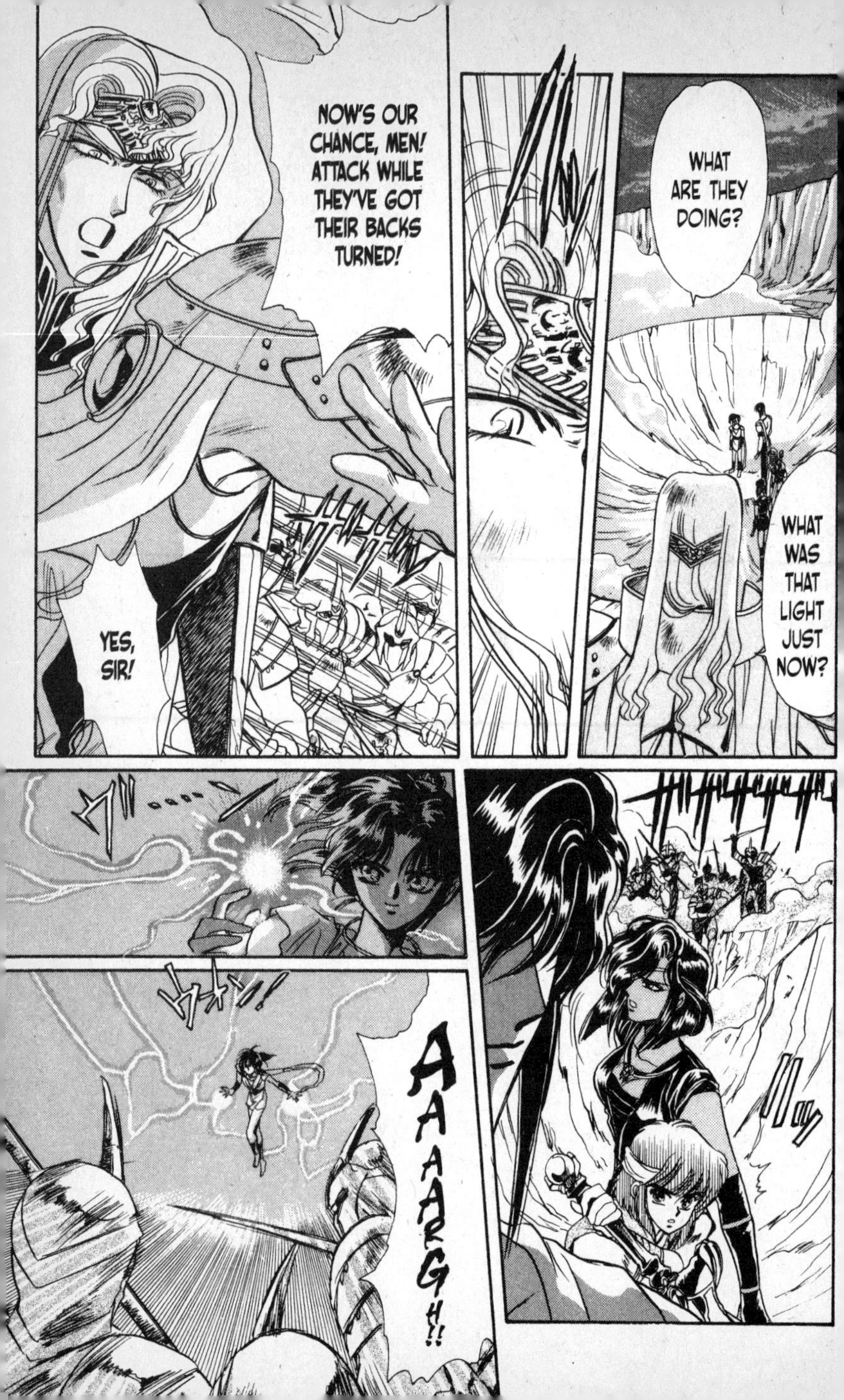
WHAT ARE THEY DOING?
WHAT WAS THAT LIGHT JUST NOW?
NOW'S OUR CHANCE, MEN! ATTACK WHILE THEY'VE GOT THEIR BACKS TURNED!
YES, SIR!
AAAAARGH!!

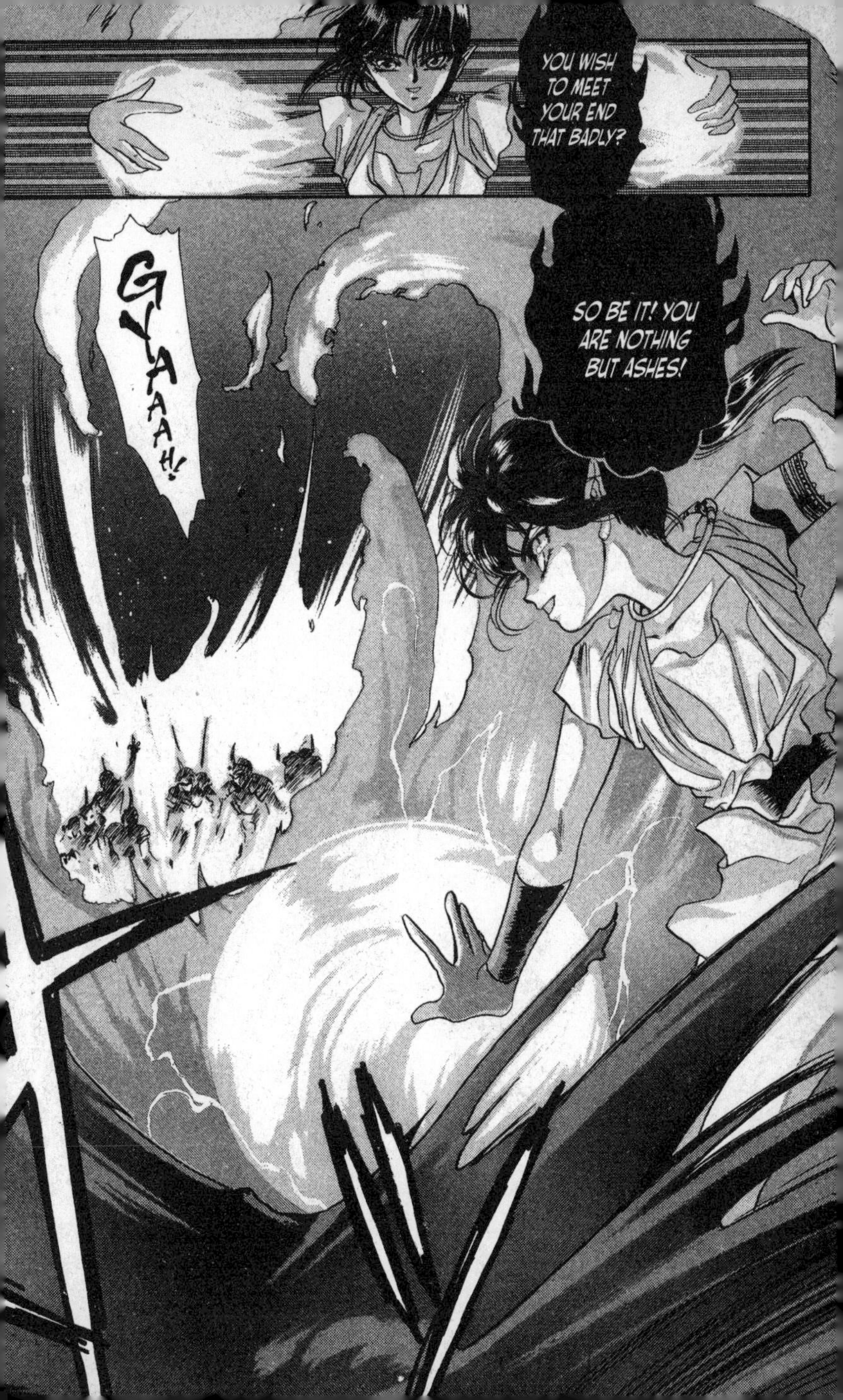
YOU WISH TO MEET YOUR END THAT BADLY?
SO BE IT! YOU ARE NOTHING BUT ASHES!
GYAAAAH!

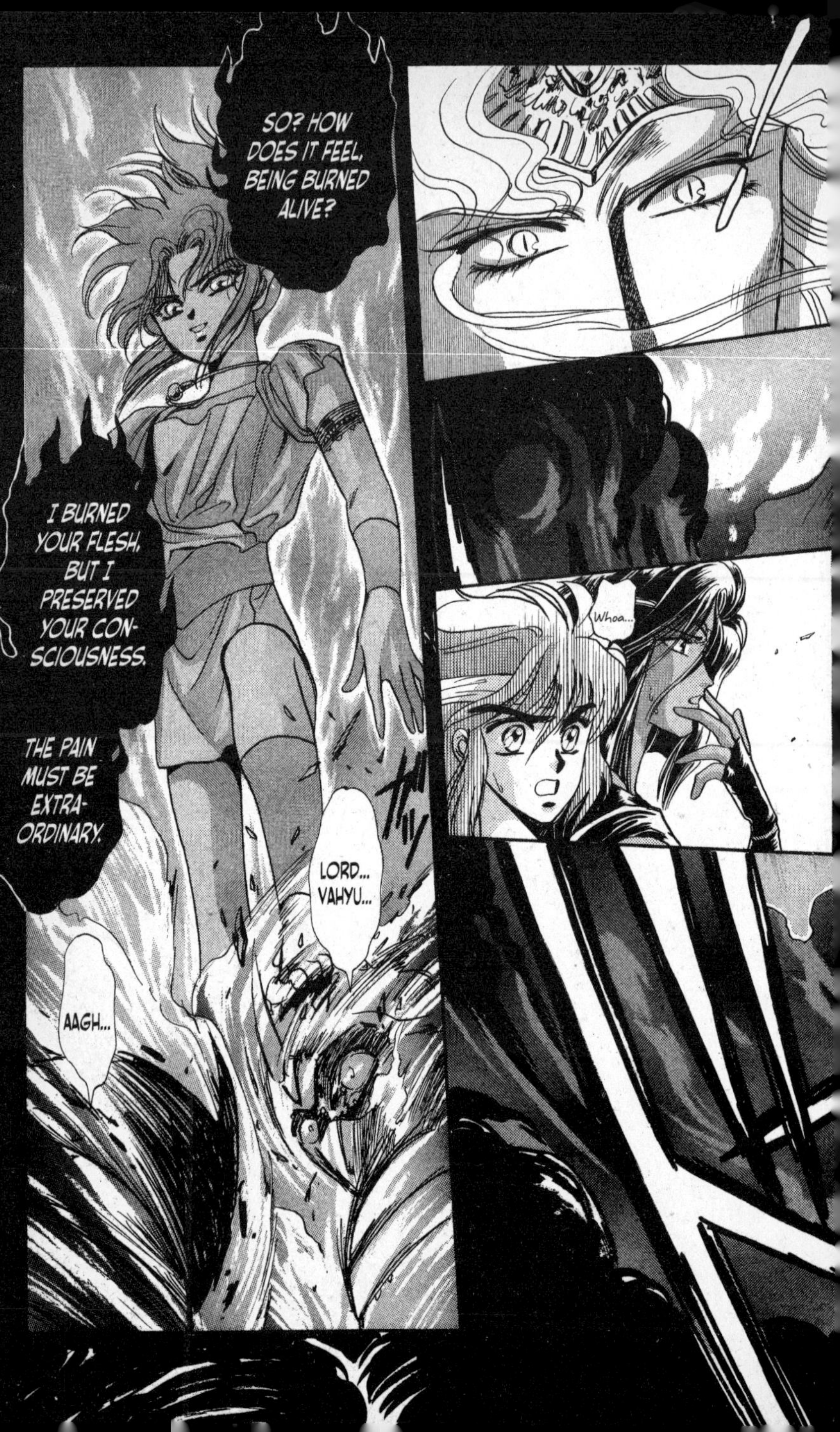
Whoa...
SO? HOW DOES IT FEEL, BEING BURNED ALIVE?
I BURNED YOUR FLESH, BUT I PRESERVED YOUR CONSCIOUSNESS.
THE PAIN MUST BE EXTRA-ORDINARY.
LORD... VAHYU...
AAGH...

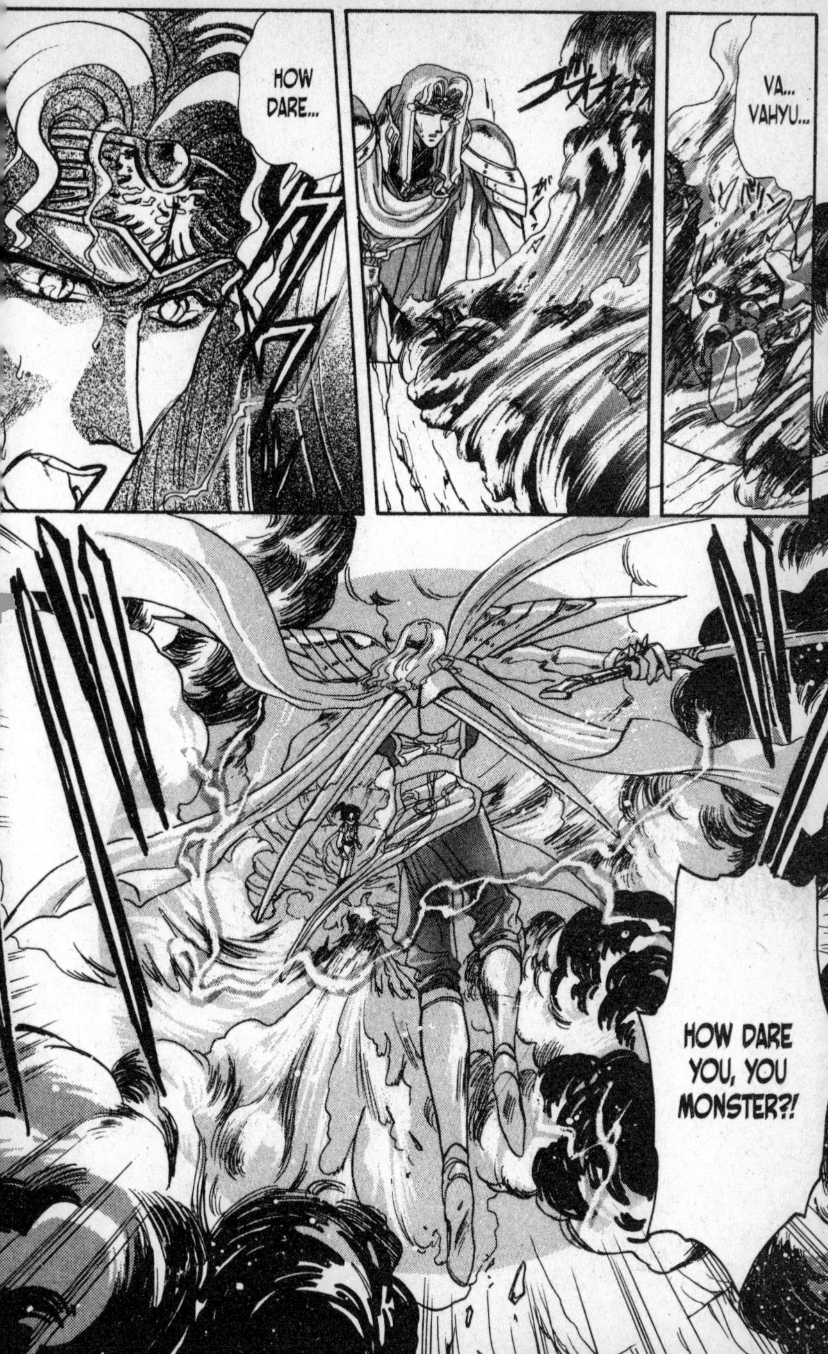
VA... VAHYU...
HOW DARE...
HOW DARE YOU, YOU MONSTER?!

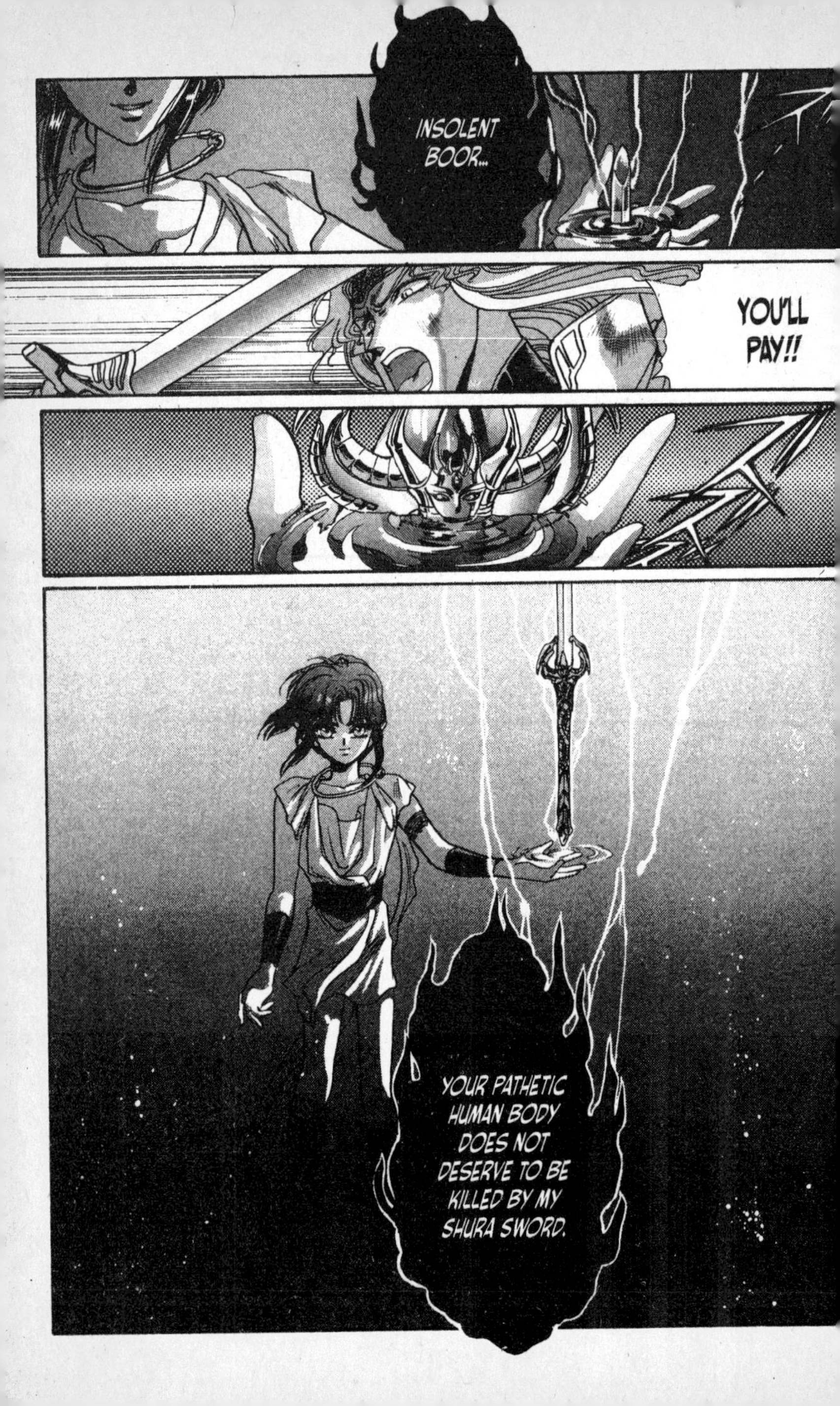
INSOLENT BOOR...
YOU'LL PAY!!
YOUR PATHETIC HUMAN BODY DOES NOT DESERVE TO BE KILLED BY MY SHURA SWORD.

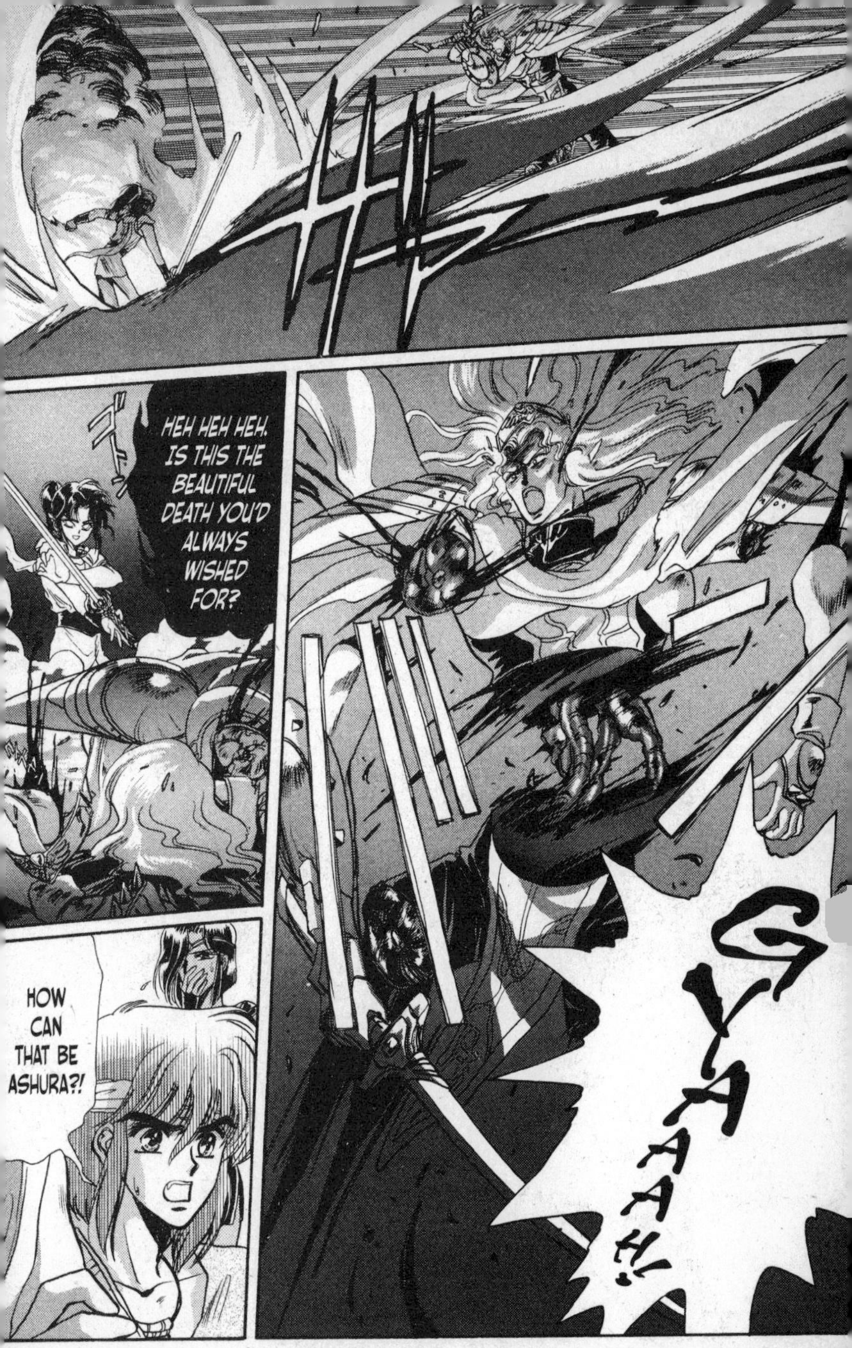
GYAAAAH?!
HEH HEH HEH. IS THIS THE BEAUTIFUL DEATH YOU'D ALWAYS WISHED FOR?
HOW CAN THAT BE ASHURA?!

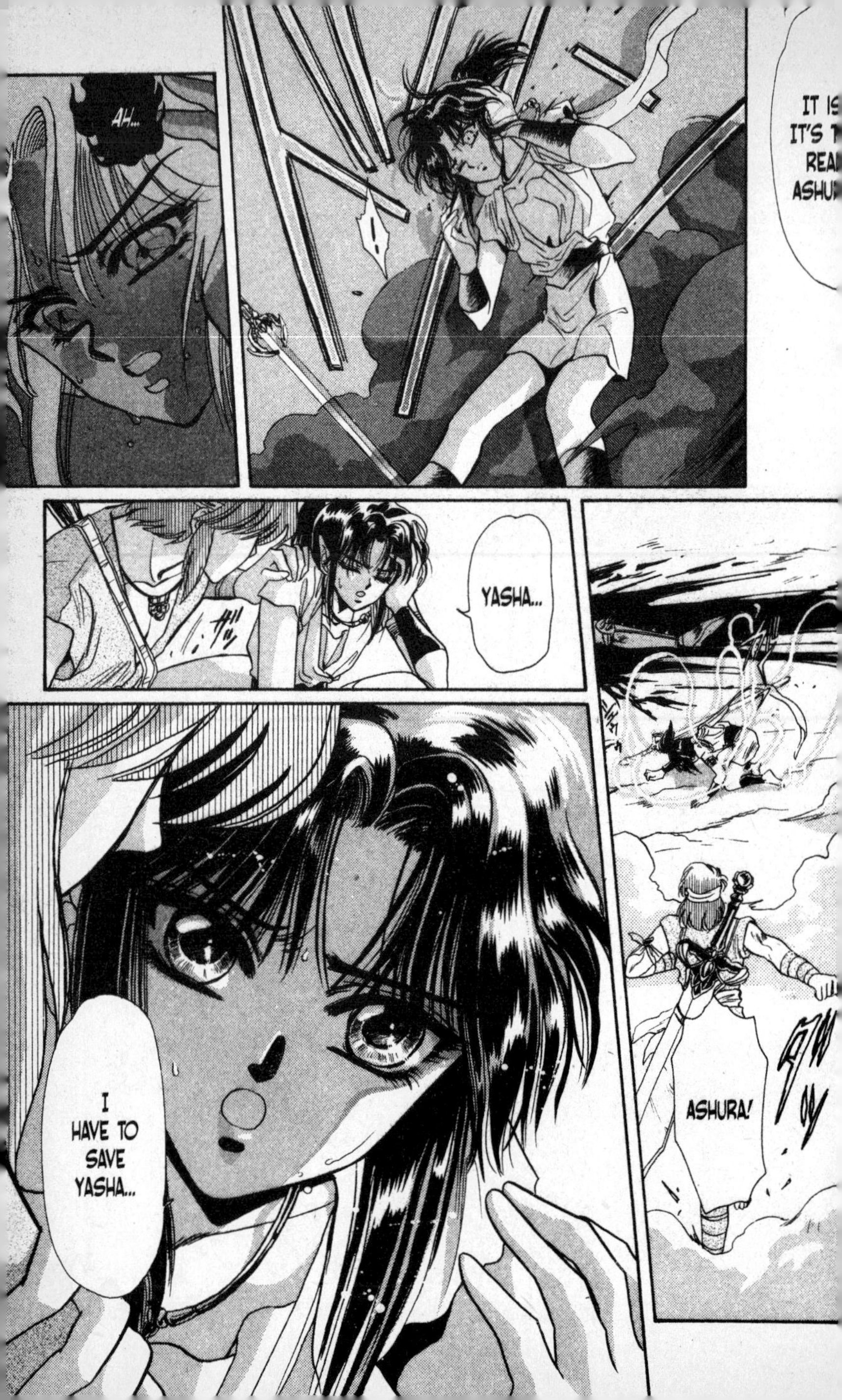
IT IS
IT'S T
REA
ASHUR
!
AH...
YASHA...
ASHURA!
I HAVE TO SAVE YASHA...

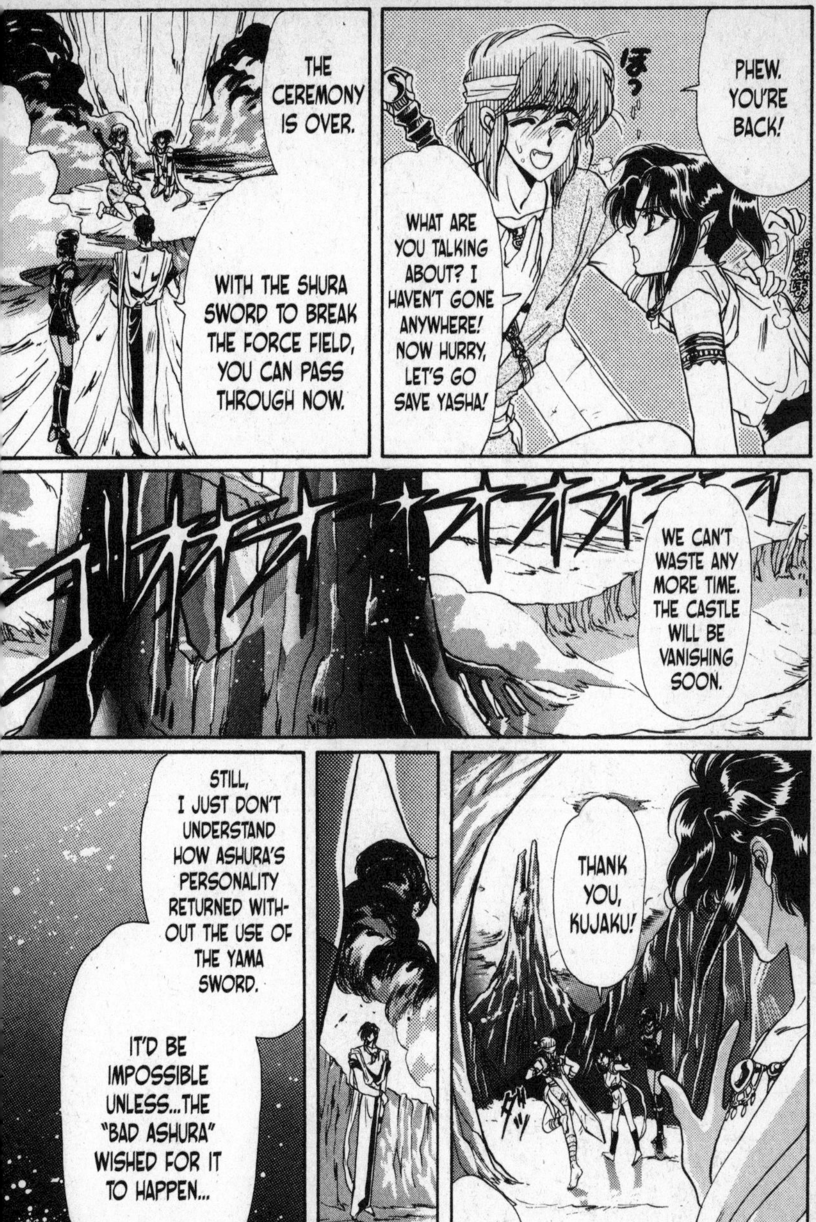
PHEW. YOU'RE BACK!
WHAT ARE YOU TALKING ABOUT? I HAVEN'T GONE ANYWHERE! NOW HURRY, LET'S GO SAVE YASHA!
THE CEREMONY IS OVER.
WITH THE SHURA SWORD TO BREAK THE FORCE FIELD, YOU CAN PASS THROUGH NOW.
WE CAN'T WASTE ANY MORE TIME. THE CASTLE WILL BE VANISHING SOON.
THANK YOU, KUJAKU!
STILL, I JUST DON'T UNDERSTAND HOW ASHURA'S PERSONALITY RETURNED WITH-OUT THE USE OF THE YAMA SWORD.
IT'D BE IMPOSSIBLE UNLESS...THE "BAD ASHURA" WISHED FOR IT TO HAPPEN...

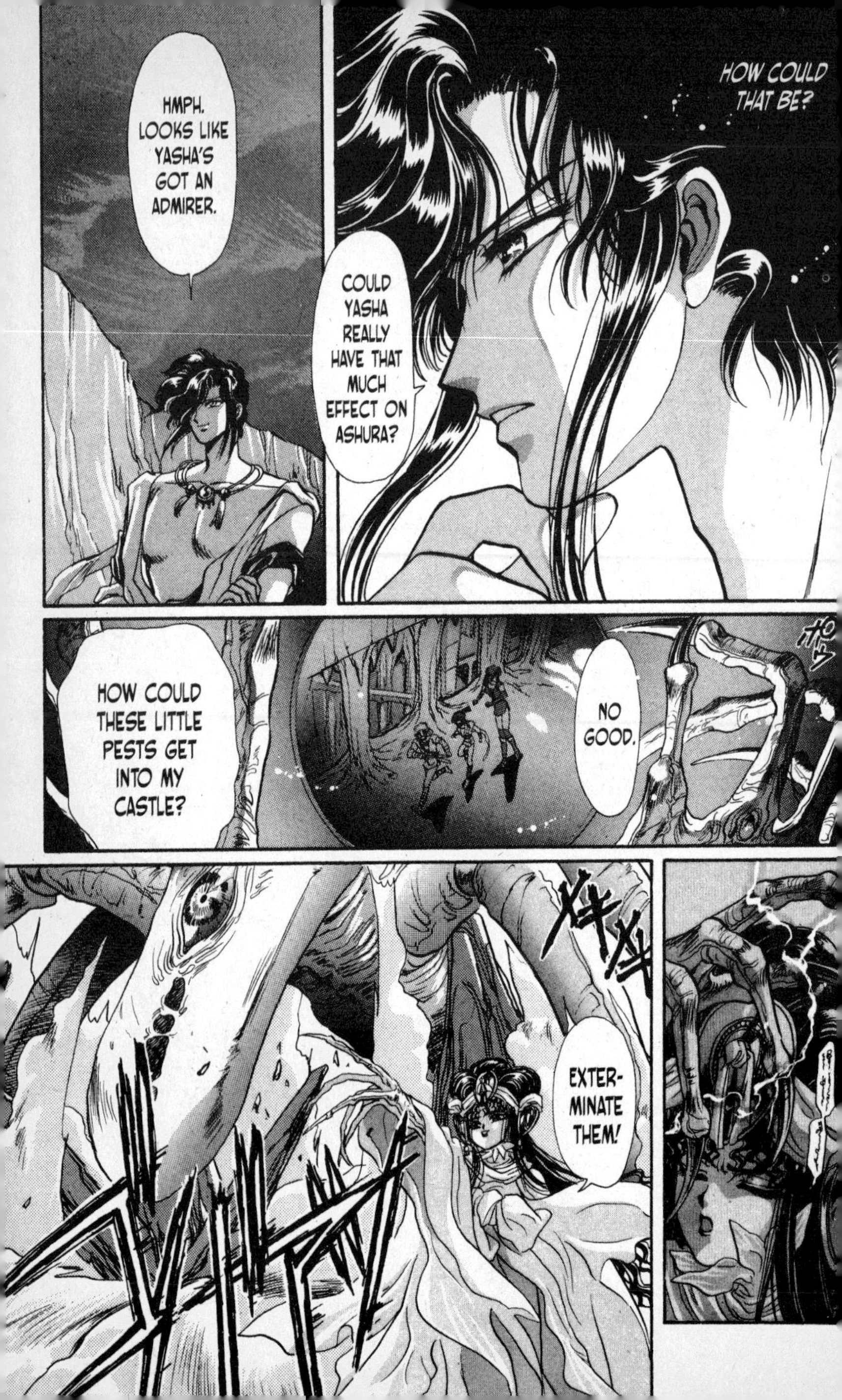
HOW COULD THAT BE?
COULD YASHA REALLY HAVE THAT MUCH EFFECT ON ASHURA?
HMPH. LOOKS LIKE YASHA'S GOT AN ADMIRER.
NO GOOD.
HOW COULD THESE LITTLE PESTS GET INTO MY CASTLE?
EXTER-MINATE THEM!

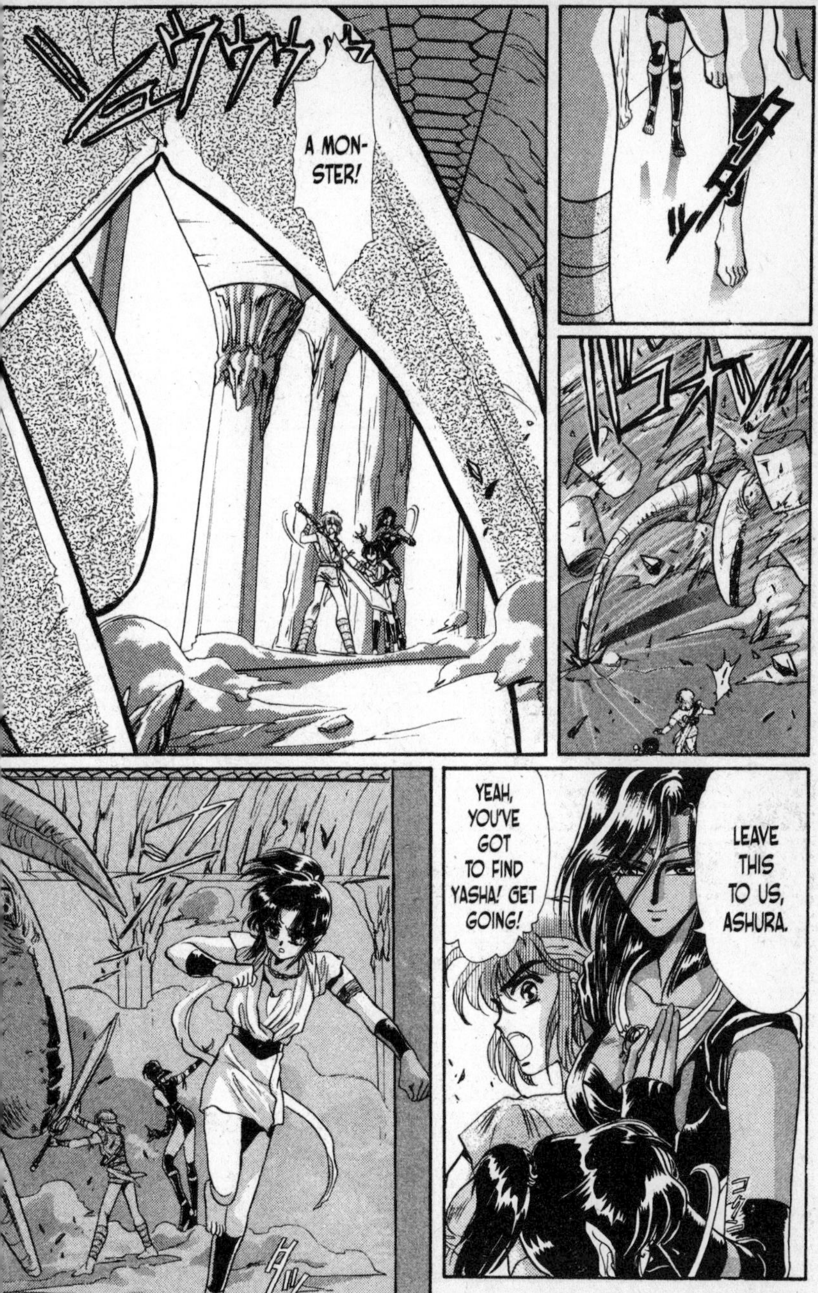
A MON-
STER!
LEAVE THIS TO US, ASHURA.
YEAH, YOU'VE GOT TO FIND YASHA! GET GOING!

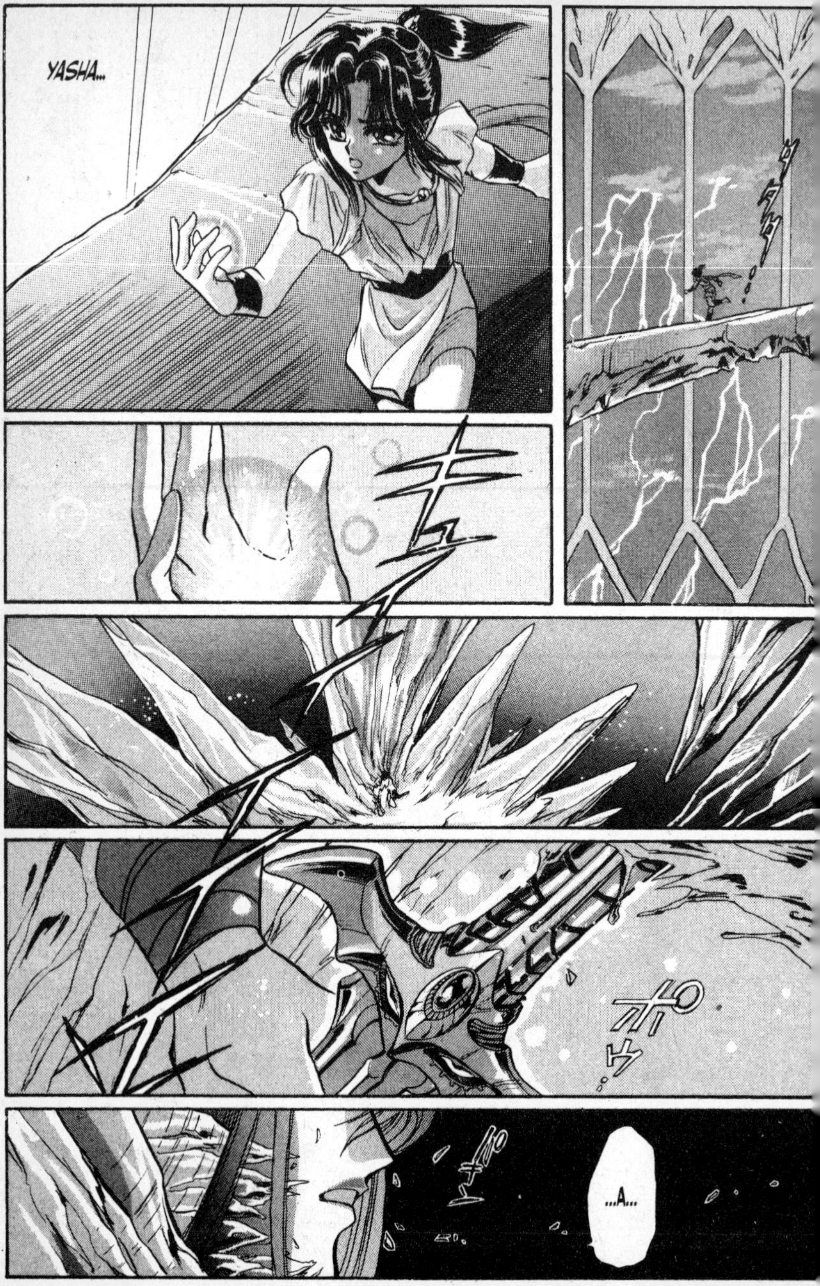
YASHA...
...A...

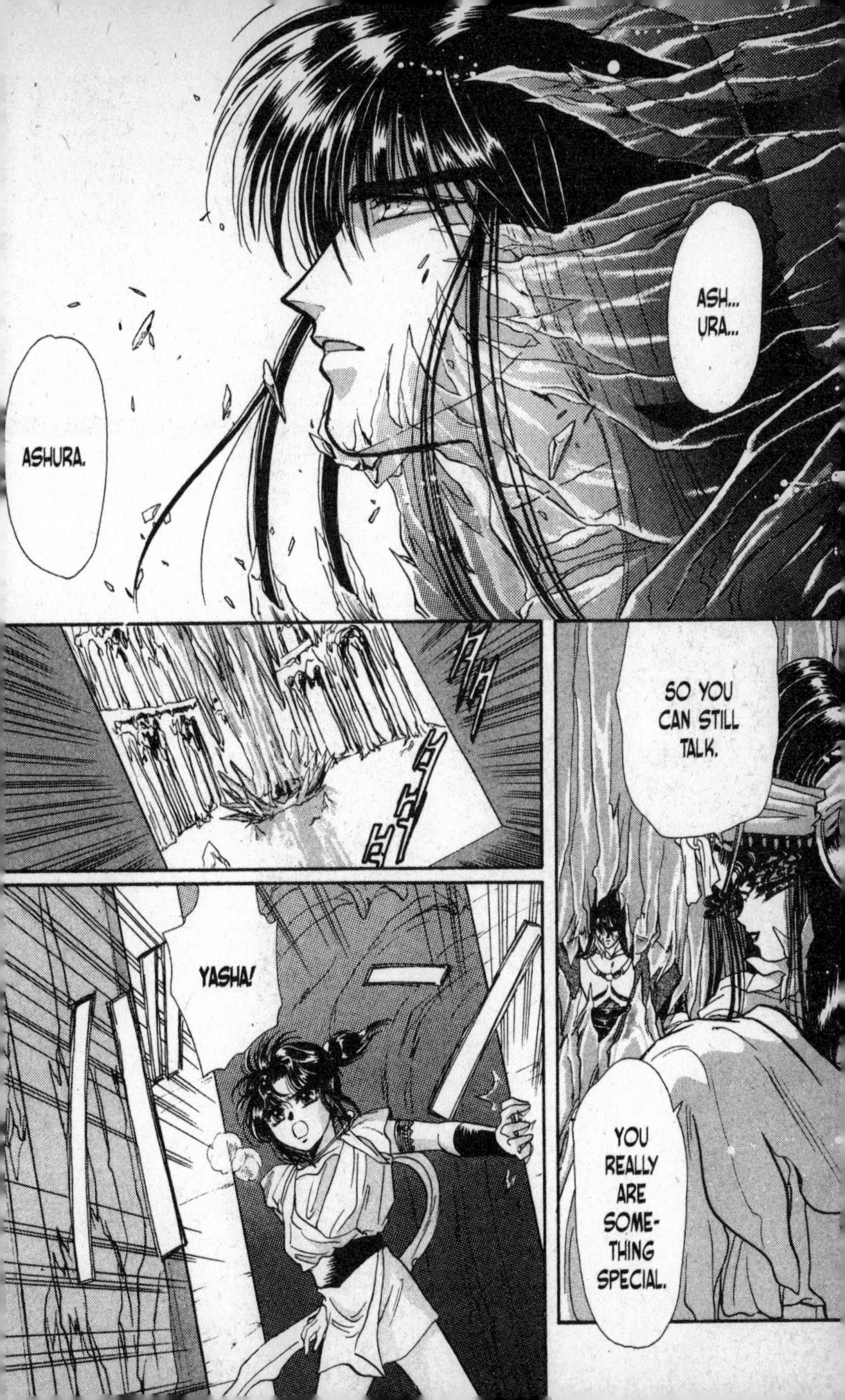
ASH... URA...
ASHURA.
SO YOU CAN STILL TALK.
YOU REALLY ARE SOME-THING SPECIAL.
YASHA!

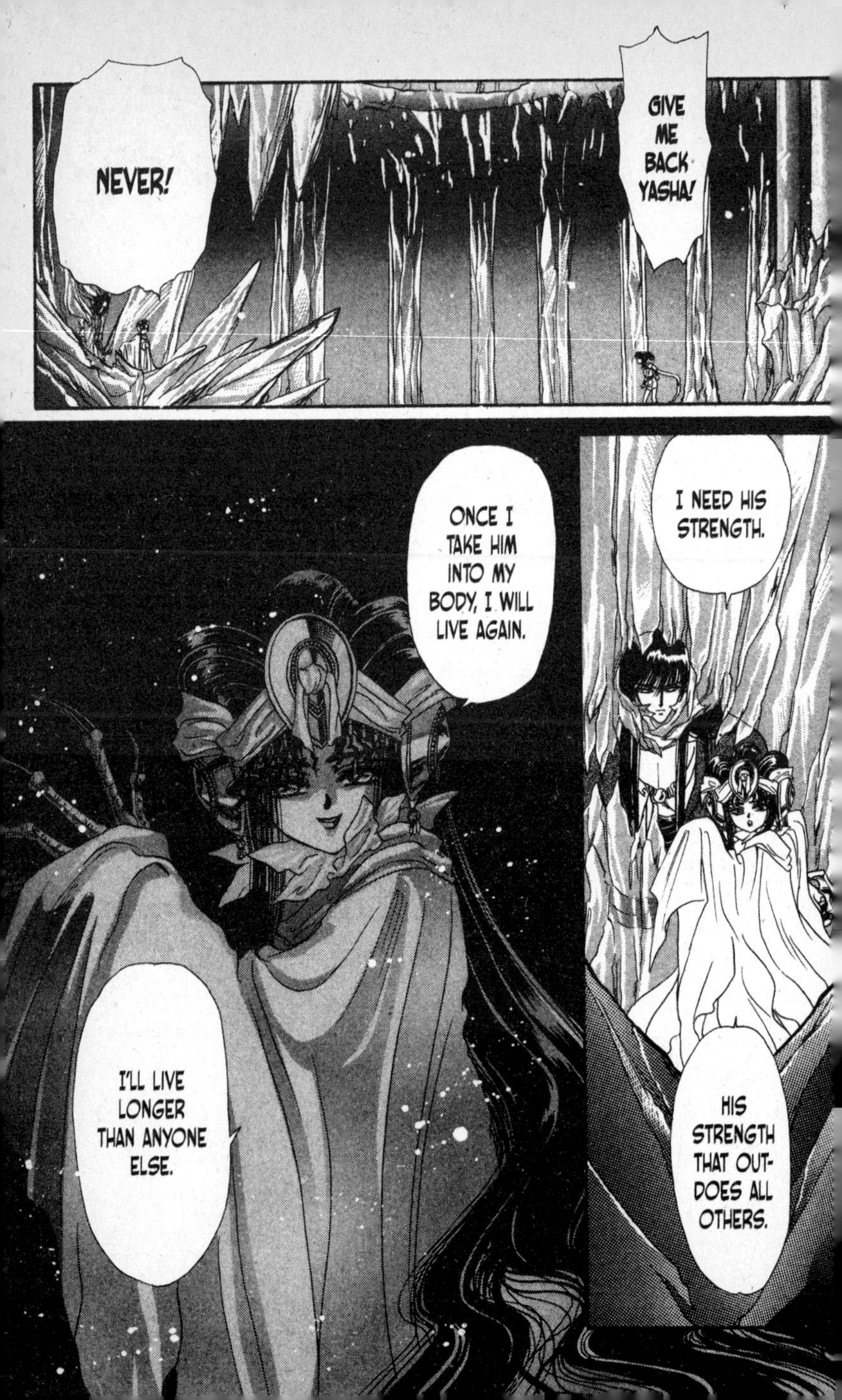
GIVE ME BACK YASHA!
NEVER!
I NEED HIS STRENGTH.
HIS STRENGTH THAT OUT-DOES ALL OTHERS.
ONCE I TAKE HIM INTO MY BODY, I WILL LIVE AGAIN.
I'LL LIVE LONGER THAN ANYONE ELSE.

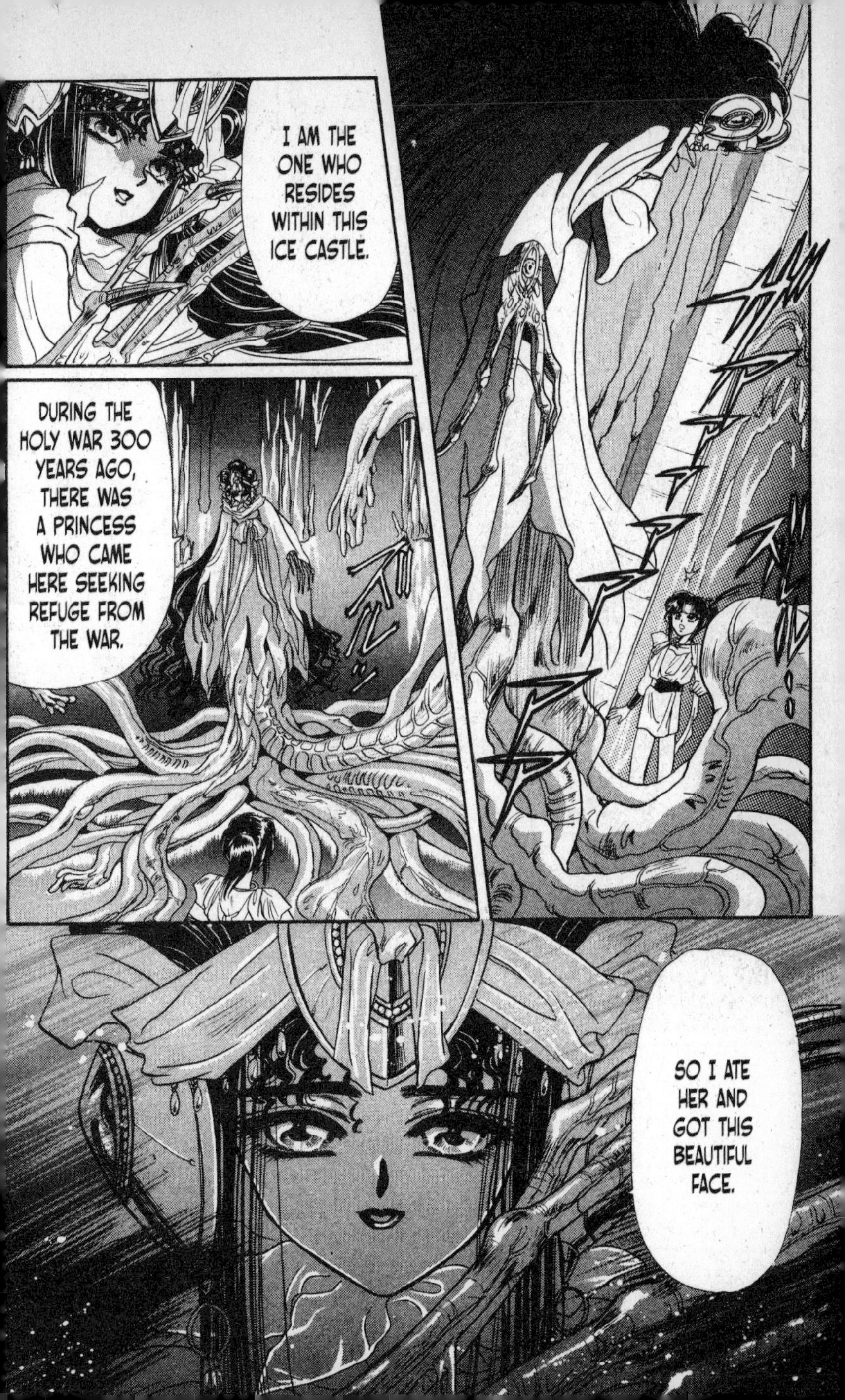
I AM THE ONE WHO RESIDES WITHIN THIS ICE CASTLE.
DURING THE HOLY WAR 300 YEARS AGO, THERE WAS A PRINCESS WHO CAME HERE SEEKING REFUGE FROM THE WAR.
SO I ATE HER AND GOT THIS BEAUTIFUL FACE.

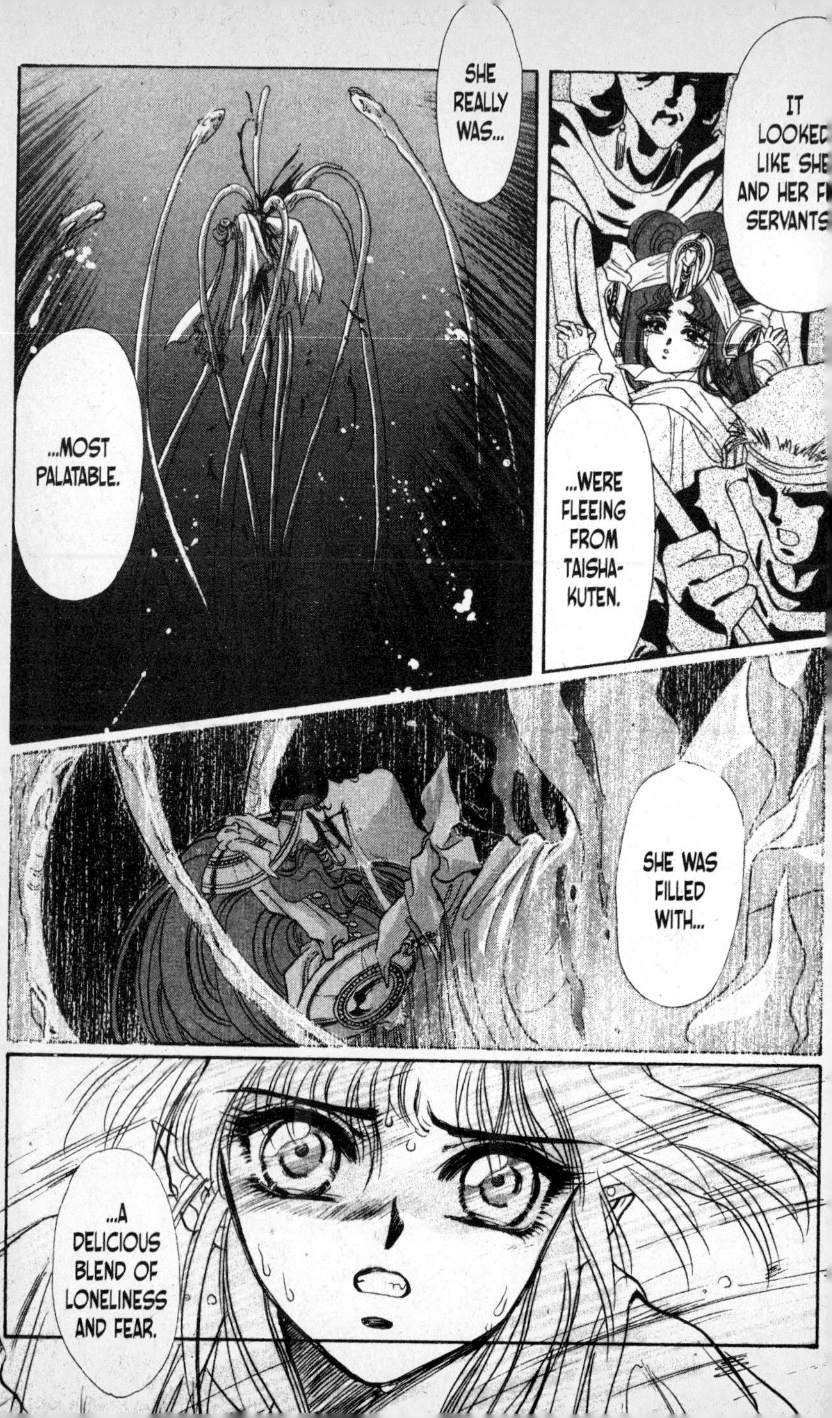
IT LOOKED LIKE SHE AND HER SERVANTS
...WERE FLEEING FROM TAISHA-KUTEN.
SHE REALLY WAS...
...MOST PALATABLE.
SHE WAS FILLED WITH...
...A DELICIOUS BLEND OF LONELINESS AND FEAR.

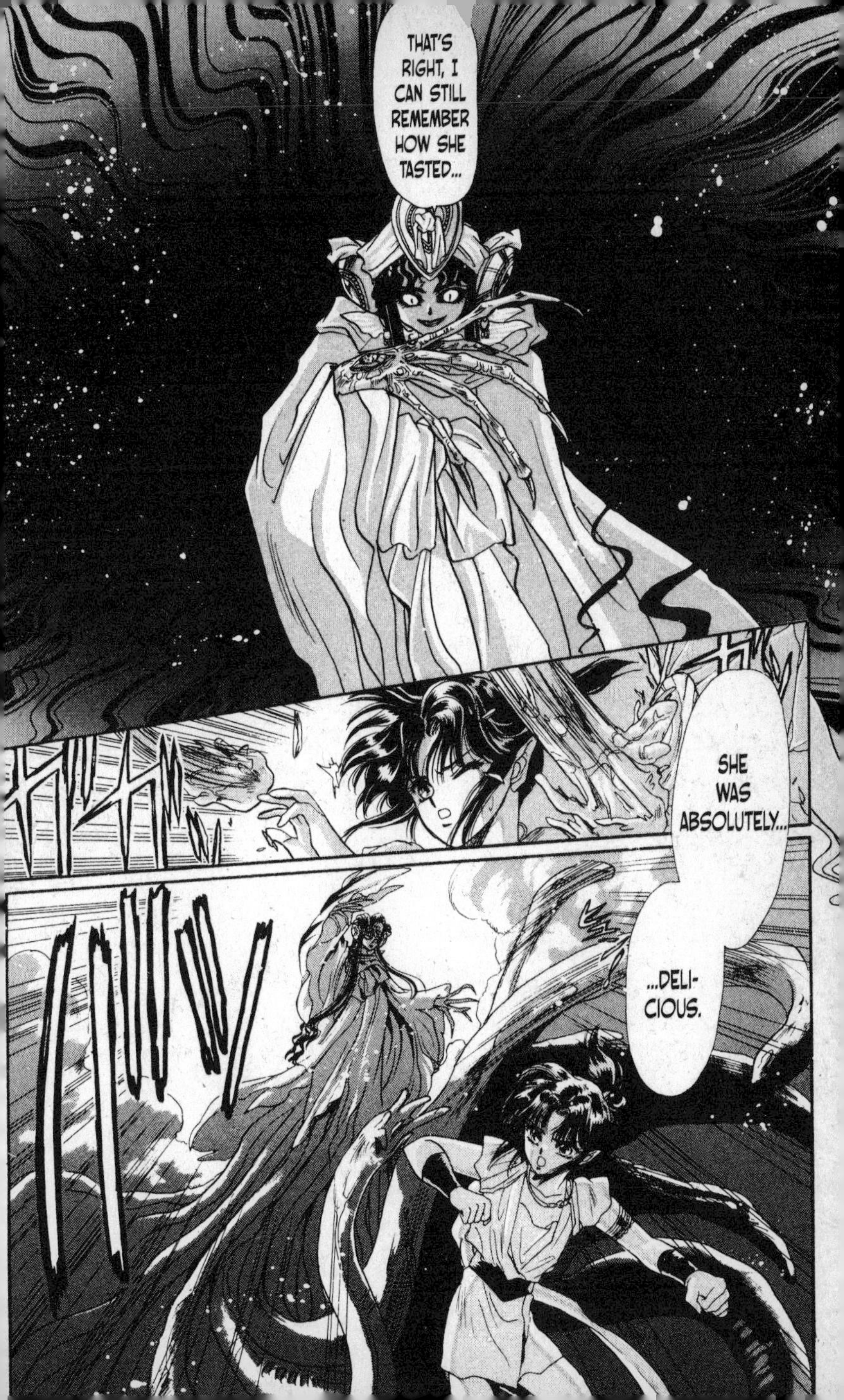
THAT'S RIGHT, I CAN STILL REMEMBER HOW SHE TASTED...
SHE WAS ABSOLUTELY...
...DELI-CIOUS.

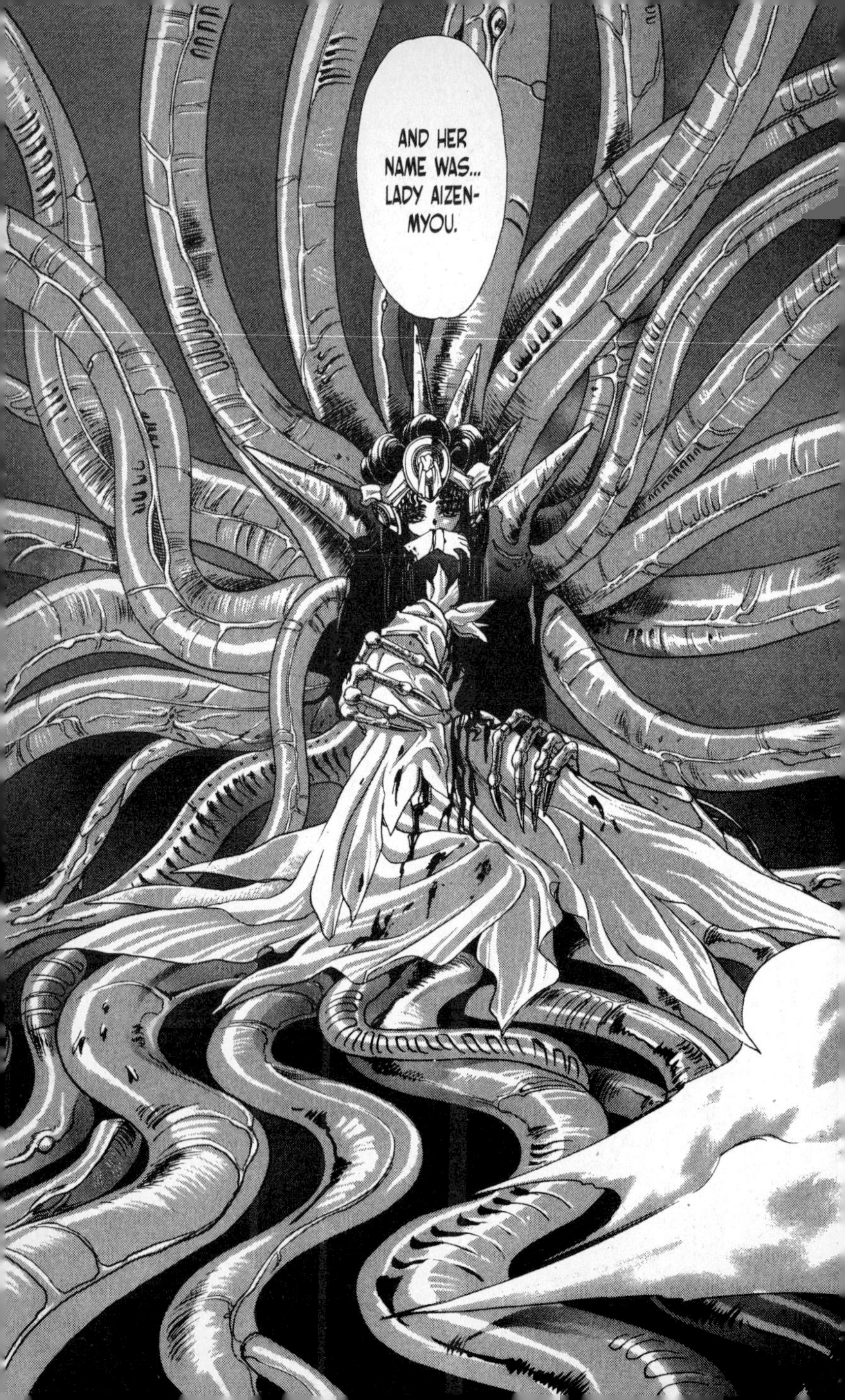
AND HER NAME WAS... LADY AIZEN-MYOU.

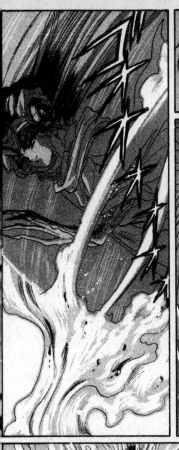

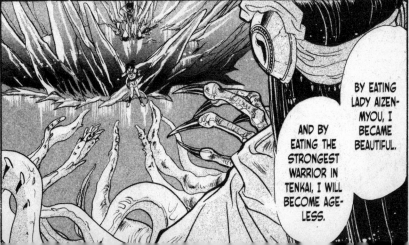

BY EATING LADY AIZEN-MYOU, I BECAME BEAUTIFUL.

AND BY EATING THE STRONGEST WARRIOR IN TENKAI, I WILL BECOME AGE-LESS.

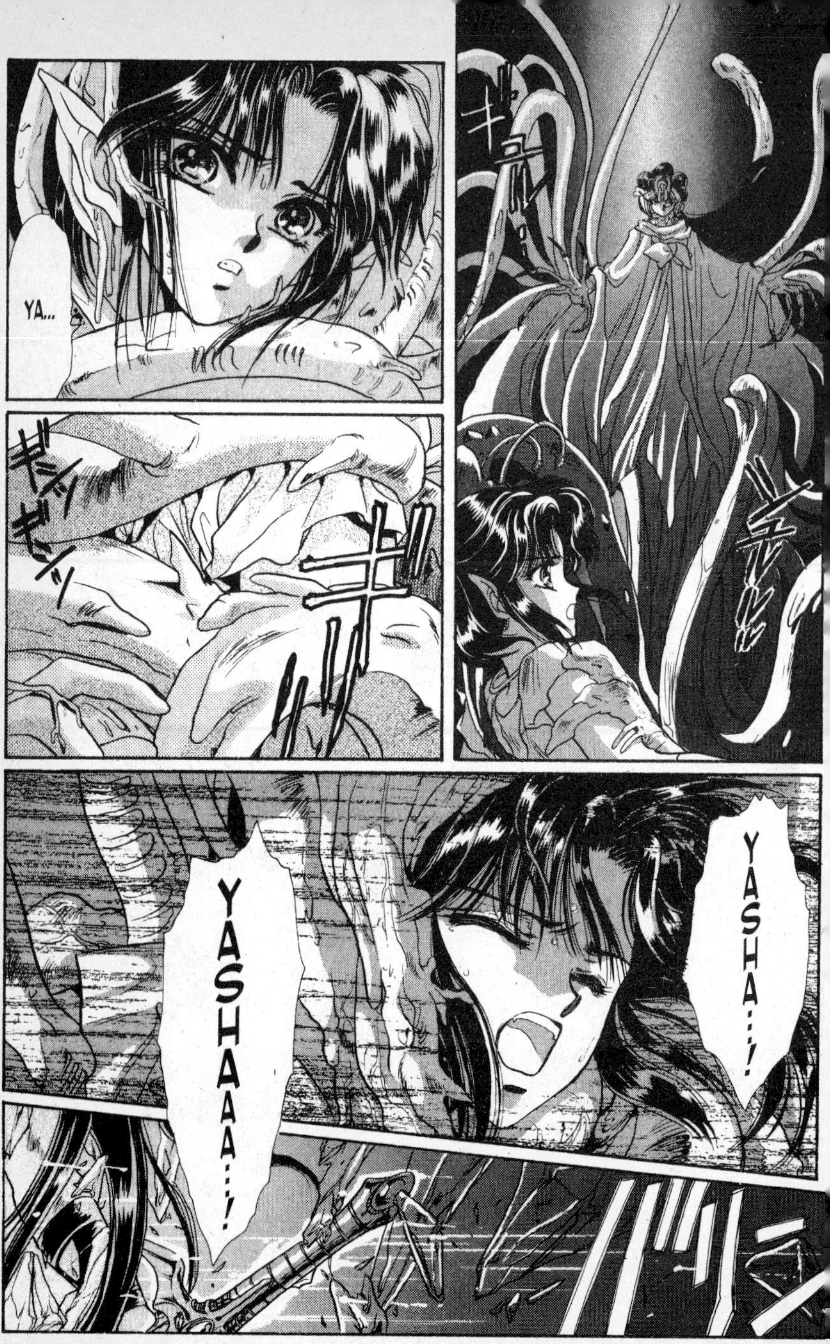
YA...
YASHA...!
YASHAAAA...!

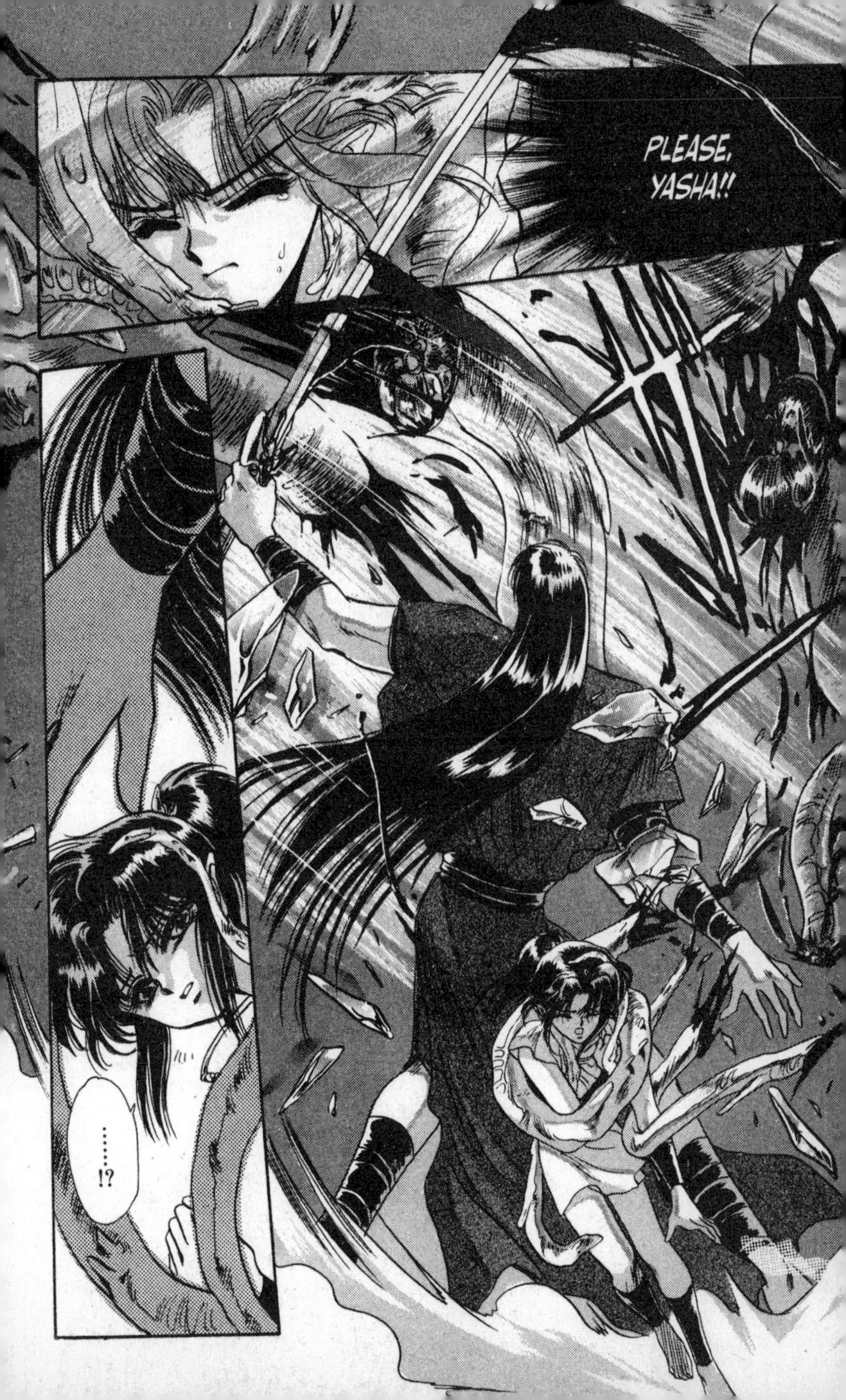
PLEASE, YASHA!!
……!?

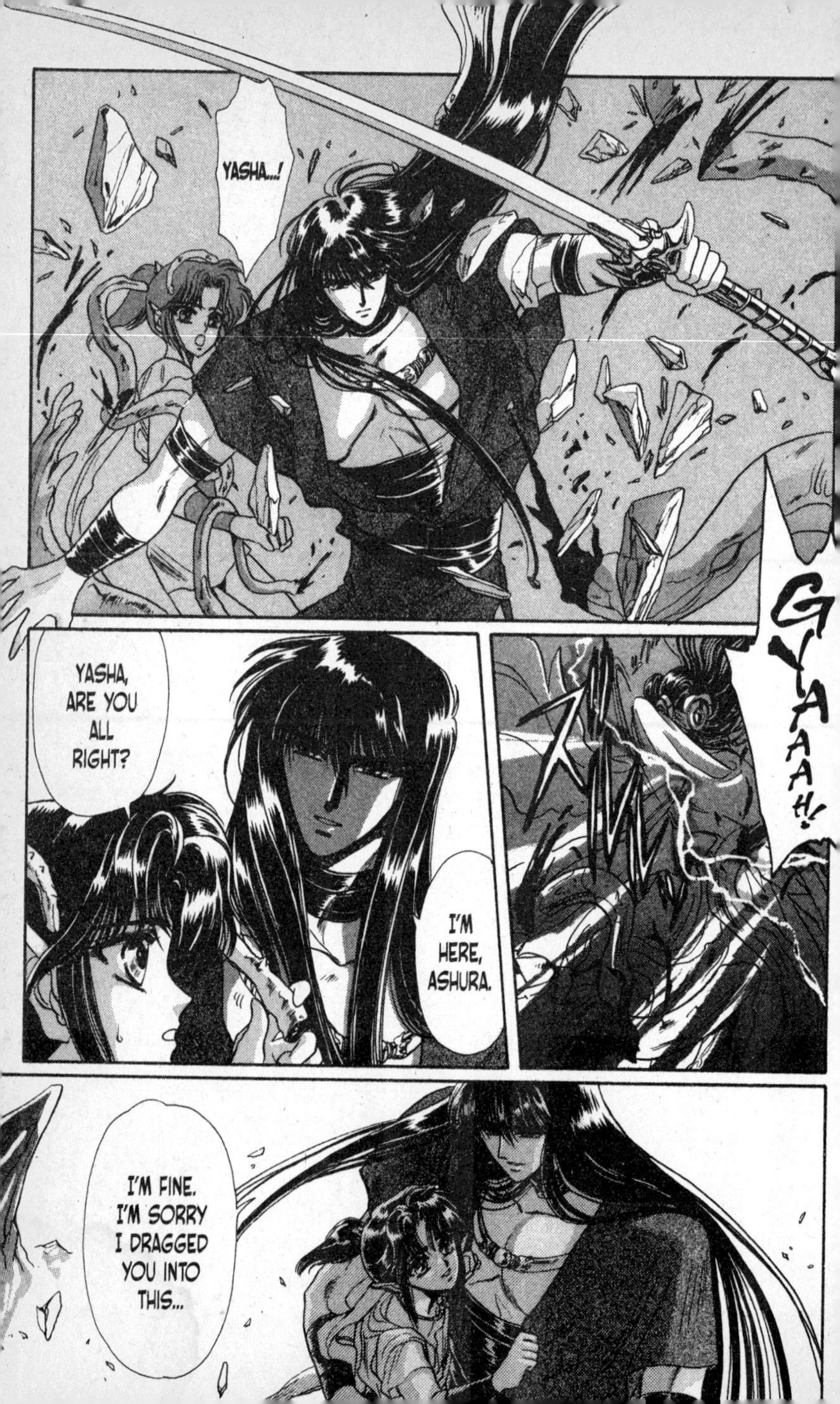
YASHA...!
GYAAAAH!
YASHA, ARE YOU ALL RIGHT?
I'M HERE, ASHURA.
I'M FINE. I'M SORRY I DRAGGED YOU INTO THIS...

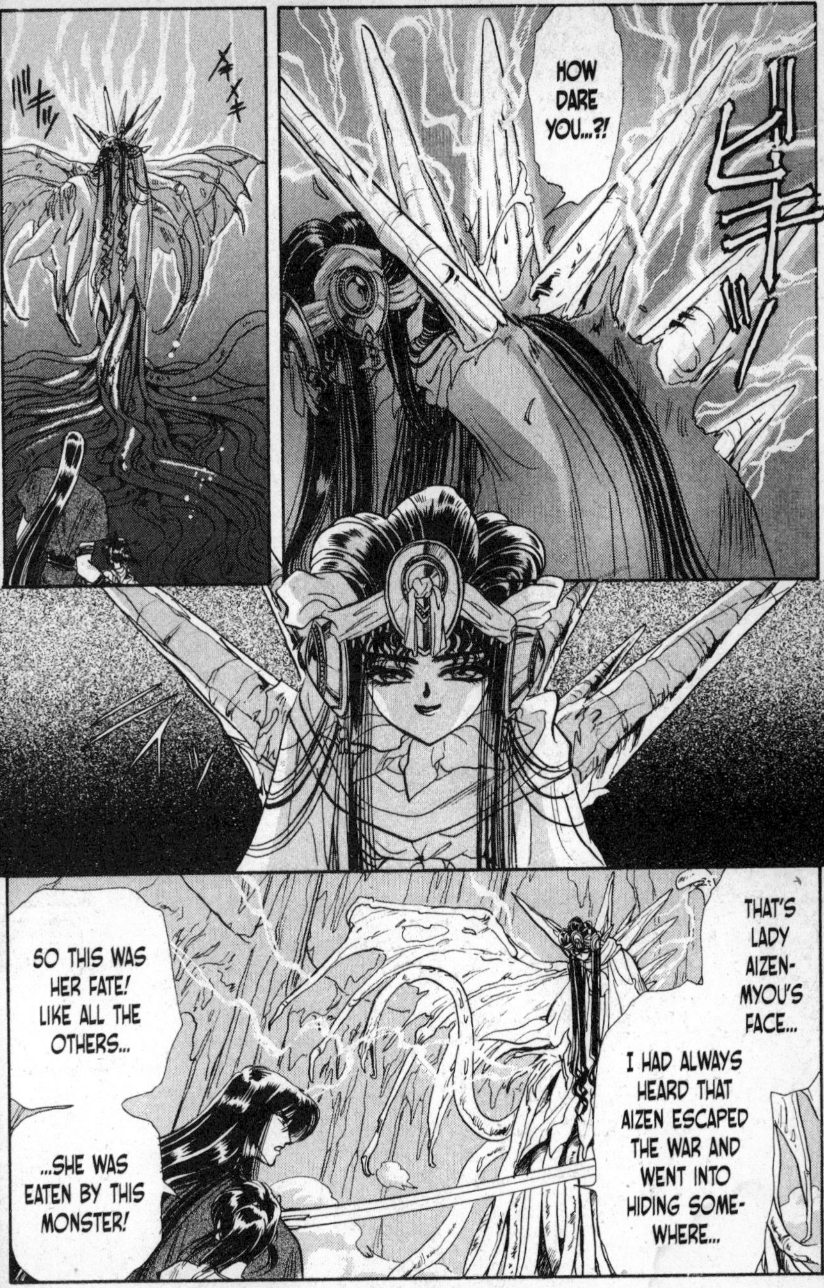
HOW DARE YOU...?!
ビキッ
メキメキ
バキッ
THAT'S LADY AIZEN-MYOU'S FACE...
I HAD ALWAYS HEARD THAT AIZEN ESCAPED THE WAR AND WENT INTO HIDING SOME-WHERE...
SO THIS WAS HER FATE! LIKE ALL THE OTHERS...
...SHE WAS EATEN BY THIS MONSTER!

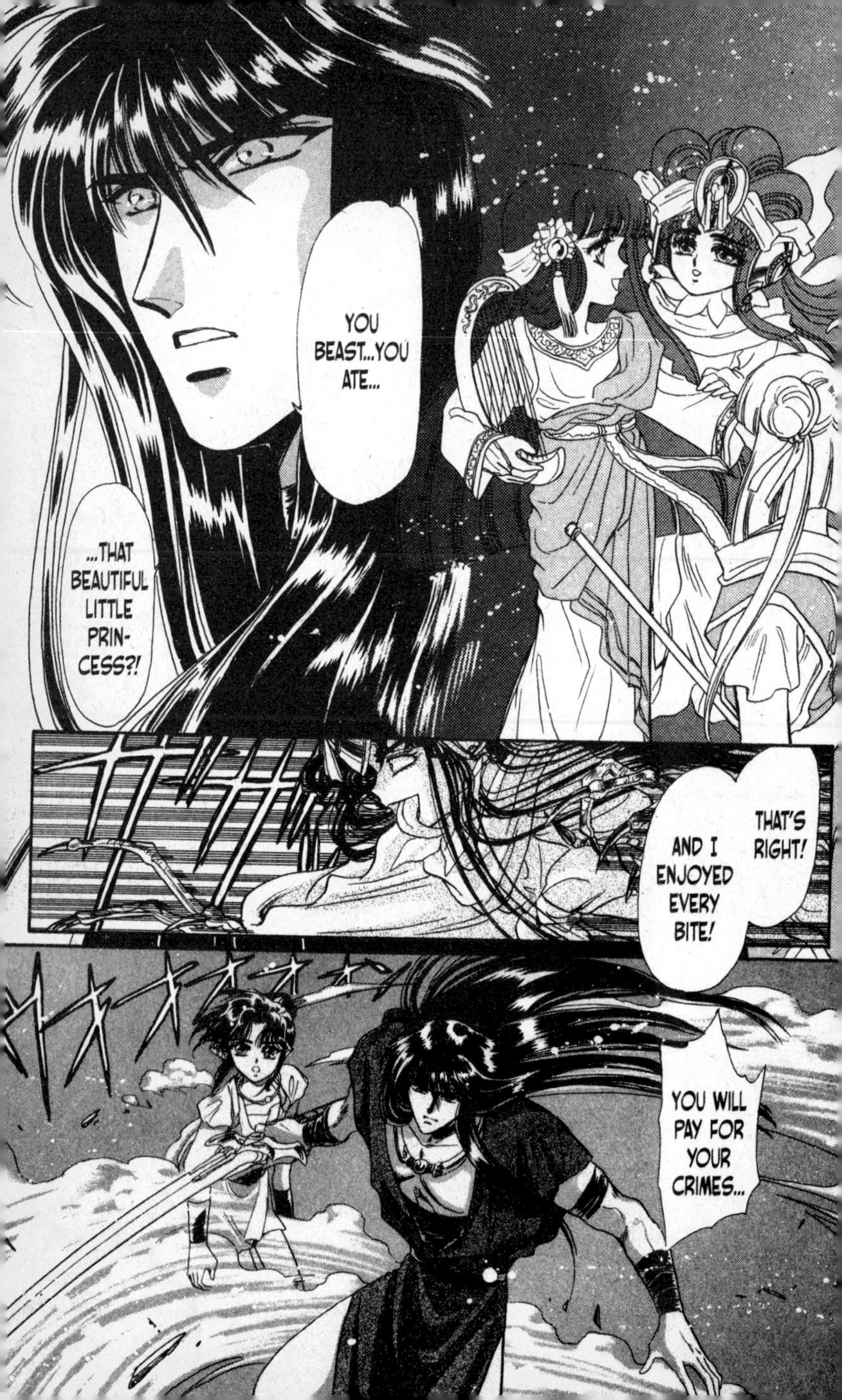
YOU BEAST...YOU ATE...
...THAT BEAUTIFUL LITTLE PRIN-CESS?!
THAT'S RIGHT!
AND I ENJOYED EVERY BITE!
YOU WILL PAY FOR YOUR CRIMES...

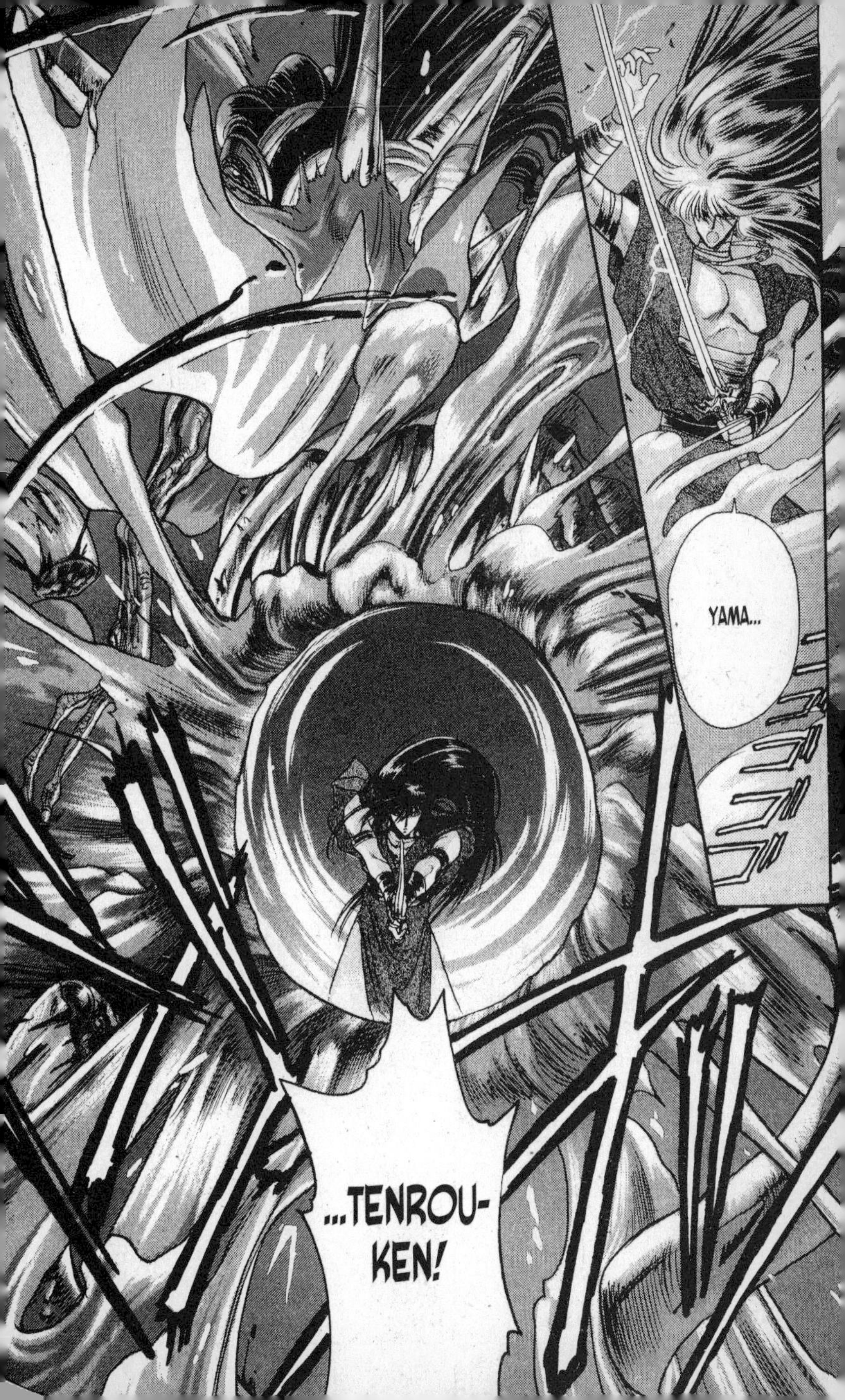
YAMA...
...TENROU-KEN!

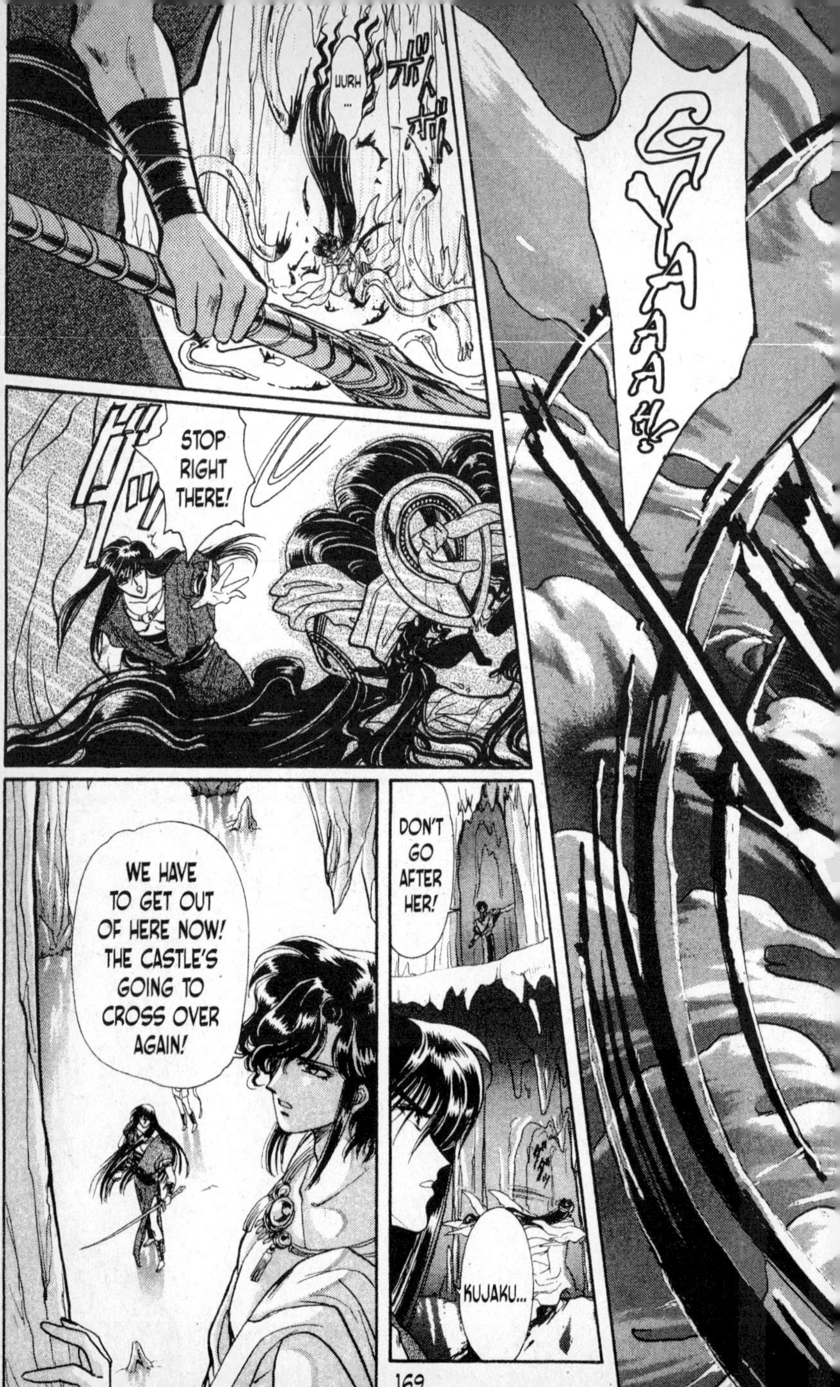
GYAAAAH!!
UURH ...
STOP RIGHT THERE!
DON'T GO AFTER HER!
KUJAKU...
WE HAVE TO GET OUT OF HERE NOW! THE CASTLE'S GOING TO CROSS OVER AGAIN!

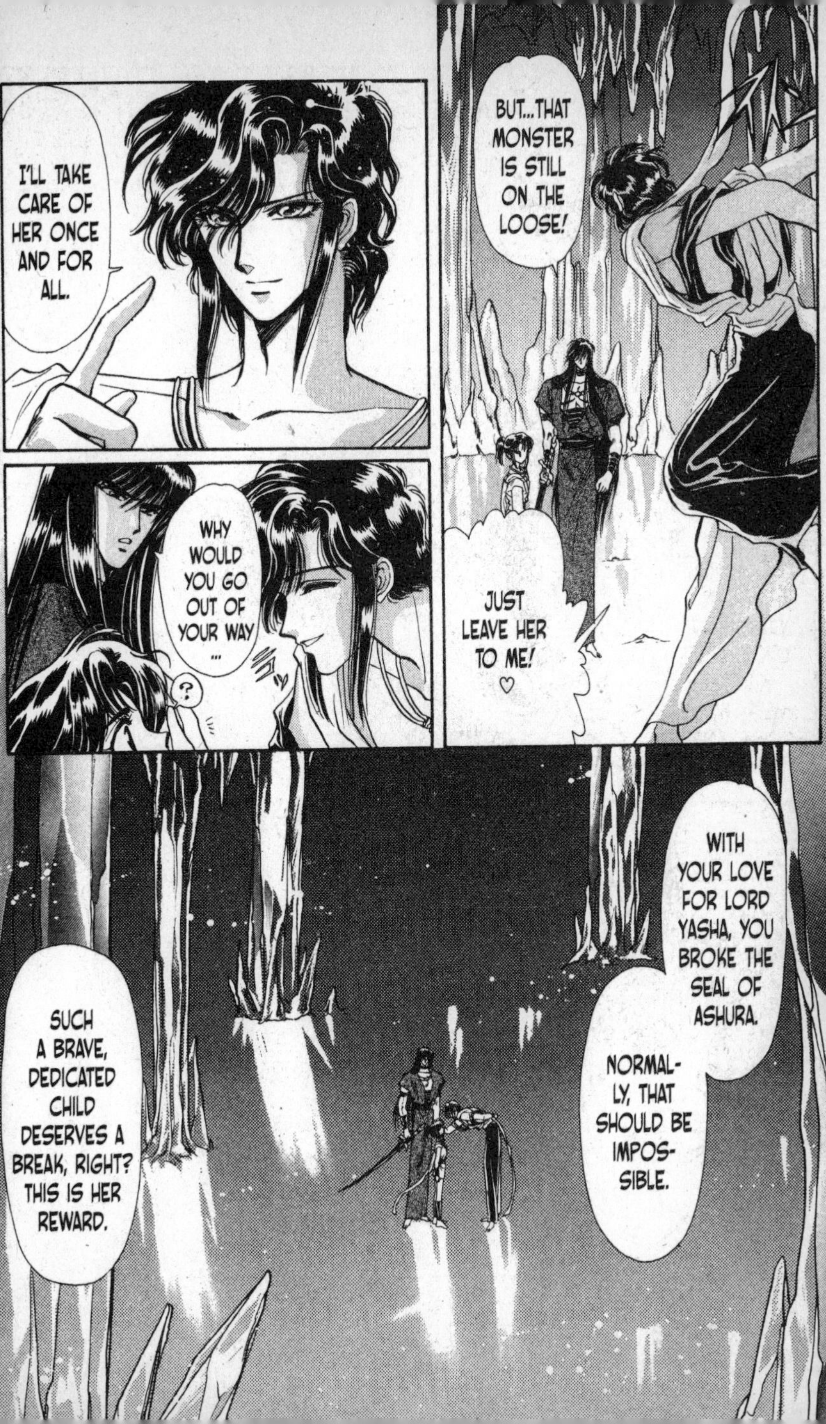
BUT...THAT MONSTER IS STILL ON THE LOOSE!
JUST LEAVE HER TO ME! ♡
I'LL TAKE CARE OF HER ONCE AND FOR ALL.
WHY WOULD YOU GO OUT OF YOUR WAY ...
?
WITH YOUR LOVE FOR LORD YASHA, YOU BROKE THE SEAL OF ASHURA.
NORMAL-LY, THAT SHOULD BE IMPOS-SIBLE.
SUCH A BRAVE, DEDICATED CHILD DESERVES A BREAK, RIGHT? THIS IS HER REWARD.

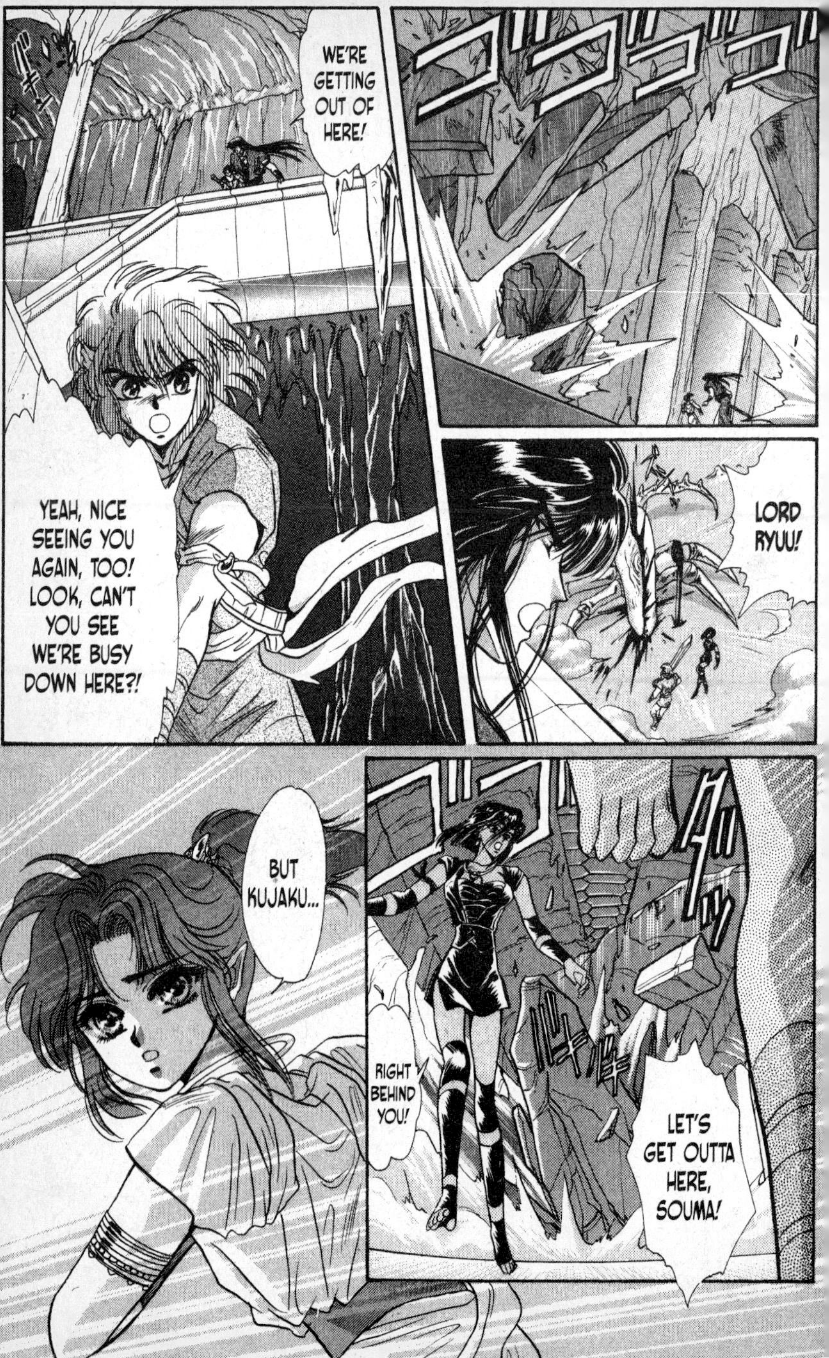
LORD RYUU!
WE'RE GETTING OUT OF HERE!
YEAH, NICE SEEING YOU AGAIN, TOO! LOOK, CAN'T YOU SEE WE'RE BUSY DOWN HERE?!
LET'S GET OUTTA HERE, SOUMA!
RIGHT BEHIND YOU!
BUT KUJAKU...

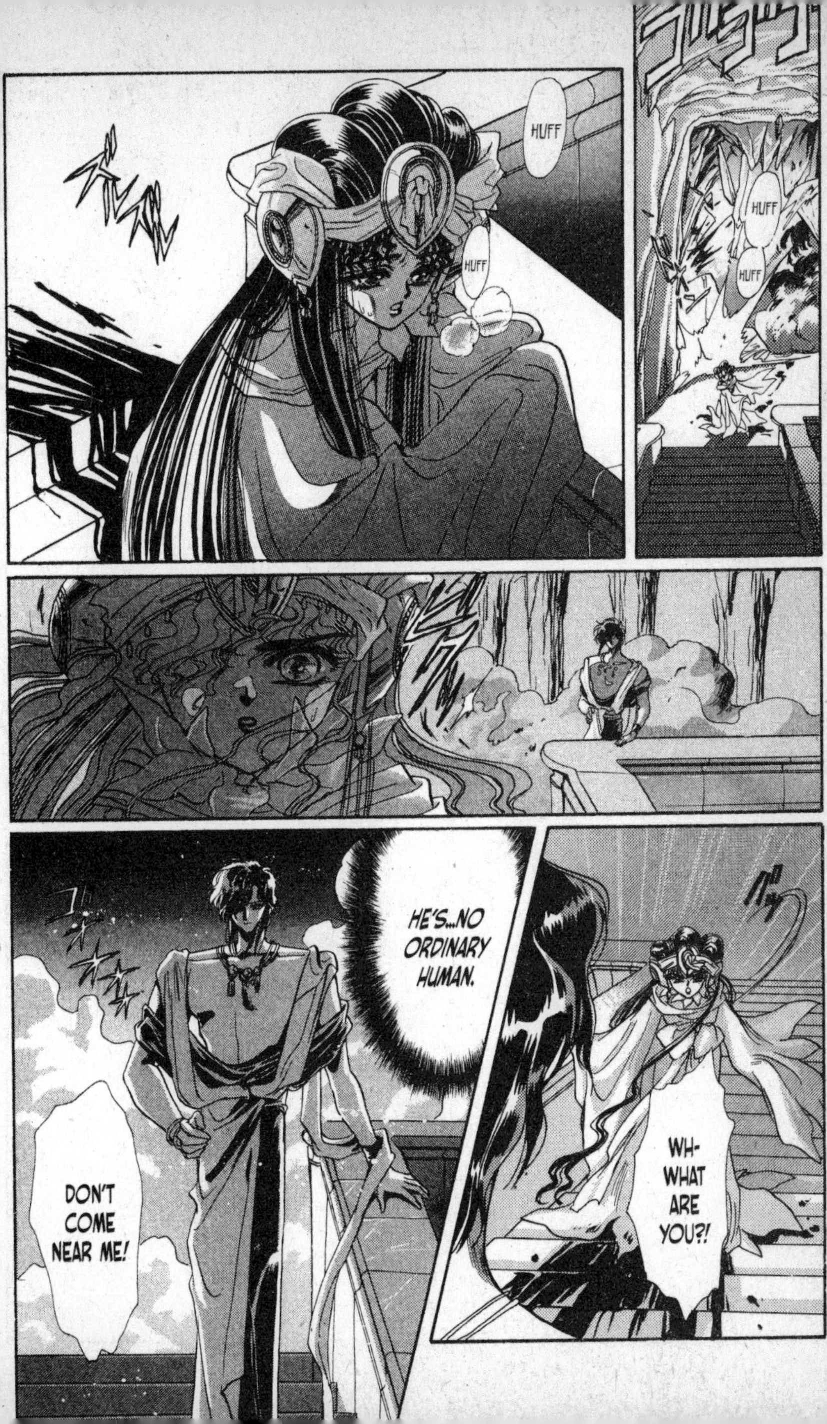
HUFF
HUFF
HUFF
HUFF
WH-WHAT ARE YOU?!
HE'S...NO ORDINARY HUMAN.
DON'T COME NEAR ME!

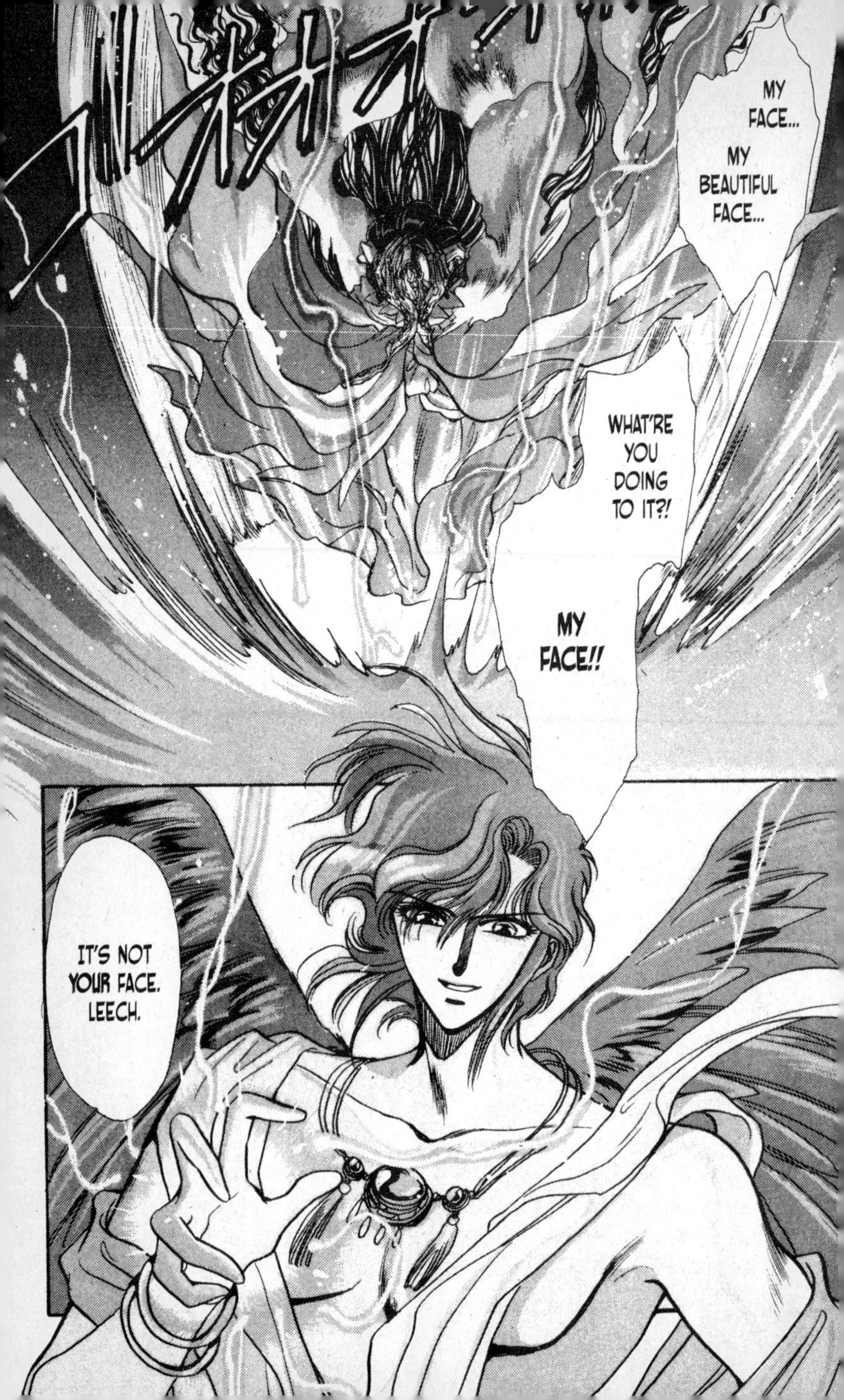
MY FACE...
MY BEAUTIFUL FACE...
WHAT'RE YOU DOING TO IT?!
MY FACE!!
IT'S NOT YOUR FACE. LEECH.

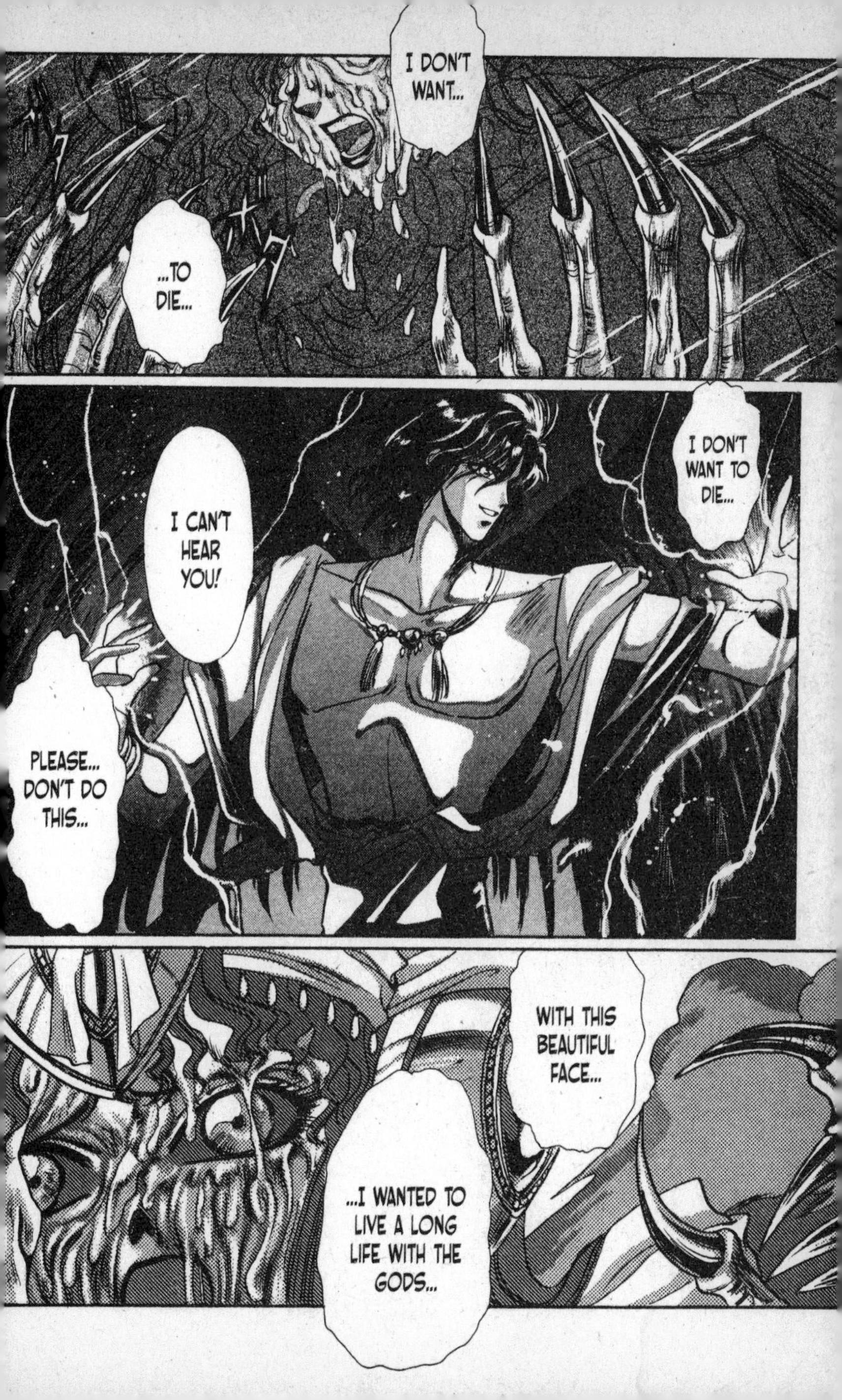
I DON'T WANT...
...TO DIE...
I DON'T WANT TO DIE...
I CAN'T HEAR YOU!
PLEASE... DON'T DO THIS...
WITH THIS BEAUTIFUL FACE...
...I WANTED TO LIVE A LONG LIFE WITH THE GODS...

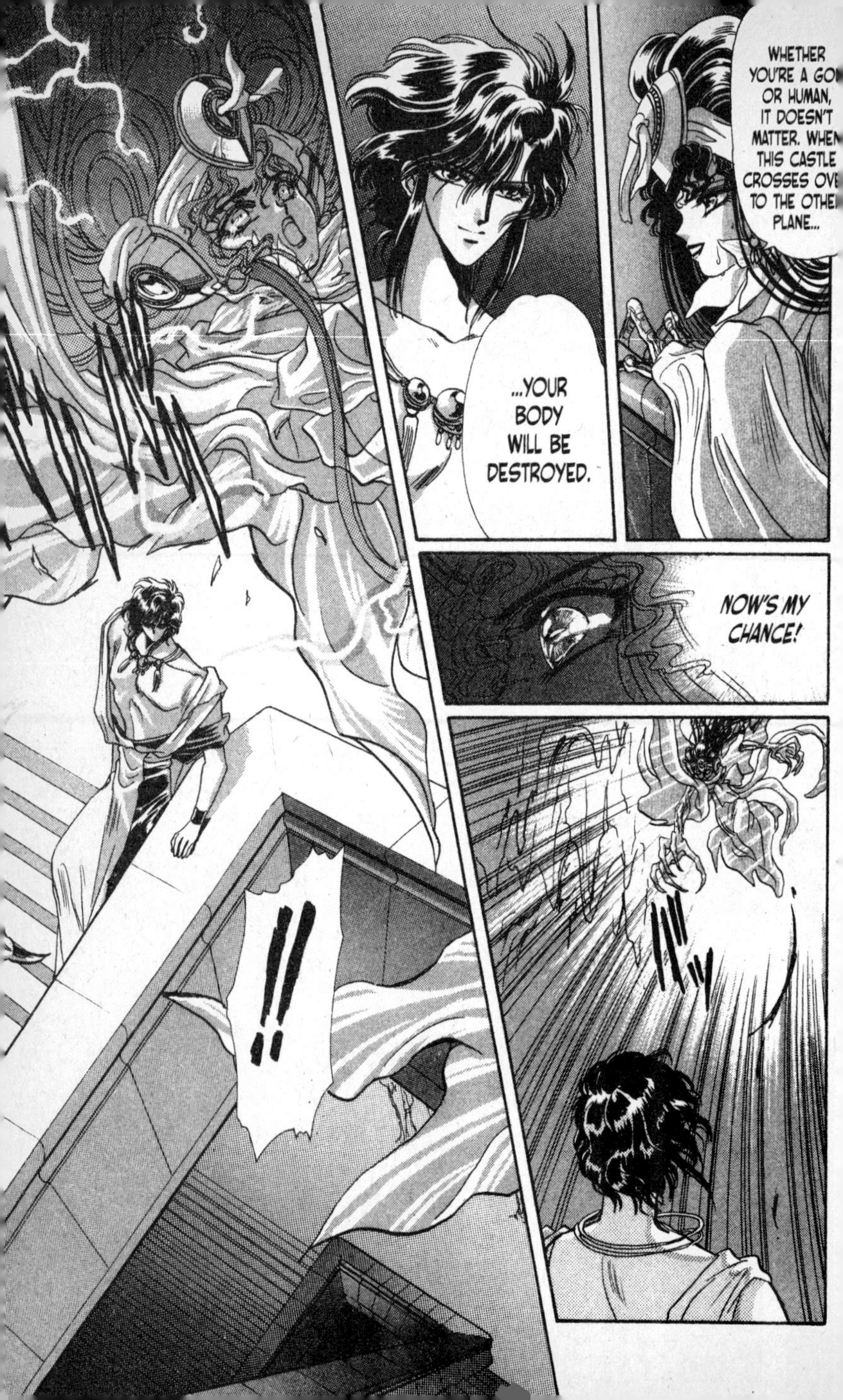
WHETHER YOU'RE A GO[D] OR HUMAN, IT DOESN'T MATTER. WHEN THIS CASTLE CROSSES OVE[R] TO THE OTHE[R] PLANE...
...YOUR BODY WILL BE DESTROYED.
NOW'S MY CHANCE!
!!

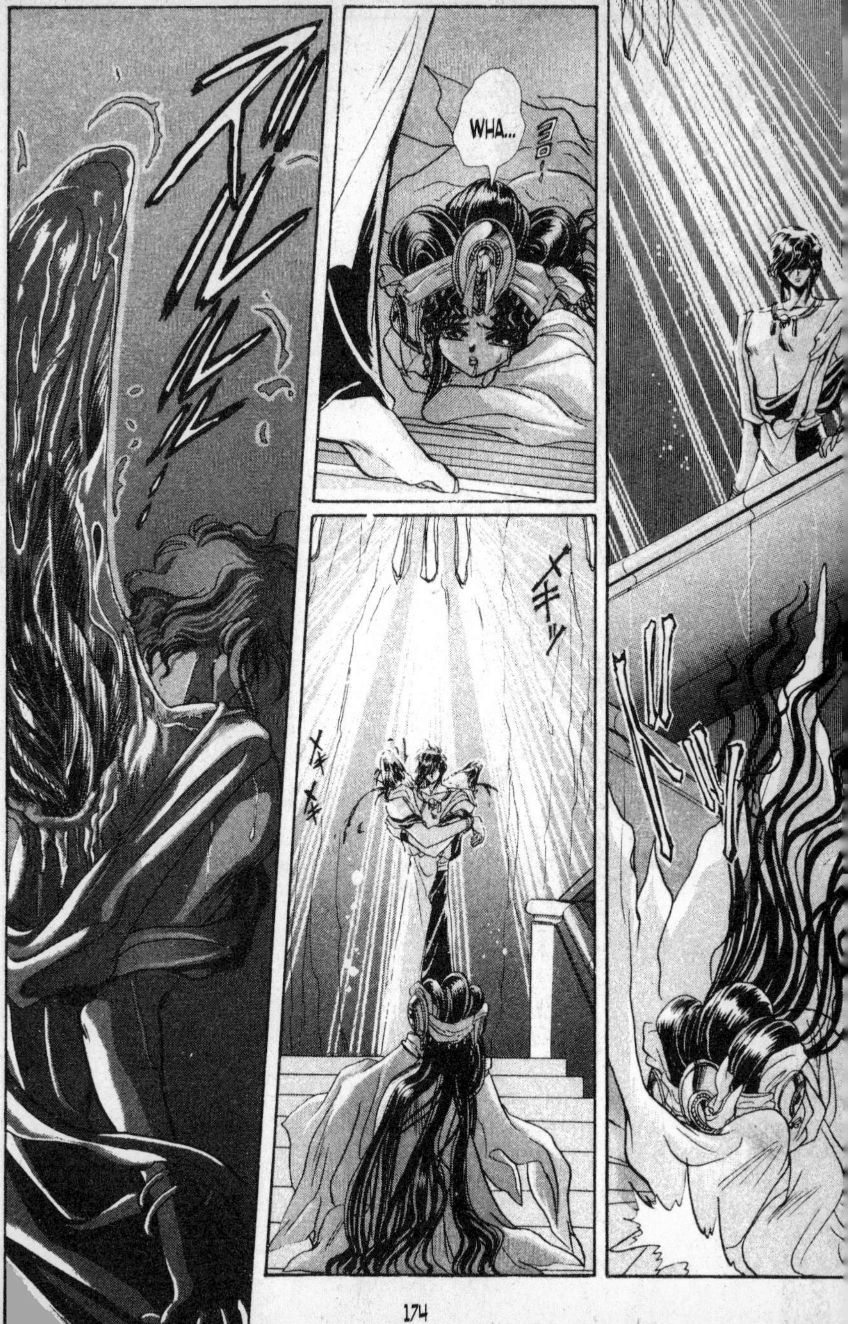
WHA...

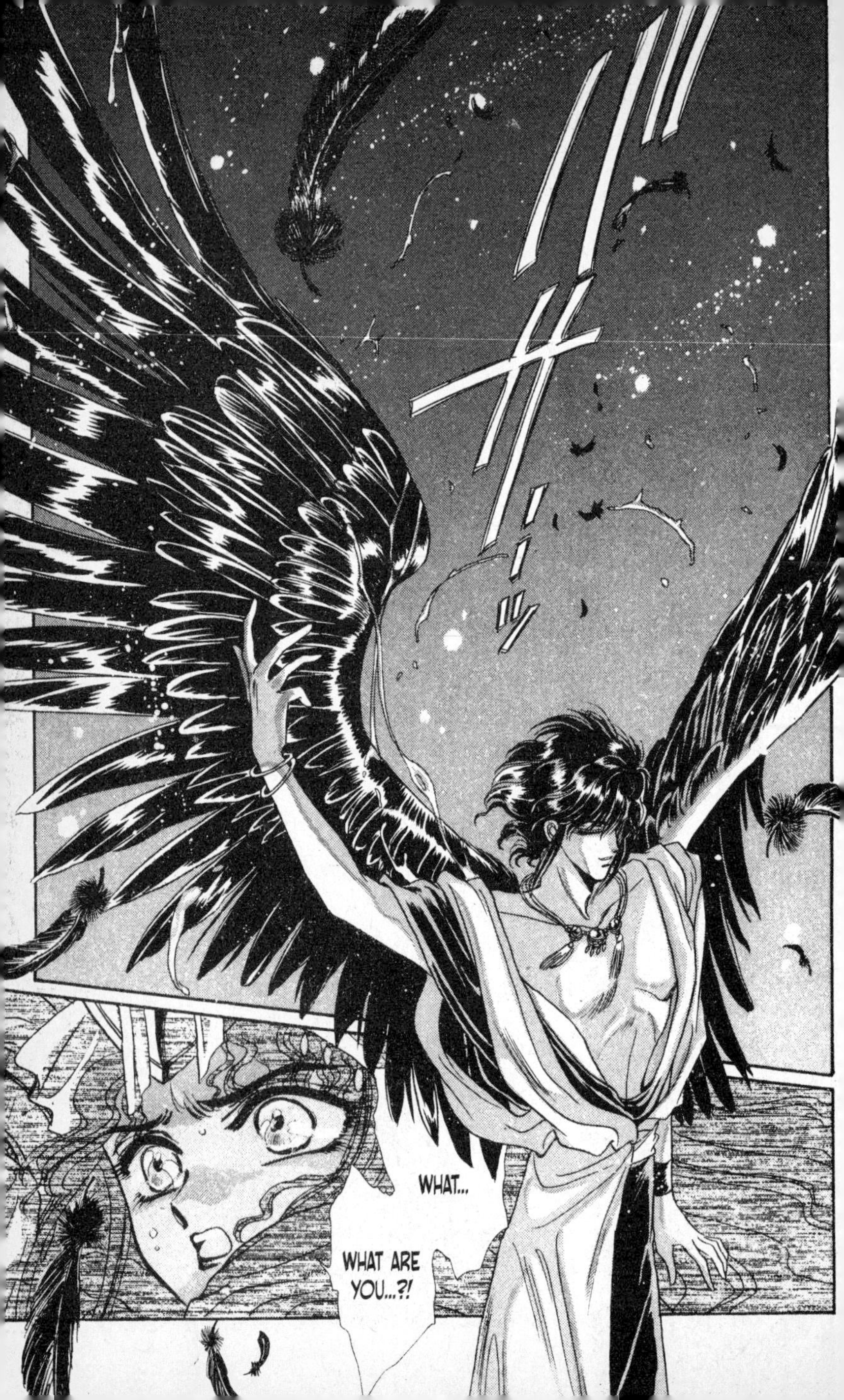
WHAT...
WHAT ARE YOU...?!

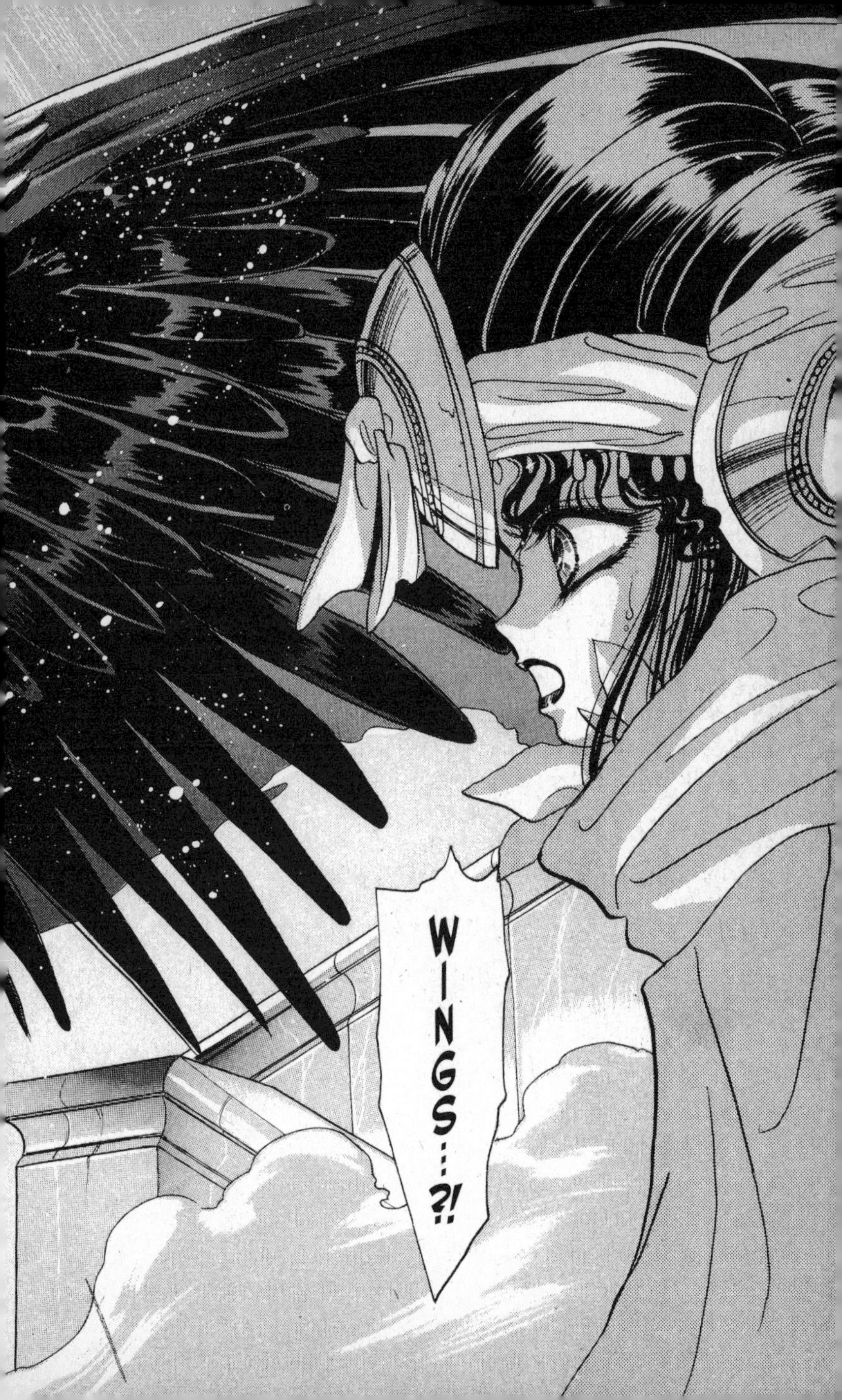
WINGS...?!

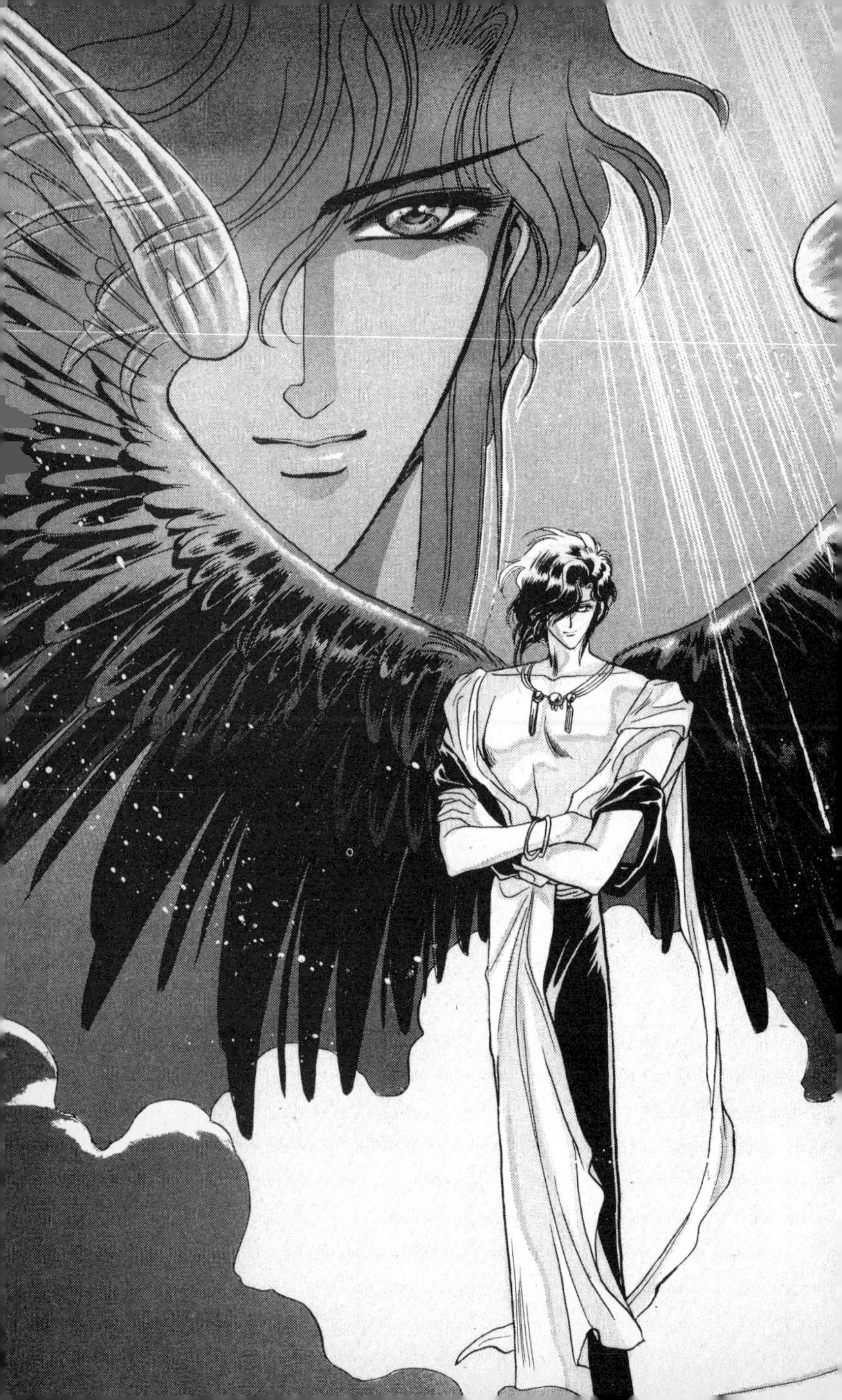

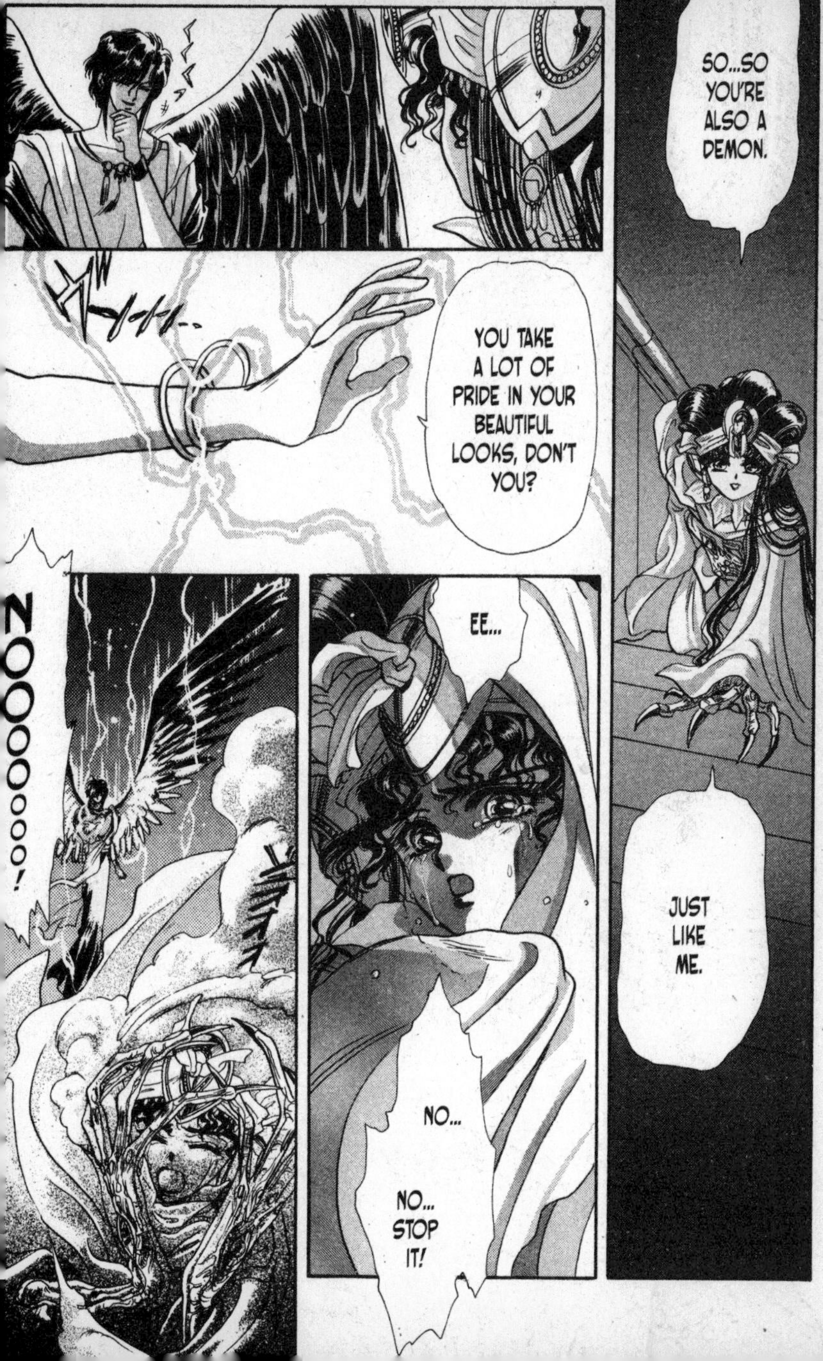
SO...SO YOU'RE ALSO A DEMON.
JUST LIKE ME.
YOU TAKE A LOT OF PRIDE IN YOUR BEAUTIFUL LOOKS, DON'T YOU?
EE...
NO...
NO... STOP IT!
NOOOOOOOOOO!

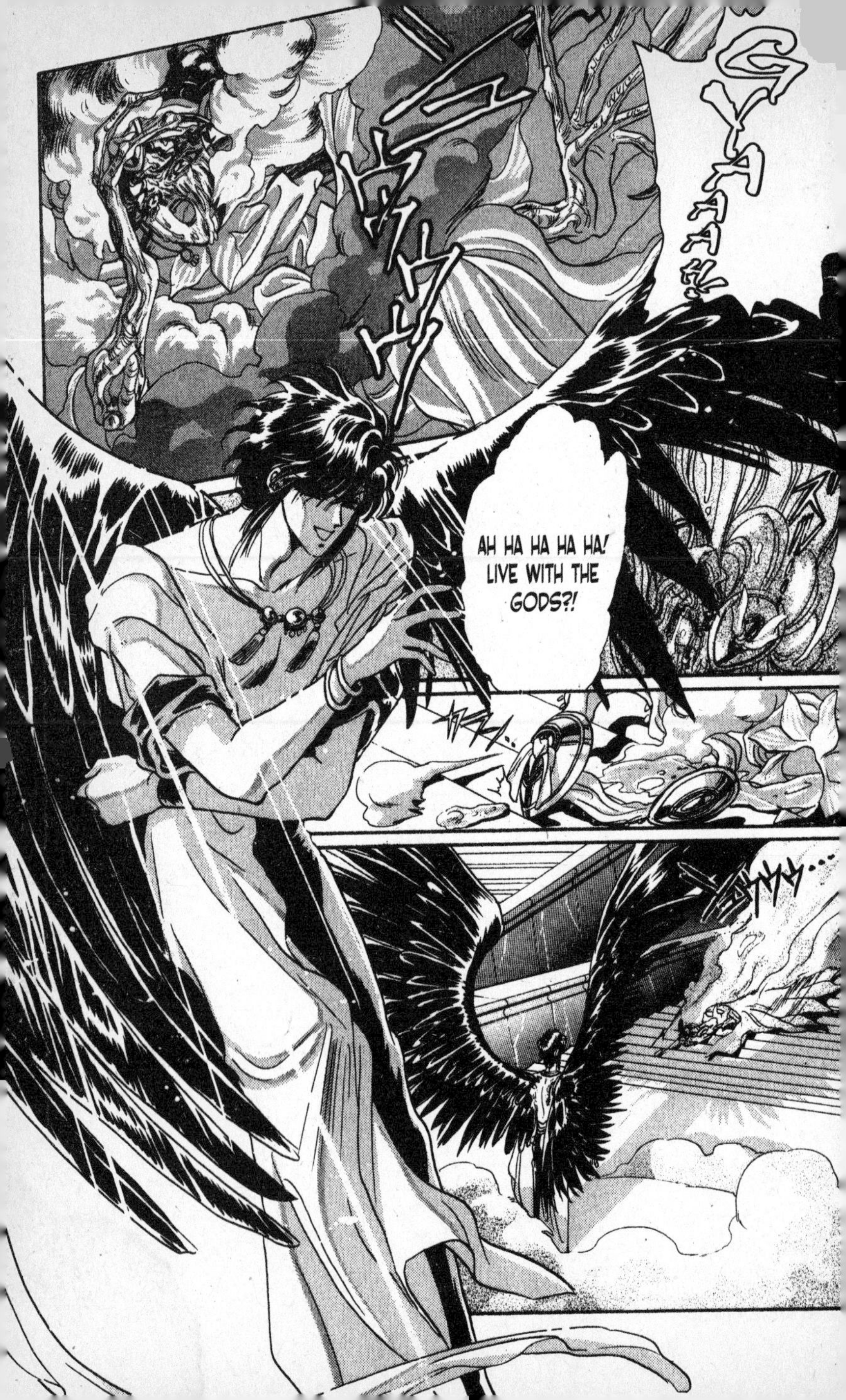
GYAAAAH!
AH HA HA HA HA! LIVE WITH THE GODS?!

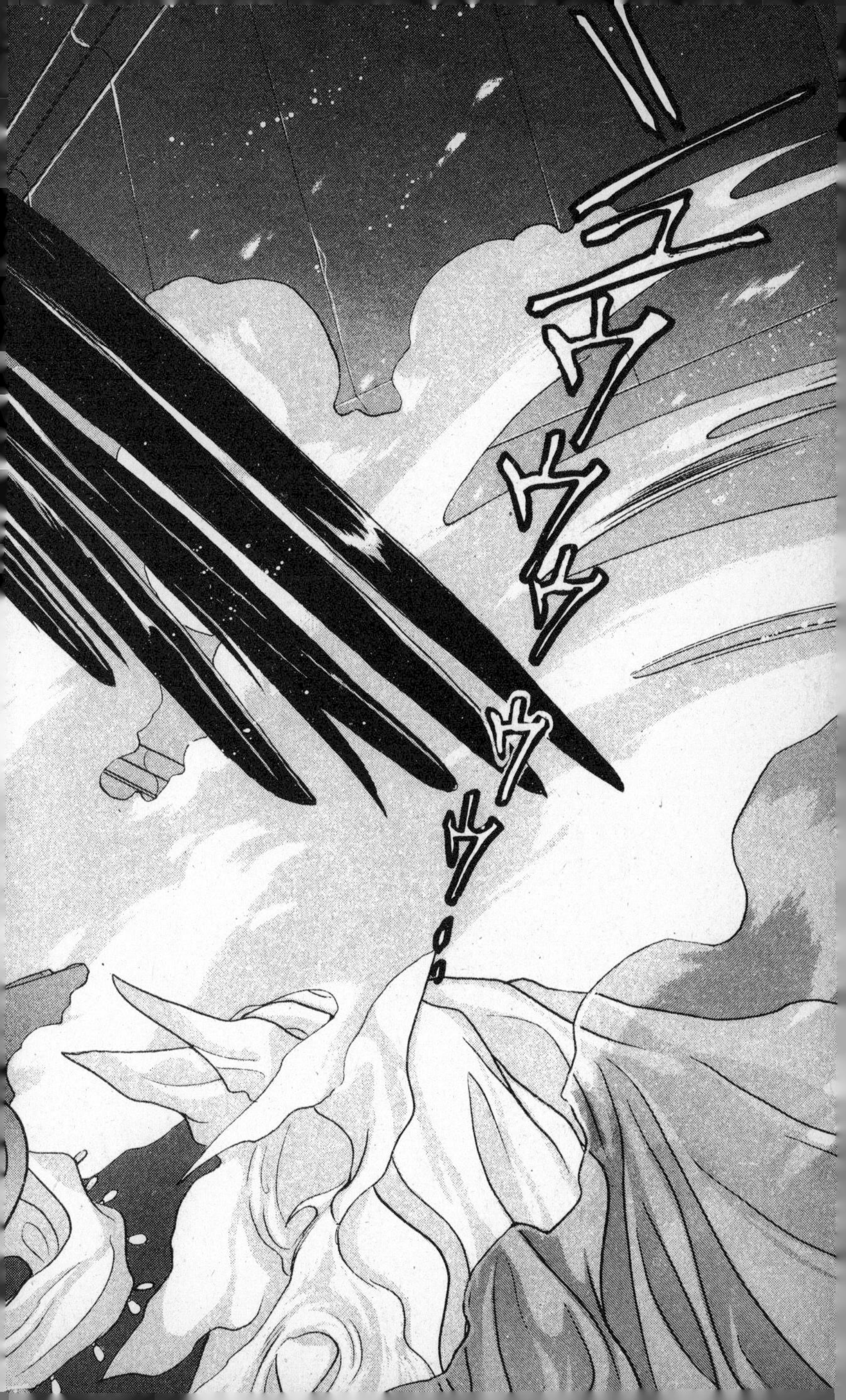
ズウウウウウ…

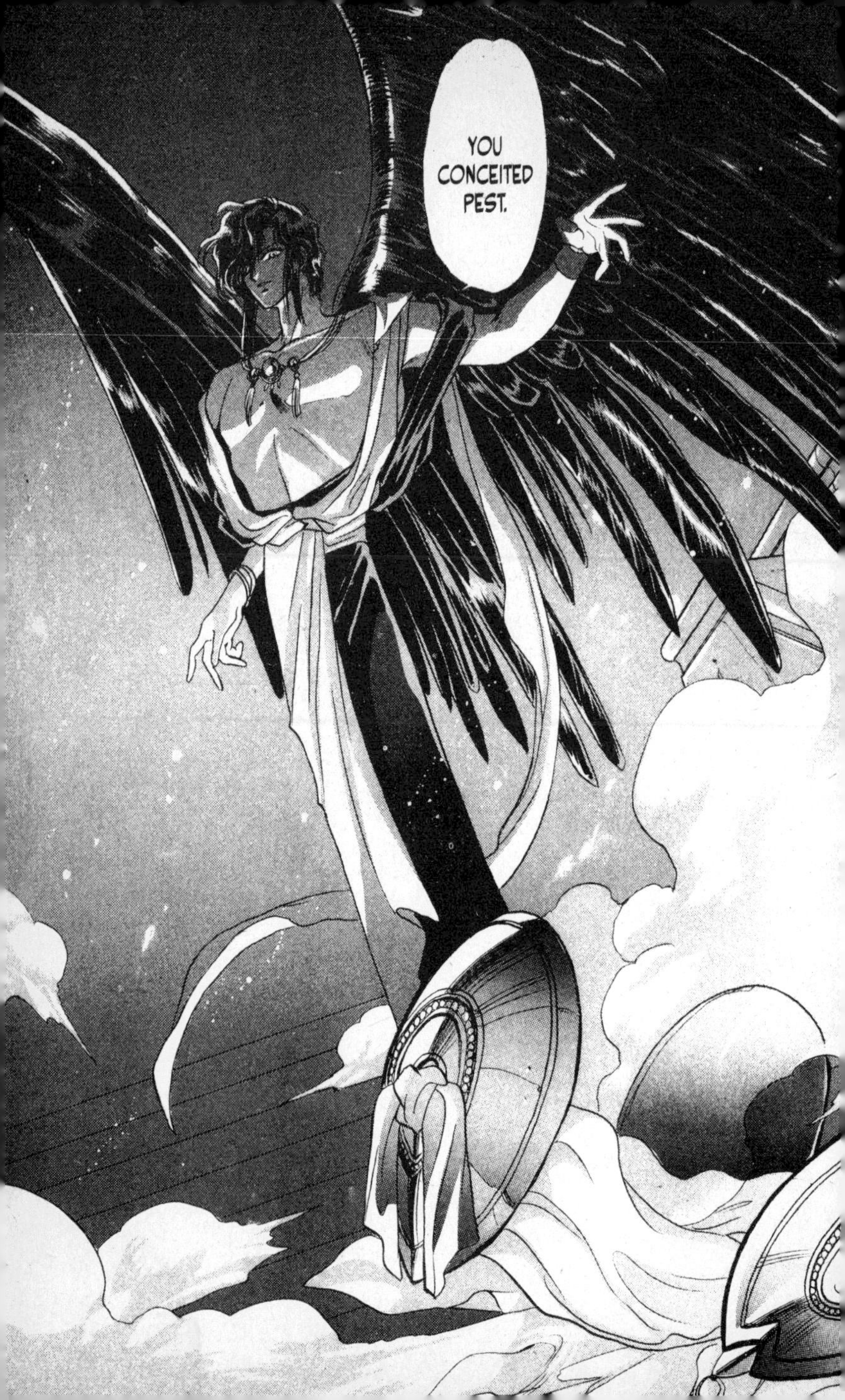
YOU CONCEITED PEST.

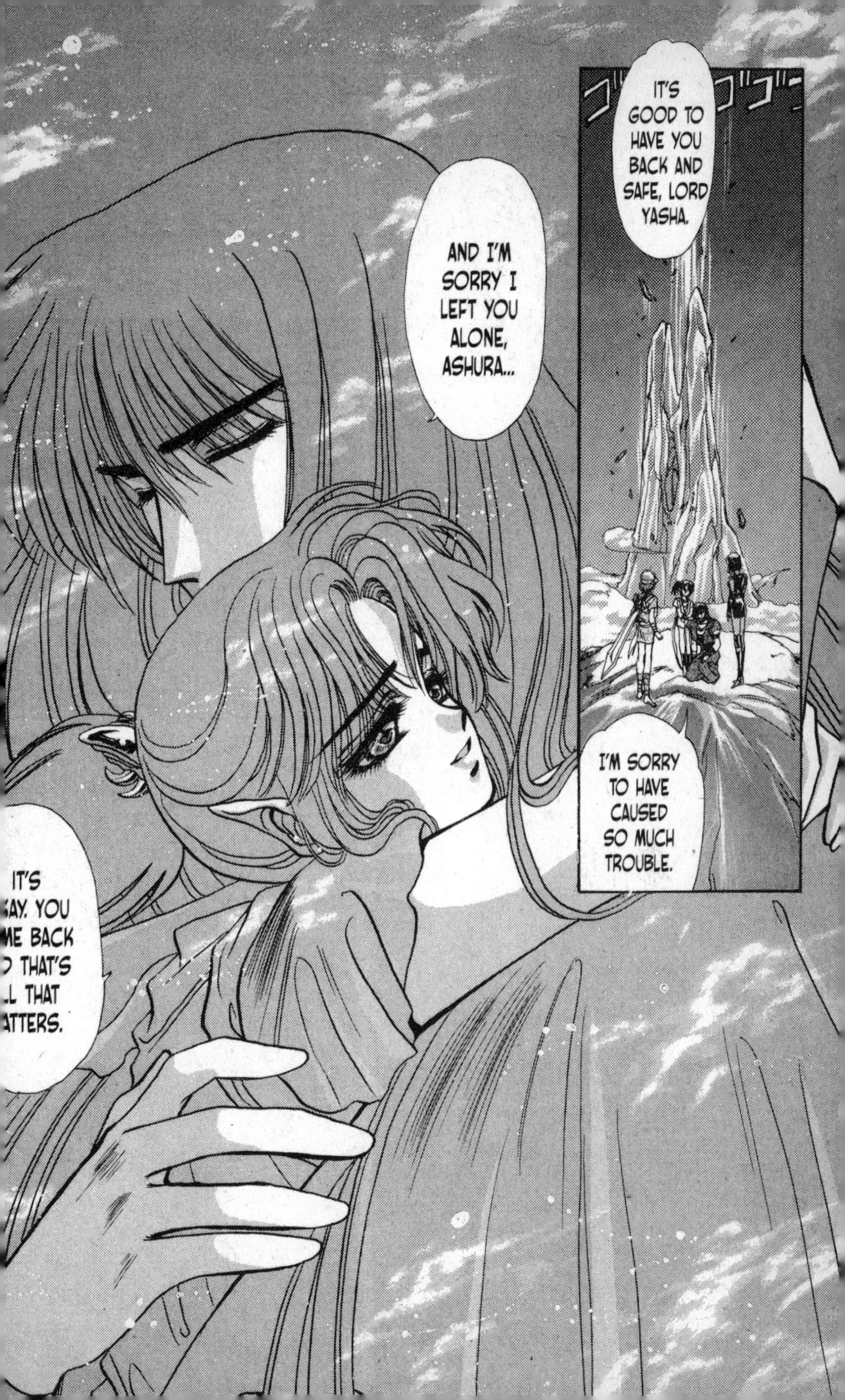
IT'S GOOD TO HAVE YOU BACK AND SAFE, LORD YASHA.
I'M SORRY TO HAVE CAUSED SO MUCH TROUBLE.
AND I'M SORRY I LEFT YOU ALONE, ASHURA...
IT'S ...AY. YOU ...ME BACK ...THAT'S ...L THAT ...ATTERS.

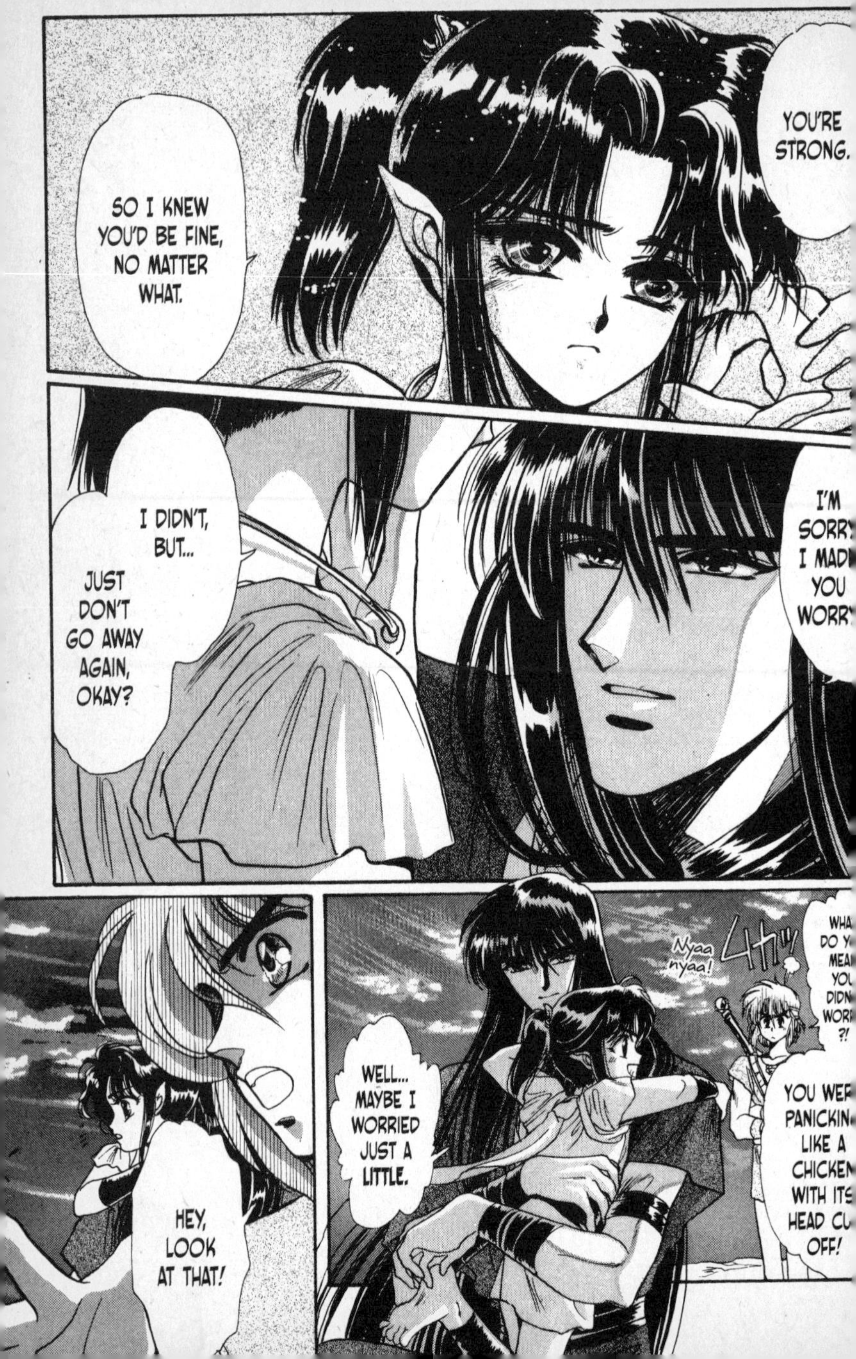
YOU'RE STRONG.
SO I KNEW YOU'D BE FINE, NO MATTER WHAT.
I'M SORR I MAD YOU WORR
I DIDN'T, BUT...
JUST DON'T GO AWAY AGAIN, OKAY?
WHA DO Y MEA YOU DIDN WORR ?!
ムカッ
Nyaa nyaa!
YOU WER PANICKIN LIKE A CHICKEN WITH ITS HEAD CU OFF!
WELL... MAYBE I WORRIED JUST A LITTLE.
HEY, LOOK AT THAT!

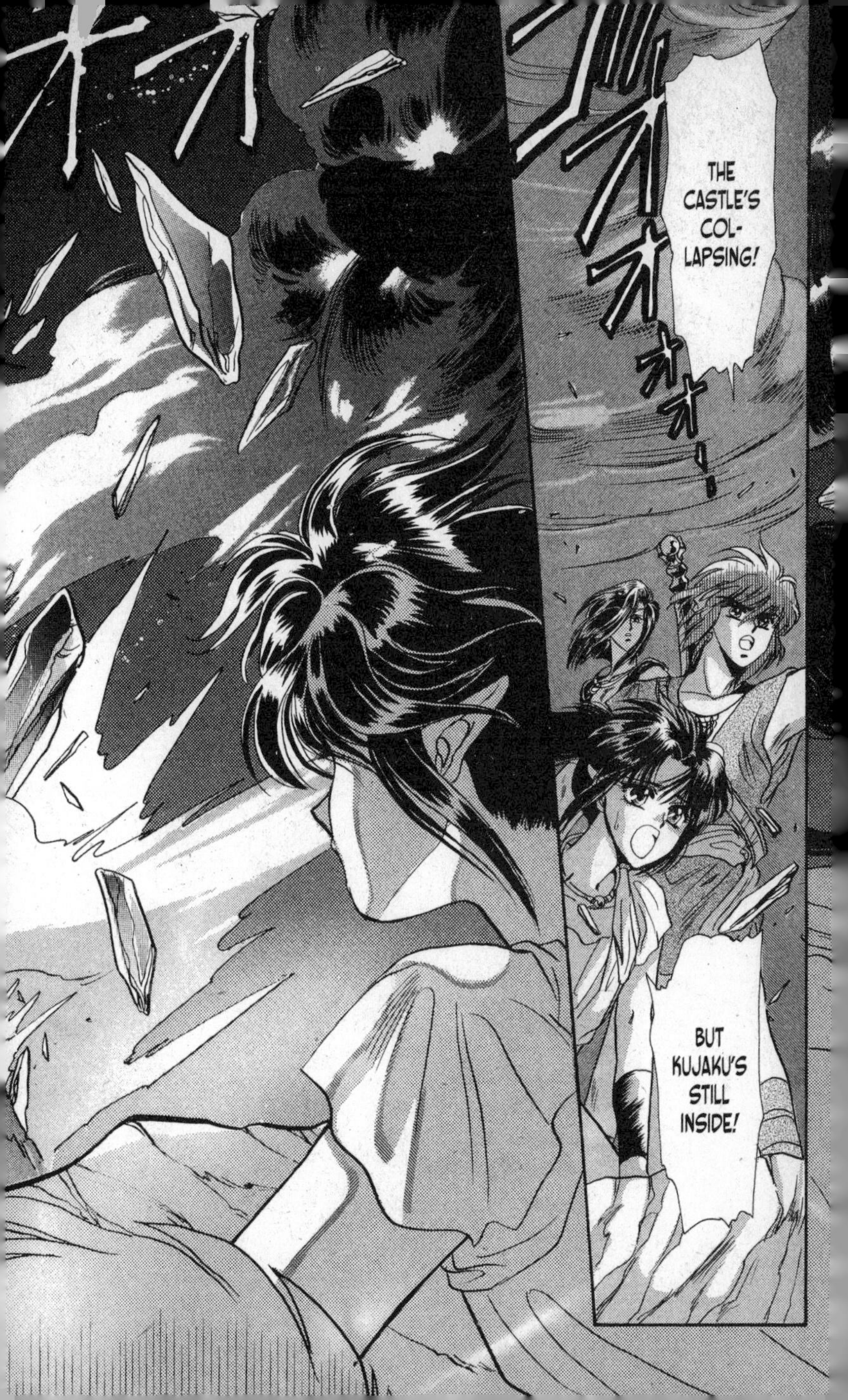
THE CASTLE'S COL-LAPSING!
BUT KUJAKU'S STILL INSIDE!

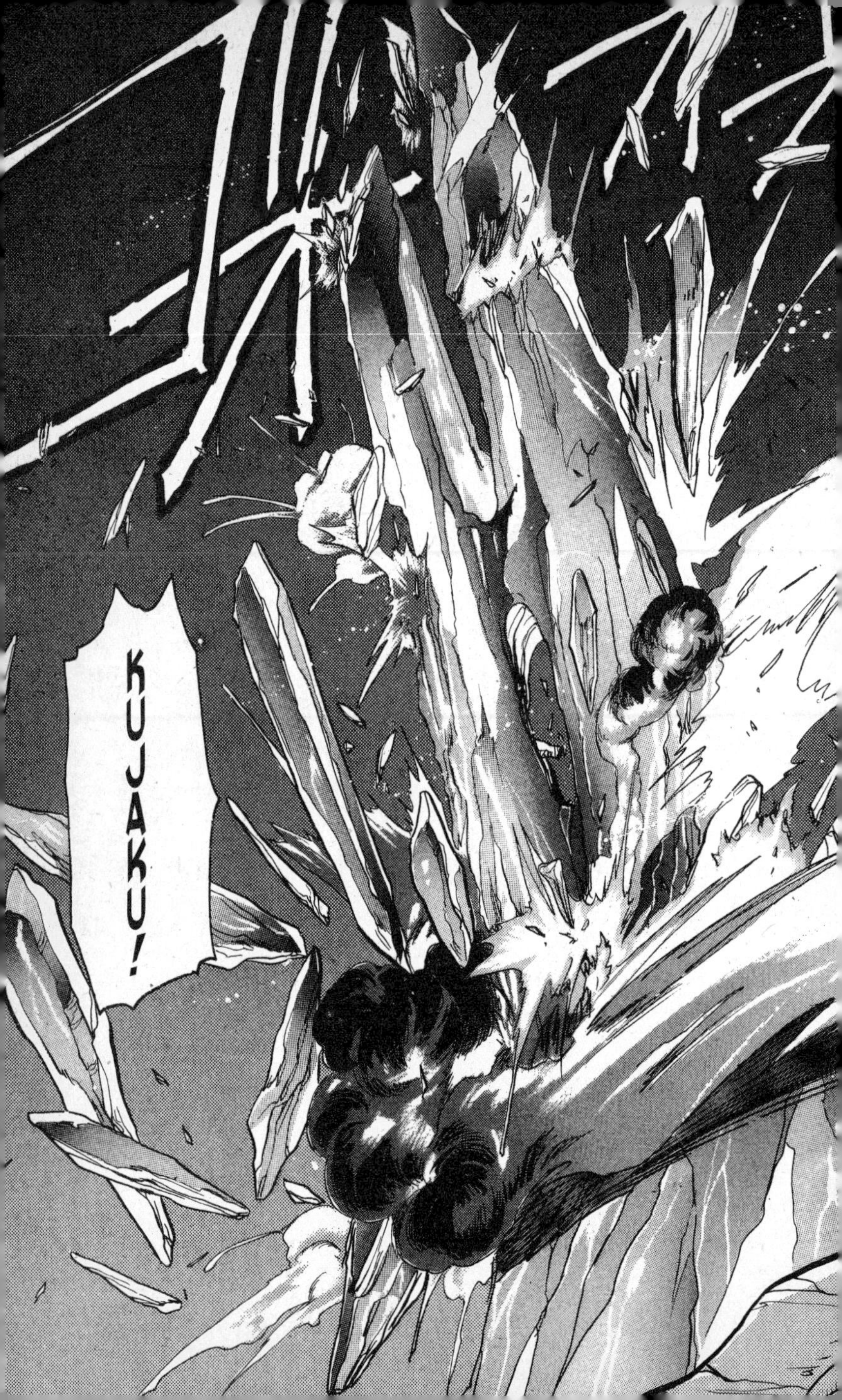
KUJAKU!

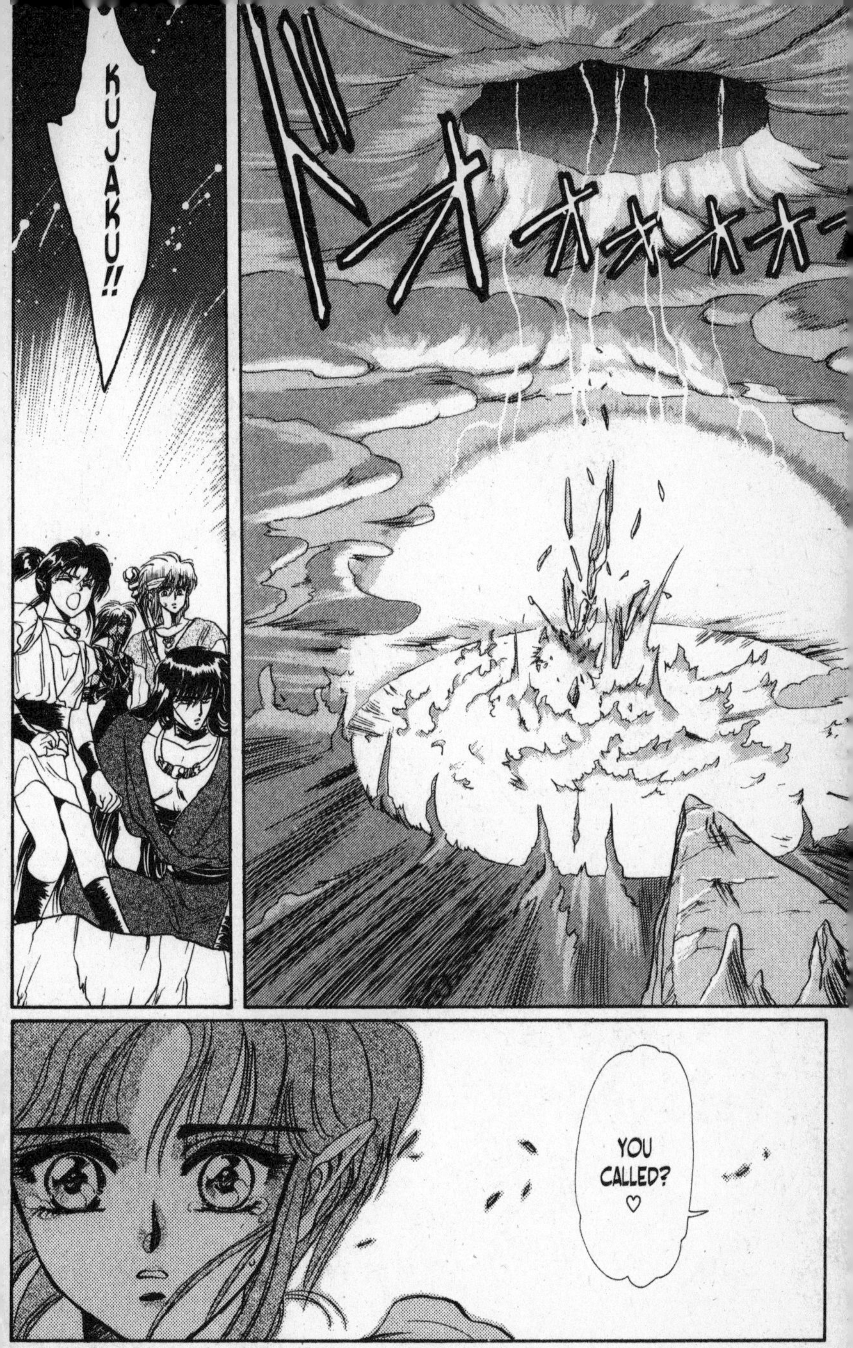
ドオオォオオー
KUJAKU!!
YOU CALLED? ♡

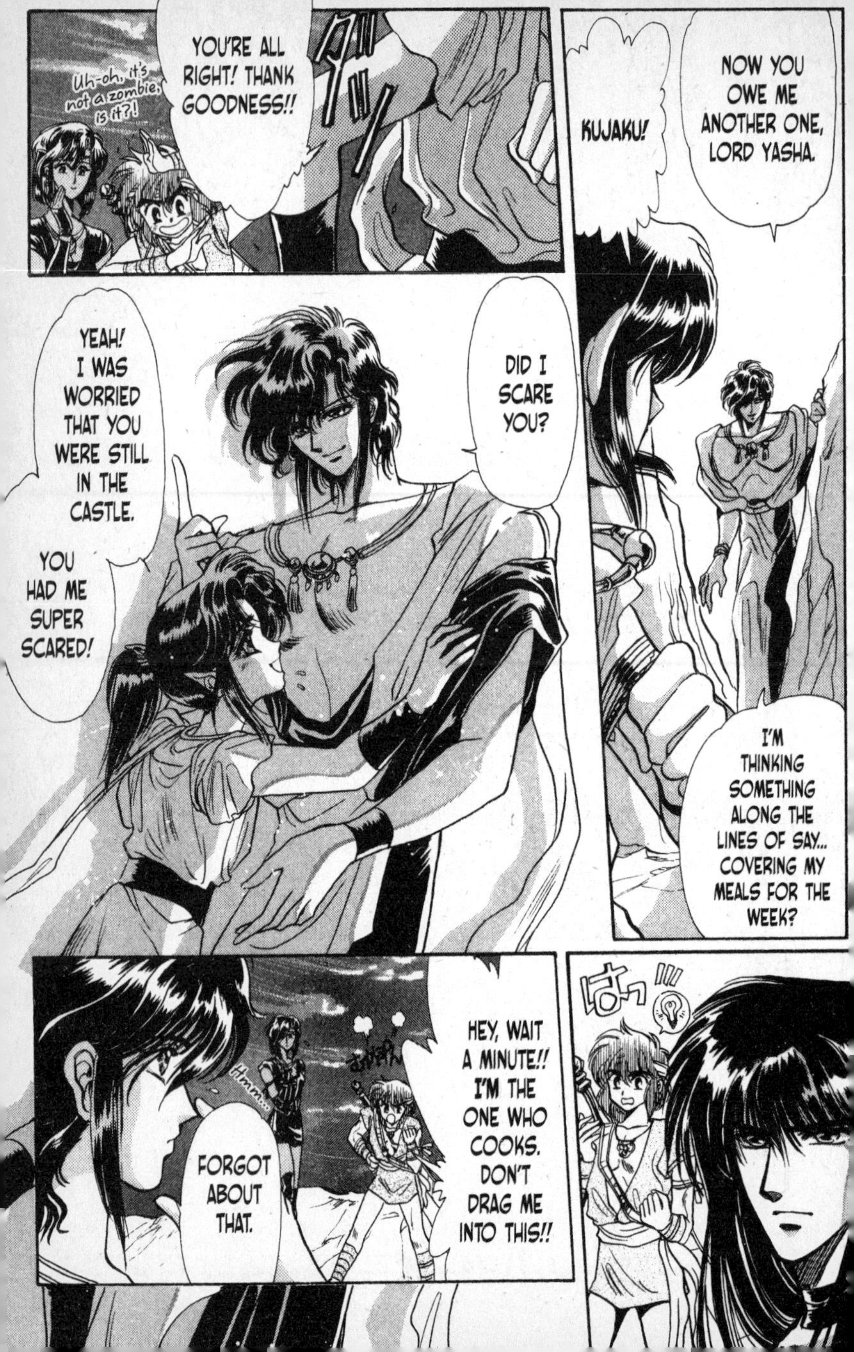
KUJAKU!
NOW YOU OWE ME ANOTHER ONE, LORD YASHA.
I'M THINKING SOMETHING ALONG THE LINES OF SAY... COVERING MY MEALS FOR THE WEEK?
YOU'RE ALL RIGHT! THANK GOODNESS!!
Uh-oh, it's not a zombie, is it?!
DID I SCARE YOU?
YEAH! I WAS WORRIED THAT YOU WERE STILL IN THE CASTLE.
YOU HAD ME SUPER SCARED!
はっ!!!
HEY, WAIT A MINUTE!! I'M THE ONE WHO COOKS. DON'T DRAG ME INTO THIS!!
Hmm...
FORGOT ABOUT THAT.

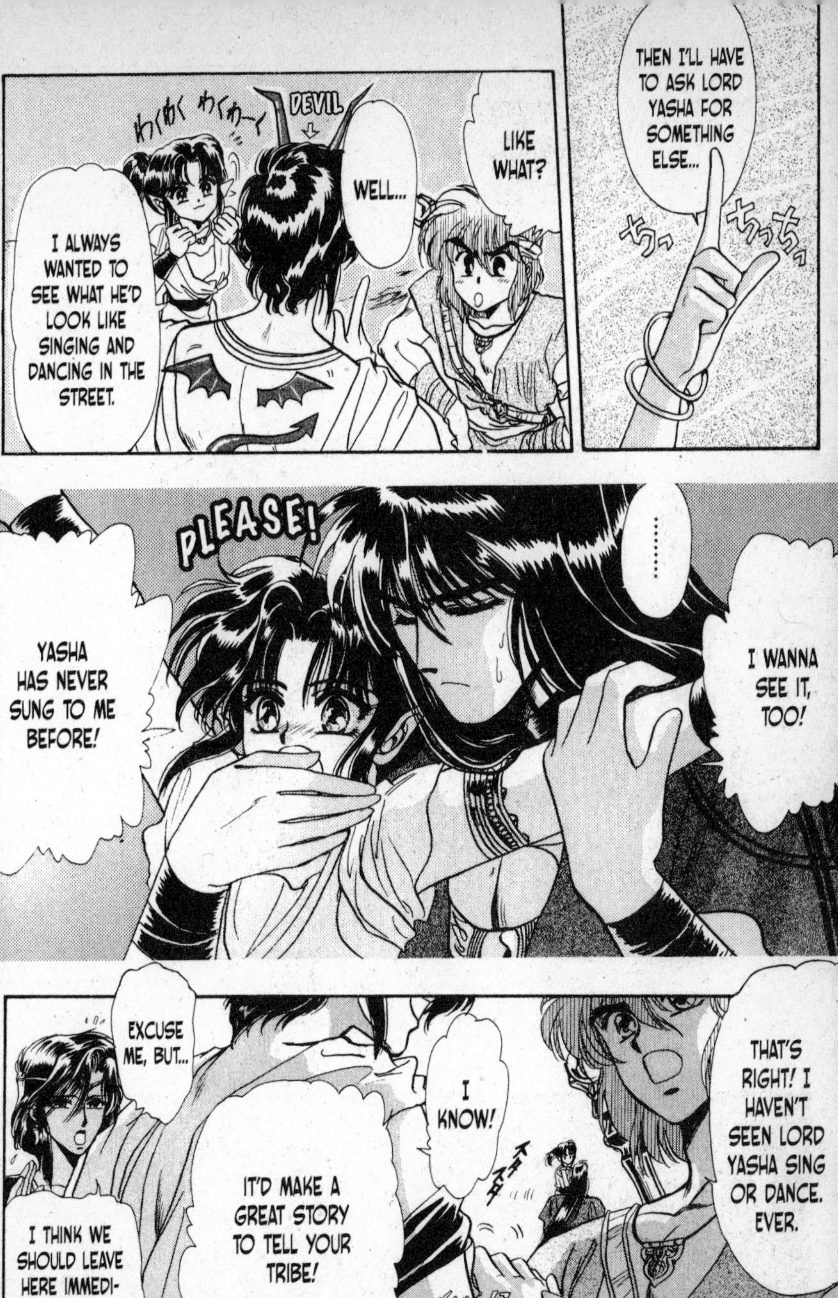
THEN I'LL HAVE TO ASK LORD YASHA FOR SOMETHING ELSE...
LIKE WHAT?
WELL...
DEVIL
I ALWAYS WANTED TO SEE WHAT HE'D LOOK LIKE SINGING AND DANCING IN THE STREET.
......
I WANNA SEE IT, TOO!
PLEASE!
YASHA HAS NEVER SUNG TO ME BEFORE!
THAT'S RIGHT! I HAVEN'T SEEN LORD YASHA SING OR DANCE. EVER.
I KNOW!
IT'D MAKE A GREAT STORY TO TELL YOUR TRIBE!
EXCUSE ME, BUT...
I THINK WE SHOULD LEAVE HERE IMMEDIATELY...

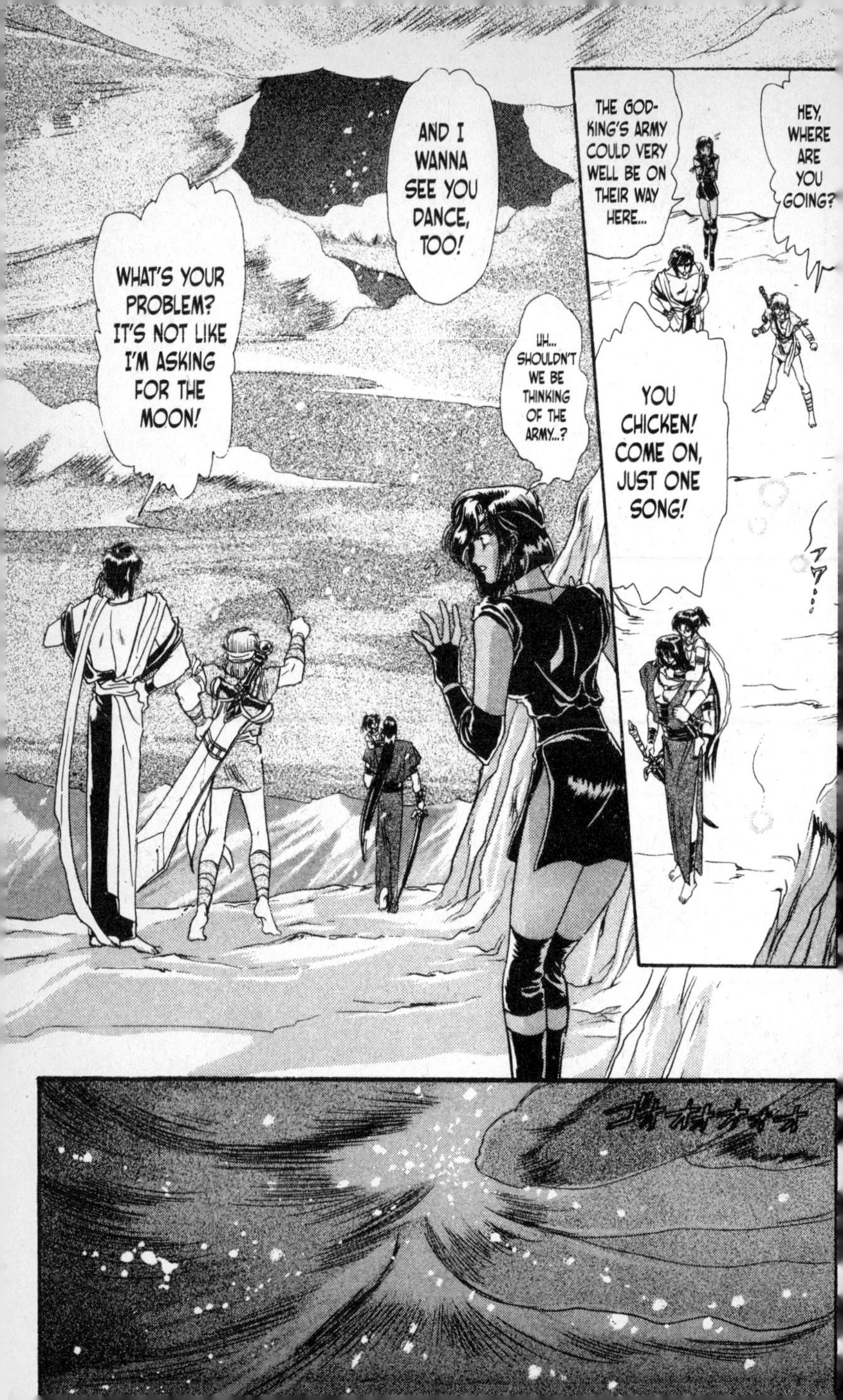
HEY, WHERE ARE YOU GOING?
THE GOD-KING'S ARMY COULD VERY WELL BE ON THEIR WAY HERE...
YOU CHICKEN! COME ON, JUST ONE SONG!
AND I WANNA SEE YOU DANCE, TOO!
WHAT'S YOUR PROBLEM? IT'S NOT LIKE I'M ASKING FOR THE MOON!
UH... SHOULDN'T WE BE THINKING OF THE ARMY...?

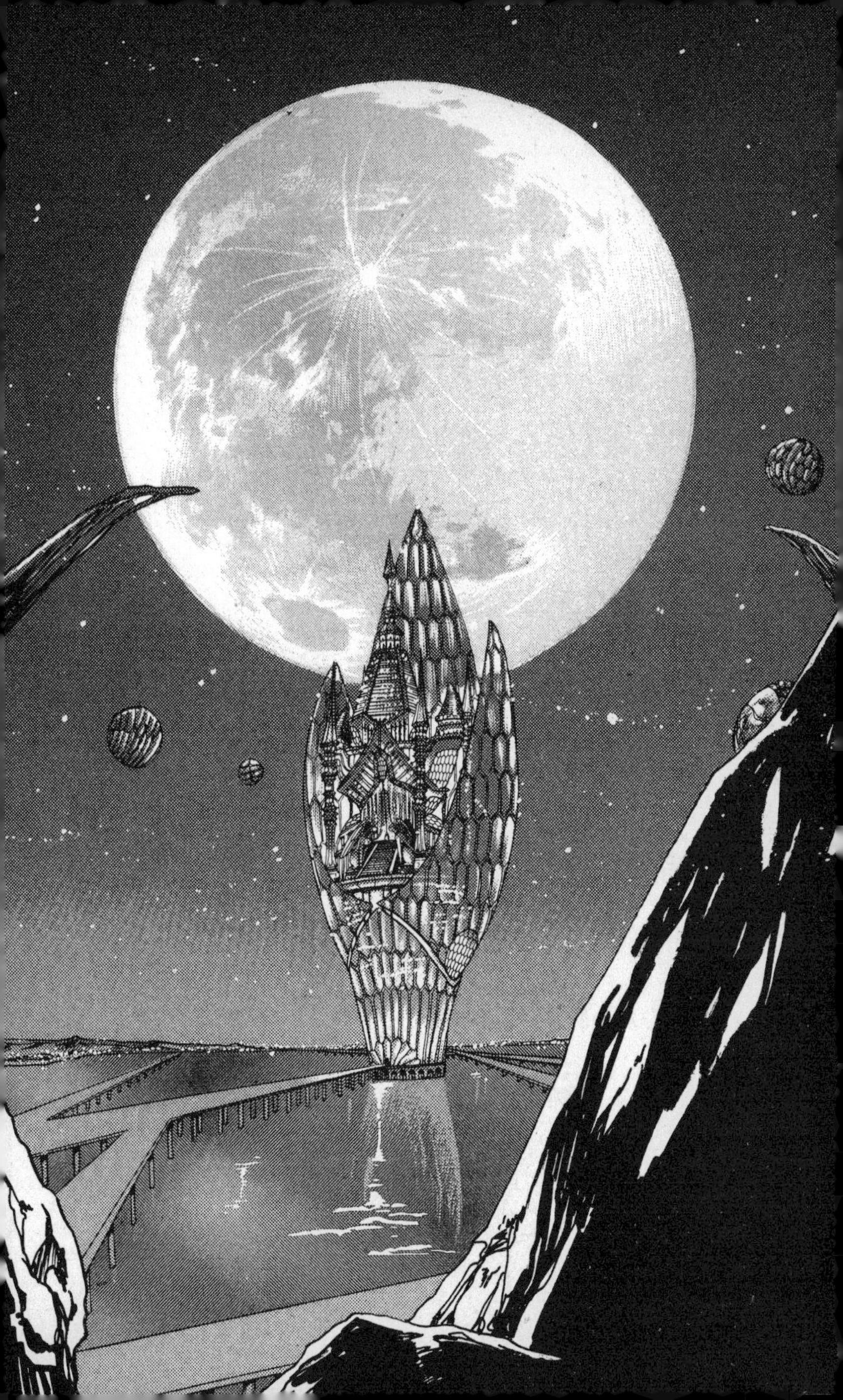

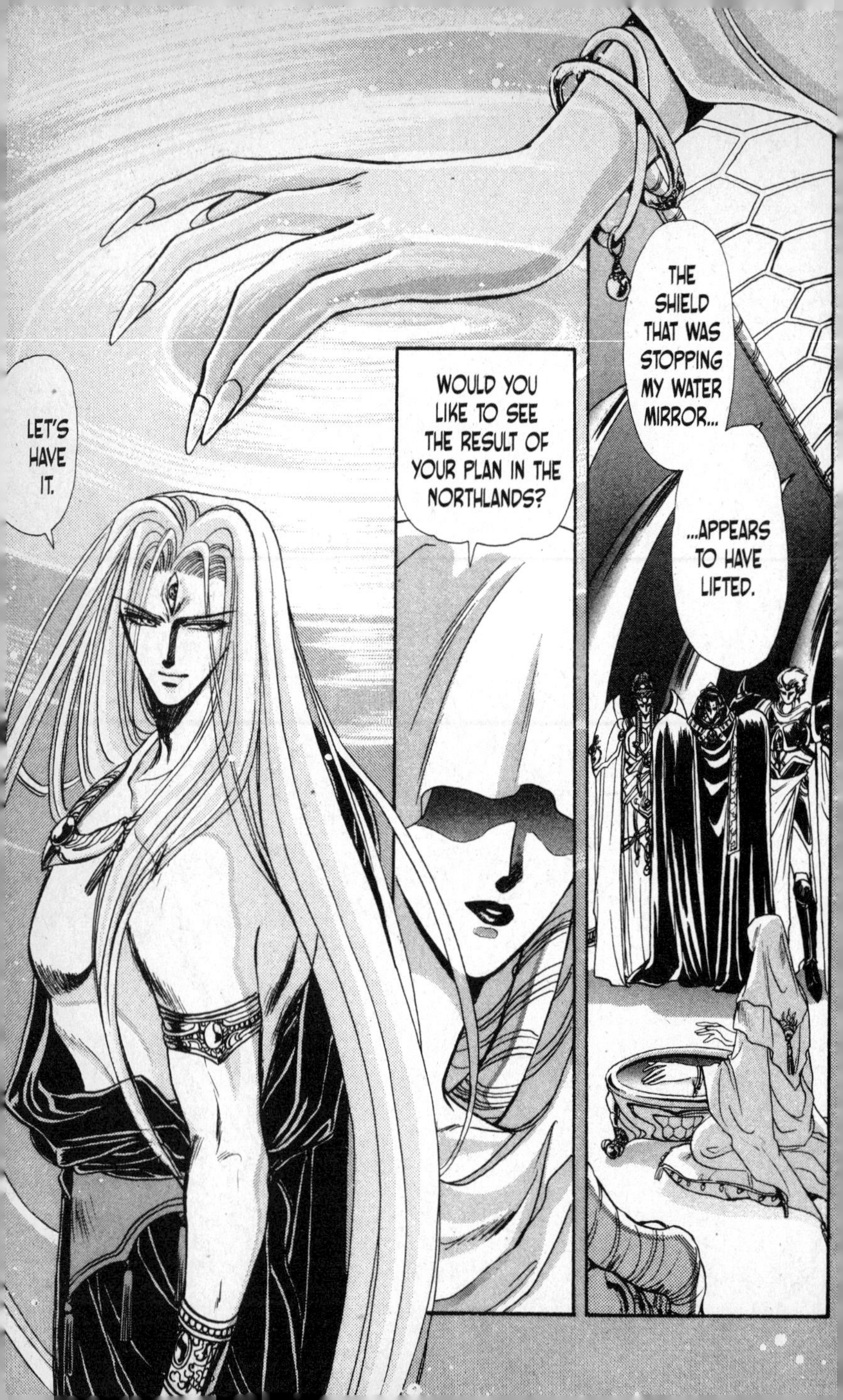
THE SHIELD THAT WAS STOPPING MY WATER MIRROR...
...APPEARS TO HAVE LIFTED.
WOULD YOU LIKE TO SEE THE RESULT OF YOUR PLAN IN THE NORTHLANDS?
LET'S HAVE IT.

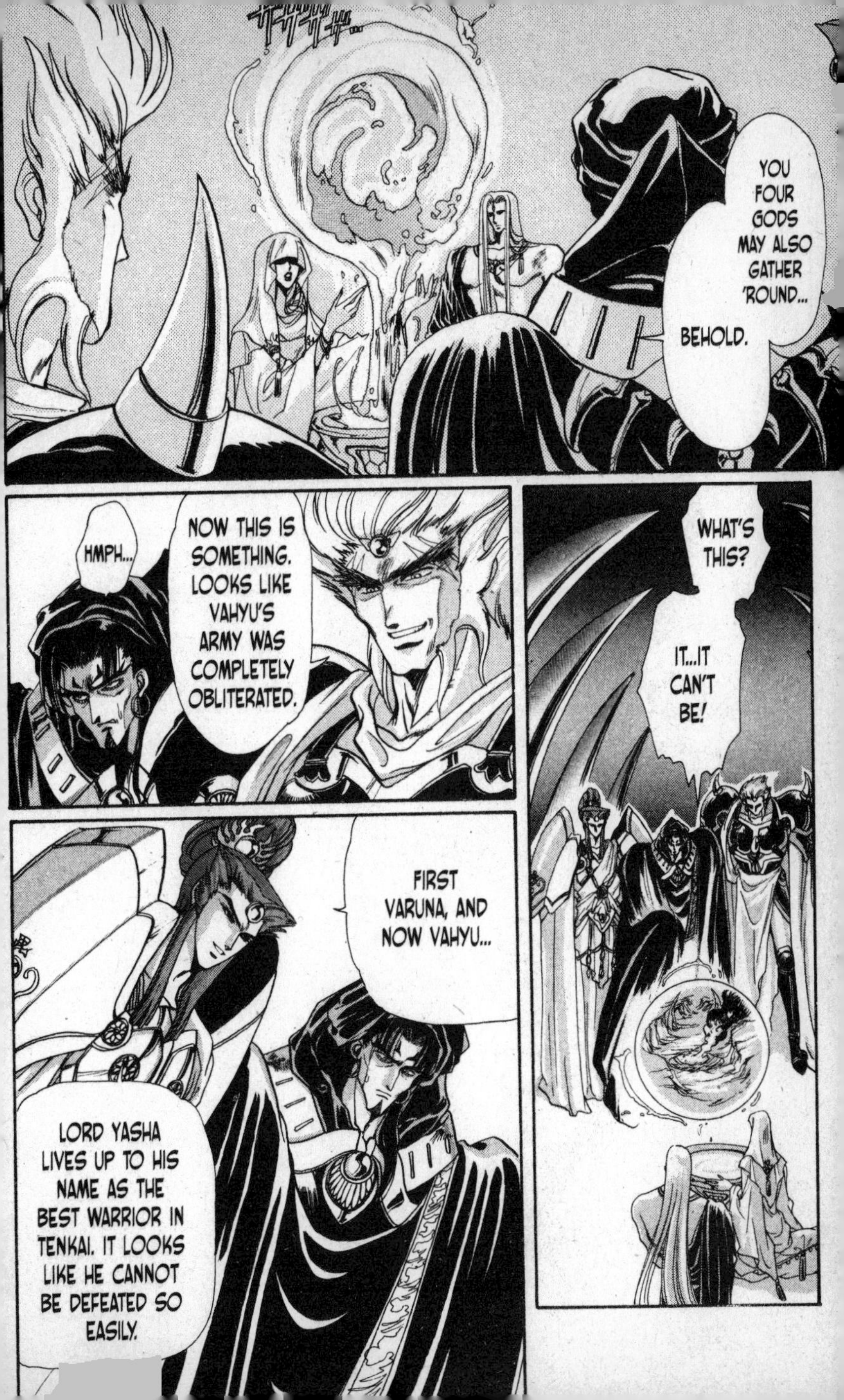
YOU FOUR GODS MAY ALSO GATHER 'ROUND...
BEHOLD.
WHAT'S THIS?
IT...IT CAN'T BE!
NOW THIS IS SOMETHING. LOOKS LIKE VAHYU'S ARMY WAS COMPLETELY OBLITERATED.
HMPH...
FIRST VARUNA, AND NOW VAHYU...
LORD YASHA LIVES UP TO HIS NAME AS THE BEST WARRIOR IN TENKAI. IT LOOKS LIKE HE CANNOT BE DEFEATED SO EASILY.

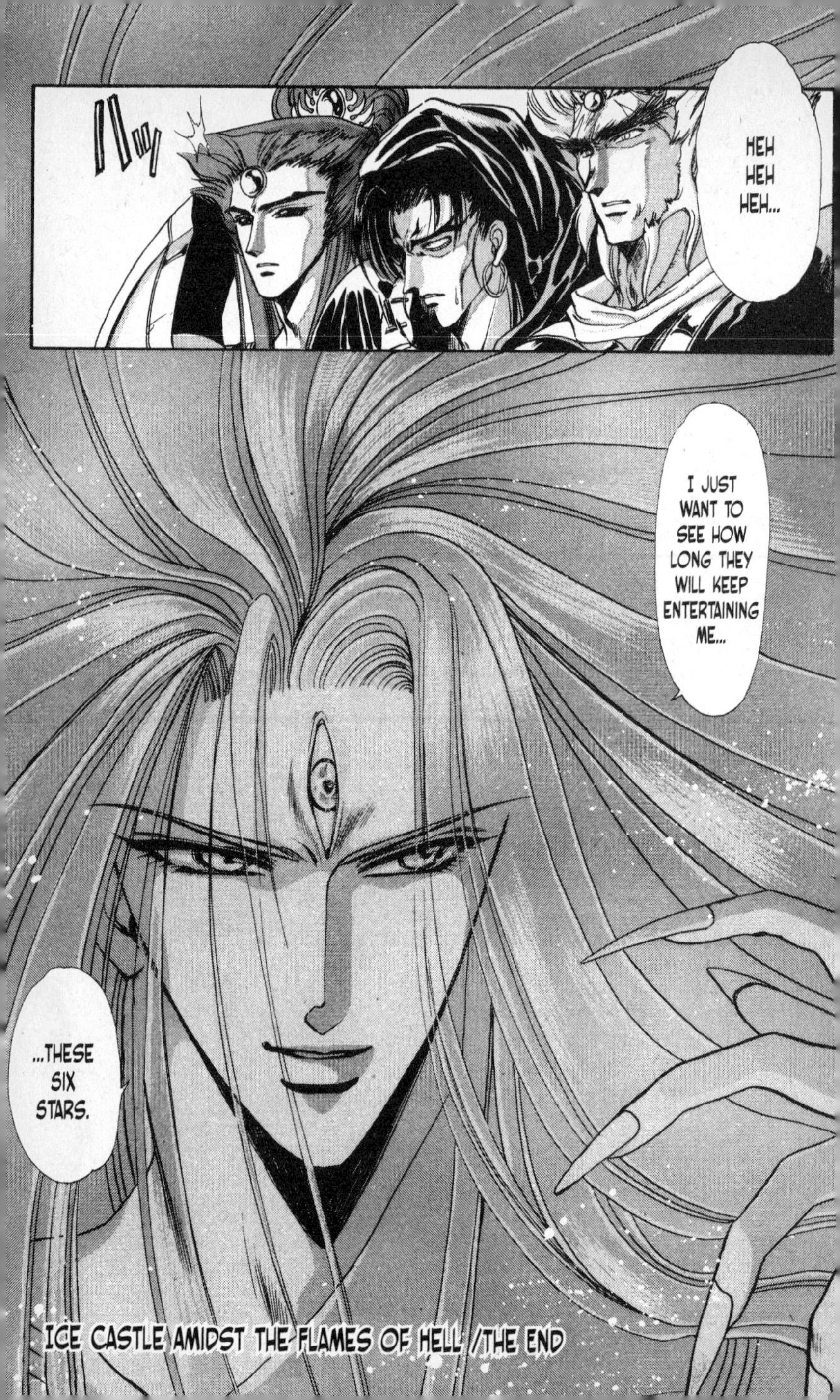
HEH HEH HEH...
I JUST WANT TO SEE HOW LONG THEY WILL KEEP ENTERTAINING ME...
...THESE SIX STARS.
ICE CASTLE AMIDST THE FLAMES OF HELL /THE END

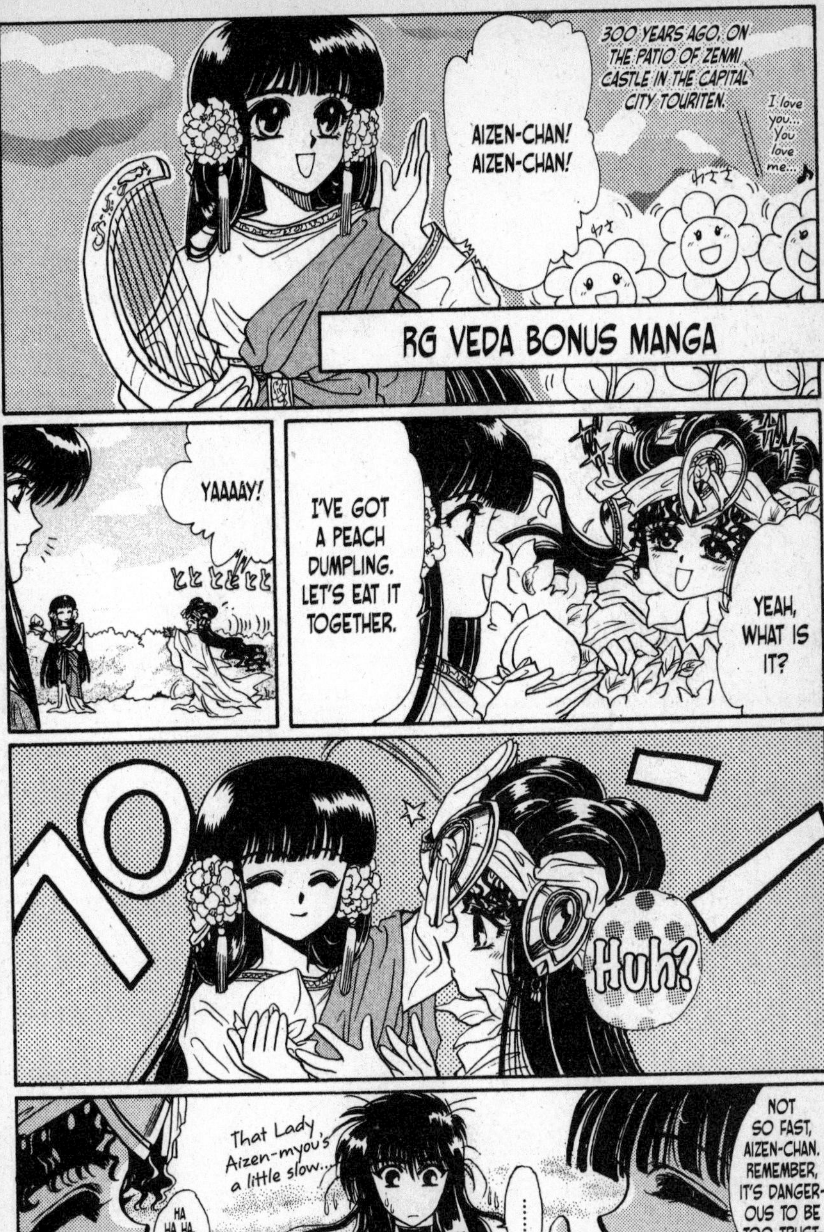
300 YEARS AGO, ON THE PATIO OF ZENMI CASTLE IN THE CAPITAL CITY TOURITEN.
I love you... You love me...
AIZEN-CHAN! AIZEN-CHAN!
RG VEDA BONUS MANGA
YEAH, WHAT IS IT?
I'VE GOT A PEACH DUMPLING. LET'S EAT IT TOGETHER.
YAAAAY!
Huh?
NOT SO FAST, AIZEN-CHAN. REMEMBER, IT'S DANGEROUS TO BE TOO TRUSTWORTHY.
......
That Lady Aizen-myou's a little slow...
HA HA HA. OOPS, YOU'RE RIGHT.

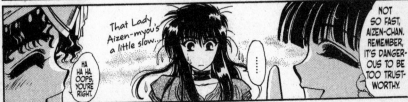

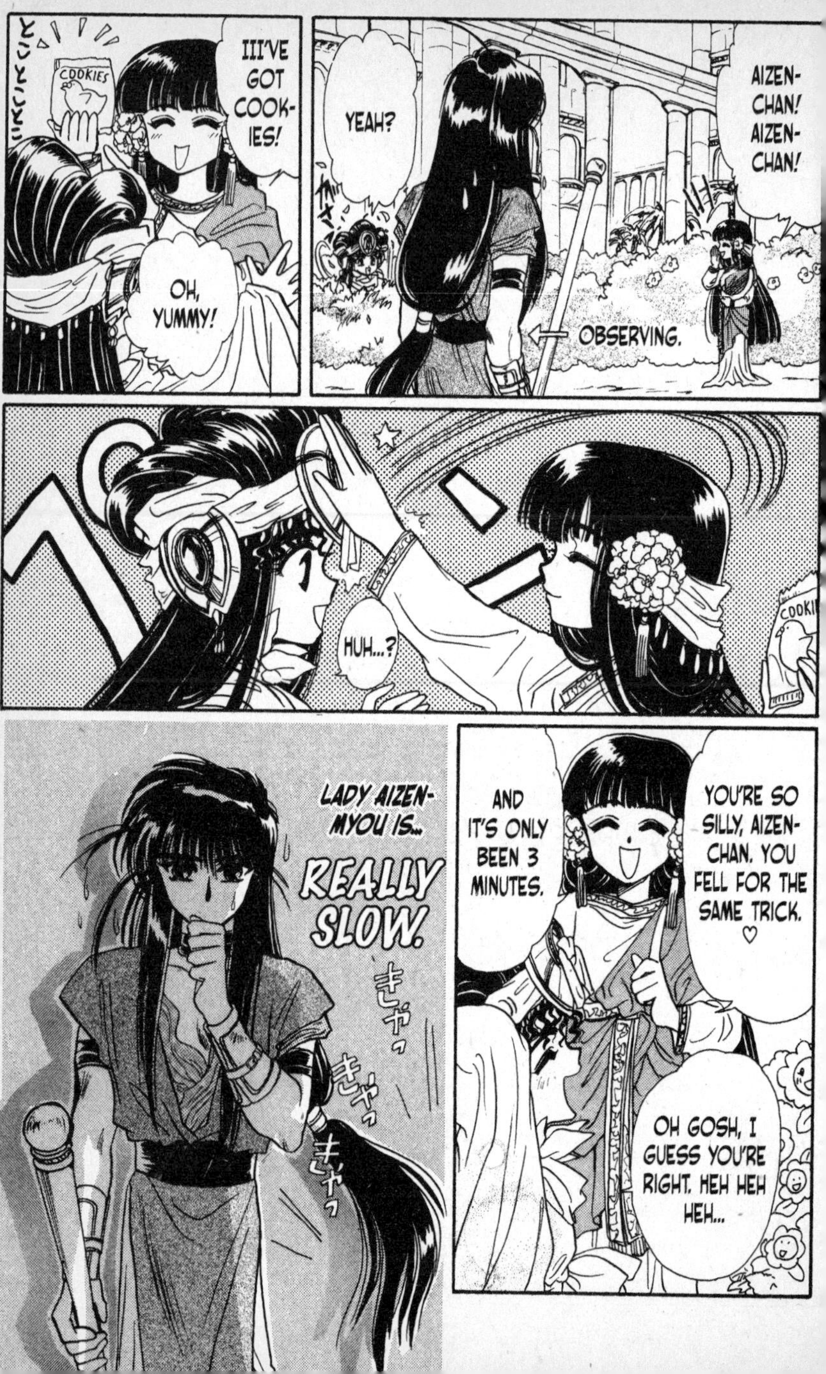
AIZEN-CHAN! AIZEN-CHAN!
YEAH?
OBSERVING.
III'VE GOT COOKIES!
COOKIES
OH, YUMMY!
HUH...?
COOKI
YOU'RE SO SILLY, AIZEN-CHAN. YOU FELL FOR THE SAME TRICK. ♡
AND IT'S ONLY BEEN 3 MINUTES.
OH GOSH, I GUESS YOU'RE RIGHT. HEH HEH HEH...
LADY AIZEN-MYOU IS...
REALLY SLOW.
きゃっ
きゃっ
きゃっ

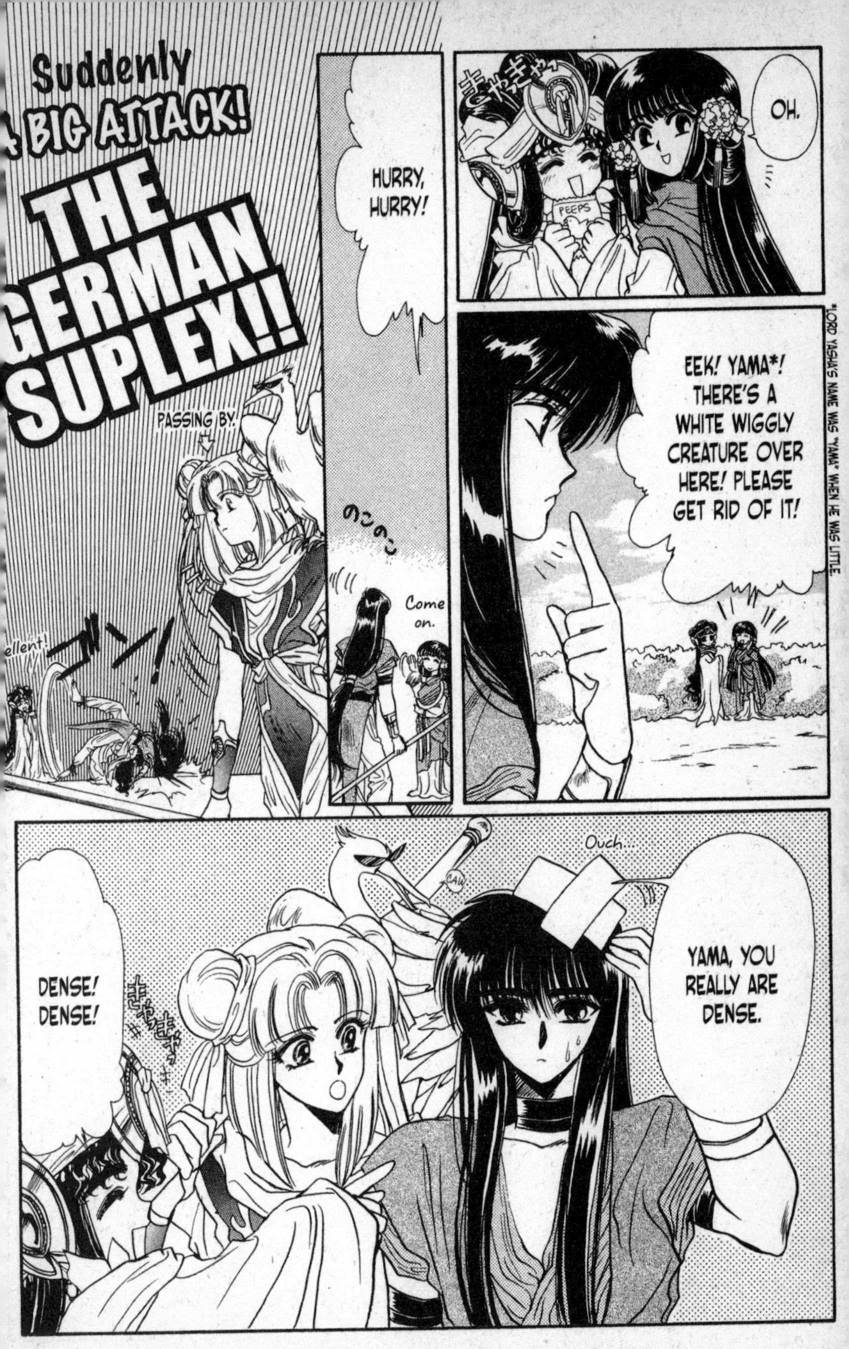
PEEPS
OH.
EEK! YAMA*! THERE'S A WHITE WIGGLY CREATURE OVER HERE! PLEASE GET RID OF IT!
*LORD YASHA'S NAME WAS "YAMA" WHEN HE WAS LITTLE.
HURRY, HURRY!
Come on.
Suddenly A BIG ATTACK!
THE GERMAN SUPLEX!!
PASSING BY.
Ouch...
CAW
YAMA, YOU REALLY ARE DENSE.
DENSE! DENSE!

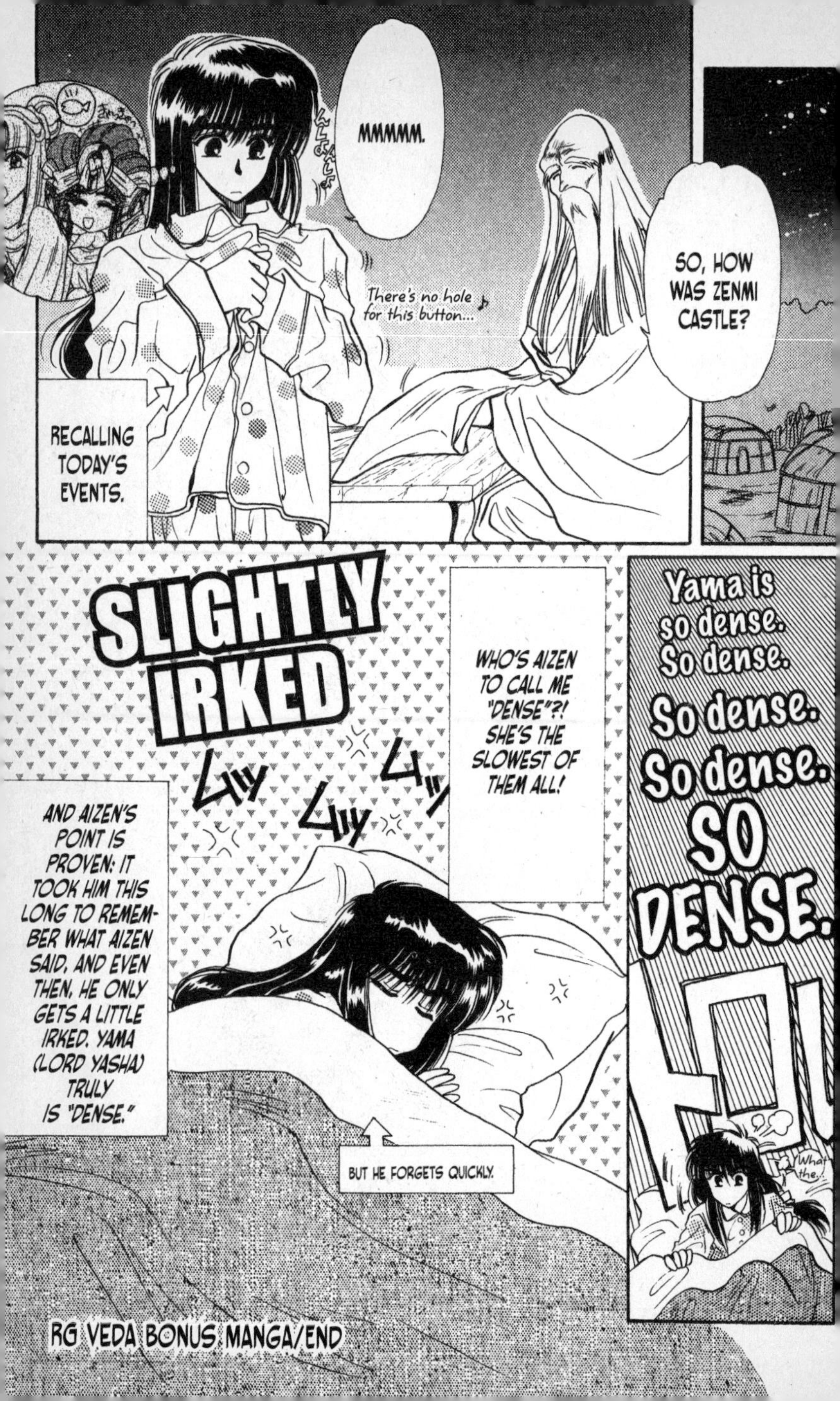
SO, HOW WAS ZENMI CASTLE?
MMMMM.
There's no hole for this button...
RECALLING TODAY'S EVENTS.
Yama is so dense. So dense. So dense. So dense. SO DENSE.
What the...
SLIGHTLY IRKED
WHO'S AIZEN TO CALL ME "DENSE"?! SHE'S THE SLOWEST OF THEM ALL!
AND AIZEN'S POINT IS PROVEN: IT TOOK HIM THIS LONG TO REMEMBER WHAT AIZEN SAID, AND EVEN THEN, HE ONLY GETS A LITTLE IRKED. YAMA (LORD YASHA) TRULY IS "DENSE."
BUT HE FORGETS QUICKLY.
RG VEDA BONUS MANGA/END

NEXT TIME IN RG VEDA

THE SKY CASTLE IS SHROUDED IN DARKNESS AS LADY KARURA GRIEVES OVER THE DEATH OF HER BELOVED SISTER. BUT SHE PLACES HERSELF IN GREAT DANGER STAYING THERE... WILL SHE LIVE TO SEE TAISHAKUTEN PAY FOR WHAT HE HAS DONE?

COMING SOON!

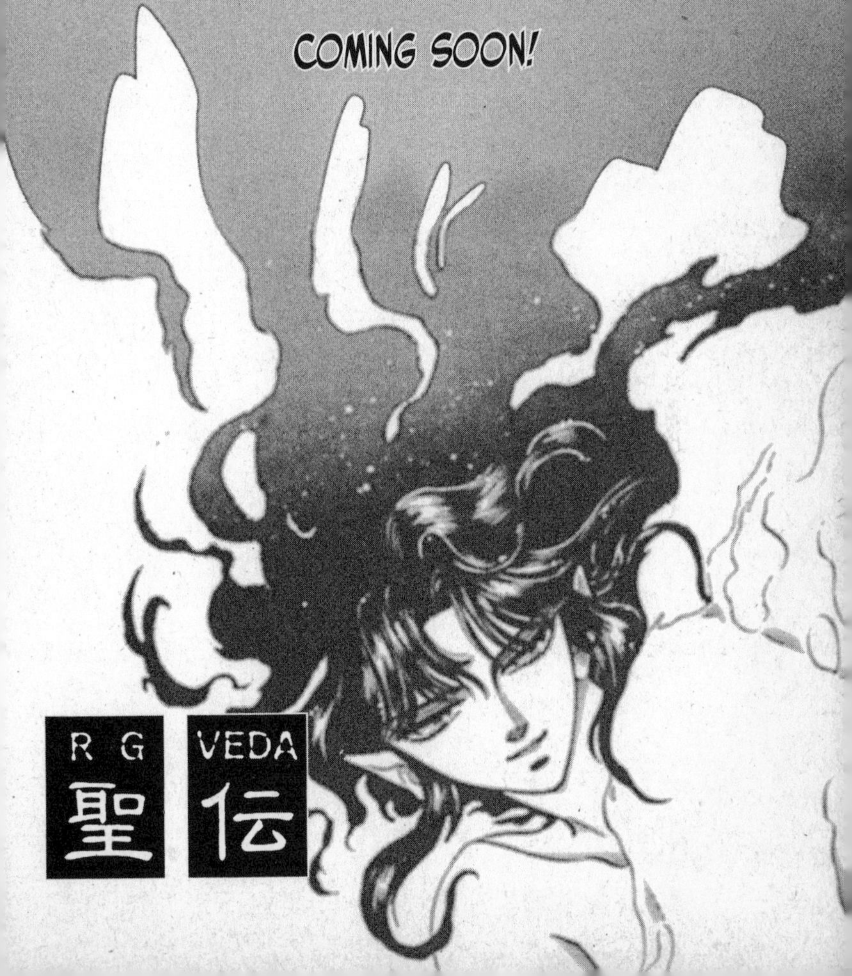
R G 聖
VEDA 伝

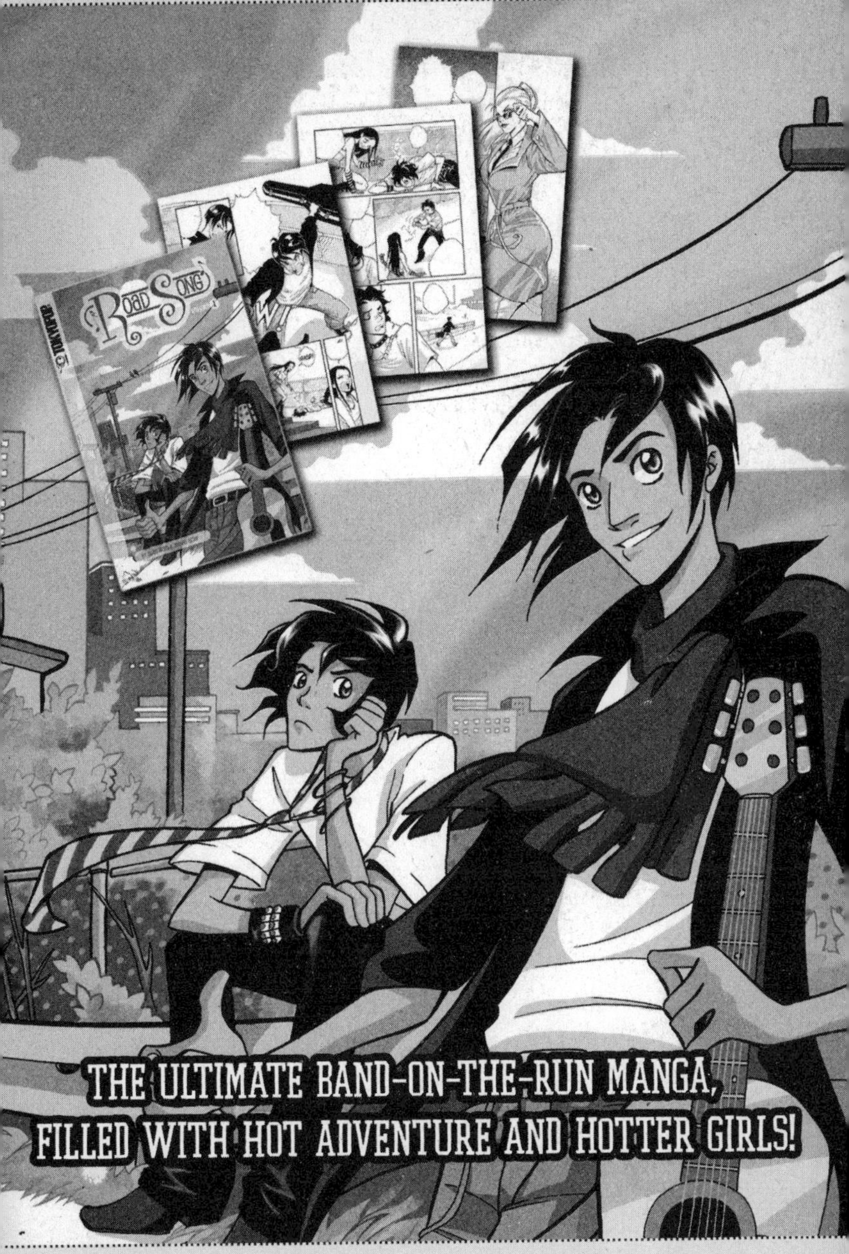
Road Song
TOKYOPOP
THE ULTIMATE BAND-ON-THE-RUN MANGA,
FILLED WITH HOT ADVENTURE AND HOTTER GIRLS!

ROADSONG

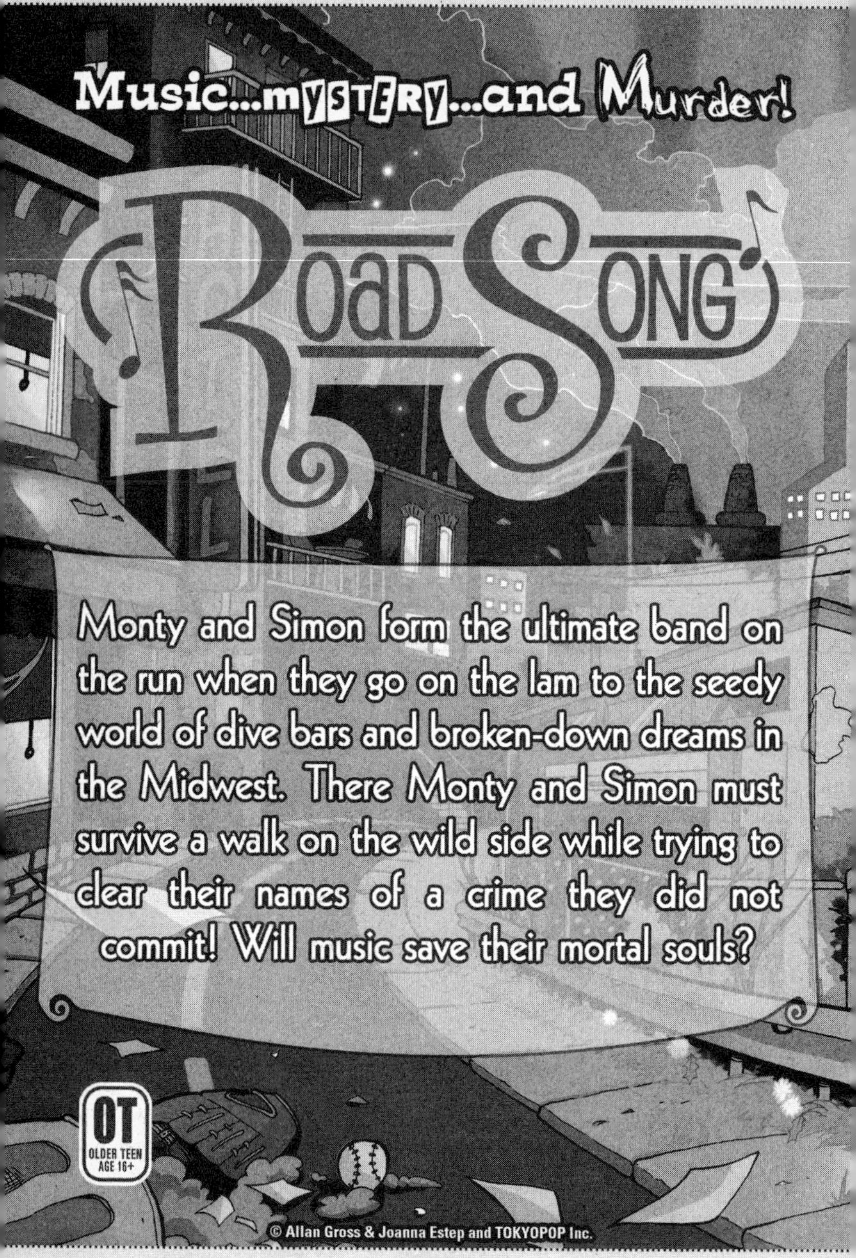

Music...mystery...and Murder!

RoadSong

Monty and Simon form the ultimate band on the run when they go on the lam to the seedy world of dive bars and broken-down dreams in the Midwest. There Monty and Simon must survive a walk on the wild side while trying to clear their names of a crime they did not commit! Will music save their mortal souls?

OT
OLDER TEEN
AGE 16+

READ A CHAPTER OF THE MANGA ONLINE FOR FREE:

TOKYOPOP SHOP